SURPRISED BY LAUGHTER

THE COMIC WORLD OF C.S. LEWIS

TERRY LINDVALL, PH.D

THOMAS NELSON
Since 1798

NASHVILLE DALLAS MEXICO CITY RIO DE JANEIRO

Published in Nashville, Tennessee, by Thomas Nelson. Thomas Nelson is a registered trademark of Thomas Nelson, Inc.

Thomas Nelson, Inc., titles may be purchased in bulk for educational, business, fund-raising, or sales promotional use. For information, please e-mail SpecialMarkets@ThomasNelson.com.

Unless otherwise noted, Scripture quotations are from the NEW AMERICAN STANDARD BIBLE®. © The Lockman Foundation 1960, 1962, 1963, 1968, 1971, 1972, 1973, 1975, 1977. Used by permission.

Scripture passages noted NIV are from HOLY BIBLE: NEW INTERNATIONAL VERSION®. © 1973, 1978, 1984 by International Bible Society. Used by permission of Zondervan Publishing House. All rights reserved.

Scripture quotations noted NRSV are from the NEW REVISED STANDARD VERSION of the Bible. © 1989 by the Division of Christian Education of the National Council of the Churches of Christ in the U.S.A. All rights reserved.

Excerpts from *That Hideous Strength* and *Perelandra* reprinted with permission of the estate of C. S. Lewis and Bodley Head.

Excerpts from *Discarded Image, An Experiment in Criticism, Spenser's Images of Life, Selected Literary Essays, Studies in Medieval and Renaissance Literature*, and *Studies in Words* by C. S. Lewis reprinted with permission of Cambridge University Press.

Originally produced for Star Song by the Livingstone corporation, Dr. James C. Galvin, Michael Kendrick, Elizabeth Winnowski, and Brenda James Todd, project staff.

ISBN 978-1-59555-478-9 (trade paper)

Library of Congress Cataloging-in-Publication Data

Lindvall, Terry
Surprised by Laughter: the comic world of C. S. Lewis/by Terry Lindvall
    p.cm.
Includes bibliographical references and index.
ISBN 0-7852-7689-0
    1. Lewis, C. S. (Clive Staples), 1898-1963—Humor. 2. Christianity and Literature—England—History—20th Century. 3. Satire, English—History and criticism. 4. Comic, The, in literature. I. Title.
PR6029. E926Z782 1995   94-42023
823' .912—dc20   CIP

Printed in the United States of America
11 12 13 14 15 QG 6 5 4 3 2 1

This book is dedicated to my parents,
John and Mae Lindvall,
whom I suspect conceived me
and my twin sister (Tessy Joy)
and my other siblings, Debby and John Mark,
in laughter and love. They bequeathed to us
all their habits of faith, hope, and loving humor.
And to my wife, Karen, who married me
with a blessed sense of farce and love and gave me
a jolly, robust son, Christopher,
and a bundle of Caroline Joy.
Soli Deus Gloria.

Contents

Acknowledgments

For the opportunity to recast this work for a paperback edition, I am indebted to Joel Miller who stumbled across the original hardback copy one night when he couldn't sleep (and this book helped cure him of his insomnia) and an amazing editor, Heather Skelton, whose name conjured up one of my favorite poet laureates and bards, John Skelton. But that is another book. Both enabled me to correct the notation system of the hardback book, add an index, and tidy up the bibliography, all academic tasks that haunt professors when they are left undone. Otherwise, even with all the fresh and excellent scholarship on C. S. Lewis since the publication of this work, I adhere to the classic principle that "if it ain't broke, don't fix it." I could have rewritten the whole darn thing, but I am getting older and have some other tasks to finish.

In the sixteenth century, a marble statue of a torso was unearthed in Rome from the third century. The fundamentalist Cardinal Carafa, notorious for his fig-leaf campaign of covering up the genitalia of Michelangelo's painting of the *Last Judgment*, allowed locals to plaster this statue with Latin epigrams, which quickly inspired mischievous Italian wits to paste their own naughty satire onto the statue. These attached ditties became known as *pasquinades*, witty verse lampooning the pope and government. Pasquino became the name of this "talking" statue, decorated with light, vernacular, and earthy verses.

This was my task here. To cover the great literary monument of C. S. Lewis with bits of jocular graffiti, with his own words on jokes and humor, in order to not let him stand as a stone idol, but be recognized as a "talking statue" for a more vulgar aspect of life, namely human laughter. In studying this Anglican icon of the twentieth century, I hoped to outline some of his key ideas of the nature and functions of laughter and to set forth some of his examples of humor as well as some old jokes that, as Aristophanes said, never fail to make his audience laugh. Of course, obeying the dictum of Cicero regarding comedy, I recognize that to make your audience laugh at the end, you must make them cry at the beginning, or at least bore them for a brief season.

The pasquinades I have scribbled here do no damage to the statue, but add a little color and character to a person who has significantly influenced Christian thinking. Hopefully, they also make us better thinkers and a bit lighter and more mischievous in our own characters.

This book owes itself to the merry band of friends, colleagues, and guides who contributed generously to my seeing and thinking and to my learning and laughter. My wife, Karen, did not complain when diapers, dust, and time piled up like mountains but made me realize why I married her every time she laughed. My son "Tophee" and daughter "Chevy" made me laugh "again and again." All my in-laws confirmed the truths of old comic stereotypes. More than a decade ago, John Lawing introduced me to someone older than himself, G. K. Chesterton, and helped me keep my insanity during the more sanitized seasons of Regent University.

An ecumenical company of friends and former students, now grown up, including Dan Holt, Steve Sylvester, Matthew Melton, and a host of others in my classes in humor and satire and film comedy, gave more than they realized (but not enough to warrant financial renumeration). Former dean Jack Keeler not only secured a sabbatical for me (in which I was able to live and study at the Kilns with the most hospitable Michael Piret, now the Reverend Doctor Dean of Divinity at Magdalen College in Oxford) but also showed me a model of sanctified sarcasm that has yet to be put to fictional character. Former Regent president Bob Slosser was himself the "breath of fresh air" I needed during stale years.

Enormous gratitude must go to those paragons of virtuous patience, Mildred Stonecypher, Sandy Horton, Karen Schindler, Suzanne Morton, and Rande Fritz, who typed into eternity and whose fingers wore out before their deeds of kindness did. A merry nod is tipped to Marjorie Mead and Barbara Reynolds, who graciously opened the doors of the Wade Collection to me. To Pam Robles, my diligent wordsmith and friend, who took out the bawdy passages that might have gotten me into trouble, I offer deep gratitude. Thanks must also be showered upon that special saint of editorial perseverance and polish and joy, Scotty Sawyer. And to that agent of mercy and mirth, son of a friend, David West, Jr., will come the reward of a few nickels and much praise.

Many others were Virgils to me through infernal pits of data: Ben Fraser spurred me on, talking trash during basketball; Michael Graves put whatever poetry he could into my prosaic soul; Bob Schihl almost persuaded me that all laughter leads to Rome; George Selig confirmed the comedy of Episcopalians; and the invisible Gene Elser muttered something legal that I didn't use. Deep appreciation ascends to my USC doctoral advisor, Walter R. Fisher, for being an Erasmus to my academic folly. Finally, thanks to Regent University.

Whatever is original in this book has come about quite by accident. This tome, destined no doubt for some dusty, old bookshop, was completed only by God's generous humor and by the perseverance inspired by Chesterton's principle that "if a thing is worth doing, it is worth doing badly."

*If any cleric or monk speaks jocular words, such as
provoke laughter, let him be anathema.*
—Ordinance, Second Council of Constance, 1418

Part 1

The Idea and the Legacy

Laughter is one of the most frequent symptoms of madness.
—CHARLES BAUDELAIRE

Introduction

Do not look dismal.
—Matthew 6:16 (nrsv)

When we read religious writing (or, what is often worse, writing by a religious person), the last thing we expect to discover is laughter. We expect the religious writer to handle truth, ethics, and other serious concerns with appropriate decorum. Treating issues of ultimate reality with levity is the habit of the fool, the mocker, the jester, the idiot.

Yet an encounter with the writings of Clive Staples Lewis turns that premise on its head. The portrait of this large, ruddy, laughing professor and author is hardly that of a dour, proper churchman. *Time* magazine portrayed the Oxford don on its September 8, 1947, cover alongside a pitchforked, horned, and tailed devil. The magazine accused Lewis of heresy. His heresy—identified in a dry mixture of whimsy and irony— was, simply and merely, Christianity in a world gone awry.

The idea of an orthodox Christian laughing heartily and giving others reason to laugh comes to too many of us as a surprise. Yet it is even more incongruous to imagine that a young boy who had lost his mother and his faith and grown into a flaming atheist would eventually somersault into the company of Christian saints. It is an incongruity that only an honest and humble heart could recognize as the work of God.

C. S. Lewis has been catalogued, footnoted, and celebrated in a variety of kingdoms: literary, theological, mythopoeic, ethical, and apologetic, among many others. He has been costumed as court poet, priest, troubadour, guard, and knight-defender of the faith. Yet too often overlooked is one other low but bright disguise in the wardrobe of this likable genius—a mask that not only fits his face but *was* his face and his heart as well. C. S. Lewis was, like G. K. Chesterton and St. Francis, a court jester, *un jongleur de Dieu*. He was a man of laughter and surprises, of jokes and joy. And he was ruddy faced because he had a sunny heart, gladness foaming and ready to burgeon out at any moment, solemn or gay. When a publisher thought to extract selections from Lewis's works, he could think of no more apt a title for the volume than *The Joyful Christian*.

Lewis has been observed by the microscopes of literary analysis, the telescopes of theological inquisitions, the bifocals of communication pedantry, and a vast array of greater and lesser lenses in their variously valuable ways. Many have contributed not only to a better understanding of the don and his writings, but also to a clearer perspective of ourselves. Whether we view him from a desk or a toolshed, we find ourselves constantly seeing through and beyond him to the greater truth of which he wrote. One bright and compelling feature we can see, sparkling in his sunlight and dancing in his moonlight, is laughter. Yet it is too large to see at once because it inhabited all Lewis was and did. Like a tree or a sock or the ticking of a clock, it is so familiar, so intrinsic and ordinary to our perceptions, that we overlook its importance.

Lewis's own progress as a pilgrim of laughter took him into many fantastic provinces and faraway lands. Yet those strange and mysterious regions were essentially like the Oxford and Cambridge he inhabited. Lewis could be characterized as Chesterton's yachtsman, who launched off to discover the East Indies only to set foot on Brighton, experiencing the delight of encountering the extraordinary and the ordinary at once.

Lewis's travels across the landscapes of laughter were never specified—never printed onto a literary road map as such—but were spontaneously jotted onto scraps of paper, recorded in letters and essays, and scattered about in various works. He left these as happy directions for weary travelers that we may rise up with wings like eagles—or, more probably, like jackdaws or cuckoos. And they remain as signposts today for other pilgrims to study, ingest, and enjoy as they plod along on their journeys.

This book aims to put those signposts and directions into a map of mirth—to make some organized sense of Lewis's "nonsense." Yet the author recognizes that, helpful as such signs and maps may be, they must never divert our attention from our enjoyment of the landscape. That is a pitfall; yet, even so, such a map is helpful—even necessary—to fully enjoy the trip. As Lewis himself observed, "To consult a map before we set out has no such ill effect. Indeed it will lead us to many prospects: including some we might never have found by following our noses."[1]

It is not the purpose of this book to argue that C. S. Lewis was a comedian. Any such attempt would itself be ridiculous. Lewis, I suspect, would mock the thought. On the other hand, this jovial man possessed an angelic mirth—a veritable inner vat of wit and humor that constantly bubbled over with the wine of laughter. Out of that jolly reservoir, gladness poured forth freely, and it is my hope that many a goblet will be filled and drunk by friends, acquaintances, and even by strangers to Lewis.

Lest I cause a grave-turning at the Headington Parish Church, I hope simply to step aside and help readers to see the laughter of Lewis as it has flowed out of his own pen and life. Lewis did advise Americans that they would be "much wiser to write about the dead, who can't answer. . . . Guesses about the dead seem plausible only because the dead are not there to refute them" and blow one's theory into smithereens.[2] His writings, even the academic and painful ones, breathe with wit and good humor.

Lewis was a wonderful dinosaur in a long tradition of good-humored dinosaurs, and to study him and the flora and fauna he ate can lead only to a renewed appreciation of his giant tracks. From Chaucer to Chesterton, a legacy of comic faith was handed down to Lewis, and he guarded it well. He freely acknowledged those sources of laughter and wit that irradiated his writings. In this encyclopedia of his mirth, one can see him borrowing from the bawdy wealth of both Rabelais and the burlesque stage of Britain. His animal characters were comic, having fed in the pastures and troughs of Aesop

and Beatrix Potter. Even the treacly, anthropomorphic cartoon characters of Disney were not without familiar connection to Lewis's
creations. We can see many shades of laughter refracting from his
prism, from light whimsy to dark satire. Traditions of both Horatian
and Juvenalian humor dwell within this house.

Lewis also stands as a model for laughter-makers. In a postmodern
age, when irrationality and absurdity reign freely and at times tyranni-
cally, it is good to remember the earth has a moral and rational foundation—to know that there is a God in heaven who is the source of
laughter. Lewis's influence can be seen in the fertile and intelligent wit
of writers such as Frederick Buechner, Peter Berger, and Madeleine
L'Engle.

Humorist Robert Benchley once observed that "defining and
analyzing humor is a pastime of humorless people."[3] So, to avoid the
danger of becoming deadly doctors of laughter, we must not lose our
own senses of humor even while studying Lewis's. Humor and wit are
two marvelous gifts God bestowed upon Lewis, and I simply would
like to share the delight of discovering them. This book, then, is not so
much an academic enterprise as it is an outburst of delight, as "when
the old poets made some virtue their theme they were not teaching but
adoring, and that what we take for the didactic is often the enchanted."[4]

I have tried to ensure that this study of Lewis's wit and humor does
not end up being an autopsy. Lewis echoed E. B. White's pithy observation that humor, like a frog, dies when we dissect it, and "the innards
are discouraging to any but the pure scientific mind."[5] Just as one
cannot contemplate passion while enjoying the nuptial embrace, Lewis
suggested, one does not laugh while studying laughter. (This is not to
say, however, as personal experience has proven, that one cannot laugh
while enjoying the nuptial embrace.) And I hope that in placing Lewis
on the operating table we will not merely handle the organs, tissues,
and entrails of the subject of laughter, but we will also see the risible
body itself awaken and laugh and cause us to laugh with the surprise of
encountering something so unexpectedly and wonderfully alive.

1

The Deadly Dissection

*The essence of all comedy is would you hit a lady
with a baby? No, I'd hit her with a brick.*
—E. E. CUMMINGS

The problem of defining what produces laughter involves a degree of wrestling with language. "A Hottentot and a Dane might hammer out an agreed definition of beauty," Lewis wrote,

> and in that sense, lexically, "mean" the same by it. Yet the one might continue, in a different sense, to "mean" blubber lips, woolly hair, and fat paunch while the other "meant" a small mouth, silky hair, "white and red," and a slender waist. And two men who agree about the [lexical] "meaning" of comic would not necessarily find the same things funny.[1]

Comedy, as the great eighteenth-century lexicographer Dr. Samuel Johnson once remarked, "has been particularly unpropitious to definers." One reason for humankind's failure to surround and capture the elusive concept can be attributed to Aristotle's observation in *The Poetics*: "Comedy has had no history, because it was not at first treated seriously."[2] Chad Walsh echoed Aristotle when he described the "awkward double predicament of trying to take the comic seriously and the serious comically. . . . To write seriously about the comic is to fail to practice what one preaches; and yet to practice what one preaches is to fail to be taken seriously."[3]

Another problem is what Lewis called the human dilemma of knowing:

Either to taste and not to know or to know and not to taste—or,
more strictly, to lack one kind of knowledge because we are in an
experience or to lack another kind because we are outside it. As
thinkers we are cut off from what we think about; as tasting, touch-
ing, willing, loving, hating, we do not clearly understand. . . . You
cannot study pleasure in the moment of the nuptial embrace, nor
repentance while repenting, nor analyze the nature of humor while
roaring with laughter.[4]

Lewis defined the two experiences or ways of knowing with two
French verbs: *savoir* and *connaitre*. *Savoir* is to know *about* something—to examine it, study it, analyze it. Lewis wrote: "But I have an
idea that the true analysis of a thing ought not to be so like the thing
itself. I should not expect a true theory of the comic to be itself funny."[5]

Yet the contemplation of an object, its *savoir*, is only one epistemo-
logical way. The other method of knowing—*connaitre*—is to enjoy an
object, to become acquainted with it intimately, to experience and taste
it. In "Meditation in a Toolshed," Lewis called this, in essence, looking
along an experience, being immersed in it.[6] For example, the spontaneous humor and banter of friends gathered on the eve of a holiday offer
one the *taste*—and not merely the outward knowledge—of humor.

A related problem in catching and defining such a slippery notion
as humor is that one can never get a firm grip on it. Like an elf in a
forest, it is gone as soon as one turns to see it. Indeed, there is a curious
and frustrating psychological law that says our postures or attitudes
toward something often inhibit the very thing they are meant to facili-
tate. Lewis noted: "You can't, in most things, get what you want if
you want it too desperately. 'Now! Let's have a real good talk' reduces
everyone to silence, 'I must get a good sleep tonight' ushers in hours of
wakefulness."[7]

This happens, too, with laughter. The king's command to the
jester to be funny ultimately may be disastrous if he does not *seriously*
fulfill his duty. Similarly, the comic writer or actor is dared by his

or her audience to be funny. Yet the quest to lasso wild and bucking laughter and keep it frisky in its stall is a futile one. As soon as one ropes and trains laughter, it becomes a manageable, wooden hobby-horse. Nevertheless, as we in the enterprise of this book attempt to corral and tame Lewis's laughter, observe and study it, we can still hope for the animal to surprise us with a snort or kick.

Yet even with all these caveats in place, categorization for an academic is irresistible—and I have not resisted (nor did Lewis, as shall be shown) putting Lewis's types of laughter into categories. Comedy can be classified in a variety of ways. It can be divided, for example, according to whether it is funny or not. But such a distinction depends upon the audience. Shakespeare noted that "a jest's prosperity lies in the ear of him that hears it, never in the tongue of him that makes it."[8] This may be why most of us laugh at our own jokes so enthusiastically; we know our audience. We've spent years fine-tuning our humor to our crowd of one.

Lewis partially adopted this approach in reminding his brother, Warnie, "you know how one classifies jokes according to the people one wants to tell them to."[9] Lewis shared with his brother a certain dry wit. Having endured a wild collection of absurdities of life with their father, the brothers possessed a sympathetic humor; they knew what each other would find amusing and funny. In a letter to his brother, Lewis told a funny, true story that embodied this shared perspective: At a college dinner, a certain undergraduate, presumably drunk, "covered the face of his neighbor with potatoes, his neighbor being a total stranger." Being hauled before the proctors (the disciplinary body in British universities), the culprit's only excuse was: "I couldn't think of anything else to do." Lewis appealed to Warnie's sense of ironic delight in imagining this

transference of the outrage from the class of positive to that of negative faults; as though it proceeds entirely from a failure of the inventive faculty or a mere poverty of the imagination. One ought to be careful of sitting near one of these unimaginative men . . . one thinks of the Mohawk bashing your hat over your eyes with the words, "Sorry old chap, I know it's a bit hackneyed, but I can't think of anything better"—or of some elderly gentleman exclaiming testily, "Ah what all these young men lack now-a-days is initiative" as he springs into the air from the hindward pressure of a pin.[10]

Lewis also likened his division of comedy to his categories of religions and soups: the thick and the clear. The *thick* includes all humor that deals with the animal side of human nature—that which grows out of the earth and blood and sex of men and women. The *clear*, on the other hand, encompasses wit, the philosophical and the intellectual, the rational realm of human nature. True comedy, ideally, brings together both—child and man, savage and citizen, head and belly.[11] Yet this system of categorizing comedy can't seem to avoid pigeonholing humor. How can one tell when laughter strikes predominantly the child or the adult? Aren't the two worlds neatly and precisely distinguishable? Is there a level of intelligence and sophistication that separates the two? It is better to ask: Must farce and slapstick remain strictly in the province of the juvenile? Do not many ribald jokes depend on an incongruous intellectual twist? Consider the evangelist's unwitting play on words in invoking the parable of the ten virgins before his audience of male, celibate seminarians: "Tell me, would you rather be with the wise virgins at the wedding feast or with the foolish virgins in the dark?"

As we grow in knowledge and understanding (though our minds ultimately operate in reverse, bringing on a jolly senility and forgetfulness), we do not simply add clear wit to thick humor. Indeed, as adults we may joyfully discover subtle ironies and paradoxes, but even a young child can delightedly recognize incongruity.

Lewis's recommendation of the two ways of thinking might be profitably applied as well to laughing. As he pointed out, "One can't think straight unless you are cool. But then neither can you think deep if you are. I suppose one must try every problem in both states.

You remember that the ancient Persians debated everything twice: once when they were drunk and once when they were sober."[12] He might easily have been speaking of clear and sober wit and intoxicating and thick comedy.

Ultimately, however, the categories that will govern this study are those defined and described in Lewis's *The Screwtape Letters*. In the eleventh letter to a junior devil, Lewis tinkered with four origins of laughter, which he labeled *joy*, *fun*, *the joke proper*, and *flippancy*. It is my purpose in this book to survey these categories, to see what Lewis had to say about them, and to examine how he used them in his own writings. A sketchy preview will draw, in broad brush strokes, the laughter of joy as a positive, spiritual experience; the laughter of fun or play as a buoyant physical expression; the laughter of the joke proper as a cognitive exercise; and the laughter of satire and flippancy as social and antisocial exchanges, respectively. A postscript on the place of love and laughter will end our study with a nice, warm glow.

2

Perspectives

This world is a comedy to those that think, a tragedy to those that feel.
—HORACE WALPOLE

Our perspectives on the species of laughter are, like all perspectives, governed primarily by training and habit. A convict looking through prison bars can gaze upon the gutters or study the stars. And looking at life, one can choose to see the tragedy or the comedy. Once, while grading a batch of papers on Chanticleer in the "Nun's Priest's Tale" from Chaucer's *Canterbury Tales*, Lewis noted dryly that the answers came from "boys whose form master was apparently a breeder of poultry. Everything was related to bird breeding."[1]

Indeed, humor is dependent upon one's perspective. Aristotle held that if the appearance of pain was actually perceived or experienced as pain, one's situation no longer was comic. If, for example, a man falling down on his hat actually broke his neck, we would not be tempted to laugh. Yet when we see a sophisticated dignitary fall on her behind, it becomes not only proper for us to laugh but sane as well. When suffering is real, one sympathizes; but when it is the superficial suffering of embarrassment, one laughs.

In reality, tragedy and comedy are so closely aligned as to be mates in a healthy marriage. "There are," wrote Chesterton,

> two rooted spiritual realities out of which grow all kinds of democratic conception or sentiment of human equality. There are two things in which all men are manifestly and unmistakably equal. They are not equally clever or equally muscular or equally fat, as the sages of the modern reaction (with piercing insight) perceive. But

this is a spiritual certainty, that all men are tragic. And this again is an equally sublime spiritual certainty that all men are comic. No special and private sorrow can be so dreadful as the fact of having to die. And no freak or deformity can be so funny as the mere fact of having two legs. Every man is important if he loses his life; and every man is funny if he loses his hat and has to run after it.[2]

Lewis thought the view that "tragedy is essentially 'truer to life' than comedy to be unfounded." The world of farce, he believed, is a "paradise of jokes where the wildest coincidences are accepted and where all things work together to produce laughter. Real life seldom succeeds in being, and never remains for more than a few minutes, nearly as funny as a well-invented farce."[3]

Yet Lewis recognized that not all the world is a comedy. This brighter and lighter view of life ignores in the comedy of the wedding the tragedy of the divorce. Even farce denies pity or compassion for its butts and fools "in situations where, if they were real, they would deserve it."[4] But neither is life the all-consuming tragedy a tragedian would like to make it. There is roaring laughter at the wake even as there are jokes on the scaffold, as was true with Thomas More.

Lewis saw gaiety and levity among even the properly serious company of King Arthur and his men when they were expecting an enemy attack. As the king and his council ascend the "spiral stairs of the Giant's Tower, Cador, who was a man of jokes, calls out merrily to Arthur who happens to be in front of him. This threat from Rome, he says, is welcome. We have had far too much peace lately. It softens a man. It encourages the young bachelors to spend too much time dressing, with an eye to the ladies. . . . Thus they jested."[5]

Similarly, Lewis recalled how his colleagues in the trenches during the First World War lived and joked as freely as their civilian counterparts. Often books about real lives that bleed with tragic events and suffering ironically can give the reader the broader impression of joy and happiness.

What could be more tragic than the main outlines of Lamb's or Cowper's lives? But as soon as you open the letters of either, and see what they were writing from day to day and what relish they got out of it, you almost begin to envy them. Perhaps the tragedies of real life contain more consolation and fun and gusto than the comedies of literature?[6]

One finds this borne out in the life of stuttering Charles Lamb. To learn that Lamb became a cheerful and beloved bachelor of letters even after his sister, in a tragic fit of bloody madness, had gruesomely slain their mother, is to find a heart of golden beauty emerging from a fiery crucible. Here was a man who playfully called his sister and himself "shorn Lambs" under the blood of the mother Lamb. Yet the humor was not so morbid as it was triumphant, coming from a gentle man whose jests, critic William Hazlitt wrote, scalded like tears.

Lewis once observed that modern youth seemed to expect a right to happiness, a life of comedy without consequences. The don quipped that one might as well ask for a right to be six feet tall. Charles Williams merrily agreed. He told Lewis that

> when young people came to us with their troubles and discontents, the worst thing we could do was to tell them they were not so unhappy as they thought. Our reply ought rather to begin, "But of course. . . ." For young people usually are unhappy, and the plain truth is often the greatest relief we can give them. The world is painful in any case: but it is quite unbearable if everyone gives us the idea that we are meant to be liking it. . . . What is unforgivable if judged as an hotel may be very tolerable as a reformatory.[7]

Williams was a brightly animated man, who had a face between an angel's or monkey's that, Lewis remembered, often "distorted into helpless laughter at some innocently broad buffoonery."[8] Williams wrote of dark and heavy things that menace and poison our lives—maiming, madness, economic insecurity, grief, torture—and yet he paradoxically spoke with high spirits, mirth, and marvelous zest. His belief in the sovereignty and grace of God mocked the perceived gloom and sufferings of the age; his head was full of comedy even as his heart held the tragic. Like Job, he was a clown in an absurd, tragic farce. He felt that God would permit him to carry his "hot complaints to the very Throne," where he would be answered, like Job, with the crocodile and hippopotamus.

> "The weight of divine displeasure had been reserved for the 'comforters,' the self-appointed advocates on God's side, the people who tried to show that all was well—the sort of people," he said [to Lewis], immeasurably dropping his lower jaw and fixing me with his eyes, "the sort of people who wrote books on the Problem of Pain."[9]

Tragedy and comedy are constructions of the raw material and stuff of real life: One gives us a cup of hemlock, the other a custard pie. Human life unavoidably includes both, and neither is a more piercing or convincing truth of the way the physical universe is than the other—though I suspect when we include the Christian vision, we come much closer to the Divine Comedy. And for Dante, a comedy was simply a play that ended well and happily.

As Lewis noted, we often cannot tell which act of the play we are in—whether our "diseases are those of childhood or senility. We can say it is an exciting story, or a crowded story, or a story with humorous characters in it."[10] But whether we are experiencing comic interludes in a tragedy, or the painful and poignant moments of a wonderful comedy, we can know only by faith. Both aspects contain common elements, but the two are radically different. In the same Chestertonian way, "a baby is bald like an old man; but it would be an error for one ignorant of infancy to infer that the baby had a long white beard. Both a baby and an old man walk with difficulty; but he who shall expect the old gentleman to be on his back and kick joyfully instead, will be disappointed."[11] More often than not our feelings convince us that life is one or the other: tragedy if we've heard bad news, comedy if we're falling in love or eating corn on the cob. "Luther surely spoke very good sense when he compared humanity to a drunkard who, after falling off his horse on the right, falls off it next time on the left."[12]

Chesterton contrasted the worldviews of the Christian and of the pagan hedonist by reversing the typically held portraits:

> It is said that Paganism is a religion of joy and Christianity of sorrow; it would be just as easy to prove that Paganism is pure sorrow and Christianity pure joy. Such conflicts mean nothing and lead nowhere. Everything human must have in it both joy and sorrow; the only matter of interest is the manner in which the two things are balanced or divided. And the really interesting thing is this, that the pagan was (in the main) happier and happier as he approached the earth, but sadder and sadder as he approached the heavens.[13]

The great mythic experiences, Lewis believed, could be sad or joyful, but they were always grave. Comic myth, in Lewis's sense of myth, would be impossible.[14] The grand myths of death and resurrection were too significant, too important and deep for jokes. Yet these wonderful myths were married to facts, and the facts of the universe are universally funny. The comedy of farce, in fact, flows from the unexpected ironies, absurdities, and surprises of real life. Life could be comic even if its stories and myths were grave.

Lewis's own experience bears this out. His initial arrival at Oxford taught him to be ready for the comic perspective even if it appeared in a great and serious place to study:

> My first taste of Oxford was comical enough. I had made no arrangements about quarters and, having no more luggage than I could carry in my hand, I sallied out of the railway station on foot

to find either a lodging house or a cheap hotel; all agog for "dreaming spires" and "last enchantments." My first disappointment at what I saw could be dealt with. Towns always show their worst face to the railway. But as I walked on and on I became more bewildered. Could this succession of mean shops really be Oxford? But I still went on, always expecting the next turn to reveal the beauties, and reflecting that it was a much larger town than I had been led to suppose. Only when it became obvious that there was very little town left ahead of me, that I was in fact getting to open country, did I turn round and look. There, behind me, far away, never more beautiful since, was the fabled cluster of spires and towers. I had come out of the station on the wrong side and been all this time walking into what was even then the mean and sprawling suburb of Botley. I did not see to what extent this little adventure was an allegory of my whole life.[15]

A fresh perspective can revive a weary soul. It can, in wonderfully Chestertonian style, turn something on its head and allow us to see it anew. Such is one aim of this book—to bring a comic focus to bear upon our understanding of our lives and the drudgery that drops in upon us.

A reversal in perspective can be a clever comic and satiric device. Lewis once imagined a lecture on revolution in which the voice was "saying all the wrong things." By simply turning everything upside down, one understood "not that the oak comes from the acorn, but that the acorn comes from the oak."[16] Indeed, one can look at facts from different angles and see another side, as Lewis did in an attack on the reductionism of psychoanalysis:

"All these moral ideals which look so transcendental and beautiful from inside," says the wiseacre, "are really only a mass of biological instincts and inherited taboos." And no one plays the game the other way round by replying, "If you will only step inside, the things that look to you like instincts and taboos will suddenly reveal their real and transcendental nature."[17]

Followed to its logical extension, this habit of "looking through things" leads to seeing nothing. In *The Great Divorce*, Lewis distinguished between *seeing through and seeing*. One cynical ghost, for example, sees through everything. Heaven, to him, is the same old lie that he heard in the nursery. He sees through the marvelous sights of the world—the Pyramids, Niagara Falls—as giant advertisement stunts and tourist traps. He sees a conspiracy behind every bush—and, he has determined, he won't be made a fool.

This kind of "seeing through," Lewis said, can actually blind one to seeing. The pilgrim of *The Pilgrim's Regress*, John, discovers this on his journey away from and toward truth. Being imprisoned in the Giant Despair's dungeon, he is given an extreme psychoanalytic vision. Like a visual King Midas, he cannot sense something as it is. Instead, his gaze X-rays and destroys everything's good nature. He sees, for instance, beyond his fellow prisoners and, more gruesomely, beyond the person of a woman: "Through the face, he saw the skull, and through that the brains and the passages of the nose, and the larynx, and the saliva moving in the glands . . . and the intestines like a coil of snakes." The giant jokes with his prisoner that eating eggs is actually—when you see through the meal—"eating the menstruum of a verminous fowl."[18]

Lewis mocked the many psychological and literary analyses of classic imagery, and even that of his own work that followed this pattern. He also resented psychology's penchant for referring everything about people to problems in potty-training and sex. In particular, the identification of gardens with the female body bothered him. He didn't mind "so much the suggestion that we are interested in the female body as that we have no interests in gardens: not what the wiseacre would force upon us, but what he threatens to take away."[19] In a similar taunting vein, Lewis satirized those who analyzed his daydreams of visiting a town of mice. "My only reason for wishing to go to it was its adorableness: there was no idea that I was to become a great man there, or marry a mouse-princess, or make my fortune out of the local trade in cheese."[20]

He further noted how inventive reviewers can be in pursuing such trails: They end up seeing all kinds of goblins or neuroses in an author's stories. All manner of allegorical meanings that were never intended can be read into a work. "Some of the allegories thus imposed on my books have been so ingenious and interesting that I often wish I had thought of them myself. Apparently it is impossible for the wit of man to devise a narration in which the wit of some other man cannot, and with some plausibility, find a hidden sense."[21]

On several occasions, Lewis found himself criticized by opposing perspectives, itself an amusing situation. This was the reaction, for instance, to his exposition of the Christian faith: "Once you are well soaked in [the different visions of Christendom], if you then venture to speak, you will have an amusing experience. You will be thought a Papist when you are actually reproducing Bunyan, a Pantheist when you are quoting Aquinas, and so forth."[22] Lewis could only chuckle when Dr. Pittenger reproved him for his callousness toward animal pain; others had charged him with extreme sentimentality. "It is hard to please all. But if the Patagonians think me a dwarf and the Pygmies a giant, perhaps my status is in fact fairly unremarkable."[23]

The problem with most human "seeing" is that our vision is clouded or narrowed or prejudiced by preconceptions. We aren't very often willing or courageous enough to see things afresh. We continually see others only as measured against ourselves, or, worse, we see only ourselves. Lewis wrote that "what we see when we think we are looking into the depths of Scripture may sometimes be only the reflection of our own silly faces."[24] Even finding or seeing "God in space depends on who you are."[25]

Lewis enjoyed how some dull, Drab Age poetry was quickened for him simply by being accompanied with music. "One that I had thought very dry and colorless came dancing into life as soon as a learned pupil (Mr. Norman Bradshaw) played me the air on his recorder." He discovered a chuckling gaiety in "Who shall have my fair lady" and enjoyed "My lady went to Canterbury" as a great nonsense ditty.[26] The fresh context of song can animate drab, dusty words into a lyrical art.

Likewise, the Christian faith offers a valuable change of perspective on the world. It treats, for example, many pressing or seemingly urgent things, such as what to eat or what to wear, almost casually. And it views such concerns as art, literature, and intellectual life as secondary at best.

F. R. Leavis, a Cambridge don, and his disciples stood out to Lewis as a solemn sort of literary coterie who would find John the Baptist too frivolous. For Leavis, "literature" was a sort of holy scripture which one should tread into soberly and in the fear of genius. His students probably were those to whom Lewis referred when he wrote of the kind of readers who were outraged that one should find Jane Austen or Chaucer's "Reeve's Tale" funny. Lewis responded to such a pompous posture that Christian perspectives on subjects such as literature

> will strike the world as shallow and flippant; but the world must not misunderstand. When Christian work is done on a serious subject there is no gravity and no sublimity it cannot attain. But they will belong to the theme. That is why they will be real and lasting— mighty nouns with which literature, an adjectival thing, is here united, far over-topping the fussy and ridiculous claims of literature that tries to be important simply as literature. And . . . it is not hard to argue that all the greatest poems have been made by men who valued something else much more than poetry—even if that something else were only cutting down enemies in a cattle-raid or tumbling a girl in bed. The real frivolity, the solemn vacuity, is all with those who make literature a self-existent thing to be valued for its own sake.[27]

Literature and all the arts are to be valued, but from the proper perspective—that they are not ultimate things. They are for instruction, inspiration, and "mere recreation." They are not an end in themselves, but they "belonged to the ornamental part of life; they provided 'innocent diversion'; or else they 'refined our manners' or 'incited us to virtue' or 'glorified the gods.'"[28]

Lewis emphasized that "the Christian knows from the outset that the salvation of a single soul is more important than the production or preservation of all the epics and tragedies in the world." And, as for the aspect of superiority, he knows that the "vulgar since they include most of the poor probably include most of his superiors. He has no objection to comedies that merely amuse and tales that merely refresh; for he thinks like Thomas Aquinas *ipsa ratio hoc habet ut quandoque rationis usus intercipiatur*. We can play, as we can eat, to the glory of God."[29]

Simply put, to gain a perspective on literature and art as opportunities for enjoyment is to liberate them from becoming themselves scriptures or sacred icons, i.e., from ultimately becoming false prophecies or graven images. Whatever temporal good is venerated and lifted up will be brought down laughably and in humility.

The dominant and pervasive perspective on modern and postmodern society, however, is dark, foreboding, ominous, and tragic. Destruction and death are inevitable and terrible; indeed, no one should doubt or dismiss the horror of the human condition. It is almost relentlessly nihilistic, and in the natural realm it is unresolvedly despairing.

The supernatural perspective, however, offers a comic ring to existence, even in pagan thought. Lewis noted that when the soul of Pompey ascended from the funeral pyre, he "looked down and saw the mockeries done to his own corpse, which was having a wretched and hugger-mugger funeral. They made him laugh." Boccaccio's Arcita also ascends to a risible height. When he ascends, he sees how tiny the earth is, and "like Pompey, he laughs; but not because his funeral, like Pompey's, is a hole-and-corner affair: it is the mourning that he laughs at." Chaucer used this same experience for the ghost of Troilus. Lewis concluded that "all three ghosts—Pompey's, Arcita's, and Troilus's—laughed for the same reason, laughed at the littleness of all those things that had seemed so important before they died; as we laugh, on waking, at the trifles or absurdities that loomed so large in our dreams."[30]

The cries of the world, trembling beneath the din of constant activity, are wailing, weeping, and mourning. Likewise, laments and complaints rumble beneath our laughing souls. Danish philosopher Søren Kierkegaard expressed this keenly in his journals when he wrote about being the life of the party, wit pouring from his lips, and then going home and wanting to kill himself.[31]

The hoarse, dreadful laughter of those who see life as a fraud—who taste it and find it bitter—is a hollow, hopeless laughter. There were those who laughed at Jesus with scorn when He said that the girl was not dead, she was only sleeping and would wake again. For them, the laughter of hope and joy is a mere illusion that evaporates like steam from a hot spring. Death is the futile end and the grave its grin; and grave laughter is silent, deadly silent.

Yet when the supernatural really breaks into the ordinary like comic epiphany, laughter breaks forth in the same way that a rainbow stretches across the heavens when the sunlight strikes the rain-drenched world. One cannot be open to God's reality, Lewis argued, without bumping into the humor of the heavens and the earth. Consider Satan in *Paradise Lost*. Even he cannot "rant and posture through the whole universe without, sooner or later, awaking the comic spirit. The whole nature of reality would have to be altered in order to give him such immunity, and it is not alterable."[32]

Laughter offers this value: *It can change and even correct one's perspective.* Ostensibly, this is the reason for the laughter of satire in Molière or Swift. It chases out the fog and mists that so cloud our minds as we try to consider what is important. When, in Lewis's *That Hideous Strength*, Mark Studdock is being deprogrammed in a "room of objectivity," he becomes aware of a wholly evil atmosphere that is meant to eradicate all moral and religious taboos. But "the built and painted perversity of his high coffin of a room had the effect of making him aware of the room's opposite." Under the unchangingly serious gaze of the institutional psychologist, who brandished "a stop watch and a notebook and all the ritual of scientific experiment," Studdock is ordered to perform indecent tasks and "petty obscenities which a very silly child might have thought funny." He becomes conscious of something sweet and straight in this sour and crooked situation—aware, that is, of a solid idea of the normal in contrast to the abnormal. And "often Mark felt that one good roar of laughter would have blown away the whole atmosphere of the thing."[33] Such a comic approach would have healed the sickness of a bent perspective. It would chase away the fog upon the mountains, providing a more sublime and glorious vision of the valley.

In his *Concluding Unscientific Postscript*, Søren Kierkegaard wrote that "the more thoroughly and substantially a human being exists, the more he will discover the comical. Even one who has merely conceived a great plan toward accomplishing something in the world will discover it."[34]

But there are those, like the fawning subjects of the king who wore no clothes, who have no eyes to see the comedy of our predicament. Chesterton fingered certain figures in the sciences as being humorless: the psychologist, the anthropologist, and the solemn scientist of the human past who see only facts and data and not meanings. "When Hiawatha was told by his nurse that a warrior threw his grandmother up to the moon, he laughed like any English child told by his nurse that a cow jumped over the moon. The child sees the joke as well as most men, and better than some scientific men."[35]

Like this child, it is the primitive human who may be more apt to truly see than the professional. Chesterton described how two groups might view one creation myth:

The Australian aborigines, regarded as the rudest of savages, have a story about a giant frog who had swallowed the sea and all the waters of the world: and who was only forced to spill them by being made to laugh. All the animals with all their antics passed before him and,

like Queen Victoria, he was not amused. He collapses at last before
an eel who stood delicately balanced on the tip of its tail, doubtless with a rather desperate dignity. . . . There is philosophy in that
vision of the dry world before the beatific Deluge of laughter. There
is imagination in the mountainous monster erupting like an aqueous
volcano; there is plenty of fun in the thought of his goggling visage
as the pelican or the penguin passed by. Anyhow the frog laughed;
but the folk-lore student remains grave.[36]

The trouble arises, Chesterton said, from the "man trying to look
at these stories from the outside, as if they were scientific objects."[37]

Lewis noted this narrow kind of perspective by using an illustration from Henri Bergson. It involved a race of people who had a
peculiar mental limitation compelling them to regard paintings as
merely mosaics of little dots. They used magnifying glasses to discover the relations and regularities among the dots, but they missed
completely the big picture.[38] "Of a sane man there is only one safe
definition," observed Chesterton. "He is a man who can have tragedy
in his heart and comedy in his head."[39] It is the balance of these two
perspectives that gave Lewis's life both a deep charity toward others
and a rational, comic view of the ironies and humors of life, and even,
eventually, toward his own father.

3

Fathers and Sons

*Men show their characters in nothing more clearly
than in what they think laughable.*
—Johann Wolfgang von Goethe

The tradition of humorous characterizations in C. S. Lewis's fiction
appears as much in rich, complex personalities as it does in true comic
sketches. The characters he knew in real life were much more interesting than anyone he could draw from imagination. His brother, Warnie,
was once described as an "amiable, baggy-trousered walrus." John Wain
called Warnie a man who had dressed up to look like Lewis with a mus-
tache. He was a jolly Watson to his rational Holmesian brother.

Their father, Albert Lewis, however, was a character out of Dickens
or Sterne. Lewis's difficulty with his father is well documented. The
strain of their relationship brought anger, anguish, and guilt upon
the son. But Lewis and his easygoing brother saw the humorous side
of it as well. On one occasion he may have been preaching to himself
when, while having lunch with a father and son, he observed "that son
would have borne patiently and humorously from any other old man
the silliness which enraged him in his father."[1] In stepping out of one's
own self-centeredness, one gains a sense of perspective that allows not
only for charity but for the comic spirit as well.

Lewis's father was notorious for his convoluted logic and misuse
of names. When Warnie spoke about a reunion dinner for the officers
of his company, the following exchange took place:

FATHER: I suppose your friend Collins was there.
BROTHER: Collins? Oh no. He wasn't in the Nth, you know.

FATHER: (after a pause) Did these fellows not like Collins then?

BROTHER: I don't quite understand. What fellows?

FATHER: The Johnnies that got up the dinner.

BROTHER: Oh no, not at all. It was nothing to do with liking or not liking. You see, it was purely a Divisional affair. There'd be no question of asking anyone who hadn't been in the Nth.

FATHER: (after a long pause) Hm! Well, I'm sure poor Collins was very much hurt.[2]

Lewis explained his affection for his utterly distinctive father by drawing parallels to the odd and whimsical spirit of son and father in Sterne's classic, *Tristram Shandy*. Lewis's Irish solicitor patriarch had "more power of confusing an issue or taking up a fact wrongly than any man I have ever known."[3] His father would retain an answer or a fact in a shape very unlike what had been given him, producing through sentiment, imagination, and lively humor his own version of the facts.

As he invariably got proper names wrong (no name seemed to him less probable than another) his *textus receptus* was often almost unrecognizable. Tell him that a boy called Churchwood had caught a field mouse and kept it as a pet, and a year, or ten years later, he would ask you, "Did you ever hear what became of poor Chickweed who was so afraid of rats?"[4]

The "ludicrous disproportion" between his father's "grandiloquent harangues and their occasions" reminded Lewis of the "advocate in Martial who thunders about all the villains of Roman history, while meantime *lis est de tribus capellis*—This case, I beg the court to note/Concerns a trespass by a goat."[5] It was a tempest in a teapot, the ridiculous dressed sublimely.

Albert Lewis seems remarkably like a model of one of Lewis's good

Narnian dwarfs, old Trumpkin. In *The Silver Chalice*, Trumpkin is the elderly Lord Regent of Prince Caspian. Two British children brought into Narnia are introduced to this aging, stubborn, and farcical dwarf in what appears to be a British music hall sketch. (Lewis did not appear to share his father's and brother's taste for vaudeville, being sensitive toward and sympathetic at the humiliation of any failed "turn" or act; but he did apparently glean the form of silly exchange of a comic old buffoon and his charge.) When an owl introduces the two strangers, the routine begins:

> "Rangers! What d'ye mean?" said the Dwarf, "I see two uncommonly grubby man-cubs. What do they want?"
>
> "My name's Jill," said Jill, pressing forward. She was very eager to explain the important business on which they had come.
>
> "The girl's called Jill," said the Owl, as loud as it could.
>
> "What's that?" said the Dwarf. "The girls are all killed! I don't believe a word of it. What girls? Who killed 'em?"
>
> "Only one girl, my Lord," said the Owl. "Her name is Jill."
>
> "Speak up, speak up," said the Dwarf.
>
> "Don't stand there buzzing and twittering in my ear. Who's been killed?"
>
> "Nobody's been killed," hooted the Owl.
>
> "Who?"
>
> "NOBODY."
>
> "All right, all right. You needn't shout. I'm not so deaf as all that. What do you mean by coming here to tell me that nobody's been killed? Why should anyone have been killed?"
>
> "Better tell him I'm Eustace," said Scrubb.
>
> "The boy's Eustace, my Lord," hooted the Owl as loud as it could.
>
> "Useless?" said the Dwarf irritably. "I dare say he is. Is that any reason for bringing him to court? Hey?"
>
> "Not useless," said the Owl. "EUSTACE."

"Used to it, is he? I don't know what you're talking about, I'm
sure. I tell you what it is, Master Glimfeather; when I was a young
Dwarf there used to be *talking* beasts and birds in this country who
really could talk. There wasn't all this mumbling and muttering
and whispering."[6]

Lewis's portrait of Trumpkin reflects somewhat an affectionate
description of his father. He and Warnie found irrepressible humor
in their father's communication and his harrumphing and blustering
and responding to corrections with an incredulous: "Hm! Well, that's
not the story you *used* to tell." One can almost imagine the two boys
gently imitating their father like the young owls who imitated dwarf
Trumpkin. At a parliament of owls, one owl remarks that Trumpkin
was "so old now he'd only say, 'You're a mere chick. I remember
when you were an egg. Don't come trying to teach me, Sir. Crabs
and crumpets!'

> This owl imitated Trumpkin's voice rather well, and there were
> sounds of owlish laughter all round. The children began to see
> that the Narnians all felt about Trumpkin as people feel at school
> about some crusty teacher, whom everyone is a little afraid of and
> everyone makes fun of and nobody really dislikes.[7]

Lewis wrote that his father, "in his armchair, sometimes appeared
not so much incapable of understanding anything as determined to
misunderstand everything." Yet he saw him as a humorist and even
occasionally a wit. "When he was dying, the pretty nurse, rallying
him, said, 'What an old pessimist you are! You're just like my father.'
'I suppose,' replied her patient, 'he has *several* daughters.'"[8]

In addition to these confusions of language were "the sheer *non
sequiturs* when the ground seemed to open at one's feet."[9] This type of
communication was pregnant with comic potential. Chesterton indicated playfully that communication, the "whole high human art of

scripture or writing, began with a joke," kings and priests exchanging hieroglyphic messages for good fun and making bad puns out of the similar picture-words for tax and pig.[10]

The conversations of the senior Lewis were dotted and decorated with "anfractuosities," which delighted his sons. The peculiar logic of their father attributed, for example, the origins of venereal disease to women, whence it spread to men. When asked why that was so, he answered: "Sure, how could a man have given it to a woman if he hadn't got it from a woman himself?"[11]

Lewis's father left him a legacy of enjoyment of "nearly all humorous authors, from Dickens to W. W. Jacobs." His passionate and rhetorical parent was, Lewis remembered,

> almost without rival the best raconteur I have ever heard; the best, that is, of his own type, the type that acts all the characters in turn with a free use of grimace, gesture, and pantomime. He was never happier than when closeted for an hour or so with one or two of my uncles exchanging "wheezes" (as anecdotes were oddly called in our family).[12]

Albert Lewis retained an enormous fund of these jokes for an evening's entertainment. And Warnie, on his travels, used to collect such wheezes as were acceptable and post them home to his father.

Jack brought to Little Lea his own wheezes from Oxford, usually about peculiar characters he had encountered. One Lewis wheeze involved an undergraduate friend doing a mugger (a sort of compulsory invitation to tea with a master) at University College. His pedantic posturing brought on an attack of malapropism. Trying to impress the ladies present, he stretched his vocabulary like allegories along the Nile, mixing the terms *salubrious* and *salacious*. When asked about places to spend a holiday, he replied: "Not Devonshire, it's not very salacious." He repeated the error when the mugger asked how he found Oxford. "Well, sir," he answered, "it isn't as salacious as I had hoped."[13]

Another chestnut of a wheeze Lewis told his father was about a professor carrying a perforated box on a train. When a woman inquired about its contents, the professor answered that it contained a snake-eating mongoose for a friend suffering from *delirium tremens,* who was seeing snakes. "But you don't mean that the snakes are real?" the lady asked. "Oh dear me, no," answered the professor, "but then neither is the mongoose."[14]

4

Grandfather of Mirth and Gladness

He can walk into the heart without knocking.
—SAMUEL JOHNSON

I found I could not keep G. K. Chesterton out of this book. It was like trying to keep Chesterton out of Lewis. The more I examined the landscape of Lewis, the more I discovered the gigantic shadows cast by the splendid sun of G. K. Chesterton.

In *The Discarded Image*, Lewis described every bookish, systematic writer of the Middle Ages as one who "based himself on an earlier writer, [who] follows an auctour."[1] Lewis, a dinosaur of Medieval and Renaissance literature, based his writing on many early writers. Yet, without doubt, in regard to humor and satire, Lewis evolved primordially from this one mammoth, Chesterton.

If a comic spirit can be breathed from one quick-witted mind into another, then Lewis and Chesterton are the clearest such models of comic inspiration constructed. Lewis breathed paradoxygen from this philosophical Peter Pan, who played a significant role in undermining his humorous protégé's early pessimism, atheism, and anti-sentimentalism.

Chesterton was famous for setting the world as we see it on its head. He turned the ordinary upside down, topsy-turvy, and breathed new breath, life, and joy into the banal and mundane. He was a cheerleader for truth, goodness, and the humorous ways of God. He entered Lewis's life as a kindly and gallant guardian angel—a giant, laughing cherub. This humorous Dr. Johnson was a sportsman who enjoyed his own enjoyment and laughed at his own laughter. Lewis and doubtless many others felt in Chesterton "the 'charm' of goodness as a man feels the charm of a woman he has no intention of marrying." After reading *The Everlasting Man*, Lewis wrote that he thought Chesterton the most sensible man alive "apart from his Christianity":

> In reading Chesterton, as in reading MacDonald, I did not know what I was letting myself in for. A young man who wishes to remain a sound atheist cannot be too careful of his reading. There are traps everywhere—"Bibles laid open, millions of surprises," as Herbert says, "fine nets and stratagems." God is, if I may say it, very unscrupulous.[2]

If the nineteenth-century Scottish Presbyterian George MacDonald baptized Lewis's imagination, it was Chesterton who turned his thinking upside down, which for an atheist would have ended right side (that is, sunny side) up.

On May 7, 1963, Sherwood E. Wirt of the Billy Graham Evangelistic Association interviewed Lewis in Cambridge. He asked Lewis: "A light touch has been characteristic of your writings, even when you are dealing with heavy theological themes. Would you say there is a key to cultivation of such an attitude?" Lewis responded by pointing to his mentor:

> I believe this is a matter of temperament. However, I was helped in achieving this attitude by my studies of the literary men of the Middle Ages, and by the writings of G. K. Chesterton. Chesterton, for example, was not afraid to combine serious Christian themes with buffoonery. In the same way, the miracle plays of the Middle Ages would deal with a sacred subject such as the nativity of Christ, yet would combine it with a farce.[3]

Lewis's initial appreciation or liking of Chesterton, however, did not derive from intellectual agreement. "Liking an author may be as involuntary and improbable as falling in love," he wrote.

I did not need to accept what Chesterton said in order to enjoy it. His humor was of the kind which I like best—not "jokes" imbedded in the page like currants in a cake, still less (what I cannot endure), a general tone of flippancy and jocularity, but the humor which is not in any way separable from the argument but is rather (as Aristotle would say) the "bloom" on dialectic itself.[4]

The peculiar "bloom" of Chesterton's dialectic unsettled young Lewis's atheism (just as the stink of burnt marshwiggle woke Puddleglum from the seductive enchantment of the Green Lady's narcotic fire). Yet, in trying to flee God, Lewis found himself stalked. "Amiable agnostics will talk cheerfully about 'man's search for God,'" wrote Lewis. "To me, as I then was, they might as well have talked about the mouse's search for the cat."[5] All the books he read were beginning to turn against him, including Chesterton's:

Then I read Chesterton's *Everlasting Man* and for the first time saw the whole Christian outline of history set out in a form that seemed to me to make sense. Somehow I contrived not to be too badly shaken. You will remember that I already thought Chesterton the most sensible man alive "apart from his Christianity." . . . I had not long finished *The Everlasting Man* when something far more alarming happened to me. Early in 1926 the hardest boiled of all the atheists I ever knew sat in my room on the other side of the fire and remarked that the evidence for the historicity of the Gospels was really surprisingly good. "Rum thing," he went on, "all that stuff of Frazer's about the Dying God. Rum thing. It almost looks as if it had really happened once." To understand the shattering

impact of it, you would need to know the man. . . . If he, the cynic
of cynics, the toughest of the toughs, were not—as I would still
have put it—"safe," where could I turn? Was there no escape?[6]

When Chesterton's faith blossomed in Lewis's soul, other fruits
were cultivated by the association, not the least of which was a bloom-
ing British humor. The second-best germ of Chesterton that infected
Lewis was a contagious sense of joy and humor.

A writer in the *Yorkshire Evening Post* once angrily reproached
Chesterton on his writing: "Mr. G. K. Chesterton is not a humorist;
not even a Cockney humorist." Chesterton launched into a defense not
of being excluded as a humorist, but being denied his standing as a
Cockney. "I do not urge that I am a humorist, but I do insist that I
am a Cockney. If I were a humorist, I should certainly be a Cockney
humorist; if I were a saint, I should certainly be a Cockney saint."[7] He
conceded his unworthiness at being numbered in the esteemed category
of Cockney humorists such as Samuel Johnson and Charles Lamb. "All
the best humor that exists in our language is Cockney humor." (Chaucer
and Dickens were also Cockney—that is, they were Londoners.) "I
need not trouble you with the long list of the Cockney humorists who
have discharged their bills (or failed to discharge them) in our noble
old City taverns." Yet, he wrote, he hoped sometime—in some strange
world beyond the stars—to become one: "In that potential paradise
I may walk among the Cockney humorists, if not an equal, at least a
companion. I may feel for a moment on my shoulder the hearty hand
of Dryden and thread the labyrinths of the sweet insanity of Lamb."[8]

The Cockney inheritance bestowed on Chesterton was left in turn
as a legacy for C. S. Lewis. Indeed, Lewis would take up not only the
faith of Chesterton, but Cockney laughter as well—in spite of the fact
that he was born in Ireland.

5

Humor of the Self

What is funny about us is precisely that we take ourselves too seriously.
—Reinhold Niebuhr

Self-effacing humor was a bright birthmark of both Chesterton and Lewis. Chesterton could not resist caricaturing himself as a figure of fun. He made jokes about his gigantic size, and in so doing reduced the height of his platform and made himself an equal with his audience. When he began a speech to the Union at Oxford, for example, he announced, "I am not a cat burglar"—and he had his audience by the whiskers. Once, when stuck in the door of a car, Chesterton compared himself to the old Irishwoman who, when asked, "Why don't you get out sideways?" replied, "I have no sideways."[1]

Edward Macdonald recalled one special anecdote Chesterton used about his image: "When Thomas Derrick drew his famous cartoon of G.K.C. milking a cow he hesitated to give it to me for fear that G.K.C. would be offended." Macdonald wanted to print it but first telephoned Chesterton and requested his permission, adding that he may not like it. "I would rather it were not printed," he replied. "I never like the idea of my name being used in the title of the paper and don't want well-intentioned but embarrassing personalities. Of course, if it were highly satirical, insulting, and otherwise unflattering I'd gladly have it on the front-page."[2]

Lewis saw himself in this sort of self-effacing comic mold as well. As a schoolboy he described himself as clumsy and unfit for games and parties. He abhorred being stuffed into his Eton suit and stiff shirt and made to endure the torment of neighborhood dances, suffering the "aching feet and burning head, and the mere weariness of being kept up so many hours after one's usual bedtime." For such persecution, "I positively felt that I could have torn my hostess limb from limb. Why should she thus pester me? I have never done her any harm, never asked her to a party."[3] What aggravated such social tortures was that Lewis didn't mix well with children his own age. Reading much more than his peers, he had "developed a vocabulary which must (I now see) have sounded very funny from the lips of a chubby urchin in an Eton jacket."[4]

Lewis portrayed with precision the embarrassing humor we all face in ill-at-ease situations when he described his young hero Shasta using the reins on an ordinary horse. Shasta "looked very carefully out of the corners of his eyes to see what the others were doing (as some of us have done at parties when we weren't quite sure which knife or fork we were meant to use)."[5] Lewis may have been confessing his lack of social poise as well in an aside about Prince Rabadash. The prince had gotten stuck on a castle wall, and "his chain-shirt was somehow hitched up so that it was horribly tight under the arms and came half way over his face. In fact he looked just as a man looks if you catch him in the very act of getting into a stiff shirt that is a little too small for him."[6]

Lewis discovered comic irony, a "curious mixture of justice and injustice," in being blamed for real faults but at the wrong time. When he used "long words," adults saw him as a conceited boy who was showing off. But these were the only words he knew; he simply hadn't yet been acquainted with schoolboy slang. "And there were not lacking adults who would egg me on with feigned interest and feigned seriousness—on and on till the moment at which I suddenly knew I was being laughed at." Lewis's defense was to affect a sillier demeanor, to develop a feigned party manner of "a giggling and gurgling imitation of the vapidest grown-up chatter."[7]

The same ironic mixture occurred when he was disliked at Wyvern College. He was not only the kind of new boy who skipped clubs, but

> I was big for my age, a great lout of a boy, and that sets one's seniors against one. I was also useless at games. Worst of all, there was my

face. I am the kind of person who gets told, "And take that look off your face too." Notice, once more, the mingled justice and injustice of our lives. No doubt in conceit or ill temper I have often intended to look insolent or truculent; but on those occasions people don't appear to notice it. On the other hand, the moments at which I was told to "take that look off" were usually those when I intended to be most abject.[8]

His own physical appearance provided Lewis with raw comic material. He described wrinkles as the "honorable insignia of long service in this warfare."[9] And his photograph in *Time* magazine was "a useful mortification; good as a hair shirt. (What an exaggeration! as if one wouldn't rather look like the Ugly Duchess than wear even ordinary tickly underclothing for half a day!)"[10]

The balding Lewis was glad to "have outgrown the muscular weakness of children; but we envy those who retain its energy, its well-thatched scalp."[11] To cover his little-thatched scalp, Lewis wore a hat that became quite famous. Warnie Lewis told one memorable anecdote about his brother's covering:

Jack's clothes were a matter of complete indifference to him: he had an extraordinary knack of making a new suit look shabby the second time he wore it. One of his garments has passed into legend. It is said that Jack once took a guest for an early morning walk on the Magdalen College grounds, in Oxford, after a very wet night. Presently the guest brought his attention to a curious lump of cloth hanging on a bush. "That looks like my hat," said Jack; then, joyfully, "It is my hat." And, clapping the sodden mass on his head, he continued his walk.[12]

Lewis compared having a body to having an old automobile— "When all sorts of apparently different things keep going wrong, but what they add up to is the plain fact that the machine is wearing out!

Well, it was not meant to last forever. Still, I have a kindly feeling for the old raddle trap."[13]

At Lewis grew older, he joked about his health and his imminent reception in heaven. "What on earth is the trouble about there being a rumor of my death? There's nothing discreditable in dying: I've known the most respectable people to do it."[14]

When this old life is finally over, Lewis wondered, how would God deal with each person individually? Perhaps by consulting reference books? "Gabriel, bring me Mr. Lewis's file."[15]

Chesterton received rebukes for similar whimsies. One indignant gentleman accused him of flippancy in degrading spiritualism.

> I thought I was defending Spiritualism; but I am rather used to being accused of mocking the thing I set out to justify. My fate in most controversies is rather pathetic. It is an almost invariable rule that the man with whom I don't agree thinks I am making a fool of myself, and the man with whom I do agree thinks I am making a fool of him.[16]

Being laughed at did not seem to bother either Chesterton or Lewis very much, particularly when the mockery was loving. Lewis's wife teased her husband merrily, and he learned "not to talk rot to her unless I did it for the sheer pleasure . . . of being exposed and laughed at. I was never less silly than as H's lover."[17]

Chesterton unexpectedly came upon a fiasco in his spiritual autobiography: that, in trying to concoct a new religion and a heresy of his own, he discovered that it was Christian orthodoxy. In his defense of Christianity, Chesterton lamented that the book could not avoid being egotistical, but then again, it could not also avoid being dull:

> Dulness will, however, free me from the charge which I most lament; the charge of being flippant. Mere light sophistry is the thing that I

happen to despise most of all things, and it is perhaps a wholesome fact that this is the thing of which I am generally accused. . . . I never in my life said anything merely because I thought it funny; though of course, I have had ordinary human vainglory, and may have thought it funny because I said it. . . . I offer this book with the heartiest sentiments to all the jolly people who hate what I write, and regard it (very justly, for all I know) as a piece of poor clowning or a single tiresome joke. . . .

For if this book is a joke it is a joke against me. I am the man who with the utmost daring discovered what had been discovered before. If there is one element of farce in what follows, the farce is at my own expense . . . no reader can accuse me here of trying to make a fool of him: I am the fool of this story, and no rebel shall hurl me from my throne.[18]

Chesterton laughed robustly at jokes at his own expense, often howling with joy. His voice, however, was unequal to his stature. Cosmo Hamilton described his high laughter as "peahen-like quarks of joy." Chesterton himself referred to the incongruity of his voice and size as "the mouse that came forth from the mountain." Yet his girth did not outsize his boisterous mirth, which Hamilton celebrated as "a sight and sound for the gods." Chesterton laughed at "his own jokes because they came to him as part of the joint findings of the quest, something he had seen and collected and brought for the pot."[19] And Lewis dipped a large soup spoon into his pot.

Humans might easily be defined as self-reflexive animals. One cannot help thinking and speaking of oneself (and even feeling oneself to be, for certain purposes as two people, one of whom can act upon and observe the other). Thus one pities, loves, admires, hates, despises, rebukes, comforts, examines, and masters (or is mastered by) "oneself." One is privy to one's own acts, as one's own conscience or accomplice. Armed with such a perspective, one is audience to one's own humanity and folly—a witness to and against oneself.

One of Lewis's dominant comic techniques was such self-reflexiv-
ity. It is a model of what Steve Seidman calls "comedian comedy," in
which the humorist steps outside the joke to comment on it, or outside
a story, a sermon, or an argument to provide a comic perspective on his
or her own role. It is the comic aside that is so robust in certain film
comedians. In the film *Horse Feathers*, Groucho Marx sees that a musical interlude is about to occur, steps forward, and says to the camera:
"I've got to stay here. But there's no reason why you folks shouldn't
go into the lobby until this thing blows over." Likewise, in *The Road
to Bali*, Bob Hope pauses, just before Bing Crosby starts to sing, and
warns: "He's going to sing, folks. Now's the time to go outside and
get the popcorn." Self-references are bracketed in these films even as
they take us out of the filmic universe. Like a comic Greek chorus, the
comedian talks directly to us, winks at us, and mutters *sotto voce*, a la
Woody Allen or Bugs Bunny, for our benefit. This breaks the illusion
of a separate world, and a new immediacy and intimacy are created
between the comic communicator and the audience.

Because Lewis wrote directly to his audience, he regularly used
the bracketed aside to establish a humorous and often more personal
relationship with his readers. He often broke out of his fiction, apologetics, or scholarly treatise to breathe in the personal, much like a
dolphin irresistibly breaking the surface of the sea to breathe and
squeal. Lewis used such opportunities to sneak in a comic avuncular
aside, much the way E. Nesbit did in her children's stories. In *Five
Children and It*, Nesbit steps out of her story to share the unknown
reason why so many children who live in towns are naughty. And
Lewis the storyteller slips out of his author's cap as well to comment
on the action: "Ten to one you have never seen a giant with his face
beaming." "Other creatures whom I won't describe because if I did
the grown-ups would probably not let you read this book."[20] He even
poked fun at his own literary invention. Discussing Mr. Beaver, he
playfully added that "he now had a sort of modest expression on his
face—the sort of look people have when you are visiting a garden

they've made or reading a story they've written."[21] With a modest expression on his face, Lewis must also have winked.

Self-reflexive humor occurs subtly in Lewis's works. He refers to a man "in our time who wrote what he intended to be a general apologetic allegory for 'all who profess and call themselves Christians,' and was surprised to find it both praised and blamed as a defense of Rome."[22] Lewis, Screwtape's stepfather, found it difficult to be merely a don in his writing output. Yet he wrote indirectly of his own low reputation at Oxford when showing how Tyndale

> repeatedly twits More with being a "poet": but everyone knew that poets were feigners and under the rules that then governed controversy the jibe was almost inevitable. Even now a writer who has ventured on any imaginative work is likely to have the fact used against him when he turns to criticism or theology.[23]

Lewis did twit his fellows back at Oxford once he moved to Cambridge. In his inaugural address, he complained that older and erroneous pictures of the Middle Ages have "survived among weaker brethren, if not [let us hope] at Cambridge, yet certainly in that Western darkness from which you have . . . bidden me emerge."[24]

His vocation as a scholar prompted much self-mocking. In writing of Martianus, who stored in his mind the knickknacks of others' philosophies and religions, Lewis confessed, "I have heard the scholar defined as one who has a propensity to collect useless information, [who] gloats and catalogues, but never dusts them for even their dust is precious in his eyes."[25] Lewis did not hide the fact that he was sufficiently of the "author's kidney to enjoy the faint smell of secular dust."[26] Yet he made light of the devoted habit of the professor's reading dry-as-dust books: "Few men at any period can have obeyed Martin's light-hearted command to 'rede ouer Doctor Bridges'; I have skipped some pages myself."[27]

Lewis laughed even at the influence that Dryden had on him,

evidenced in his going through the "Essay of Dramatick Poesie" and altering every sentence that ended with a preposition. Lewis detested this "frenchified schoolroom superstition," which often plucked at his elbow, knowing this curious and unwelcome grammatical taboo would not have happened without Dryden. He wrote, with a twinkle in his eye (and a preposition dangling): "It is so alien from the language that it has never penetrated into the conversation of even the worst prigs, and serves no purpose but to increase those little bunches of unemphatic monosyllables that English was already prone to."[28]

Lewis frequently inserted inside jokes into his essays. In one, he spoke of two young boys who stole a cigar and smoked it before its time: "And may I add the important moral of the story? One of these boys has been permanently punished by a life-long inability to appreciate cigars."[29] Lewis played gamely also with his heritage. It is true, he wrote, that Spenser "hated the Irish and they him: but, as an Irishman myself, I take leave to doubt whether that is a very un-Irish trait. ('The Irish, sir,' said Dr. Johnson, 'are an honest people. They never speak well of one another')."[30]

In *That Hideous Strength*, Lewis created a fictional character, Dr. Dimble, who as a college don was a not-so-dim reflection of the author. His delight in Arthurian legend and gardening and his distrust of psychoanalysis paralleled Lewis's. Even more revealing was an attitude toward mediocre students—as, for example, when Dr. Dimble looked out of a window: " 'There is my dullest pupil just ringing the bell,' he said. 'I must go to the study, and listen to an essay on Swift beginning, "Swift was born." Must try to keep my mind on it, too, which won't be easy.' "[31]

Lewis bemoaned the answers he received from many students on questions such as, "contrast the characters Uriah Heep and Mr. Micawber." One student would write: "U. H. is the finished type of a rogue; Mr. M. on the other hand is the portrait of a happy-go-lucky debtor." The next paper would simply reverse the answer. There was "too much maddening jargon on 'the finished portrait of a rogue.'"[32]

John Lawlor remembered Lewis as Oxford tutor and scholar, and recalled that upon first encountering pupils Lewis would ask: "What have you been reading?"[33] Lewis reconstructed one initial meeting in a breezy, jovial letter to his father:

SELF: "Well, S., what Greek authors have you been reading?"
S: (cheerfully) "I can never remember. Try a few names and I'll see if I get on to any."
SELF: "Any Sophocles?"
S: "Oh yes."
SELF: "What plays of his have you read?"
S: (after a pause) "Well—the Alcestis."
SELF: (apologetically) "But isn't that by Euripedes?"
S: (with the genial surprise of a man who finds £1 where he thought there was only a 10/-note) "Really. Is it now? Then by Jove I have read some Euripedes."[34]

Most students were not so cheery and blissfully ignorant. Still, even in their cowering or awe they found good humor in their relations with Lewis. Adam Fox recalled that when one student was questioned about the matter of a date, he "referred to his own manuscript and said with some assurance, 'Well, it says so here.'"[35] Another interrupted Lewis during his prayers and Lewis told him he couldn't enter the room but should instead "kneel down and pray for me." The student obeyed. Another apologetically asked if he could turn in his unfinished essay the next day. Lewis responded: "Oh, that's quite all right, my dear boy, quite all right, but you must bring me a suitable bribe."[36] The next day Lewis received the finished essay and a bottle of whiskey.

Tutoring girls sent shivers up Lewis's bachelor spine. One colleague confided that Lewis had been worried by a woman who repeatedly approached him at the end of his lectures. She eventually proposed, afterward pretending it was a joke, but, his friend said, "It wasn't. And she wasn't the only one either. A man who lectures to women takes his life in his hands."[37] Lewis feared this prospect of the Abelard and Heloise relation. Engagement was "that fatal tomb of all lively and interesting men."[38] His concern escalated particularly when he was called upon to lecture at a women's college. He wrote:

> However I am not engaged to be married yet, and there are always seven of them there together, and the pretty ones are stupid and the interesting ones are ugly, so it is all right. I say this because as a general rule women marry their tutors. I suppose if a girl is determined to marry and has a man alone once a week to whom she can play the rapt disciple (most fatal of all poses to male vanity) her task is done.[39]

George Bailey compared the Lewis of the university to a "school book description of Friar Tuck," with a pronouncedly hearty manner and a booming voice "given to what someone once called 'rhetorical guffawing' ('Ho, ho, ho, so you think Milton was ascetic, do you? Ho, ho! You are quite wrong there.')."[40]

His lecture style at the rostrum was disciplined, deceptively easy, and deadpan. Bailey recalled one instance in which Lewis, who never "threw away a line," displayed his discrete humor. In a prolegomenon, Lewis said with dry, casual asides: "Reason can see truth in sleep with three kinds of clarity: . . . in the oracle kind (oraculum) some venerable person (an ancestor, wise-man, parent, or *even* a tutor) appears and announces truth otherwise unknown."[41] He garnered good laughs in his lectures, as his lines were perfectly "timed with all an actor's skills."[42] Upon lecturing an audience of women who were expected to wear academic gowns but hadn't, he began with mock modesty: "Oh! I must apologize for wearing a gown!" At the next meeting, gowns were in fashion again.[43]

The habitat of Oxford encouraged the cult of wit among its dons. Witty, casual remarks were designed, even "elaborately contrived," as ripostes or rejoinders. What was called for, said Bailey, was "dry, desultory, almost surreptitious humor, the nonchalant riposte . . . and best of all—whimsy." Such was Lewis's gift. Once knocking his pipe ashes out of a window overlooking a garden, Lewis was abruptly interrupted by a lively stranger who dashed into his room, shouting: "Do you real-ize that you almost blinded my baby?" "No," said Lewis, "I didn't even know you were married"—a rim-shot line worthy of W. C. Fields.[44]

Owen Barfield testified to the predominance of Lewis's comic spirit in conversation. His was a friendly playfulness, like that of Charles Lamb. (Lamb once responded to the poet Coleridge, when the latter asked if he'd ever heard him preach a sermon: "My dear fel-low, I never heard you do anything else!") Lewis's humor was a loud hint of an intellectual intimacy given to his close friends. Barfield observed that "a good deal could be said about the absolute necessity of humor, as an available ingredient, to any really deep thinker, as distinct from . . . a merely solemn one."[45]

Indeed, humor can be useful as a form of "packaging," of typing up a whole argument and its parts into a memorably comic complex—like Lewis's discussion of Bluspels and Flalanspheres. His longtime friend Barfield faithfully stressed Lewis's "irrepressible bent for comedy, simply because without that emphasis one would miss altogether the typical flavor of his company."[46] This humor was not buffoonery, flip-pancy, or even "professional" jesting, but, rather, fun—hearty, healthy, good-natured fun, evident in the "almost habitual breeze of irony at his own, and of sarcasm at his friends' expense." Yet his humor was never mean, bitter, or bitingly sarcastic. In a letter to Barfield, Lewis teased that the villainous characters in *That Hideous Strength* (Wither, Frost, Feverstone, even Fairy Hardcastle) were all portraits of Barfield. If he didn't mention this, he wrote, "that may have been because it isn't true. By gum, though, wait until I write another story."[47]

Lewis followed and echoed Aristotle's exhortation to his pupils "to play in order to become generous or noble." Above all, one should play! For Lewis, the Germanic idea of "humor" contained too much gravity and thus offered only a pretense to play. A weighty concept like *Schadenfreude*, delighting in the misfortunes of others, could almost crush laughter. Yet if humor must not be too heavy, it also must not be too flippant. Although Lewis

> would readily make fun of the great men of the past and exhibit them in a nonsensical light, he would only do so with those who knew and revered them as he did himself. A joke at the expense of Shelley or Goethe is a joke precisely because they were great men. "In the mouth, or in the presence, of those who have never experienced that greatness, it is merely boorishness."[48]

Lewis used a tangy, dry wit to gently puncture those who presumptuously assumed an air of knowledge. He observed, for example, that "every week a clever undergraduate, every quarter a dull American don, discovers for the first time what some Shakespearean play really meant."[49] He found absurdity even in the tomes he dusted in the library. He thought one reference work particularly intriguing: *Every Man His Own Lawyer—Illustrated*. Lewis looked in vain, however,

> for a portrait of a tort or a south aspect of Habeas Corpus—the pictures consisting entirely of courthouses and famous judges. Can you imagine anything more infuriating than, on turning to such a book to try to extricate yourself from an Income Tax muddle or an injudicious betrothal (and for what other purpose would you ever open it?) to be met with the bland features of Lord Darling?[50]

Not surprisingly, Lewis found the rites and rituals of the academic community funny. He perceived his formal admission to Magdalen College as a ceremonial event of unacknowledged comedy. Ushered into a grand room, he saw a red cushion laid before the feet of the college president. "I realized with some displeasure that this was going to be a kneeling affair." After several minutes of an incomprehensible Latin address and his own uncertain responses, Lewis was raised up by the hand as the president pronounced, "I wish you joy." Lewis wrote:

"It sounds well enough on paper but it was hardly impressive in fact; and I tripped over my gown in rising." The ordeal included the blessing from all the members, and the multiple repetitions of "I wish you joy" sounded odd: "English people have not the talent for graceful ceremonial. They go through it lumpishly and with a certain mixture of defiance and embarrassment, as if everyone felt he was being rather silly, and was at the same time ready to shoot down anyone who said so."[51]

Lewis revealed a similar attitude toward the college administration:

Yes we have the word "dither" and the thing too. And our offices are in a dither too. This is so common that I suspect there must be something in the very structure of a modern office which creates Dither. Otherwise why does our "College Office" find full time work for a crowd of people in doing what the president of the College, 100 years ago, did in his spare time without a secretary and without a typewriter? (The more noise, heat, and smell a machine produces the more power is being wasted!)[52]

Lewis satirized in his fiction the college office and its members and meetings. "Fellows of colleges," he wrote, perhaps partly as confession, "do not always find money matters easy to understand: if they did, they would probably not have been the sort of men who became Fellows of colleges."[53]

Lewis's fiction also sketched outlines of his own professorial quirks. He knew his students found him amusing and eccentric, as all Oxford dons were supposed to be. A trace of this role found its way into *The Last Battle*. Professor Digory Kirke acts the role of the quintessential professor when he instructs the children on the end of the old Narnia. He compares the old country to a shadow or a dream,

but when he added under his breath "It's all in Plato, all in Plato: bless me, what *do* they teach them at these schools!" the older ones laughed. It was so exactly like the sort of thing they had heard him say long ago in that other world where his beard was grey instead of golden. He knew why they were laughing and joined in the laugh himself.[54]

Self-effacing humor was a common rhetorical device Lewis used in addressing his audiences. He once began an address to theological students: "The proper study of shepherds is sheep, not (save accidentally) other shepherds. And woe to you if you evangelize. I am not trying to teach my grandmother. I am a sheep, telling shepherds what only a sheep can tell them. And now I start my bleating."[55] Appearing before a Shakespearean audience, Lewis modestly indicated he felt "rather like a child brought in at dessert to recite his piece before the grown-ups."[56] So he decided to bestow all his childishness upon them.

Lewis saw his own spiritual responsibilities with more honesty and humor than do most of us. In a letter to an American child, Laurence Krieg, whose mother worried that her son was worshiping Aslan more than Christ, Lewis composed a prayer for the boy. It ended with a postscript: "And if Mr. Lewis has worried any other children by his books or done them any harm, then please forgive him and help him never to do it again."[57] Writing on the call to holiness in Thomas à Kempis's *Imitation of Christ*, he found it, to an almost comic degree, "not addressed to my condition." When Kempis warned against "chatting in the kitchen when you ought to be in your cell," Lewis confessed that "our temptation is to be in our studies when we ought to be chatting in the kitchen. (Perhaps if our studies were as cold as those cells it would be different.)"[58]

Lewis faithfully reminded himself that we must learn to love those we don't naturally like. Even pagans knew "that any beggar at your doorstep might be a god in disguise: and the parable of the sheep and the goats is Our Lord's comment."[59] He acknowledged that "it's so much easier to pray for a bore than to go and see him."[60] And both Lewis and his brother, Warnie, saw the wisdom in the New Testament's exhortation to "visit the widows, not to let them visit us."[61]

Chesterton in the same spirit quipped: "The Bible tells us to love our neighbors, and also to love our enemies; probably because they are generally the same people."[62] This comic perspective equipped him and his godson of humor, Lewis, to view the spirit and the flesh with the same sense of balance. Their laughter liberated them from the prisons of both their times and their selves. They were given a vantage point from which to see and understand more clearly the folly of humanity, yet a folly divinely overseen and repaired.

Part 2

Joy

Introduction

Surprised by joy,
impatient, as the wind
I turned to share the transport.
—WILLIAM WORDSWORTH

Of Lewis's four causes of laughter, the highest and most sublime is joy. Yet its arrival, as Frederick Buechner observes, is as "notoriously unpredictable as the one who bequeaths it."[1] God in His wisdom withholds it from His children at some moments, and in His mercy pours it out on them at others. Fun, the joke proper, and flippancy can be planned and produced by any person. But joy can be received only from the One whose presence is absolute joy.

For C. S. Lewis, the purest laughter on earth dwells in the kingdom of joy. When joy reigns in the land, the sound of laughter is never far away. Silvery volleys of laughter fall on every dale and in every valley of the countryside where the King of joy rules. In Lewis's underworld kingdom of pride and selfishness, the devil Screwtape reserved some of his sharpest criticism for this seemingly hallowed laughter of joy. He found it utterly repulsive and repugnant to the ego-infested environs of hell. He attacked its exhilaration and merriment as inappropriate for creatures whose cardinal value is self-importance. This offensive jocundity, Screwtape wrote in a letter classifying the types of laughter, was what one would see

among friends and lovers reunited on the eve of a holiday. Among adults some pretext in the way of jokes is usually provided, but the facility with which the smallest witticisms produce laughter at such a time shows that they are not the real cause. What the real cause is we do not know. . . . Laughter of this kind does us no good and should always be discouraged. Besides, this phenomenon is of itself disgusting and a direct insult to the realism, dignity, and austerity of hell.[2]

For Screwtape, the affront of this laughter carried a mystery that runs counter to the fallen nature of human beings. For Lewis, joy is at the heart of Christianity—it is the gigantic secret that compels women and men into the company of the Cross and characterizes the fruit of their sufferings. It converts a wide, diverse throng of sad, lonely pilgrims into a fellowship of blessedness, bringing all into a dance of comedy. Indeed, if there is any laughter that expresses the character of God, it may be presumed to be that of joy. In His season of much anguish with trouble brewing, Jesus promised His disciples that His joy might be in them and that their joy might be full (John 15:11). The promise intimated that laughter would yet rush into the vale of tears and bring this motley gang of proud and competing disciples together into a fellowship of joy.

The heavens teem with life, singing the glories and joys of God. Thunder resounds the cosmos's hearty laughter (and not, as Aristophanes called it, divine flatulence) from the throne room of God, and lightning could be the flash of wit. Laughter reigns in the heavenlies in unmasked and unmeasured abundance; there is celestial joy forevermore. When Ransom, Lewis's protagonist in *Out of the Silent Planet*, is on the way to Malacandra (Mars), he is overwhelmed by a joyous "exaltation of heart," which spins out of his realization that space is not dead and empty, but rather that the heavens are as alive and nourishing as a womb.

Beneath the heavens, on the humble earth, joy descends. When angels appear with the incredible good news for the geriatric couple in Genesis, Sarah falls down and breaks out laughing. The gospel of Luke bursts with joy, as messengers of God interrupt daily life. When an angel spears in that narrative, people usually break forth in song and joy. The *Magnificat* of Mary celebrates all that is good and blessed: "My soul exalts the Lord, and my spirit has rejoiced in

God my Savior" (Luke 1:46–47). The Queen of Perelandra echoes the blessed Mary and sings her own version of the *Magnificat*, in which praise, delight, and blessing swirl about in a great dance of glory.

Joy dominated Lewis's life and characterized his deepest longings. Life to him was a wandering toward the source of this joy—toward one's real home. The journey may be rough and tiring and even tedious, but it offers surprises to a traveler at those very hours when he or she ought to be miserable. Lewis rightly noted that "one is more often happy than wretched without apparent cause."[3] Each surprise is a free sample of joy, foretastes of heavenly pleasure, offered without explanation. On a train trip from London, Lewis discovered he was invited to experience a moment of Eden:

> I am free to take it or not as I choose—like distant music which you need not listen to unless you wish, like a delicious faint wind on your face which you can easily ignore. One was invited to surrender to it. And the odd thing is that something inside me suggested that it would be "sensible" to refuse the invitation; almost that I would be better employed in remembering that I was going to do a job I do not greatly enjoy and that I should have a very tiresome journey back to Oxford. Then I silenced this inward wiseacre. I accepted the invitation—threw myself open to this feathery, impalpable, tingling sensation. The rest of the journey I passed in a state which can be described only as joy.[4]

A greedy impatience to snare, grasp, and keep joy, however, is the surest way to lose it. It can be instantly frightened away by introspection. It also can be vulgarized. "Those who think that if adolescents were all provided with a suitable mistress we should soon hear no more of 'immortal longings' are certainly wrong."[5] Lewis's character John in *The Pilgrim's Regress*, made this mistake repeatedly, seeking joy through fornication with the brown girl. Pleasure can be found in sexual experience, but John discovered that pleasure was not what he was seeking.

Lewis said the offer of sexual pleasure as an alternative to the desire of joy compared to offering a mutton chop to a man dying of thirst: "Joy is not a substitute for sex; sex is very often a substitute for Joy. I sometimes wonder whether all pleasures are not substitutes for Joy."[6] Lewis distinguished what he technically defined as joy both

> from Happiness and Pleasure. Joy (in my sense) has indeed one characteristic, and one only, in common with them; that fact that anyone who has experienced it will want it again. Apart from that, and considered only in its quality, it might almost equally well be called a particular kind of unhappiness or grief. But it is a kind we want. I doubt whether anyone who has tasted it would ever, if both were in his power, exchange it for all the pleasures in the world. But then Joy is never in our power and pleasure often is.[7]

When joy did appear in Lewis's life, it stripped away the veneer of all his erotic and magical perversions of it. The latter were distinctly separate experiences, he recognized, and in contrast looked like "sordid trumpery."[8] True joy had a vastly different effect: It did not disenchant the ordinary. The "bread upon the table or the coals in the grate" became sharper and more splendidly themselves.

What distinguished joy from happiness or pleasure was, for Lewis, a defining characteristic of longing—a deep yearning or poignant desire for something agonizingly elusive. Just as one's pleasure in spring contains a memory of winter longings, joy for Lewis always contained "the stab, the pang, the inconsolable longing." This underlying quality of joy in Lewis's system, then, was "that of an unsatisfied desire which is itself more desirable than any other satisfaction."[9]

The German language has a word for this joy-ward longing that Lewis describes: *Sehnsucht*. This is the haunting longing that touched Lewis throughout his life, that full, heavy, enveloping nostalgia for a fulfillment that awaited him—in something, somewhere.

6

Sehnsucht

He who binds to himself a joy
Does the winged life destroy;
But he who kisses the joy as it flies
Lives in eternity's sunrise.
—WILLIAM BLAKE

C. S. Lewis's joy was intimately connected to his experience of poignant longing. This longing could be sparked simply by the idea of autumn or an encounter with a "squirrel and a fat old rat in Addison's walk" just steps from his room at Magdalen College.[1]

In his pilgrimage into Christianity, Lewis met Owen Barfield, who quickened this longing in an "idea of the spiritual world as home— the discovery of homeliness in that which is otherwise so remote—the feeling that you are coming back tho' to a place you have never yet reached." Barfield found such spiritual nostalgia in the writings of George MacDonald and G. K. Chesterton. He protested against the abuse of R. L. Stevenson's romantic saying that "it is better to travel hopefully than to arrive." It is nonsense to imagine traveling hopefully with no hope of arriving. "It's like saying 'What a bore. I see we shan't be able to go to the opera after all. However we can still enjoy looking forward to going!'"[2] Picking up on this idea, Lewis explained that his tastes of joy were pointers, hints, and clues of what he truly sought.

For now, our joy is rough and unsteady. It cannot be held or kept. Any attempt to grasp it is to try to grasp Gerard Manley Hopkins's dim and faint echo of beauty. It dies in our clutch, becoming like lead. But the golden echo, which gives beauty back to beauty's maker and joy to the fount of joy, rings clear and true and eternal. It whispers in the wind, calling us to remember the word we first heard. The proverb reminds us, "Like cold water to a thirsty soul, so is good news from a far country" (Prov. 25:25 NRSV). So the voice from our home country comes to us while we are aliens and sojourners in a strange land. The merry characters of Kenneth Grahame's *Wind in the Willows* were, while separated from their homes, struck with sweet wantings—a deep longing for home, for the place each was designed to be.

In a letter to Dom Bede Griffiths (November 1959), Lewis expressed his feelings behind his desire for his real country:

> About death I go through different moods, but the times when I can desire it are never, I think, those when this world seems harshest. On the contrary, it is just when there seems to be most of Heaven already here that I come nearest to longing for a patria. It is the bright frontispiece which whets one to read the story itself. All joy (as distinct from mere pleasure, still more amusement) emphasizes our pilgrim status; always reminds, beckons, awakens desire. Our best havings are wantings.[3]

Lewis balanced the human pilgrimage on the razor edge between these two possible ways: "Apparently, then, our lifelong nostalgia, our longing to be reunited with something in the universe from which we now feel cut off, to be on the inside of some door which we have always seen from the outside is . . . the truest index of our real situation."[4] The old ache and inconsolable longing will be gloriously healed as we are summoned and ushered into the bright and luminous joy. We shall be bathed in the beauty of God's presence, and, as children know, a bath can be a hilarious thing. But for now, we travel the long, dusty road as a company of Chaucerian pilgrims on our way to Canterbury.

Our pilgrims' status is demonstrated, among other things, by the ever-present restlessness in the human heart. We move from town to town, from job to job. Wanderers among us take to the road and sometimes live that way for months or years. But what are we seeking? We often describe it as looking for "home," by which we don't mean the place we were born. In *Till We Have Faces*, Lewis's character Psyche uses the analogy of homesickness to express a *Sehnsucht* that is painful: "It almost hurt me like a bird in a cage when the other birds of its kind are flying home . . . to find the place where all the beauty came from—my country, the place where I ought to have been born. The longing for home."[5] Lewis quoted the same simile in Chaucer's "The Knight's Tale," in which the knight addresses the human journey: "All men know that the true good is Happiness, and all men seek it, but for the most part by wrong routes—like a drunk man who knows he has a house but can't find his way home."[6]

Once again, out of the experiences of his growing up, Lewis remembered a simple, childlike example of the homeward longing in which the capacity for joy grows: the end of a school term. He never forgot his anticipation of that blessed date, marked on the little penciled calendar on his desk. He later likened his feelings about it to that of the pilgrims as they approached their heavenly home (Beulah Land) in Bunyan's *Pilgrim's Progress*:

> Bunyan tells us that when the Pilgrims came to the land of Beulah, "Christian with desire fell sick; Hopeful also had a fit or two of the same disease." How well I know that sickness! It was no mere metaphor. . . . It was . . . a dizzying exaltation. . . . One had to think hard of common things lest reason should be overset. I believe it has served me ever since for my criterion of joy, and especially of the difference between joy and mere pleasure. Those who remember such Ends of Term are inexcusable if even, in later life, they allow mere pleasure to fob them off. One can tell at once when that razor-edged or needle-pointed quality is lacking: that shock, as if one were swallowing light itself.[7]

Old or young, human beings generally feel a longing of this type—for something they find difficult to describe. It is difficult because the longing is intangible and ineffable. Thus, *Sehnsucht* remains in human nature, no matter how settled one may become; it is one of the things that mark our humanity. No other creature is so inherently dissatisfied as the human being.

From his childhood, Lewis connected joy with this deeply felt but indescribable nostalgia. The main object of his longing, however, was not some type of elusive "home." Rather, surprisingly, it was a longing associated first with a season and then with a mythology. Lewis's first taste of this "sweet desire" came before he was five years old, when reading Beatrix Potter's story about Squirrel Nutkin who loses his tail. Why Squirrel Nutkin? Lewis answered,

> It troubled me with what I can only describe as the Idea of Autumn. . . . It sounds fantastic to say that one can be enamored of a season, but that is something like what happened and . . . the experience was one of intense desire. And one went back to the book, not to gratify the desire (how can one possess Autumn?) but to reawaken it.[8]

Then autumn was supplanted by something else—by a longing and a quest for joy that sustained Lewis through a convoluted path of youth and early adulthood shrouded with atheism, and which helped lead him eventually to faith in God. This heavenward longing was a passion for "Northernness," for something distant and other-worldly—a passion awakened by the *Twilight of the Gods* (joy was an arrow shot from the north) and by the poetry of Longfellow (based on the Swedish *Frithiof's Saga*). It was unexpected. The precocious young Lewis, nine or ten years old, was idly turning the pages of Longfellow's *King Olaf* when he read for the first time the enchanting verse that began: "I heard a voice, that cried, 'Balder the Beautiful / Is dead, is dead!'"[9]

The poem continues, enchanting evermore: "And through the misty air / Passed like the mournful cry / Of sunward sailing cranes." Of this poetry Lewis wrote:

I knew nothing about Balder; but instantly I was uplifted into huge regions of northern sky. I desired with almost sickening intensity something never to be described (except that it is cold, spacious, severe, pale and remote) and then . . . found myself at the very same moment already falling out of that desire and wishing I were back in it.[10]

From that point onward until his conversion, and perhaps even afterward, this Northern longing was a cold, intense fire that chance seemed to keep stoking in young Lewis. He pursued this "Northernness" mainly by reading books. But Lewis later pointed out that books were not the thing. They were mainly the channel:

The books or the music in which we thought the beauty was located will betray us if we trust to them; it was not in them, it only came through them, and what came through them was longing. These things—the beauty, the memory of our own past—are good images of what we really desire; but if they are mistaken for the thing itself they turn into dumb idols, breaking the hearts of their worshippers. For they are not the thing itself; they are only the scent of a flower we have not found, the echo of a tune we have not heard, news from a country we have never yet visited.[11]

Not long after Lewis hit on this Northern longing, his mother died. She had become ill with cancer, recovered for a while, then became ill again and died. As he describes it, "With my mother's death all settled happiness, all that was tranquil and reliable, disappeared from my life."[12] Lewis had prayed and prayed that God would heal his mother, but He did not. Whether this affected Lewis's childhood faith (Lewis infers that it didn't) one is left to wonder. Nevertheless, the next year, when he began the normal British boy's progression through boarding schools, his faith in the God of Christianity began to decrease in inverse proportion to his increasing age and education. He comments that the impression he got during his early formal education was that "religion, in general, though utterly false, was a natural growth, a kind of endemic nonsense into which humanity tended to blunder." In his early teens, the intellectual young Lewis decided he did not believe in the silly faith of his fathers. He "became an apostate, dropping [his] faith with no sense of loss but with the greatest relief."[13]

Nevertheless, the Northern longing, a spiritual longing of a kind, continued to smolder. One day, when he was about fourteen years old, Lewis chanced to see the words "Siegfried and the twilight of the Gods" under an illustration from that volume.

> Pure [Northernness] engulfed me. . . . There arose at once, almost like heartbreak, the memory of Joy itself. . . . The distance of the Twilight of the Gods and the distance of my own past Joy, both unattainable, flowed together into a single, unendurable sense of desire and loss. . . . And at once I knew that to "have it again" was the supreme and only important object of desire.[14]

And have it again he did, soon thereafter, when he heard in a record shop one day "The Ride of the Valkyries" from Wagner's *Ring of the Nibelungen* cycle. "To a boy crazed with 'Northernness,' whose highest musical experience had been [Gilbert and] Sullivan, the Ride came like a thunderbolt."[15]

Northernness became like a religion for Lewis. It awoke in him a capacity, not yet experienced in the context of Christianity, for true worship—not that he really believed in the Norse gods whose music and literature he now devoured. He didn't at all believe them to be real, but he felt for them "some kind of quite disinterested self-abandonment to an object which securely claimed this by simply being the object it was." Looking back on this period later, Lewis wondered if God hadn't kept that capacity for worship alive for His own purposes. "Sometimes," Lewis wrote in his autobiography, "I can almost think that I was sent back to the false gods there to acquire some capacity for worship against that day when the true God should recall me to himself."[16]

Over the next ten years Lewis became an expert in Norse literature and mythology. He read everything there was to read on the subject in English while he was still in secondary school. When he reached Oxford, he studied Old Norse and read what hadn't yet been translated. But Lewis noticed that his expertise did not heighten that joy he had felt, "Northernness." It did rather the opposite. "From these books again and again," he wrote, "I received the stab of Joy. I did not yet notice that it was, very gradually, becoming rarer. I did not yet reflect on the difference between it and . . . merely intellectual satisfaction."[17]

Joy, however, was still Lewis's quest. Patches of remembered boyhood could be stirred and awakened by some sudden smell or sound or image. Exquisite Proustian or Wordsworthian moments sometimes carried for Lewis stabs of "an almost unbearable pleasure."[18] Such joys could be "so sharp that they might sting." These momentary tastes of joy were like "seconds of gold scattered in months of dross." Sweet pangs of joy "passed along the spine with delicious, yet harrowing thrills: took away the appetite: made sleep impossible." But that distinguishing sleeplessness—the "sting," those "razor-edged," "needle-pointed" qualities—became more and more elusive. "Northernness," philosophy (which Lewis loved), wine, women, and song were not producing them. Something was missing.

At Oxford, Lewis, who had been an avowed atheist for years, met for the first time Christians whom he liked and whose intellects he respected. To this vexation was added a similar one when, as Lewis puts it, "all the books were beginning to turn against me." He began to notice that many of the authors he most liked were Christians. Previously he had been rationalizing away that fact by saying of Chesterton, for instance, that "he had more sense than all the other moderns put together; bating, of course, his Christianity."[19] But now these defenses were beginning to show cracks.

Soon afterward Lewis read Chesterton's *The Everlasting Man*. "Somehow I contrived," he says, "not to be too badly shaken." But someone was closing in. God had apparently determined to reveal Himself to Lewis, this hardheaded, atheistic philosopher. Resist as Lewis might, God's approach was inexorable. "You must picture me," Lewis wrote, "alone in that room in Magdalen, night after night, feeling, whenever my mind lifted even for a second from my work, the steady, unrelenting approach of Him whom I so earnestly desired not to meet."[20]

Finally, in 1929, Lewis gave in—not yet to Christianity, but to theism. He "admitted that God was God, and knelt and prayed: perhaps, that night, the most dejected and reluctant convert in all England."[21] He began to attend church and to read the Gospels. He was surprised to find that they did not have the flavor of myth. They read like histories. Lewis had acknowledged God; now God was after him to acknowledge His Son. The subject was on Lewis's mind constantly. In a now famous passage of *Surprised by Joy*, Lewis related his final step into real joy: "I know very well when, but hardly how, the final step was taken. I was driven to Whipsnade one sunny morning. When we set out I did not believe that Jesus Christ is the Son of God, and when we reached the zoo I did."[22]

So C. S. Lewis was drawn into the kingdom of God by joy—by a taste of this blessed fruit and divine gift. Joy was the divine carrot that persuaded such a self-proclaimed donkey as Lewis to plod down the road toward Jerusalem. It was the soft, disturbing kiss of God that unmade all of Lewis's world. Joy compelled Lewis toward the resurrection laughter of Easter, yet it was a path that had to pass through Good Friday. As Lewis grew in his faith, there would be no detour around the tears and tribulations of life—of being stomped, pressed down, and crushed like grapes—so that the sweet wine of intoxicating laughter could be poured out on dry, thirsty souls.

After his conversion, Lewis went on to build a successful academic career, publish excellent work in his field, and become a celebrated apologist for Christianity. He had passed contentedly into late middle age, when, once more, he was surprised—ambushed—by joy. Professor Lewis fell in love with and married an American woman named Joy Davidman. The coincidence of Lewis's wife's name was compounded by the fact that his autobiography, *Surprised by Joy*, was published at the time she was becoming an integral and happy part of his life.

A few years later Joy became ill. At first, Lewis wrote of the experience that "you would not believe how many joys have been experienced amid these troubles. And what wonder? For has He not promised to comfort those who mourn? . . . I am in much trouble. Nevertheless let us lift up our hearts: for Christ is risen."[23] The vale of tears is also a well of living waters. "If we are happy, then we remember that the crown is not promised without the Cross and tremble."[24]

However, after a joyful but short remission in her cancer, Lewis's Joy, his beloved wife, died. His faith was seared and scarred, and, for a while, it seemed a hopeless and perhaps even pointless struggle to retain it. Who cared anymore? Some of the depth of Lewis's sorrow can be read in a poem he wrote about Joy's death, entitled, "Joys That Sting":

> *Oh do not die, says Donne, for I shall hate*
> *All women so. How false the sentence rings.*
> *Women? But in a life made desolate*
> *It is the joys once shared that have the stings.*
> *To take the old walks alone, or not at all,*
> *To order one pint where I ordered two,*
> *To think of, and then not to make, the small*
> *Time-honoured joke (senseless to all but you);*
> *To laugh (oh, one'll laugh), to talk upon*
> *Themes that we talked upon when you were there,*
> *To make some poor pretence of going on,*
> *Be kind to one's old friends, and seem to care,*

While no one (O God) through the years will say
The simplest, common word in just your way.[25]

Joy's early death by cancer initiated a piercing personal struggle for Lewis. He had literally and metaphorically lost his Joy. The pain of this earthly separation was recorded in painfully raw candor in *A Grief Observed*. Now Lewis not only knew about pain but also had come to know it intimately. And in his bereavement, he shook his puny little fist at the brass heavens.

"It was too perfect to last," so I am tempted to say of our marriage. But it can be meant in two ways. It may be grimly pessimistic—as if God no sooner saw two of His creatures happy than He stopped it ("None of that here!"). As if He were like the Hostess at the Sherry party who separates two guests the moment they show signs of having got into a real conversation.[26]

In his grief, Lewis longed for his wife.

[She is what] I am mourning for, homesick for, famished for. You tell me "she goes on." But my heart and body are crying out, come back, come back. . . . But I know this is impossible. I know that the thing I want is exactly the thing I can never get. The old life, the jokes, the drinks, the arguments, the lovemaking, the tiny, heartbreaking commonplace.[27]

Nights became desolate, sleepless trails that descended into lonely valleys—dark places of sorrow and despair. Then, to this man in total darkness, who imagines he is in a cellar or dungeon, comes a small, faint sound.

He thinks it might be a sound from far off—waves or windblown trees or cattle half a mile away. And if so, it proves he's not in a cellar, but free, in the open air. Or it may be a much smaller sound close at hand—a chuckle of laughter. And if so, there is a friend just beside him in the dark. Either way, a good, good sound.[28]

Hope—the thing with feathers that perches in the soul—lived in a cage of ache and agony in anticipation of joy. It took flight, finally, in one of Lewis's remembrances:

> Once very near the end I said, "If you can—if it is allowed—come to me when I too am on my death bed." "Allowed," she said. "Heaven would have a job to hold me; and as for Hell, I'd break it into bits." She knew she was speaking a kind of mythological language, with even an element of comedy in it. There was a twinkle as well as a tear in her eye. But there was no myth and no joke about the will, deeper than any feeling, that flashed through her.[29]

Remembering this exchange was the beginning of Lewis's recovery. The memory scourged his soul but also purified it. It would do little good to turn to his wife's memory with morbid sadness and increasing anger; the facts were hard as nails. The most difficult leap for Lewis came in his weakness of will: "I will turn to her as often as possible in gladness. I will even salute her with a laugh. The less I mourn her the nearer I seem to her."[30]

Just as suffering was as certain as night, joy was as sure as the coming morning. In the crucible of watching his wife die, Lewis remembered the incredible happiness and "gaiety we sometimes had together after all hope was gone."[31] It was a hint of dawn. The moment became a savoring of what the Germans call *Das Erhabene*, the instant of being moved and feeling pain in a positive way, of allowing the laughter and the tear to cohabit the tomb of the eye. Death, Lewis remembered now, was by no means a permanent separation. There was heaven—joy would be there. Both "Joys." No farewells are final. In a letter to Father John, an Italian priest in Verona with whom he carried on a correspondence in Latin, Lewis expressed the view that comforted him in his wife's death: "Now indeed mountains and seas divide us, nor do I know what your appearance is in the body. God grant, on that day hereafter, day of the resurrection of the body, yes, and of all things made, beyond our telling, new—God grant us, on that Day, to meet."[32]

Later, in a letter to Dom Bede Griffiths about friendship (November 1959), Lewis expressed his understanding of the meaning and enduring joy of his short marriage:

> Are not all lifelong friendships born at the moment when at last you meet another human being who has some inkling (but faint and uncertain even in the best) of that something which you were born desiring, and which, beneath the flux of other desires and in all the momentary silences between the louder passions, night and day, year by year, from childhood to old age, you are looking for, watching for, listening for? You have never had it. All the things that have ever deeply possessed your soul have been but hints of it—tantalizing glimpses, promises never quite fulfilled, echoes that died away just as they caught your ear. But if it should really become manifest—if there ever came an echo that did not die away but swelled into the sound itself—you would know it. Beyond all possibility of doubt you would say "Here at last is the thing I was made for." We cannot tell each other about it. It is the secret signature of each soul, the incommunicable and unappeasable want, the thing we desired before we met our wives or made our friends or chose our work, and which we shall still desire on our deathbeds, when the mind no longer knows wife or friend or work. While we are, this is. If we lose this, we lose all.[33]

When his dear friend Charles Williams died suddenly, Lewis observed that it wasn't his idea of Charles Williams that changed as much as his idea of death. Death became to him the final barrier or separation before the final reunion—the grand, glad reunion. Death could only be feared, ignored, or desired, and Lewis opted for the last. It would be like stripping off the hair shirt of this life or getting out of a dungeon. To Mary, an American woman, he compared their sickly, bedridden lives as being drowsy seeds awaiting the Gardener's good time to come up as real flowers. "It will be fun when we at last meet" in a better place.[34]

Throughout his life, stabs of joy were to C. S. Lewis like faint whispers from beyond the world, a meek and plaintive call from "the horns of elfland" for lost, aimless, weary pilgrims to "come home, come home." For Lewis, this special happiness we seek can be found only in God. Or, as Augustine professed, "Our hearts are restless until they rest in Thee." What our hearts seek and hunger after is the overwhelming joy of homecoming and reunion with a Beloved.

The terror, however, is that we may never find our way to this heavenly home we are looking for. We may be utterly and hopelessly lost, stumbling like Dante into a dark wood. Or we may even choose to be deliberately prodigal. We may plod and trod what Keats called "the journey homeward to habitual self." Moving downward toward ourselves, we see we suffer from the law of spiritual gravitation— of falling away from God. Yet an incredible hope sneaks into our consciousness that we will be found, called in, reeled up, received, welcomed. Lewis certainly was that—not just passively found, but actively hunted down by God. Lewis had searched and searched for joy. And when God found him, the object of his desire, grand as it was, paled in comparison.

7

Joy and Suffering

Joy and woe are woven fine,
A clothing for the soul divine.
Under every grief and pine
Runs a joy with silken twine.
It is right it should be so;
Man was made for joy and woe;
And when this we rightly know,
Through the world we safely go.
—WILLIAM BLAKE

Within the darker moments of life—twilight, winter, sadness, death—are buried the seeds of joy. Promises of joy to come are inherent in the very nature of these things. For every twilight there is a dawn; for every winter, a spring; for periods of sadness, periods of happiness; for every death, a birth (and sometimes even a resurrection).

An integral part of the joy we feel when the dawn comes is the memory of the darkness we suffered beforehand and the despair we felt of its approach. Darkness, suffering, and longing are part of the very definition of joy. That is why joy is not the same as unadulterated happiness or uninhibited pleasure. It is not the culmination of these things or the greatest in degree among them, because it is different in kind. And it is not so easily achieved; the price of joy is, indeed, greater. Lewis wrote:

> A little sense of labor is necessary to all perfect pleasures I think: just
> as (to my palate at least) there is no really delicious taste without a
> touch of astringency—the "bite" in alcoholic drinks, the resistance

to the teeth in nuts or meat, the tartness of fruit, the bitterness of mint sauce. The apple must not be too sweet, the cheese must not be too mild.[1]

Similarly, the salt of joy is sorrow, a touch of tears. If we in our present mortal state met joy in her fullness, we would drown in laughter. We would be blinded and struck dumb by gladness and mirth. This may sound a pleasant way to die, but it probably would be unendurable. To be struck by unmanageable shafts of infinite sweetness would quake and crack our being into a billion pieces—it would break our hearts. Thus, instead of being explosive in us, joy is calmed and watered down like a potent wine with a note of gravity, loss, and sorrow.

Joy is prepared for by suffering. God accomplishes that preparation by interrupting our material and superficial happiness. He shatters, through suffering, our illusions and pretenses that all is well. He has to do this because, as Lewis says, quoting Augustine: "God wants to give us something, but cannot, because our hands are full—there's nowhere for Him to put it."[2]

The keenest pleasures and joys of life cannot be given us without interruption, simply because we tend to cling to them. Yet such toys are not meant to take the place of real treasures. Joy comes only when the toys are put away. However, we don't want to put them away; and, more often than not, the toys must be taken from us. People are thus persuaded, sometimes none too gently, to surrender to a Ruler who knows of His subjects that their "modest prosperity and the happiness of their children are not enough to make them blessed."[3]

This is not to say that God does not bless us with plenty of happiness and with many periods of sweet—albeit temporal—joy. Of course He does. After all, He intends for us, ultimately, to be extremely happy (a fact that disgusts Screwtape: "In His presence are joys forevermore," he complains. "Ugh!"). But Lewis pointed out that the Christian doctrine of woe and suffering explains both why God gives us some happiness in life and why He never seems to give us as much as we want.

The settled happiness and security which we all desire, God with-holds from us by the very nature of the world: but joy, pleasure, and merriment He has scattered broadcast. We are never safe, but we have plenty of fun, and some ecstasy. It is not hard to see why. The security we crave would teach us to rest our hearts in this world and oppose an obstacle to our return to God: a few moments of happy love, a landscape, a symphony, a merry meeting with our friends, a bathe or a football match, have no such tendency. Our Father refreshes us on the journey with some pleasant inns, but will not encourage us to mistake them for home.[4]

As Lewis admitted, Christianity is not the religion you want if you want uninterrupted happiness. He was once asked what kind of religion gives its followers the greatest happiness. "While it lasts," Lewis answered, "the religion of worshiping oneself is best."[5] But while the worship of self may for a season protect one from the tragedy of seeing oneself honestly as a hopeless sinner, it also restricts one from entering the joyous fellowship of the hoping saints. Lewis recalled a man who practiced the religion of the self:

I have an elderly acquaintance of about eighty, who has lived a life of unbroken selfishness and self-admiration from the earliest years, and is, more or less, I regret to say, one of the happiest men I know. From the moral point of view it is very difficult! . . . As you perhaps know, I haven't always been a Christian. I didn't go to religion to make me happy. I always knew a bottle of Port would do that. If you want a religion to make you feel really comfortable, I certainly don't recommend Christianity.[6]

No, the saints are not uninterruptedly happy. On the contrary, they are, as Jesus was, "acquainted with grief" (Isa. 53:3) even in their hope of joy. While they weep over their sin and its inevitable wages, however, they can at the same time rejoice and laugh for their salvation. And they discover, as Henry Ward Beecher preached, that "joy is more divine than sorrow, for joy is bread and sorrow is medicine."[7] Lewis wrote that he received letters from "saints, who have no notion they are any such thing, showing in every line radiant faith, joy, humility and even humor, in the midst of appalling suffering."[8] As one writer once observed, only those souls deep enough for grief are wide enough for joy.

Suffering is God's message to summon us to our true home, where real food and drink and joy abound. It is, however, like other communication from God, a message too often left unanswered by its recipients. Yet, Lewis emphasized, "Pain insists upon being attended to. God whispers to us in our pleasures, speaks in our conscience, but shouts in our pains: it is His megaphone to rouse a deaf world."[9] Pain shatters the illusion that all is well. To be wakened from our deadly slumber, the splash of cold water in our faces must sting. These pains that wake us, of course, need not always be momentous; it all depends on how sleepy we are. Mere tweaks of the ear or pinches on the behind may be sufficient. Yet even these are tiny, vivid reminders of our sinfulness and our mortality.

Lewis recalled some pains as "instantaneous, but not fearful. They may be intense: but they are gone as we recognize their intensity. In my own case I do not find anything in them which demands pity; they are, rather comical. One tends to laugh."[10] One imagines a schoolteacher catching a schoolboy dozing or goofing when he should be studying, and tweaking his ear as a serious and surprising reminder (and one no doubt amusing to his fellows) that he should be about better business. Like Lewis, we behave "like a puppy when the hated bath is over—I shake myself as dry as I can and race off to reacquire my comfortable dirtiness, if not in the nearest manure heap, at least in the nearest flower bed."[11]

In his own life, of course, Lewis did not set out looking for these corrective pains and sorrows. An honest man, Lewis reminded his readers that although he understood the need for suffering (the only path to joy), the sufferings he endured himself were not due to his personal wishes. He did not enjoy suffering, and in writing about it did not intend to recommend it to people. He wanted only to illustrate the Christian doctrine of being made "perfect through suffering." How did he respond to pain in real life? He confesses:

> I am a great coward. But what is that to the purpose? When I think of pain—of anxiety that gnaws like fire and loneliness that spreads out like a desert, and the heartbreaking routine of monotonous misery, or again of dull aches that blacken our whole landscape or sudden nauseating pains that knock a man's heart out at one blow, of pains that seem already intolerable and then are suddenly increased, of infuriating scorpion-stinging pains that startle into maniacal movement a man who seemed half dead with his previous tortures—it "quite o'ercrows my spirit." If I knew any way of escape I would crawl through sewers to find it.[12]

Crawl through sewers we may, but we will not escape pain. Life cannot but be painful; it is brought forth in pain. And our suffering cannot cease until God sees us remade (or sees that our transformation is hopeless). If it were at all possible, all of us except the masochist would cry, "Let this cup pass from me. Allow me to enter directly into joy." Although we are fallen and selfish creatures, we are more than animals, for we have been made in the image of God. He therefore takes pains to train us. "He does not," noticed Lewis, "house-train the earwig or give baths to centipedes."[13] Love demands our cleansing, that we might enjoy love's joy. Love may be forgiving of all faults, but He is not condoning. A loving God must labor to make us perfectly lovable. Lewis wrote:

> When He said, "Be perfect," He meant it. He meant that we must go in for the full treatment. It is hard; but the sort of compromise we are all hankering after is harder—in fact, it is impossible. It may

be hard for an egg to turn into a bird: it would be a jolly sight harder for it to learn to fly while remaining in the egg. We are like eggs at present. And you cannot go on indefinitely being just an ordinary, decent egg. We must be hatched or go bad.[14]

Ultimately, we are called to be like God and share in His goodness and His joy, or to be miserable. The fact of our inherent human wickedness will continually tug us toward the misery. That is our natural gravitational direction—downward and inward, toward ourselves, away from God. Thus, being turned back to God and to joy means being twisted and pulled in an unnatural—or supernatural—direction. It means being pulled up and extricated from a very comfortable place. And going against the grain hurts. What is good for us (and joy for us) must first mean primarily a corrective and even painful ultimate good. We must first confront our sins. Before we enter freely into God's joy, our chains and fetters must be cut, and before they can be cut, they must be confronted.

> Our souls demand Purgatory, don't they? Would it not break the heart if God said to us, "It is true, my son, that your breath smells and your rags drip with mud and slime, but we are charitable here and no one will upbraid you with these things, not draw away from you. Enter into the joy!" Should we not reply, "With submission, sir, and if there is no objection, I'd rather be cleaned first." "It may hurt, you know." "Even so, sir."[15]

Our instruments must be tuned up here, at the door to eternity. To be prepared for the laughter and joy of the wedding feast and bridal chamber, we must first be cleansed.

Lewis had heard the complaint that it is not at all pleasurable, but rather gloomy, to think of one's sins. It is much more fun to attend to the problems of others, he said—their jealousy, stupidity, selfishness, hypocrisy. The problem is that each of us remains unaware of our own fatal flaws. "Does the person with smelly breath know it smells? Or does the Club bore know he is a bore?"[16] Others will recognize the problem before we do. "And it is almost certainly something you don't know about—like what the advertisements call 'halitosis,' which everyone notices except the person who has it."[17]

To become aware of our own sins may be gloomy and depressing initially, but soon the reverse begins to dawn on us: It is healthy to know of our sins and repent. After a necessary deal of pain, terror, anguish, and dismay, we stumble into a "lightening and relieving process." Indeed, the world is a valley of soul-making, and to be brought into the holy city of God, we must travel through the tribulations of this life. But the preparation is painful. Two examples serve us well. In the first, Lewis, anteceding Margery Williams's *The Velveteen Rabbit,* wrote that

> all the rabbit in us is to disappear—the worried, conscientious, ethical rabbit as well as the cowardly and sensual rabbit. We shall bleed and squeal as the handfuls of fur come out; and then, surprisingly, we shall find underneath it all a thing we never imagined: a real Man, an ageless god, a son of God, strong, radiant, wise, beautiful, and drenched in joy.[18]

Lewis borrowed the second parable from George MacDonald:

> Imagine yourself a living house. God comes in to rebuild that house. At first, perhaps, you can understand what He is doing. He is getting the drains right and stopping the leaks in the roof and so on: you knew that those jobs needed doing and so you are not surprised. But presently He starts knocking the house about in a way that hurts abominably and does not seem to make sense. What on earth is He up to? The explanation is that He is building quite a different house from the one you thought of—throwing out a new wing here, putting on an extra floor there, running up towers, making courtyards.

You thought you were going to be made into a decent little cottage: but He is building a palace. He intends to come and live in it Himself.[19]

The awareness that we are sinners in need of major reconstruction does lead to confusion and to despair. Lewis believed that we must be remade and made ready for paradise and its joys. Our whole lives are preparation for eternal, ecstatic delight; yet, even knowing that, we still don't want the suffering and raw rubbing that would polish us into radiant and shining joy.

For Christians, the only thorough cleansing is a type of death—death to self. As the apostle Paul wrote, "Our old self was crucified with Him, in order that our body of sin might be done away with" (Rom. 6:6). When we are baptized, our immersion symbolizes our death to ourselves and our identification with Christ's death. "Our life as Christians," Lewis observed, "begins by being baptized into a death; our most joyous festivals begin with, and centre upon, the broken body and the shed blood. There is thus a tragic depth in our worship which Judaism lacked. Our joy has to be the sort of joy which coexists with that."[20] The joy of the Resurrection, the greatest reunion that will ever be, was preceded by the separation of the Crucifixion. And to know the richness of joy in the Resurrection, one must have tasted the excruciating pain and tragedy of the Crucifixion. It is thus with compassion that Christ foretold His death and spoke to His disciples:

Truly, truly, I say to you, that you will weep and lament, but the world will rejoice; you will grieve, but your grief will be turned into joy. Whenever a woman is in labor she has pain, because her hour has come; but when she gives birth to the child, she no longer remembers the anguish because of the joy that a child has been born into the world. Therefore you too have grief now; but I will see you again, and your heart will rejoice, and no one will take your joy away from you. (John 16:20–22)

When we see Him again, we will be home at last. At this the weary heart rejoices—it is what we desired all along. That is why to the Christian, physical death is the door of "tragic splendor" that ushers us into a divine coronation, where creatures of dust and decay will be crowned with the glory and goodness of God. Yet we now walk through the furnace of affliction, the fires of trouble and pain.

Lewis and Chesterton, as well as J. R. R. Tolkien, believed that the simple reading of fairy tales could provide for us a taste of the bitter medicine we must swallow and the ecstatic experience of joy that arises out of our rescue from our sickness unto death. Imaginative literature gives what Tolkien called the "consolation of the Happy Ending." This he named the *Eucatastrophe*—"the joy of the happy ending: or more correctly of the good catastrophe, the sudden joyous 'turn.'"[21] The fairy tale does not deny suffering, pain, sorrow, or other calamities, but it does deny a final defeat. It acknowledges death, as in "The Steadfast Tin Soldier" or "The Happy Prince," but it does not admit death's victory. It becomes good news, "giving a fleeting glimpse of Joy, Joy beyond the walls of the world, poignant as grief," giving each "child or man that hears it . . . a catch of the breath, a beat and a lifting of the heart, near to (or indeed, accompanied by) tears."[22] Joy, Tolkien wrote, is the mark of the true fairy tale, a far-off gleam or dim reflection of the real, historical fact of the Resurrection. This Joy "looks forward to the Great Eucatastrophe."[23]

Lewis's personal correspondence and other writings reflect his firm conviction of the reality of this view of death. In a letter to his American woman friend, he asked, "What in Heaven's name is 'distressing' about an old man saying to an old woman that they haven't much more to do here?" When the American woman wrote back, worrying and moaning about impending death in response to his "morbid subject," Lewis wrote her again and said playfully: "If this is Goodbye, I am sure you will not forget me when you are in a better place. You'll put in a good word for me now and then, won't you? It will be fun when we at last meet."[24] The joys of heaven can only be an exclamation point to the sufferings of earth. We understand now that before we can hear the laughter of reunion, we have to weep of our separation. Before we can rejoice over our rescue, we have to despair of our lostness. But there, in heaven, every tear will be wiped away; there will be no more death or mourning or crying or pain, for the new joy will have come. For when the pain "is over, it is over, and the natural sequel is joy."[25] "I hope to come to you and speak face to face, so that your joy may be made full" (2 John 1:12). When we are face-to-face with Jesus, joy will be completely full—a sensation that the partial joys of earth do not even prepare us to imagine. But to know the heights of laughter, one must taste the depths of tears.

When we hear that God laughs, we must not suppose the reason is because of His sadistic superiority over His creatures of clay, but because He knows how it will all turn out in the end. He is the author of the Great Eucatastrophe. God does not safely chortle from a divine distance at our suffering; He does not jest because He knows no pain. His laughter is born in the same heart that has also known rejection, betrayal, hunger, whipping, ridicule, torture, and all manner of suffering. The One who laughs is the One who wept.

8

Laughter of Reunions

But we had to be merry and rejoice, for this brother of yours was
dead and has begun to live, and was lost and has been found.
—LUKE 15:32

In the same way that reconciliations are built upon broken relations, so
reunions occur only after separations. When C. S. Lewis was growing
up, his relationship with his father was often strained and painful. Yet
his brother, Warnie, remembered wonderful times of reunion. During
one particularly stressful season for each of the Lewis men, all three of
them were unexpectedly home together. Warnie said the gathering gave
birth to gladness. "It was a joyful reunion on all sides, a recovery of old
days, the first occasion moreover on which I had champagne at home."[1]

Reunions revive laughter like dips into the cold waters of the Parson's
Pleasure. They are a time for remembering and reliving. Lewis noted
the Shakespearean scene in which "Falstaff meets his old acquaintance
Shallow in the country—one of the best 'Do you remember' conversations in any book I know."[2] Indeed, remembering and cherishing
are the joyous completion of every pleasure we experience. Each great
experience is, as Owen Barfield wrote, "a whisper which Memory will
warehouse as a shout."[3]

In *Out of the Silent Planet*, a creature called a "hross" tells Ransom,
"A pleasure is full grown only when it is remembered. You are speaking, Hman, as if the pleasure were one thing and the memory another.
It is all as one thing."[4] He was explaining the delights of a single sexual
act, for the purpose of reproduction. Unlike terrestrial beings in heat,
who crave sexual feeling again and again, the hrossa have the act of
sex as a memory, and as such it satisfies fully.

In Narnia, when the four children return to Cair Paravel where they once reigned as kings and queens, they stumble upon treasures of their past. It was like "meeting very old friends. If you had been there you would have heard them saying things like 'Oh look! Our coronation rings—do you remember first wearing this? . . . do you remember drinking out of that horn?—do you remember, do you remember?"[5]

Small details, fragrances, and sounds may awaken the delicious memories of yesterday. When Susan rediscovers her old bow, she gives one little pluck to the string. Its twang vibrates through the room, and "that one small noise brought back the old days to the children's minds more than anything that had happened yet. All the battles and hunts and feasts came rushing into their heads together."[6]

Lewis believed that "any moment may sink an artesian well right down into one's past self, and old joy, even old power, may come rushing up. That is why I think resurrection is so much profounder an idea than mere immortality."[7] In *The Last Battle*—the final book of *The Chronicles of Narnia*—Peter, Edmund, Lucy, and their parents all have been killed in a railway crash (although they aren't yet aware of it having happened). As Edmund describes it, "There was a frightful roar and something hit me with a bang, but it didn't hurt. And I felt not so much scared as—well, excited. Oh—and this one queer thing. I'd had a rather sore knee, from a hack at rugger [rugby football]. I noticed it had suddenly gone. . . . And then—here we were."[8]

There they are, reunited with their parents and all their dear friends, Narnian and Tellurian, "all walking together—and a great, bright procession it was—up towards mountains higher than you could see in this world."[9] The joyous company of reunited friends suddenly stops jesting with one another, and all become grave. What overwhelms them, Lewis tells us, "is a kind of happiness and wonder that makes you serious. It is too good to waste on jokes."[10] The promised land is at hand—every hope is to be realized. And for a moment, on the edge of a glorious and uproarious eternity where jesting will surface in fresh and lively surprises, there is a sober silence. Aslan is there. "There was a real railway accident," he explains to them. "Your father and mother and all of you are—as you used to call it in the Shadow-Lands—dead. The term is over: the holidays have begun. The dream is ended: this is the morning."

And as He spoke He no longer looked to them like a lion; but the things that began to happen after that were so great and beautiful that I cannot write them. And for us this is the end of all the stories, and we can most truly say that they all lived happily ever after. But for them it was only the beginning of the real story. All their life in this world and all their adventures in Narnia had only been the cover and the title page: now at last they were beginning Chapter One of the Great Story, which no one on earth has read: which goes on for ever: in which every chapter is better than the one before.[11]

9

Joy and Hierarchy

*Only if we are secure in our beliefs can we see
the comical side of the universe.*
—FLANNERY O'CONNOR

There is utter joy in finding and filling one's proper place in the divine dance of the cosmos. Chesterton once saw in a printer's mistake of leaving out the letter *s*, a truth of God—that the cosmic and comic are intimately related: "Whatever is cosmic is comic."[1] The stars and planets, obeying their ordained paths, participate in the divine comedy and summon all of life to join them. In a letter to an American boy, Lewis wrote that

> gaiety at its highest may be an (intellectual) creature's delighted recognition that its imperfection as a being may constitute part of its perfection as an element in the whole hierarchical order of creation. I mean, while it is a pity there should be bad men or bad dogs, part of the excellence of a good man is that he is not an angel, and of a good dog that it is not a man. This is an extension of what St. Paul says about the body and the members. A good toe-nail is not an unsuccessful attempt at hair; and if it were conscious it would delight in being simply a good toe-nail.[2]

Just as each organ has its proper place in the body, so each person finds joy in his fit relation to God and to his neighbor. "The dog becomes really doggy only when he has taken his place in the household of man."[3] Lewis provided an apt illustration of this ordering in *The Magician's Nephew*, at the coronation of King Frank of Narnia and Helen, his queen. Here everyone finds his proper and good place, and each finds his ordained task. The dwarfs, who love mining and working with metal, take precious stones and shape them into light, delicate, beautiful crowns. The moles, who love digging, root out the jewels from the ground. Even the jackdaw enjoys being the jester of this new kingdom. All find their calling and find joy in being obedient to that calling.

The holy game in which we human creatures are invited to find our place is a wild but orderly romp, a tumbling, somersaulting sport like rugby that appears to the uninitiated to be a rough, madcap free-for-all. But the disciplined player knows the order and the rules. The first rule, Lewis wrote, concerns the ball or golden apple of selfhood:

> Every player must by all means touch the ball and then immediately pass it on. To be found with it in your hands is a fault: to cling to it, death. But when it flies to and fro among the players too swift for the eye to follow, and the great master Himself leads the revelry . . . then indeed the eternal dance "makes heaven drowsy with the harmony." All pains and pleasures we have known on earth are early initiations in the movement of that dance. . . . As we draw nearer to its uncreated rhythm, pain and pleasure sink almost out of sight. There is joy in the dance, but it does not exist for the sake of joy.[4]

Hierarchy was a pivotal concept for Lewis. One finds joy, he believed, when one finds one's place in the hierarchy of the universe and obediently fulfills it. In *That Hideous Strength*, Ransom showed how joyful good order could be even in a simple game with mice (which looked like tiny kangaroos). After Ransom blew a whistle, the little mice scampered out and cleaned up some crumbs. "There," he said, "a very simple adjustment. . . . Humans want crumbs removed; mice are anxious to remove them. It ought never to have been a cause of war. But you see that obedience and rule are more like a dance than a drill—specially between man and woman where the roles are always changing."[5]

The discipline that Lewis respected in hierarchy was not military but musical; not legalistic but regal and artistic. It led to the liberty of leaping and bowing and dancing as order does in a dance. Lewis drew a splendid sketch of obedience in action in the Great Dance of *Perelandra*. The queen, having blessedly obeyed the law of the land and resisted the temptation of the villain Weston, is united with her king in a holiday of joy. Their coronation is a wedding and a birth, and the celebration awakens all creation in that new Eden (endowed with a regular Noah's Ark): "Romping, prancing, fluttering, gliding, crawling, waddling, with every kind of movement—in every kind of shape and colour and size—a whole zoo of beasts and birds was pouring into a flowery valley." They came in pairs, male and female, "fawning upon one another, climbing over one another, diving under one another's bellies, perching upon one another's backs."[6] Paradise unfolds before Ransom with songs of joy and lights that shine like emeralds. An awesome pageant of beauty, goodness, ripeness, wonder, virility, splendor, and joy parades on Perelandra. Then the grand and exalted ceremony is interrupted by a wonderful sound.

> Unexpectedly the King laughed. His body was very big and his laugh was like an earthquake in it, loud and deep and long, till in the end Ransom laughed too, though he had not seen the joke, and the Queen laughed as well. And the birds began clapping their wings and the beasts wagging their tails, and the light seemed brighter and the pulse of the whole assembly quickened, and new modes of joy that had nothing to do with mirth as we understand it passed into them all, as it were from the very air, or as if there were dancing in Deep Heaven. Some say there always is.[7]

Thus begins the Great Game and the Great Dance. It offers a place for every creature. All things were made for this dance, and one must find his proper place in it to receive the abundant joy awaiting him.

To Lewis, dancing was a bodily expression of joy and of universal order. The dance he honored was not the wild, orgiastic, undisciplined dancing with which we moderns are familiar, but rather a dance that issued out of the divine order of the universe.

> The pattern deep hidden in the dance, hidden so deep that shallow spectators cannot see it, alone gives beauty to the wild, free gestures that fill it. . . . The heavenly frolic arises from an orchestra which is in tune; the rules of courtesy make perfect ease and freedom possible between those who obey them. Without sin, the universe is a Solemn Game: and there is no good game without rules.[8]

There is excellent symbolism in such dance. The dancer bows in one movement and is lifted up in the next; the one who is exalted and reverenced is brought down, even as the one who is low is raised up.[9] ("We become," Chesterton said, "taller when we bow; we become lowlier when we instruct."[10])

Dance was, for Lewis, a very *solempne* game. This Middle English word conveyed a word like and yet unlike the modern word *solemn*. Both words denote an atmosphere opposing the free and easy familiarity of ordinary life. *Solempne* differs from *solemn*, however, in that it does not suggest things gloomy, oppressive, or austere. In this sense, waltzes are more *solempne* than military marches, feasts more *solempne* than fasts. "The ball in the first act of *Romeo and Juliet* was a 'solemnity.' The feast at the beginning of *Gawain and the Green Knight* is very much of a solemnity. A great mass by Mozart or Beethoven is as much a solemnity in its hilarious Gloria as in its poignant crucifixus est. . . . Easter is *solempne*, Good Friday is not."[11]

The quality conveyed here is one of glorious pomp and festal ceremony—not that of the dull, academic rituals that many of us dread like a plague of cockroaches (or a convention of religious broadcasters). To recover the stately yet joyous idea of the *solempne* one "must think of a court ball, or a coronation, or a victory march, as these things appear to people who enjoy them; in an age when every one puts on

his oldest clothes to be happy in, you must re-awake the simpler state
of mind in which people put on gold and scarlet to be happy in."[12] One
throws oneself into the rite, fully forgetting oneself, and finds proper
pleasure in the public festivity and holiday. The *solempne* ceremony
could be gay and lively, but it can never be colloquial or commonplace.

> The desire for simplicity is a late and sophisticated one. We moderns
> may like dances which are hardly distinguishable from walking
> and poetry which sounds as if it might be uttered ex tempore. Our
> ancestors did not. They liked a dance which was a dance, and fine
> clothes which no one could mistake for working clothes, and feasts
> that no one could mistake for ordinary dinners.[13]

The stately beauty of the order of the ceremony or dance strikes
one as a piece of art, perfectly fit and fitting. This order was governed
in earthly realms by the goddess "Ceremonie," to whom dance was
related. Yet Lewis was aware that, unfortunately, modern Englishmen
"do not—at least that class of Englishmen who study literature do
not—perform ceremonies gracefully, nor attend them with much
enthusiasm. . . . Elizabethan sentiment was very different. . . . One
quarreled, loved, dined, and even played by ceremonial rule."[14]

Lewis regretted his clumsiness with ceremony. His friend Charles
Williams, however, had no such problem. He was a ritualist who exhibited a mixture of elaborate courtesy and playful delight.

> Had modern society permitted it he would equally have enjoyed
> kneeling and being knelt to, kissing hands and extending his hand
> to be kissed. . . . Even while enjoying such high pomps he would
> have been aware of them as a game: not a silly game, to be laid aside
> in private, but a glorious game, well worth the playing.[15]

Lewis saw in dance a symbol not only of order in the universe, but
also of order in the relationship of the sexes. Those who would resist

their place in the dance, like a child fighting a father, would only find misery until they humbled themselves. In Shakespeare, after all, the alternative to hierarchy is not equality but tyranny: "If you will not have authority you will find yourself obeying brute force."[16] The comedy of *The Taming of the Shrew* is grounded in Katharina's unwilling submission to the hierarchy of marriage. The awful rule and right supremacy of marriage, Petruchio says, bodes peace and love and quiet life and all that's sweet and happy. Such words may be startling to a modern audience, Lewis acknowledged, but perhaps those who cannot handle them should not read old books. The correction of Katharina, who pretends to hate men and bullies her sister, puts her in her proper place in the dance and puts her into comedy as well.

The Great Dance would include all. It would gather in any created thing willing to join in this hymn to the universe, this great dance and pageant: sheep, cattle, trees, mountains, Leviathan. Even the very stones themselves would sing. In his own literature, Lewis, like Spenser and Tolkien, invited all creatures to take their place in the dance. Joy and revelry are at the core of his imaginative worlds and often are expressed in music and its accompanying dance. Aslan sings Narnia into existence, and throughout the Chronicles dancing erupts continually, like hiccups. Dancing becomes the outward expression of joy, for fauns and giants as well as the children of Adam and Eve.

In *Prince Caspian*, Caspian meets the fauns on the Dancing Lawn, playing a wild yet dreamy tune, and he finds himself joining in the dance. The alter ego of the clumsy Lewis, the old dwarf Trumpkin, "with heavier and jerkier movements, did likewise and even Trufflehunter hopped and lumbered about as best he could."[17] The chief means of celebration in Narnia, in fact, is probably dancing (although it could be argued successfully that most enjoyment and fun in Narnia is connected to eating). The liberation of Narnia from the Telmarines, for example, inaugurates an assembly of dances: trees doing a complicated country dance, fauns and satyrs romping and frolicking—all creatures great and small reveling in a wild and magic victory dance, a dance of plenty. This scene in Lewis's fantasyland recalls Spenser's joyous wood, where one might meet "joy, veiled or perhaps unveiled. Anywhere you may hear angels singing—or come upon satyrs romping. What is more, the satyrs may lead you to the angels."[18] The euphoric dance of all such creatures escorts one into the rhythms and raptures of the heavens.

In *The Silver Chair*, a bedraggled and desperate pack of pilgrims try to dig themselves out of a living grave. Finally breaking out of their underground prison, Eustace, Jill, Prince Rilian, and Puddleglum run smack into a party of Narnians dancing the Great Snow Dance. Their rhythmical movement upward into dancing becomes a movement from death and despair into life and laughter. The Great Snow Dance was celebrated "every year in Narnia on the first moonlit night when there is snow on the ground." It was a dance with complicated steps and figures and choreographed throwing of snowballs. And it was as much a game as a dance "because every now and then some dancer will be the least little bit wrong and get a snowball in the face, and then everyone laughs."[19]

Obedience to the rules of the dance is more poetic than military, more pomp than mundane legalism—for skilled dancers are less concerned with the jot and tittle of their regimen than with the perfect harmony of their movement. Like hierarchy, dance is a physical expression of order and discipline—expressions of the order and law created by God that, unfortunately, the inanimate things of the universe obey better than human beings. When Prince Caspian worries about two stars colliding, his tutor, Dr. Cornelius, allays his fears: "The great lords of the upper sky," he says, "know the steps of their dance too well for that."[20]

10

A Joyful Noise

When I think upon my God, my heart is so full of joy
that the notes dance and leap from my pen.
—FRANZ JOSEPH HAYDN

Music, like Northernness, provided Lewis in his early days with an inconsolable stab of joy. He wrote Arthur Greeves that he found his musical soul again in the wonderful preludes of Chopin. "Although Mrs. K. [Kirkpatrick] doesn't play them well, they are so passionate, so hopeless, I could almost cry over them; they are unbearable."[1]

When he was fifteen, Lewis sunk himself into music, writing the skeleton of a mythic opera on Odin, Thor, Loki, and other dark Norse gods. He imagined soul-stirring music, some themes majestic and mournful, others inexpressibly sad and yearning. In a letter to Sister Penelope, he admired Holst's *Planets*:

> I heard Mars and Jupiter long ago and greatly admired them . . .
> but his characters are rather different from mine I think. . . . On
> Jupiter I am closer to him; but I think he is more "jovial" in the
> modern sense of the word. The folk tune on which he bases it is not
> regal enough for my conception.[2]

Lewis disagreed with the idea that music and books were " 'vanity and vexation.' Really imaginative (or intellectual) pleasure is neither the one nor the other: the bad element is the miserly pleasure of possession, the delight in this book because it is mine."[3] Music that takes itself seriously with gloriously heroic sentiment, he said, aspires to become holy music—much in the way wars may pretend to be holy crusades instead of honest, heroic wars.

> And (delightfully) the same sentiment which could be so serious in a rearguard action could also in peacetime take itself as lightly as all happy loves often do. It could laugh at itself. Our older patriotic songs cannot be sung without a twinkle in the eye; later ones sound more like hymns. Give me "The British Grenadiers" (with a tow-row-row-row) any day rather than "Land of Hope and Glory."[4]

As a young man, Lewis compared the difference between books and music to that between friendship and love. "The one is a calm and easy going satisfaction, the other a sort of madness: we take possession of one, the other takes possession of us: the one is always pleasant, the other in its greatest moments of joy is painful."[5] In this sense music was the highest of the arts for Lewis, as it could express pure, ineffable feeling. For him, music began where the other arts left off. "And you know all day sitting at work, eating, walking, etc. you have hundreds of feelings that can't . . . be put into words or even into thought, but which would naturally come out in music."[6]

Certain music, such as that of Richard Wagner, could transport Lewis into other worlds. Yet Lewis saw that over time—little by little, note by note—he was "losing by degrees my musical faculty; already as you know, I cannot enjoy things that used to drive me wild with delight."[7] Part of this was due, no doubt, to being spoiled by a gramophone. He was disappointed by everything he heard live; it all seemed stale after he'd heard and learned to expect certain standards of performance from the gramophone.

His musical tastes became increasingly philistine except for Chopin's preludes; here he found enough transcendence to place music (and not books) in the realm of joy. The music of Chopin's preludes, Duparc's *Chanson Triste*, Beethoven's *Moonlight Sonata*, Chopin's *March Funebre*, and the *Peer Gynt Suite* all gave him double pleasures—that of beautiful harmonies well executed, coupled with nostalgic memories of happy afternoons with his friend Arthur Greeves. Lewis's experience with music came primarily through three sources: Arthur, Mrs. Kirkpatrick's piano playing, and the gramophone. In his letters he clamored to know the name of the "Galloping Horse" piece by Chopin (Op. 53 Polonaise) for Mrs. K. to play. But when she played it for him, he rued that it didn't have Greeves's frank, fiery, and sympathetic enjoyment. She merely "sat there, amiable, complacent and correct as if she were pouring out tea."

Lewis's fun with music seemed to come in the ways in which he used it, much of which was for amusement. In a letter to Greeves, he compared a pretty girl he met to that grave movement in the *Hungarian Rhapsody*: "Of course to you I needn't explain how a person can be like a piece of music. . . . By the way that would be a rather interesting amusement, trying to find music interpretations for all our friends."[8] Thus, he proceeded to describe friends as the Valkyries, "only not so loud"; as a dance-movement in the Dance Macabre; or as a Salvation Army hymn. He confessed that being an ignoramus in his musical education gave him license to exercise a mischievous inclination to amuse himself in the middle of *Aida* by talking to Greeves or coughing loudly.[9]

The making of joyful noises was not one of Lewis's preferred tastes. He emphasized that "music means not the noises it is nice to make, but the noises it is nice to hear."[10] The operative term here is "noise." He did like Wagner's operatic *Ring* (and he points out "how operatic the whole building up of the climax is in Perelandra."[11]). But in general he commended music very little. He overcame his prejudice for the word over the chord, however, in allowing Screwtape to describe the laughter of joy as something akin to "that detestable art which the humans call Music, and something like it occurs in Heaven—a meaningless acceleration in the rhythm of celestial experience, quite opaque to us."[12]

When Warnie Lewis acquired both an excellent gramophone and a complete set of Beethoven symphonies in March 1933, the Lewis brothers' household sat through a whole symphony each Sunday

evening. These symphonies revived Lewis's dormant musical enjoyment. In fact, for him this became some of the best hours of the week.
Some two years later, he exulted in "a magnificent philharmonic performance of the Ninth Symphony. . . . You know I used to dislike the
choral part of it. I was completely converted and have seldom enjoyed
anything more. How tonic Beethoven is, and how festal—one has the
feeling of having taken part in the revelry of giants."[13]

Lewis believed there was a twofold response to musical tunes:
"First, and most obviously, a social and organic response. One wanted
to 'join in'; to sing, to hum, to beat time, to sway one's body rhyth-
mically. How often the many feel and indulge this impulse we all
know only too well."[14] During Christmas of 1952, he, Joy, and Warnie
attended a holiday program where they laughed at some old jokes of a
Christmas pantomime and joined in the choruses of the songs. Lewis
especially let loose on such ditties as: "Am I going to be a bad boy?
No, no, no! Am I going to be awful? No, no, no! I promise not to put
some crumbs in Aunt Fanny's bed. I promise not to put gravy over the
baby's head. . . ."[15]

No matter how silly, this communal music could be both an expression of and a vessel for joy. What music and joyful laughter have most in
common is that they are at their best when they are ensemble—when
the instruments of the orchestra play together, when the community
lets loose a roar of laughter. This, for Lewis, was an expression of real
joy. "People like to shout their old favorite hymns and bellow 'Auld
Lang Syne.' To make a communal, familiar noise—whether song or
laughter—is certainly a pleasure to human beings. Both are not only
good for the lungs but also promote food fellowship."[16]

Music, unlike poetry, Lewis wrote, "has often reached that jocundity" of communicating joy. "Those who have attempted to write poetry
will know how very much easier it is to express sorrow than joy."[17] The
merry songs of the people indicate the merry health of the people. Songs
come out of happy people, even when they are poor. Indeed, music
is made by the blessed poor in spirit, for they have nothing but joy.

Chesterton wrote that as he ambled homeward one day, he "passed a lit-tle tin building of some religious sort, which was shaken with shouting as a trumpet is torn with its own tongue. They were singing anyhow; and I had for an instant a fancy I had often had before: that with us the super-human is the only place where you can bind the human."[18] Truly, in joy—a heavenly music—human laughter can be heard.

Chesterton contrasted the simple people who tend to sing at their tasks with the more sophisticated who do not: "There were songs for reapers reaping and songs for sailors hauling ropes. . . . Why is a mod-ern newspaper never printed by people singing in chorus? . . . If reapers sing while reaping, why should not auditors sing while auditing and bankers while banking?" Perhaps, Chesterton thought, it is because they have no songs. So, obligingly, he wrote a "thundering chorus in praise of simple addition" for the work of bank clerks fiddling with financial columns: "Up my lads, and lift the ledgers, sleep and ease are o'er. Hear the stars of Morning shouting: 'Two and Two are Four.' Though the creeds and realms are reeling, though the sophists roar, Though we weep and pawn our watches, Two and Two are Four."[19]

Submitting these verses to a friend who worked in a bank, Chesterton was told that the bank's atmosphere was not spiritually conducive to singing. So he left the private sector and approached the socialistic post office with this rhyming ditty for the collective, a post office hymn:

> O'er London our letters are shaken like snow,
> Our wires o'er the world like the thunderbolts go,
> With the news that may marry a maiden in Sark,
> Or kill an old lady in Finsbury Park.
> [Chorus (with a swing of joy and energy):]
> Or kill an old lady in Finsbury Park.[20]

"Judge of my surprise," wrote Chesterton, "when the lady in my local post office (whom I urged to sing) dismissed the idea with far more coldness than the bank clerk had done." The conclusion Chesterton reached after his exertions was that there is "something spiritually suffocating about our life. . . . Bank-clerks are without songs not because they are poor, but because they are sad."[21] And, one should add, because they are alone. Bank clerks should at least form quartets, like barbers. Both songs and laughter flourish within merry bands of people.

Second, Lewis wrote, we respond emotionally to music, becoming "heroic, lugubrious, or gay as the tune 'seemed' to invite us." The aroused emotional responses are by no means universal. Lewis confessed that a certain Zulu war song sounded wistful and gentle to him, not like the charged, bloodthirsty cry of advancing Impi. Such emotions then beget imaginings: "Dim ideas of inconsolable sorrows, brilliant revelry, or well-fought fields, arise."[22]

Yet ironically, the music that excites delight in one person may have been borne in another's suffering. Such is the image drawn by Kierkegaard in defining a poet:

> A poet is an unhappy being whose heart is torn by secret sufferings, but whose lips are so strangely formed that when the sighs and the cries escape them they sound like beautiful music. His fate is like that of the unfortunate victims whom the tyrant Phalaris imprisoned in a brazen bull and slowly tortured over a steady fire; their cries could not reach the tyrant's ears so as to strike terror into his heart; when they reached his ears they sounded like sweet music.[23]

Music mixes tears and laughter, pain and pleasure, in its making and in its hearing.

Music such as that of bagpipes could become to Lewis intoxicating, heartrending, orgiastic, even transcending. He noted that Boswell reacted this way to all music:

> "I [Boswell] told him [Johnson] that it affected me to such a degree, as often to agitate my nerves painfully, producing in my mind

alternate sensations of pathetic dejection, so that I was ready to shed tears, and of daring resolution, so that I was inclined to rush into that thickest part of the battle." Johnson's reply will be remembered: "Sir, I should never hear it, if it made me such a fool."[24]

Music, like wine, can make one such a fool. As a character in Noel Coward's *Private Lives* quipped: "Strange how potent cheap music could be." But Lewis encouraged audiences to go beyond using music for emotional surges and imaginative meanderings to receiving something lastingly delightful. Yet, even so, he reminded that we need not reject our ordinary human responses to the various emotional suggestions of music: "To sing and dance round a fiddler at a fair (the organic and social response) is obviously a right-minded thing to do. To have 'the salt tear harped out of your eye' is not foolish or shameful. And neither response is peculiar to the unmusical. The cognoscenti too can be caught humming or whistling."[25]

Lewis would not unequivocally condemn what he viewed as bad music, merely because it struck him as vulgar or treacly. "Perhaps," he suggested,

the emotional invitation of certain airs to vulgar swagger or lacrimose self-pity so overpowers me that I cannot hear them as neutral patterns of which a good use might possibly be made. I leave it to true musicians to say whether there is no tune so odious (not even Home Sweet Home) that a great composer might not successfully make it one of the materials of a good symphony.[26]

Lewis bluntly acknowledged what he considered disagreeable: those hymns used by the Anglican Church—those "fifth-rate poems set to sixth-rate music."[27] "What I, like many other laymen, chiefly desire in church are fewer, better, and shorter hymns; especially fewer."[28] Yet his aesthetic tastes were tempered by moral and spiritual influences. As time went on, Lewis changed, and saw the merit of hymn-singing:

> I came up against different people of quite different outlooks and different education, and then gradually my conceit just began peeling off. I realized that the hymns . . . were, nevertheless, being sung with devotion and benefit by an old saint in elastic-side boots in the opposite pew, and then you realize that you aren't fit to clean those boots.[29]

Lewis incorporated the power of music in his fiction. Its sweet, compelling intoxication, for instance, appears in *The Voyage of the Dawn Treader* in a passage straight out of Homer's *Odyssey*. As Prince Caspian's ship passes an exotic island far out at sea, Caspian issues orders that he be tied to the mast so that he will not jump into the water when he hears the sweet, seductive music of the Sirens. Their music would, like a stab of false joy, drive a man to his death. In Narnia, on the other hand, music is often so sweet and lovely that it would break one's heart to hear it. In *The Silver Chair*, for example, Jill escapes from the narcotic thrumming of the witch to the flute, fiddle, and drum music of the Great Snow Dance. She could have "fainted with delight" to be in Narnia and hear "the music—the wild music, intensely sweet and yet just the least bit eerie too."[30]

Joy and music are wedded in the moving and beautiful ceremony of the creation of Narnia. In the beginning of Narnia was the song, the music of the lion's voice, calling everything into existence: stars, constellations, planets, hills, mountains, golden skies, green valleys. As Aslan sings with Chestertonian gusto, the sun of Narnia appears in its glorious and virile youth, almost like a young bridegroom ready to run to the wedding chamber. With open mouths and shining eyes, the Cabby and the children drink in the song and watch the sun rise for the first time. "You could imagine that it laughed for joy as it came up."[31] Then the song of creation gathers new harmonies and variations to itself, becoming soft and lilting. Aslan then sings gentle and rippling music, and it brings forth green grass, heather, trees, daisies, buttercups, willows, lilac, and wild roses. Polly sees the connection between the lion's song and the things that are appearing:

> When a line of dark firs sprang up on a ridge about a hundred yards away she felt that they were connected with a series of deep, prolonged notes which the Lion had sung a second before. And when he burst into a rapid series of lighter notes she was not surprised to see primroses suddenly appearing in every direction.[32]

This psychophysical parallelism of Creation joins the musical word with the thing itself. Polly saw, with an "unspeakable thrill," that "all the things were coming . . . 'out of the Lion's head.' When you listened to his song you heard the things he was making up: when you looked around you, you saw them."[33]

Then suddenly the lion's song changes again, becoming a wild, lively tune that "made you want to run and jump and climb. It made you want to shout." Patches of grassy land swell and bubble like water in a pot. And the humps and swells burst forth into animals—moles and dogs, stags and frogs. And then "you could hardly hear the song of the Lion; there was so much cawing, cooing, crowing, braying, neighing, baying, barking, lowing, bleating, and trumpeting."[34] The responses to this music also indicate the character of each one who hears it. And those who receive the divine music with humility and delight are those who are received into paradise. Joy and awe overwhelm the children and the Cabby; but anger, envy, hatred—even pain—fill the wicked Queen Jadis and Uncle Andrew.

The effect of music, observed Lewis, can be worthwhile and blessed as well as worthless.

> [It] can be a preparation for or even a medium for meeting God, but it can also be a distraction and impediment. In that respect music is not different from a good many other things, human relations, landscape, poetry, philosophy. The most relevant one is wine

which can be used sacramentally or for getting drunk or neutrally. I think every *natural* thing which is not in itself sinful can become the servant of the spiritual life, but none automatically so.[35]

Lewis established a simple test that could help discern whether music or religion or laughter contributed to the sanctification of a person, or to his or her corruption: "Do they make one more obedient, more God-centered and neighbor-centered and less self-centered. 'Though I speak with the tongues of Bach and Palestrina and have not charity, etc.!'"[36]

Music resembles laughter and wine in its sublime talent to transport the soul, massage the body, and to intoxicate. All are good medicines, which can become mere drugs. All potentially become addictive and destructive. Music, laughter, and wine can make the heart glad and free; they can also depress and enslave one to the passions and moods of their enchantments. None must be given a false transcendence. While they are gifts that can glorify God, they still suffer under the curse of the Fall. Music may cause one's soul to soar like Icarus, to sense the splendor of the heavens, but our world's melodies wax and wane as the distant sighs of God. The true music of the heavens, like the divine laughter of joy, is "too loud for us to hear."[37]

Upon leaving purgatory, the first sound that Dante heard was strange but refreshing music that sounded like celestial laughter. So those who have ears to hear pick up the distant music of heaven: the music of joyous laughter.

11

Laughter as Thanksgiving

It is pleasing to the dear God whenever thou rejoicest
or laughest from the bottom of thy heart.
—MARTIN LUTHER

The proper response to the laughter and fun of life is praise and thanksgiving. Such worshipful acts give rational expression to the outbursts of hilarity that overwhelm us. They are moments of laughter translated into words. The mirth of glossolalia is interpreted in our thanksgiving.

Thanksgiving itself is the spilling over of joy. Our gratitude stems from the awareness of being given amazing gifts, from ripe vegetables to amusing friends. All of life, in fact, bubbles over with the possibilities of praise. Often, all we need is a gentle twist of perspective to turn our hearts from grumbling to gladness. Chesterton illustrated this principle in a typical domestic frustration: "A gentleman trying to get a fly out of the milk or a piece of cork out of his glass of wine often imagines himself to be irritated. Let him think for a moment of the patience of anglers sitting by dark pools, and let his soul be immediately irradiated with gratification and repose."[1] When we see all things uprightly, we can give thanks in all things.

Whenever unexpected or undeserved delights enter our lives, our purest response is grateful praise. Every tiny courtesy is purposed as a kind conquering of our hearts. A cup of cold water or an unexpected second chance calls forth our meek but merry thanksgiving. And the *practice* of praise can usher in gratitude as an effect.

In Lewis's story, the surprise of being healed or made new brings laughter, humility, and gratitude to Trumpkin the dwarf. When Lucy heals his wound with her magic cordial, Trumpkin cries: "Giants and junipers! It's cured! It's as good as new." After that he bursts into a great laugh and says, "Well, I've made as big a fool of myself as ever a Dwarf did. No offence, I hope? My humble duty to your Majesties all—humble duty. And thanks for my life, my cure, my breakfast—and my lesson."[2] In *The Magician's Nephew*, the Cabby is jerked out of London and into cold darkness. Not knowing what else to do, he recommends singing a hymn—and the hymn is one of thanksgiving.

The Psalms illuminated colorful and deep passions for Lewis, not the least of which was mirth. As Lewis translated it, unrestrained delight in the Lord rewarded the worshiper with the freedom of becoming a holy fool. When David danced with abandon before the Lord, one of his wives, Michal (whom Lewis described as "presumably a more modern, though not a better, type" than David) disapproved of his making a fool of himself. But as Lewis observed, "David didn't care whether he was making a fool of himself or not. He was rejoicing in the Lord."[3]

The Psalms express that same delight in the "fair beauty of the Lord" that made David dance, and that called for the grain of the fields and the trees of the wood to rejoice. Lewis discovered in the Jewish acts of praise more than what might be distinguished ("rather dangerously") as a spiritual love of God. (It is a common religious danger where the creature tries to become more spiritual than the Creator.) Praise in the Psalms contrasts with the routine duties of "church-going" and laboriously "saying our prayers" as "something astonishingly robust, virile, and spontaneous." The nearest we can understand this state of mind is if we

> think of a pious modern farm-laborer at church on Christmas Day or at the harvest thanksgiving . . . you would do him wrong by asking him to separate out . . . some exclusively religious element in his mind from all the rest—from his hearty social pleasure in a corporate act, his enjoyment of the hymns (and the crowd), his memory of other such services since childhood, his well-earned anticipation of rest after harvest or Christmas dinner after church.[4]

It is, Lewis suggested, much like the inseparable connection in a child's mind between the religious and festal character of Christmas or Easter: "I have been told of a very small and very devout boy who was heard murmuring to himself on Easter morning a poem of his own composition which began 'Chocolate eggs and Jesus is risen.' This seems to me, for his age, both admirable poetry and admirable piety."[5]

Many of the Psalms are natural, spontaneous responses of mirth and good cheer in the discovery of an "appetite for God," much like the initial response of a man or woman discovering their human love and that the attraction is reciprocated. The psalmists' cheerful spontaneity is

> gay and jocund. They are glad and rejoice (9:2). Their fingers itch for the harp (43:4), for the lute and the harp—wake up, lute and harp!—(57:8); let's have a song, bring the tambourine, bring the merry harp with the lute, we're going to sing merrily and make a cheerful noise (81:1, 2) you may well say. Mere music is not enough. Let everyone, even the benighted gentiles, clap their hands (47:1). Let us have clashing cymbals, not only well tuned, but loud, and dances too (150:5). Let even the remote islands (all islands were remote, for the Jews were no sailors) share the exultation (97:1).[6]

The music, the noise, the laughter are filled with gusto, even rowdiness. As the rowdy evangelist Billy Sunday preached, "If you have no joy in your religion, there's a leak in your Christianity."[7] This exultation of enjoying God is more like a rodeo than a modern church service. Joy and fun are abundant, and the congregation enjoys the rollicking romp, like lambs frolicking in the springtime or children jumping on their father.

In dealing with praise to God, however, Lewis confessed to a problem:

> Those who were never thick-headed enough to get into the difficulty it deals with may even find it funny. I have not the least objection to

their laughing; a little comic relief in a discussion does no harm, however serious the topic may be. (In my own experience the funniest things have occurred in the gravest and most sincere conversations.)[8]

Lewis hoped this comedy of errors, on so circuitous a journey of finding the obvious truth about praise, would "furnish occasion for charitable laughter."[9] He came to realize that praise was not merely religious duty, but a genuine and proper response to something or someone deserving or meriting admiration. Conversely, not to admire God and not to appreciate Him is not to be fully awake. To fail to praise is too frequently to fail to see the praiseworthy. For example,

the incomplete and crippled lives of those who are tone deaf, have never been in love, never known true friendship, never cared for a good book, never enjoyed the feel of the morning air on their cheeks, never (I am one of these) enjoyed football, are faint images of having lost the greatest experience of admiring and loving God.[10]

For Lewis it was a fundamental fact of human nature that all of our enjoyment "bubbles up and overflows into praise."

Just observe how the world rings with praise—lovers praising their mistresses, readers praising their favorite poet, walkers praising the countryside, players praising their favorite game—praise of weather, wines, dishes, actors, motors, horses, colleges, countries, historical personages, children, flowers, mountains, rare stamps, rare beetles, even sometimes politicians or scholars.[11]

The humble one praises more frequently than the crank. The optimist celebrates the good more often than the pessimist. "The healthy and unaffected man, even if luxuriously brought up and widely experienced in good cookery, could praise a very modest meal: the dyspeptic and the snob found fault with all."[12] Those who complain and grumble find their mouths filled with toads and worms and rocks rather than the sweet, refreshing breath of praise.

Praise is simply appreciation made public. When we enjoy an experience fully, we burst into happy, spontaneous praise. And we invite others to join in that praise: "Wasn't that a great meal?" "Isn't she beautiful?" "Isn't this a surprisingly good book?" We urge others to add their instruments to our grand symphony of delight, to play and sing and laugh with us, because we believe in its delightfulness. Our hymns of joy invite heaven and earth to sing and a sound of joy to be repeated.

Like laughter and music, praise works best when it is experienced ensemble. Just as the more people laugh the more uproarious and hilarious the laughter, so the more people praise the more uproarious and hilarious the praise. Laughter should include rather than exclude others, bringing a crescendo of voices together in holy laughter.

Lewis thought that we delight to praise what we enjoy because the praise "not merely expresses but completes the enjoyment; it is its appointed consummation. It is not out of compliment that lovers keep on telling one another how beautiful they are; the delight is incomplete till it is expressed."[13]

It is frustrating, Lewis noted, to enjoy something immensely and not have the company to enjoy it with: to "hear a good joke and find no one to share it with."[14] When Lewis and his brother lost a friend, they noted that "we keep on hearing jokes for which she would have been exactly the right recipient."[15]

Like lovers marveling at each other, overflowing with delight and laughter, overwhelming enjoyment and the ensuing praise are a tiny hint of what heaven will be. No, being in heaven is *not*, as it might dismally seem, like "being in church." (In his autobiography, Lewis confessed: "Though I liked clergymen as I liked bears, I had as little wish to be in Church as in the zoo.") Rather, the doctrine of heaven is a doctrine of being in perfect love with God—"drunk with, drowned in, dissolved by, that delight which . . . flows out from us incessantly in effortless and perfect expression." It is bliss, liberating and bright and joyous. It is thanksgiving in its fullness. It is the completion of the Scottish catechism that identifies man's chief end as glorifying God and enjoying Him forever—for these are the same things. "Fully to enjoy is to glorify. In commanding us to glorify Him, God is inviting us to enjoy Him"[16]

The laughter of praise is part of the appreciation, for it communicates the gratitude to a particular person. "No doubt we experience sorrow when we repent and joy when we adore. But those were by-products of our attention to a particular object."[17] Our laughter thanks God, and in this it finds its proper home. It is thus more the pity, as Rossetti remarked, that when an atheist is filled with thanksgiving and praise for life, he has no one to thank.

After the death of his wife, Lewis found some solace in praise.

> I see that I have nowhere fallen into that mode of thinking about either [God or Joy] which we call praising them. Yet that would have been best for me. Praise is the mode of love which always has some element of joy in it. Praise in due order; of Him as the giver, of her as the gift. Don't we in praise somehow enjoy what we praise? . . . By praising I can still, in some degree, enjoy her, and already, in some degree, enjoy Him.[18]

To see a model of true gratitude, Chesterton says, one must look back to the Middle Ages and forward to heaven: "We should turn to St. Francis; in the spirit of thanks for what he has done. He was above all things a great giver; and he cared chiefly for the best kind of giving which is called thanksgiving."[19] The great saints, Chesterton wrote, were those like St. Francis, who was said "to mix all his thoughts with thanks."[20]

All of life is a gift, and God has given it for joy. The servant shares the master's delight—thus, dependence and obedience become our pleasure and joy. Saint Francis gave us a grammar of gratitude and a theory of thanks, showing us it is a gift to be simple, a gift to be free, a gift simply to be.

The ineffable abundance of the universe presents at our feet all manner of good and physical gifts. And in this fullness of tasting and experiencing, Lewis expressed how humans are better off than angels. In his poem, "On Being Human," Lewis sings how angels can "by simple intelligence / Behold the Forms of nature. . . . / The Tree-ness of the tree they know. . . . / But never an angel knows the knife-edged severance / Of the sun from shadow where the trees begin, / The blessed cool at every pore caressing us / –An angel has no skin." In the same way, angels can see the form of air, but mortals breathe it in the pleasure and pang that angels cannot measure, because "an angel has no nose" nor taste buds that receive the tingling taste of oranges. Seraphim and cherubim are too bright and rich and knowing, "Yet here, within this tiny, charm'd interior, / This parlour of the brain, their Maker shares / With living men some secrets in a privacy / Forever ours, not theirs."[21]

We earthlings are given the gift of flesh, a gift that God would later give Himself, a gift for which our most ordinate response is gratitude and, when we closely study it, laughter.

12

Heaven

Love divine, all loves excelling,
Joy of heaven to earth come down.
—Charles Wesley

In *Voyage of the Dawn Treader*, the valiant mouse, Reepicheep, vows to fulfill the prophecy that has haunted him from his wee youth like a stab of joy. His heart's desire is to "go on into the utter east and never return to the world."[1] The water of the waves grows sweet and lovely as Reepicheep travels along, and a breeze from the east brings a fragrance and a musical sound that, as Lucy described it, "would break your heart." These sensual stabs of joy are invitations to the paradise of Aslan's country. Reepicheep is called to leave the old world behind and come home to joy by a compelling beauty, mystery, and wonder that appear in images of the sea of the utter east, distant hills, exotic gardens, and lovely white lilies.

The laughter of joy is one of these fleeting divine moments on our weary journeys. It appears like an oasis in arid deserts. It refreshes and renews our vigor to persevere to paradise, to plod steadfastly on through the sands of time to the Eternal Rock. Yet to seek laughter for its own sake is to wander aimlessly and wishfully, and to see only mirages. When Dr. Johnson said, "To be happy at home is the end of all human endeavor," Lewis added that this meant "first to be happy to prepare for being happy in our own real home hereafter; second in the meantime to be happy in our houses."[2] Where we go wrong, however, is in trying to preserve the happiness of our home here and now—of trying to make permanent a thing that is passing, to freeze a brook that necessarily must flow. We must receive a thing for what it is. Chesterton put forth a "Doctrine of Conditional Joy," in which joy is promised in fairy tales only if certain conditions are followed and obeyed. If we seek to grasp and keep the chalice, we shall lose it. One must give away one's bread or life to save it. The gift of joy cannot be kept, even in fairyland.

Fallen creatures that we are, we often reject a passing good that God offers us because we want or expect some other good. No, when stabs of joy come, they must be enjoyed and passed on like a summer breeze. Wind cannot be kept like stone idols. It blows where it will. Lewis saw that any attempt to circumvent the cosmic law of joy—to keep or repeat what is freely given to us—has a truly tragic shortcoming.

> On every area of our lives—in our religious experience, in our gas-tronomic, erotic, aesthetic, and social experience—we are always harking back to some occasion which seemed to us to reach perfec-tion, setting that up as a norm, and depreciating all other occasions by comparison. But these other occasions, . . . are often full of their own new blessings if only we would lay ourselves open to it. God shows us a new facet of the glory, and we refuse to look at it because we're still looking for the old one.[3]

This selfish desire to seize and clutch, to hoard and possess some-thing so as to have it again and again, whenever one demands, carries its own ironic twist. The joke of it all, for Lewis,

> is that these golden moments in the past, which are so tormenting if we erect them into a norm, are entirely nourishing, wholesome, and enchanting if we are content to accept them for what they are, for memories. Properly bedded down in a past which we do not miser-ably try to conjure back, they will send up exquisite growths. Leave the bulbs alone, and the new flowers will come up. Grub them up and hope, by fondling and sniffing, to get last year's blooms, and you will get nothing.[4]

Such temporal pleasures are "shafts of glory" that strike our sensibility to remind us of the pleasure of God. These flashing beams of gladness and glory descend on us and drench us in light and goodness. Lewis tried to "make every pleasure into a channel of adoration"—to humbly receive the pleasure and recognize its Giver as part of a single experience. The "heavenly fruit is instantly redolent of the orchard where it grew. This sweet air whispers of the country from whence it blows. It is a message. We know we are being touched by a finger of that right hand at which there are pleasures for evermore."[5] Indeed, it is immediate, pure, and spontaneous joy to experience such "tiny theophanies" as the first taste of fresh air or the feel of one's "soft slippers at bedtime"; we taste them and see that the Lord is good.

Any patch of sunlight in a dark and deep wood could well be described as a "patch of Godlight." Yet it is easy to stop and stare at the same hint of light when one has been in the darkness for a long time. When God surprises us with laughter, we may well forget that the gift is to remind us of the Giver of joy.

> Indeed the best thing about happiness itself is that it liberates you from thinking about happiness—as the greatest pleasure that money can give us is to make it unnecessary to think about money. . . . To how few of us He dare send happiness because He knows we will forget Him if He gives us any sort of nice things for the moment.[6]

To those who may object that our present homey pleasures might obscure the true pleasure of our eternal home, Lewis reminds us of their very nature:

> As long as we live in merry middle earth it is necessary to have middle things. If the round table is abolished, for every one who rises to the level of Galahad, a hundred will drop plumb down to that of Mordred. Mr. Eliot may succeed in persuading the reading youth of

England to have done with robes of purple and pavement of marble. But he will not therefore find them walking in sackcloth on floors of mud—he will only find them in smart, ugly suits walking on rubberoid. It has been tried before. The older Puritans took away the maypoles and mince-pies: but they did not bring in the millennium, they only brought in the Restoration.[7]

The simple, natural pleasures of this world contain secrets to the meaning of existence that extend beyond themselves. Even Screwtape recognized that the sorts of pleasures books and walks can give are "the most dangerous of all. That it would peel off from his sensibility the kind of crust you have been forming on it, and make him feel that he was coming home, recovering himself."[8] After the prodigal wakes up in the pigsty, he realizes he has a home and a father waiting for him. Shaking off the crust of filth, he crawls home and is unexpectedly met with all the merriment, feasting, dancing, joy, and laughter that surely will fill every heavenly reunion.

Joy celebrates the rebirth of relationships, whether between God and His creatures or between one person and another. While it arrives with healing and hopes fulfilled, it is never far away from a tear or a sigh or a sense of warmth and care. Lewis's fiction was full of such reunions. The reunion in *The Great Divorce*, particularly, carries the promise of joy. The ghosts from the netherworld generally behave with decorum, but without joy. Yet they are met by angels who brim, shake, and shine with laugher.

When joy arrives or descends, it offers the incomparable experience of being washed, enfolded, swathed, enveloped, and overwhelmed, even as it wrapped up Adam "like a blanket or a bandage."[9] It brings a bit of heaven down to us. In this way, joy on earth suggests the laughter of the heavens, of which it is a reminder, "a copy, or echo, or mirage. I must keep alive in myself," wrote Lewis, "the desire for my true country, which I shall not find till after death."[10] Joy inhabits every corner in heaven; in the new heavens and the new earth it is the native language.

"Rejoice," exhorted the apostle Paul, "and again I say rejoice." Learn to speak this heavenly language of joy.

However, Lewis warned, "the joys of Heaven [are] an acquired taste."[11] Facetious people joke about heaven as a place where people will "spend eternity playing harps." But Lewis suggested that people who mock such scriptural imagery as harps, crowns, and precious jewels do not understand the symbolic attempt to communicate the inexpressible, to express the ineffable ecstasy, infinity, splendor, beauty, and joy of heaven. "People who take these symbols literally," he wrote, "might as well think that when Christ told us to be like doves, He meant that we were to lay eggs."[12] In the seventeenth century, Thomas Fuller also shook his audiences out of their moral stupor of literalisms. He proclaimed that "hee who is so sootish as to conceive that Christ was a materiall Doore showeth himself to be a Post indeed."[13] In *Mere Christianity*, Lewis said,

> Heaven is different, too, than a club of good people singing hymns and taking offerings. (That kind of gathering would not appeal to many of us.) All Christians would agree with me if I said that though Christianity seems at first to be all about morality, all about duties and rules and guilt and virtue, yet it leads you on, out of all that, into something beyond. One has a glimpse of a country where they do not talk of those things, except perhaps as a joke.[14]

Heaven is as different from what we think it will be as these two views of Christianity are different from each other. We must suppose the end of life to be blessed. In the paradox of paradise, heaven reconciles spontaneous and boundless liberty with delicate and intricate order. Perfection in both freedom and obedience is offered in the hilarious hope of heaven. Yet there is no image of this in the "serious" activities of our natural and present spiritual life. Heaven is a place where people want to go; it is not conceivable that it would be a place to where, like church, people must be dragged. ("Oh no, Mom, do we have to go to Heaven? Can't we just stay at home?") On the contrary, Lewis pointed out that the symbols under which heaven is presented to us in Scripture are "(a) a dinner party, (b) a wedding, (c) a city, and (d) a concert."[15] As a Christian society, heaven is "to be a cheerful society: full of singing and rejoicing, and regarding worry or anxiety as wrong."[16] Such imagery was packed with astonishing and piquant appeal for the early church; and if modern Christians could grasp the point, it would appeal to us too. If modern tastes are too satiated to be overwhelmed by the promising pleasure of heaven, then that may be our fault for being too fat and unimaginative. The pleasure is lost on us much as the taste of a ripe apple is lost on the drunkard.

Lewis believed that while we are in this "valley of tears," certain qualities of heaven cannot break through to us "except in activities which for us, here and now, are frivolous." Yet in those times when we are allowed to be festive, we catch an analogous whiff of heaven. It seems so heartless, Lewis wrote in a letter to Malcolm, that the use of

> images like play and dance for the highest things is a stumbling block to you. . . . And you add that it comes with a ludicrously ill grace from me who never enjoyed any game and can dance no better than a centipede with wooden legs. . . . Dance and game are frivolous and unimportant down here—for "down here" is not their natural place. Here, they are a moment's rest from the life we were placed here to live. But in this world everything is upside down. . . .
> *Joy is the serious business of Heaven.*[17]

One of the matchless expressions of this heavenly joy occurred for Lewis in Edmund Spenser's imagery of the wedding celebration. His "Epithalamion," that jolly, happy, buoyant poem of the festal bridal day, carries the reader from the couple's expectant awakening on their wedding morning to the tired lovers' falling asleep after a blessed connubial celebration (and the bride being sent, after the nine-month wait, the "timely fruit of this same night").[18] Joy is born in love, and the steady progression of the nuptial day introduces laughter of every good sort. The early strophes in the morning call: "Awake," "Bid her awake," and announce with expectation, "Hymen is awake." (Hymen was the god of marriage.) "The wished day is come at last." Joy begins to be accompanied by merriment with a lively "medieval chorus of birds" at strophe five, breaking forth in the fourteenth into "lustiness, Bacchanalian or fescennine jollity."[19] These broad, coarse, and licentious poems or songs of bridal festivals add louder laughter to the celebration, without diminishing the holy laughter of the two becoming one. The promised fruit of all this joy, mirth, and bawdy laughter is a child, a new life. The joy of bridegrooms everywhere praising love is lifted up by angels, nymphs, priests, boisterous English boys, chirping birds, and a choir of croaking frogs. Everything that has breath praises love.

Such a poem held for Lewis a truer hint of heaven than all of what he saw as the banal songs of the hymnbook. Such poetry gives us a glimpse of the glorious joy of heaven. So, too, does Jean de Meun in "Romance of the Rose," when he touches on the idea of eternity. Lewis commented: "No one who remembers the fatuity of most poetical attempts to describe heaven—the dull catalogues of jewelry and mass singing—will underrate this green park, with its unearthly peace, its endless sunshine and fresh grass and grazing flocks—and the delightful joyous unending laughter."[20]

In heaven, "the whole man," Lewis envisioned, "is to drink from the fountain of joy. As St. Augustine said, the rapture of the saved soul will 'flow over' into the glorified body."[21] This *torrens voluptatis* is, as yet, marvelously unimaginable. For many it is unintelligible. Although the experience of joy in God's presence dwarfs all the earthly pleasures that we are too familiar with, those pleasures nevertheless may be all that we know in this life, which makes joy hard to understand. Lewis illustrated this problem well. The dilemma is like the "small boy who, on being told that the sexual act was highest bodily pleasure, should immediately ask whether you ate chocolates at the same time."[22] Trying to explain why lovers in carnal ecstasy don't bother about chocolates would be in vain. "The boy knows chocolates: he does not know the positive thing that excludes it." In the same way, many of us know the fleeting and momentary pleasures of this existence and yet cannot imagine the incredible and breathtaking joy that awaits and beckons us.

Earthly joys were never meant to satisfy our deepest needs. Yet they do perform a good task; they arouse the appetite for something better, filling, fulfilling, complete, eternal. The appetite for heavenly joy, however, seems too distant to most of us. We do not attend to this yearning or its staggering promises and rewards. It seems, observed Lewis, "that our Lord finds our desires, not too strong, but too weak. We are half-hearted creatures, fooling around with drink and sex and ambition when infinite joy is offered us, like an ignorant child who wants to go on making mud pies in a slum because he cannot imagine what is meant by the offer of a holiday at the sea. We are far too easily pleased."[23]

The afterlife that Lewis invented for the new Narnia bubbled over with laughter. Being flung through the door of the stable after a resounding and brutal defeat, the last Narnians discover the ecstatic joy of the Narnian heaven. And that's not even mentioning their wonderful change in clothing. Prince Tirian finds himself dressed in good clothes that are not uncomfortable, for "there was no such thing as starch or flannel or elastic to be found."[24] The passage of death into new life leads through the Stable, where one is reunited with old friends and older ancestors. Kisses, glad tears, and uproarious laughter are mixed in abundant measure. A great joy puts everything else out of Eustace's head as he sees a crowd of happy creatures whom he has thought dead. Everyone races to the heart of heaven, hearing the cry, "*Further up and further in.*" Bears waddle, dogs wag their tails, and little Poggin the dwarf shakes hands with everyone and grins all over his honest face. Moving from the darkness of a dead old Narnia, the company discovers "blue sky above them, flowers at their feet, and laughter in Aslan's eyes."[25]

The other Narnia was only a shadow or copy of Aslan's real world.

Now everyone entered the real, sunlit Narnia, full of vivid color and living beauty. Here they met all the characters of all the stories and histories of Narnia. "And there was greeting and kissing and handshaking and old jokes revived (you've no idea how good an old joke sounds when you take it out again after a rest of five or six hundred years)."[26] Here in Narnia Lewis rejuvenated one of his fondest notions from childhood, what Chesterton had called the "slow maturing of old jokes."[27] The laughter of joy transcends but does not deny the jokes of earth.

Aslan tells the children that their life in the Shadow-Lands is over. "The term is over: the holidays have begun. The dream is ended: this is the morning."[28] Lewis breathes into his invented Narnia heaven-swirls of glory, cascading joy, and living waterfalls of luminous laughter. As he would acknowledge, this is but a hint or peek at the unimagined splendor of God's own heaven, prepared (oh wondrous surprise!) for us.

The sound of laughter in heaven is tremendous. In *The Great Divorce*, the Dreamer (Lewis himself as a character) notices that everything is drenched with delight. He discovers that the plains and forests shake "with a sound which in our world would be too large to hear, but here I could take it with joy."[29] The voices of earth, woods, and water resound with songs of joy: "The noise, though gigantic, was like giant laughter: like the revelry of a whole college of giants together laughing, dancing, singing, roaring at their high works."[30] The native language of heaven is the laughter of joy. Speaking in this new tongue will be laughing as well as blessing, adoring, and worshiping:

> Then the new earth and sky, the same yet not the same as these, will rise in us as we have risen in Christ. And once again, after who knows what aeons of silence and dark, the birds will sing out and the waters flow, and lights and shadows move across the hills and the faces of our friends laugh upon us with amazed recognition.[31]

Part 3

Fun

*I'd rather learn from one bird how to sing than
teach ten thousand stars how not to dance.*

—E. E. CUMMINGS

Serve the LORD with gladness.

—PSALM 100:2

Introduction

When the voices of children are heard on the green
And laughing is heard on the hill,
My heart is at rest within my breast
And everything else is still.
—William Blake

The universe teems with Lewis's second category of laughter—the adventure of fun. On Lewis's scale, this is just one step down from joy—full of goodness, but less transcendent. If joy is the serious business of heaven, then fun is the serious business of earth. Joy, in fact, often turns into fun—just as a parent's joyful adoration over a baby turns into silly faces and gurgling, cooing noises.

The ridiculous charm of making funny faces at a child is that it makes a child out of the person making the faces. Grandparents gladly get on their arthritic knees to play "horsey" because they remember the glimpses of Eden in the play of their own youth. Indeed, the laughter of fun rings eternally of being young, carefree, and under the rainbow of grace. It is not without significance that the first shared act of communication between parent and child is the smile. Likewise, the blessings of God are bestowed upon His children when His face shines upon us—when He communicates with a smile.

Fun finds its natural province in the activity of play, and people play at a variety of things: walking, talking, sports, tag, tickling, hide-and-go-seek, reading, writing, chasing, climbing, eating, drinking, dancing, singing, and rolling down a grassy hill. It is in play and fun that we find ourselves closest to our biological natures. We laugh from the rush of speed and wind in our faces; we laugh from splashing into cold, bracing water; we laugh in hugging and being hugged. The laughter of fun emanates from our being creatures of the earth—being physical, being creatures sensitive to touch, taste, sound, smell, and sight, and being able to breathe and bounce in this adventure of life. Play allows us to be eternally young, to be like children even when we are old and wrinkly. (It is amazing how closely a bald, wrinkled, toothless newborn boy resembles a bald, wrinkled toothless old man.)

The laughter of our leisure (i.e., the laughter of fun), comments Screwtape, is "a sort of emotional froth arising from the play instinct." Screwtape regretted that laughter had very little use for pulling a soul to hell, other than possibly being "used, of course, to divert humans from something else which the Enemy would like them to be feeling or doing."[1] Had Screwtape reflected on the idea of fun a bit more, he might have remembered that there are some kinds of fun that might be deliciously forbidden. Some playgrounds would prove dangerous and deadly. The laughter from the fun house could be full of dread. And some people, Lewis pointed out, "talk as if meeting the gaze of absolute goodness would be fun. They need to think again. They are still only playing with religion."[2]

But Screwtape knew what dastardly deeds this heavenly fun could do to his work. In itself, fun is too closely related to joy and has "wholly undesirable tendencies; it promotes charity, courage, contentment, and many other evils."[3]

The fun of fun is that it is available wholesale on this planet. It is to be had by anyone who keeps his senses open to the amazing earth. This world is a marvel. It's full of laughter, dancing, and singing. It invites beggars and cripples and orphans to join in a game, packed with pain and hunger, no doubt, but promising something more, something miraculous, and something festive.

In the following discussion of fun, I freely switch between various synonyms for fun. That's because Lewis did as well. He talked about fun and play and pleasure—as gifts from God. He believed so strongly in the sanctification of innocent pleasures, in fact, that even in a church uncomfortable with the concept, he championed the cause in his conversation and writing. Lewis was an apologist for the faith *and* for fun in the faith. Although not a Reformed Calvinist, Lewis most assuredly would celebrate the doctrine of the sober work of faith, the Westminster Confession, that the chief end of man is to glorify God and to *enjoy* Him forever. Whether or not a creeping hedonism brought a contagious happiness to his theology, Lewis viewed God as a Person to enjoy, as both a duty and a delight. (This is not to say, however, that Lewis would trade the biblical image of God the Father for a more malleable image of God as grandfather—what Lewis described as a "senile benevolence who, as they say, 'liked to see young people enjoying themselves,' and whose plan for the universe was simply that it might be truly said at the end of each day, 'a good time was had by all.'"[4]) On the other hand, in contrast to the solemn religiosity of many churchgoers, Lewis would argue for seeing God as One who made play and pleasure and declared them, along with the rest of Creation, "good."

One way to enjoy God is to appreciate the kind of creatures He made us, and to delight and frolic in the gardens and goods He has bestowed upon us. Through play, Aslan—the parallel to Christ in the world of Narnia—shows an agnostic dwarf named Trumpkin that not only does God exist but He playfully invades our lives as well. Aslan pounces on the dwarf, as Lewis describes it: "Have you ever seen a very young kitten being carried in the mother-cat's mouth? It was like that." After the lion throws Trumpkin up in the air and catches him with his huge, velveted paws, he "set him (right way up, too) on the ground. 'Son of Earth, shall we be friends?' asked Aslan."[5]

The wholehearted experience of pleasure needed an apologist in the church. The idea that one can sinlessly experience pleasure in this world has often been rejected, even condemned, in some quarters of Christianity. It has been seen as something that is at best frivolous, inconsistent with the sobriety required to live a godly life, or, at worst, downright wicked. Lewis, of course, rejected this view entirely and addressed this issue forcefully (albeit often playfully) in his work. Several passages in *The Screwtape Letters* supply suitable examples. In one passage, Lewis—who confessed he found it exhausting doing the upside-down thinking necessary to approximate a devil's point of

view—has the chief tempter, Uncle Screwtape, growl over the fact that
God created pleasure. On the surface this seems strange. One would
think that the devil would see pleasure in general (and several forms of
it in particular) simply as an effective means to tempt people into sin.
Not Screwtape. Lewis's devil is more perceptive (and, therefore, probably more realistic) than other diabolic portrayals. Although Screwtape
does acknowledge that many souls have been won to hell through
twisted pleasure, he reminds his demonic nephew:

> Never forget that when we are dealing with any pleasure in its
> healthy and normal and satisfying form, we are, in a sense, on the
> Enemy's ground . . . it is His invention, not ours. He made the
> pleasures: all our research so far has not enabled us to produce one.
> All we can do is encourage the humans to take the pleasures which
> our Enemy has produced, at times, or in ways, or in degrees, which
> He has forbidden.[6]

In a later letter, echoing the psalmist, Screwtape complains that
"at His right hand are 'pleasures for evermore.' Ugh!"[7]

Throughout Lewis's work, the tempters understand the nature
of pleasure better than most people do. They realize that pleasure,
as it is purposefully created, is not people's property but God's. And
the demons know that their position on the subject is the opposite of
God's: He made pleasure; He intends man and woman to enjoy it forever; they didn't and don't. God, to the devils, is a hedonist at heart.[8]

Lewis believed that simple pleasures are so much God's province
that he puts the tempters in *Screwtape* in the ironic position of having to discourage their enjoyment. Uncle Screwtape actually warns
Wormwood that he must "eradicate any strong personal taste which is
not actually sin, even if it is something quite trivial such as a fondness
for county cricket or collecting stamps or drinking cocoa." Screwtape
gave Wormwood this advice because, although he knew there was
nothing innately virtuous in such things, he recognized and feared the

effects of the kind of "innocence and humility and self-forgetfulness" that accompanies their enjoyment. It produces, Screwtape felt, "the man who truly and disinterestedly enjoys any one thing in the world, for its own sake, and without caring twopence what other people say about it."[9]

Lewis also believed that God is pleased to see us enjoy His created abundance of simple pleasures. Most of the time, however, we take these pleasures for granted, seldom, if ever, thanking Him for them. Consider eating, for example. Does it occur to us that God didn't have to build nearly so much pleasure into the process of eating? What is the functional purpose of our ability to distinguish such a great number of flavors and to enjoy so many of them so much? Certainly, the Creator could have made all edible things taste much more alike than they do. Instead, we have been given a wide, wild range of taste sensations, from those that make us retch to those that make us hug ourselves and float into the air. Why did God do it? Lewis would answer that he did it for fun—*our* fun. "There are," Screwtape complains, "things for humans to do all day long without His minding in the least—sleeping, washing, eating, drinking, making love, playing, praying, working."[10]

Lewis enjoyed and advocated the enjoyment of fun, play, and pleasure, but he also understood the potential for their misuse. An invitation to play does not remove guests from the sphere of moral action. Lewis punctuated his belief in God's sovereignty over these areas of enjoyment by claiming that "our leisure, even our play, is a matter of serious concern. There is no neutral ground in the universe: every square inch, every split second, is claimed by God and counter-claimed by Satan."[11]

Although it is a fundamental part of human nature, play is nevertheless a challenged activity in the realm of spiritual warfare. The playground is as much a battleground for God's reign as is any other territory in the kingdom because, as we all know, fun can go berserk. Merriment, merrymaking, and their attendant laughter can become tyrants reigning over reason and righteousness. Laughter can sour and spoil. In *The Bridal of Triermain*, Sir Walter Scott warned, "how mirth can into folly glide, and folly into sin." Every good gift can be used wrongly. God contrived so much of what we need for our biological and social life (food, drink, rest, sleep, exercise, companionship, laughter) to be positively delightful to us; yet we can spoil it all by twisting its right enjoyment into crookedness through things such as quarreling, jealousy, pride, excess, hoarding, tomfoolery, cruelty, and flippancy.[12] In these cases, our pleasures become perverse, our laughter demonic.

Lewis wrote, "Unfortunately, we enjoy thinking about other people's faults: and in the proper sense of the word 'morbid,' that is the most morbid pleasure in the world."[13] Our laughter, like our whole lives, can be ruined by any number of fatal flaws (envy, spite, lust, greed, pride, idleness, gluttony), morbidity being just one of many vices.

> And while we are governed by this vice, there can be no Heaven for you, just as there can be no sweet smells for a man with a cold in the nose, and no music for a man who is deaf. It's not a question of God "sending" us to hell. In each of us there is something growing up which will of itself be Hell unless it is nipped in the bud.[14]

For all his advocacy of pleasure and fun, discipline of their enjoyment was a principle Lewis never forgot. There are times, as the church has always known, when "we must practice in abstaining from pleasures which are not in themselves wicked. If you don't abstain from pleasure, you won't be good when the time [for enduring trials, temptations, and unpleasant things] comes along."[15] Chesterton commented on the need for such self-denial:

> The fact is that purification and austerity are even more necessary for the appreciation of life and laughter than for anything else. To let no bird fly past unnoticed, to spell patiently the stones and weeks, to have the mind in a storehouse of sunset, requires a discipline in pleasure and an education in gratitude.[16]

When the pleasure becomes an end in itself, it falls from its proper place. When this is the case, pleasure—as those of us who have ever overindulged ourselves know—ceases to be pleasurable. When it falls short of its proper place it becomes, by definition, sin—that is, a "missing of the mark" it was intended to hit. Therefore, the practice of "discipline in pleasure" is the key to its proper enjoyment.

Even in some of these most bacchanalian moments in Lewis's fiction, this "discipline in pleasure" is present. In the golden new world of Perelandra, an Eden that never had known (and never would know) sin, Lewis's hero, Ransom, tastes a yellow fruit shaped like a toy balloon.

> He had meant to extract the smallest, experimental sip, but the first taste put his caution all to flight. . . . It was like the discovery of a totally new *genus* of pleasures, something unheard of among men, out of all reckoning, beyond all covenant. For one draught of this on earth wars would be fought and nations betrayed. . . . As he let the empty gourd fall from his hand and was about to pluck a second one, it came into his head that he was now neither hungry nor thirsty. And yet to repeat a pleasure so intense and almost so spiritual seemed an obvious thing to do. . . . Yet something seemed opposed to this "reason." . . . For whatever cause, it appeared to him better not to taste again. Perhaps the experience had been so complete that repetition would be a vulgarity—like asking to hear the same symphony twice in a day.[17]

In Ransom, Lewis offers a model of temperance. He knew that we all must learn to handle the temporal pleasures God provides on earth as Random did on Perelandra—with restraint. Our gratitude and enjoyment of the pleasures God has created must always be balanced by temperance. After all, "Who will trust us with the true wealth if we cannot be trusted with the wealth that perishes?" Lewis summed up this issue with an analogy:

Who will trust me with a spiritual body if I cannot control even an earthly body? These small and perishable bodies we now have were given to us as ponies are given to schoolboys. We must learn to manage their pleasures: not that we may some day be free of horses altogether but that some day we may ride bare-back, confident and rejoicing, those greater mounts, those winged, shining and world-shaking horses which perhaps even now are waiting for us impatiently, pawing and snorting in the King's stables. Not that the gallop would be of any value unless it were a gallop with the King; but how else—since He has retained His own charger—should we accompany Him?[18]

The preparation for the pleasures and joy of heaven must be rehearsed here on earth. Spiritual joy need not be rescued or protected from men and women of flesh and blood, for God is the Giver of flesh and blood, of wine and corn and all created pleasures. He is the glad Creator, giving us His mighty and merry gifts. And rather than running away from the horses of pleasure, we should be learning how to ride them, even if we start by riding on a simple hobbyhorse.

An invitation to accompany the King on one of His romps through forests of fun requires that one ride with restraint and balance. There are obstacles in the race, and one can either acknowledge them and enjoy their challenge, or trip over them. It is in learning the art of play in a gloriously amateurish way—discovering the rules of pleasure—that one fully and wisely delights in fun. And for Lewis, the world was ripe with the possibility of stumbling into the laughter of fun—through dogs, cats, books and games, adventures, people, and funny names.

13

The Quiddity of Life

All Thy works with joy surround Thee,
Earth and heaven reflect Thy rays,
Stars and angels sing around Thee,
Center of unbroken praise.
—HENRY VAN DYKE

To surrender to the quiddity of life—which means, to surrender to whatever life sends you—can be an adventure of unexpected and neglected delight. The commonplace becomes quite startling and marvelous when one actually pays attention to it and forgets oneself. Lewis believed that simple, everyday life presents us with countless opportunities to have fun.

Take the enjoyment of the weather, for instance. Lewis himself was introduced to the wild games of wind and rain by Sirrah, his schoolmaster, whom he called "a wise madcap: a boisterous, boyish hearty man. . . . He communicated (what I very much needed) a sense of the gusto with which life ought, whenever possible, to be taken. I fancy it was on a run with him in the sleet that I first discovered how bad weather is to be treated—as a rough joke, a romp."[1]

We Americans can apply this same treatment to the crickets that flood the South (where I live) and keep us up at night with their infernally irritating creaking. Their droning buzz is worse (and funnier) than a sore conscience accusing and berating us all night. You might call them a conscience incarnate, in the form of Jiminy Cricket. There is no rest for the wicked; so the righteous must laugh.

In adulthood, the lessons Lewis received from his schoolmaster, Sirrah, were reinforced by two of his friends, Arthur Greeves and A.

K. Hamilton Jenkin, and later by his wife, Joy. From Greeves and Jenkin, Lewis first acquired an "education as a seeing, listening, smelling, receptive creature."[2] Greeves had a preference for the homely. But Jenkin seemed to be able to enjoy everything, even ugliness.

> I [Lewis] learned from him that we should attempt a total surrender to whatever atmosphere was offering itself at the moment; in a squalid town to seek out those very places where its squalor rose to grimness and almost grandeur, on a dismal day to find the most dismal and dripping wood, on a windy day to seek the windiest ridge. There was no Betjemannic irony about it; only a serious, yet gleeful determination to rub one's nose in the very quiddity of each thing, to rejoice in its being (so magnificently) what it was.[3]

By surrendering to the ordinary objects of this world—sun, rain, and snow alike—we may catch a glimpse or hint of the mystery beyond the world. Delights thrown broadcast as clues to the nature of the universe—a universe that almost seems friendly at times. The commonplace becomes quite startling and marvelous; but only by tasting the given can we begin to recognize the Giver. Our "happiest moments are those when we forget our precious selves and [receive] everything else (God, our fellow humans, animals, the garden and the sky) instead."[4]

Lewis championed Edmund Spenser's genius in awakening the imagination to rejoice not only in the ugliness of giants and the loveliness of ladies, but in the green carpet of grass as a sort of magic carpet. Lewis saw how we are given the very sheen and "radiance of the reality of the greenness of Spenser's graves and glades, lawns, hills, and forests."[5] In reading works such as those of Spenser, Lewis found a renewed appreciation of the *being* of things. Having visited magical forests, we discover in our return to the real world that all woods are in some sense enchanted. The playful imagination offers fresh spectacles for effete eyes to see brightness, sheen, gladness, glory, and joy in the ordinary things, people, and places of our daily routine. And it offers, with a twist of mischief, a glimpse of the humorous in familiar things seen slightly askew, such as Lewis's childlike vision of "how nasty the sugar cottage in Hansel and Gretel must have been in wet weather."[6]

Lewis pointed out in a similar way how the psalmists themselves have bequeathed to us an enjoyment of nature. With sensuous delight they, too, reveled in the very feel of weather—enjoying it almost as a vegetable might be supposed to enjoy it. "Thou art good to the earth . . . thou waterest her furrows . . . thou makest it soft with the drops of rain . . . the little hills shall rejoice on every side . . . the valleys shall stand so thick with corn that they shall laugh and sing."[7]

Lewis once commented to someone on his ability to enjoy a dismal day and was surprised by the response: "My claim to be rather fond of all sorts of weather was received with the stunning information that psychologists detected the same trait in children and lunatics."[8] Nevertheless, he persisted in his enjoyment of the quiddity of each moment. Later in life, when he had grown into middle age, Lewis's new wife, Joy, revitalized his childlike vision, his habit of inhaling life. "Her palate for all the joys of sense and intellect and spirit was fresh and unspoiled. Nothing would have been wasted on her. She liked more things and liked them more than anyone I have known."[9] The marriage of Lewis's fictional characters Denniston and Camilla came about because, according to Denniston:

> We both like weather. Not this or that kind of weather, but just Weather. It's a useful taste if one lives in England. . . . Everyone begins as a child by liking Weather. You can learn the art of disliking it as you grow up. Haven't you ever noticed it on a snowy day? The grown-ups are all going about with long faces, but look at the children—and the dogs. They know what snow's made for. . . . And [how] a child loves to paddle about in rain.[10]

The patriarch in the Lewis family of adult puddle-splashers was G. K. Chesterton. Chesterton delighted in the given moment so immensely that he often forgot all else—even, at times, where he was supposed to be. In a letter to his wife, Chesterton paid homage to the essence of life, lauding how "the startling wetness of water excited me; the fierceness of fire, the steeliness of steel, the unutterable muddiness of mud."[11] Chesterton believed fun comes when we learn to see unexpected things, even things usually considered dull, as opportunities for play, as children are able to do. When confined to hanging around a railway station to wait for a train, for instance, most adults complain. (Chesterton once observed that the best way to catch a train is to miss the one that went before.) But one would never hear such a complaint from a small boy in the same situation: "No, for him to be inside a railway station is to be inside a cavern of wonder and a palace of poetical pleasure. Because to him the red light and the green light on the signal are like a new sun and a new moon."[12]

Chesterton stumbled upon the rare experience of seeing this world as home and yet as a strange and astonishing land. He combined the ideas of comfort and welcome with the senses of curiosity and wonder. "How can this queer cosmic town, with its many-legged citizens, with its monstrous and ancient lamps, how can this world give us at once the fascination of a strange town and the comfort and honour of being our own town?"[13] Like Shakespeare and Dickens in their creations of Falstaff and Sam Weller, God poetically fashioned both a positive thing and a round thing called the earth (much as Falstaff is a positive and round thing on the stage). The fun of the world must be seen with childlike, innocent eyes—even with the vision of Eden. Then all things become new and fresh and sparkling: yes, even a dreary, steady downpour of gray rain.

Like Lewis, Chesterton simply could not find rain depressing. "A shower-bath is not depressing; it is rather startling. And if it is exciting when a man throws a pail of water over you, why should it not also be exciting when the gods throw many pails?"[14] Chesterton handed down to Lewis this blessed knack to see the extraordinary and even breathless quality of the ordinary. Both men wanted people to see everything with the eyes of a child and to enjoy it all as a child would.

Although Lewis said he was taught to enjoy the quiddity of life, this was actually something he had not to learn but to relearn. Enjoying the quiddity of life seems an innate ability of all children; at the same time, it is an ability that many lose as adults. To counteract this tendency, Lewis advised his adult readers to make a point of holding on to the things they enjoyed as children. To grow up does not mean one should leave behind old pleasures but rather should acquire and learn new delights.

Part of the pity of our age is that children try too hard and too soon to act grown up, to taste pleasures that they are not spiritually or emotionally ready to fully enjoy. There is a season for chocolates and a season for sex. One must not rush too quickly into the fierce heat of summer when the young and tender buds of springtime have only begun to sprout. To rush into adulthood (and into all the grave and very important "matters of consequence" about which Saint-Exupéry's Little Prince was warned) is to forever deny oneself the delights of youth.

We may even forfeit our ability to lose ourselves in laughter. Max Eastman, in his book *The Enjoyment of Laughter*, quoted the doleful Balzac: "As children only do we laugh, and as we travel onward, laughter sinks down and dies out like the light of the oil-lit lamp."[15] Lewis would not permit himself such a handicap. He remained a child, albeit a large one, all his life, even as he grew into manhood. To his taste for lemon squash, he added a taste for hock (but never for prunes). "I now enjoy Tolstoy and Jane Austen and Trollope as well as fairy tales and I call that growth; if I had had to lose the fairy tales in order to acquire the novelists, I would not say that I had grown but only that I had changed. A tree grows because it adds rings; a train doesn't grow by leaving one station behind and puffing on to the next."[16] If we are to lose the laughter of childhood and be congratulated, Lewis asked, should we not also "be congratulated on losing our teeth and hair?"[17] Fortunately, even though he lost his hair, Lewis did not lose his laughter or his childlike delight.

Through his works Lewis hoped to help his readers retain the delights of childhood. He sought to inject the spirit and delight of youth into his audience. Simple events, he believed, could and should become major adventures. A man waiting for his soup to cool, or his wife to return from shopping, for example, was like a fisherman patiently waiting for a fish to bite his line. For those who have ears to hear, the sound of the rooster crowing should be the sound of a trumpet, a glad announcement of not only a new morning but a new life as well, a roar of reveille and resurrection all at once.

This perspective allowed Lewis to poke fun at humdrum things that most people overlook. Even the fantastical and whimsical can be brought to the level of the humorous humdrum. One rarely considers the dietary habits of fabulous creatures as much as did Lewis, a sort of imaginative Pliny. In *The Silver Chair*, a faun watches in awe as Eustace gobbles mouthfuls of eggs and toast.

> No need to hurry *quite* so dreadfully as that. I don't think the Centaurs have quite finished *their* breakfasts yet . . . [for] a Centaur has a man-stomach and a horse-stomach. And of course both want breakfast. . . . That's why it's such a serious thing to ask a Centaur to stay for the weekend. A very serious thing indeed.[18]

Enjoying the quiddity of life includes seeing the humor in our messy chores. In *The Silver Chair*, Lewis exposed the ignorance of the character Jill, who "thought that when, in books, people live on what they shoot, it never tells you what a long, smelly, messy job it is plucking and cleaning dead birds, and how cold it makes your fingers."[19] Jill also finds disgusting, and shudders at, the normal eating habits of the owl who snaps at something in flight: "I was just nabbing a bat. There's nothing so sustaining, in a small way, as a nice plump little bat. Shall I catch you one?"[20] Lewis also acknowledged a real but often forgotten aspect of rescuing prisoners from dungeons: the stench. When a trap door is opened to liberate friends, a voice exclaims: "Phew! How it smells in here." Humor lies in wait in the humdrum. When the Beavers and the children need to escape the White Queen with utmost urgency, Mrs. Beaver hesitates, wanting to bring along her heavy sewing machine. In the rush of life, it behooves those who wish to discover the comedy of everyday life to pause and receive it.

Lewis found some of the world's simplest things to be the most pleasant, such as going on a journey. William Hazlitt's words in *Table Talk* might have been Lewis's motto: "Give me the clear blue sky over my head, and the green turf beneath my feet, a winding road before me, and a three hours' march to dinner—and then to thinking." Everyone enjoys a walk now and then, but what about learning to enjoy monotony? In this age of impatience, it seems heretical to suggest that the repetitive may be received simply as an opportunity for repeated enjoyment. Lewis once shocked a *Time* magazine reporter who inquired whether the don's quiet routine was not somewhat monotonous. Lewis replied: "I like monotony."[21] His answer would have been an affront not only to contemporary pleasure seekers but to Lewis's character, Screwtape, who pointed to the human horror of the "Same Old Thing" as "one of the most valuable passions we have produced in the human heart—an endless source of heresies in religion, folly in counsel, infidelity in marriage, and inconstancy in friendship."[22]

Chesterton, however, suspected that there was a sense of delight in this "Same Old Thing" within the divine character.

> The sun rises every morning. . . . It might be true that the sun rises regularly because he never gets tired of rising. His routine might be due, not to a lifelessness, but to a rush of life. The thing I mean can be seen, for instance, in children when they find some game or joke that they specially enjoy. . . . Because children have abounding vitality . . . they want things repeated and unchanged. They always say, "Do it again"; and the grown-up person does it again until he is nearly dead. For grown-up people are not strong enough to exult in monotony. But perhaps God is strong enough to exult in monotony.

It is possible that God says every morning, "Do it again" to the sun;
and every evening, "Do it again" to the moon.[23]

That God has never tired of doing it again and again may mean
that "He has the eternal appetite of infancy; for we have sinned and
grown old, and our Father is younger than we."[24]

One example of pleasure in repetition is found in reading a
great book again and again. To reread is to remain forever young as
reader (more about this later). Lewis pitied those who said they'd read
Pickwick or Boswell as though once were enough. "It is as if a man
said he had once washed, or once slept, or once kissed his wife, or
once gone for a walk."[25] Yet even this simple repetition can be ruined
by sin—the sin of wanting to be like God, of controlling what comes
to us. Lewis cautioned that in the repetition of our pleasures a desire
can arise to have "it" again, which can lead to a compulsion to clamp
a regulator on what happens to us in life, restricting or cutting off (if
possible) its quiddity, and thereby controlling our pleasures. Is this
not the sweet poison of the false infinite, that we devour and gorge
ourselves on every earthly imitation of heaven's eternal joy? We are
drawn to and taken in by every false disguise of eternal gladness.

There is a world of difference between the quality we experience
when we surrender to the quiddity of life and the quality of enjoyment
repeated pleasures bring when we try to control our experience. One
is the joy of a child abroad in a field, soaking up sweet sunshine one
minute and squealing delightedly at the cool kiss of raindrops the
next. The other is the joy of a miser locked in his dark vault counting
and recounting the same coins. One puts a child in touch with the
generosity of God. The other puts a man in touch with nothing but
his own greed.

Setting out to enjoy life's quiddity can lead to an encounter with
its meaning. The apostle Paul was speaking of food when he wrote
the following words to Timothy, but they could apply equally well
to so many of the experiences life brings us: "For everything created

by God is good, and nothing is to be rejected if it is received with gratitude" (1 Tim. 4:4). It amazes grown-ups the number of "unpleasant" things children can enjoy: dirt, rain, mud, lizards, bugs, etc. But we should all be such children, reveling in what God gives us. G. K. Chesterton was one such child. It came to him one day (perhaps one windy day) that grown-ups were mistaken about chasing hats:

> Why should it be unpleasant to run after one's hat? Why should it be unpleasant to the well-ordered and pious mind? Not merely because it is running, and running exhausts one. The same people run much faster in games and sports. The same people run much more eagerly after an uninteresting little leather ball than they will after a nice silk hat. There is an idea that it is humiliating to run after one's hat; and that when people say it is humiliating they mean that it is comic. It certainly is comic; but man is a very comic creature, and most of the things he does are comic—eating for instance. And the most comic things of all are exactly the things that are most worth doing—such as making love. A man running after a hat is not half so ridiculous as a man running after his wife.[26]

Inconveniences may be embraced as upside-down opportunities for fun. Chesterton predicted that hat chasing could just as well become the sport of the future—a wild and riotous hat race made especially for over-the-hill, older gentlemen on gusty, windy days. Rather than inflicting pain on some unwilling rabbit, these men would be

> inflicting pleasure, rich, almost riotous pleasure, upon the people who were looking on. When last I saw an old gentleman running after his hat in Hyde Park, I told him that a heart so benevolent as his ought to be filled with peace and thanks at the thought of how much unaffected pleasure his every gesture and bodily attitude were at that moment giving to the crowd.[27]

Chesterton virtually squeezed the drabness out of the daily grind and weekly routine. Life has such spice for us to enjoy, but our taste buds are deadened with artificial seasonings. God gave the wonder of the world to the children of man, but we have continually ignored the marvels. "What did a week mean?" Chesterton asked. For many, it meant only seven, dull days. But the real meaning—the secret of the calendar—was the secret of the universe. "Seven times we have been dissolved into darkness as we shall be dissolved into dust; our very selves, so far as we know, have been wiped out of the world of living things; and seven times we have been raised alive like Lazarus, and found all our limbs and sense unaltered, with the coming of the day."[28] The sound of the cock crowing is like the sound of the trumpet—a glad announcement of new life, a roar of resurrection now and to come.

Lewis and Chesterton offer us the possibility of finding delight (and play) in all that we work at and do. For some tasks, this would mean a mammoth, even Herculean, transformation into pleasure. Yet the imagination must be quickened in these monotonous modern times. Forget trying to turn rain into sunshine by positive thinking; relax and enjoy the rain. Dance in it. Sing in it. Even cry in it, and believe that the lachrymose heavens lament and weep with you. Experience each offering of life for what it is, Lewis tells us. Look for the fun in it, and while you're at it you will probably find some meaning in it and something to be thankful for.

14

Humor and Humility

However, a good laugh is a mighty good thing, and rather too scarce
a good thing; the more's the pity. So, if any man, in his own proper
person, afford stuff for a good joke to anybody, let him not be backward,
but let him cheerfully allow himself to spend and be spent in that way.
And the man that has anything bountifully laughable about him,
be sure there is more in that man than you perhaps think for.
—HERMAN MELVILLE

The plain, ordinary activities of life not only are meant to supply most of our fun, but are symbols of goodness in human society as well. Regarding the value of such simple natural moments, Lewis lauded how

> the sun looks down on nothing half so good as a household laughing together over a meal, or two friends talking over a pint of beer, or a man alone reading a book that interests him; and that all economics, politics, laws, armies, and institutions, save in so far as they prolong and multiply such scenes, are a mere ploughing the sand and sowing the ocean, a meaningless vanity and vexation of spirit.[1]

In Lewis's stories, goodness bathes those fictional characters who enjoy the simple and honest pleasures of eating, drinking, talking, or reading. Mrs. Beaver fixes tasty, hearty meals, and the Green Lady of Perelandra enjoys the pleasure prepared for her: "The fruit we are eating is always the best fruit of all."[2] To receive the good that is given and taste the fruit that is found is to enjoy the joys that God has prepared for His creatures.

Lewis wrote that the attitude on the front lines during the war was, "They're not shelling us at the moment, and it's not raining, and the rations have come up, so let's enjoy ourselves."[3] We learn, as the Green Lady did, that to find our proper joy, one must "turn from the good expected to given good." As she tells Ransom: "You could send your soul after the good you had expected, instead of turning it to the good you had got. You could refuse the real good; you could make the real fruit tastes insipid by thinking of the other."[4]

A main problem for devils, Pharisees, and ascetics is that God created pleasure and play as good things. Screwtape acknowledged that though many souls have been won to hell through pleasure, the devils must remember that everything is created by God and therefore is good. Before pleasure can be used for sin, it must be twisted, contaminated by excess, greed, perversion, and self-centeredness. This fact discouraged Screwtape.

> The health and spirits which you want to use in producing lust can also, alas, be very easily used for work or play or thought or innocuous merriment. . . . It is the same with other desires of the flesh. You are much more likely to make your man a sound drunkard by pressing drink on him as an anodyne when he is dull and weary than by encouraging him to use it as means of merriment among his friends when he is happy and expansive.[5]

The ascetic rightfully warns us against the tendency in ourselves to be consumed with pleasure. The ascetic demands we die to ourselves, to be made humble in denial. We would, if we could, give ourselves over to laughter until we rolled in it like clover. Yet the same ascetic would whip himself rather than whip cream: he connects self-abasement to divine humility. It is not so connected. Such self-cruelty is a dark shadow of pride. The ascetic who would remind us of the important spiritual fast at the expense of the important natural feast must himself be reminded of the goodness of God's creation, and it is in the face of God's goodness that one is humbled.

In contrast to the proud denizens of the underworld are those who live lightly and humbly. Laughter is a divine gift to the human who is humble. A proud man cannot laugh because he must watch his dignity; he cannot give himself over to the rocking and rolling of his belly. But a poor and happy man laughs heartily because he gives no serious attention to his ego. The proud person may at best smile like Buddha, with the controlled half-smile of moral or psychological superiority. Yet it is one of the vices of our culture that we honor and commend the smile in sophisticated or polite company and save the laughter for more common arenas. Even Confucius warned, "Beware the man whose belly does not move when he laughs."

If forced to choose between smiling or laughing, Chesterton would campaign for the latter. The gentle, polite smile of the Victorian who held her head high above the world was sure to come smack up against this crusader of the laugh. Chesterton believed that at least three strikes can be thrown against the smile: First, it can "unobtrusively turn into the sneer"; second, it remains an individual and even secretive act; and, finally, it tends to be guarded and tinged with cynicism. Laughter, however, can be communal, social, and gregarious. Furthermore, Chesterton argued,

> laughing lays itself open to criticism, is innocent and unguarded, has the sort of humanity which has always something of humility. . . . Therefore, in this modern conflict between the Smile and the Laugh, I am all in favor of Laughing. Laughter has something in it in common with the ancient winds of faith and inspiration; it unfreezes pride and unwinds secrecy; it makes men forget themselves in the presence of something greater than themselves; something (as the common phase goes about a joke) that they cannot resist.[6]

The smile, for Chesterton, is the product of wit, while laughter is the child of mirth. Wit is a weapon to overpower one's enemies; mirth is a way to see oneself overpowered.

As long as a man is merely witty he can be quite dignified; in other words, as long as he is witty he can be entirely solemn. But if he is mirthful he at once abandons dignity, which is another name for solemnity, which is another name for spiritual pride. A mere humorist is merely admirable; but a man laughing is laughable. He spreads the exquisite and desirable disease by which he himself is convulsed. But our recent comedians have distrusted laughter for exactly the same reason that they have distrusted religion or romantic love. A laugh is like a love affair in that it carries a man completely off his feet; a laugh is like a creed or church in that it asks that a man should trust himself to it. [The humble man] must sacrifice himself to the God of laughter, who has stricken him with a sacred madness. As a woman can make a fool of a man, so a joke makes a fool of a man. And a man must love a joke more than himself, or he will not surrender his pride for it. A man must take what is called a leap in the dark, as he does when he is married or when he dies, or when he is born, or when he does almost anything else that is important.[7]

Chesterton noted that only clever or flippant people make jokes without participating in them, without turning themselves over to the blessed absurdity of their creation. The creator of a joke who then stands outside the laughter and does not take part in it is a Manichaean. "It is unpardonable conceit not to laugh at your own jokes. Joking is undignified; that is why it is so good for one's soul. Do not fancy you can be a detached wit and avoid being a buffoon; you cannot. If you are the Court Jester you must be the Court Fool."[8] Only the truly humble belong in this kingdom of divine laughter. The proud are not allowed—or, rather, the proud will not deign to enter and join the vulgar throng. Voltaire, in his enlightened wit, stands outside the rollicking company of these like Rabelais and Chaucer. He smiles and smirks with his mind, while the humble, common man laughs with his body, soul, heart, and belly.

Humor dwells in the stable, with the lowly, the humble, and, by definition, the common and the vulgar. This relation comes about as humility shares etymological roots (and isn't it just like humility to share?) with humor and humanity. It is play itself, as well as a play on words, that the origins of these words are buried in the basic elements of earth and water. The roots of this laughter are in *humus*, that rich, dark soil from which humankind has come and *humere*, that fluid, liquid moisture that wets and refreshes that soil. God had breathed upon this dust. (Adam's name in Hebrew, *Adamah*, literally means "clay" and "earth." Here then is our first earthly father, a veritable clod.) Out of the *humus* and *humere* grow humanity, humility, and humor. The laughter of humor inhabits the earth and is of the earth, like humankind coming from dust and going back to dust, but dampened with a few drops of divine dew.

The joy of heaven incarnates in the humor of the earth. Lewis pointed out that when this happens, the spiritual grows lighter upon assuming a load of good earth. Quoting William Langland's satirical poem *Piers Plowman*, he noted that

> love, incarnate became as "merry as a lark." Love is the plant of peace and the most precious of powers, for heaven could not contain it, it felt so heavy, until it had poured itself out on the earth. After that, no leaf on a lime/tree was lighter (gayer, more mobile) than it, when it had taken flesh and blood from the clay.[9]

Humus, as a rich, dense mixture of minerals, forms a simple base for all that is laughable in character and incident. The character of the simpleton, idiot, or moron, for example, has a simple mind—and each is, quite literally, a half-wit and a clod. Each is also potentially a source for loving humor or for ridicule. The idiot, Lewis wrote, "may indeed raise uneasiness or disgust in a modern; but he does not seem to have done so in our ancestors. They loved 'fools' and kept them as pets."[10] "Good" humor finds a common humanity with idiots. Laughter at fools is essentially laughter at oneself. Citing Thomas Carlyle's observation that men were mostly fools, Chesterton expanded the truth, noting:

"Christianity, with a surer and more reverent realism, says that they are all fools. This doctrine is sometimes called the doctrine of original sin. It may also be described as the doctrine of the equality of men."[11] If men or women cannot make fools of themselves, then we may be assured their efforts are superfluous.

Even Lewis saw the folly of his own pride. Having once become silently irritated from a mild tiff with Mrs. Moore, Lewis puffed himself up into some temporary relief through a bit of symbolic savagery by "jabbing violently at a piece of pastry. As a result I covered myself in a fine shower of custard and juice; my melodramatic gesture was thus deservedly exposed and everyone roared with laughter."[12]

Humor and humility should keep good company. Self-deprecating humor can be a healthy reminder that we are not the center of the universe, that humility is our proper posture before our fellow humans as well as before almighty God. One reason people enjoy seeing authority humiliated is that authority rarely carries itself with either humility or humor. "I suppose," wrote Lewis, "(tho it seems a hard saying) we should mind humiliation less if [we] were humbler. . . . It is the humble and the meek who have all the blessings of the Magnificat."[13]

Humility for Lewis was not a sort of bootlicking hypocrisy or fawning obsequiousness, such as one might find in an unctuous Dickens character or in Lewis's country of Calormen. Rather, humility was an open, happy, and outward-looking habit.

Do not imagine that if you meet a really humble man he will be what most people call "humble" nowadays: he will not be a sort of greasy, smarmy person, who is always telling you that, of course, he is a nobody. Probably all you will think about him is that he seemed a cheerful, intelligent chap who took a real interest in what you said to him.[14]

The truly humble person is a cheerful and merry man or woman who listens to others. Her concern is completely apart from herself and wholly toward others. Humility, like good humor, embodies a charisma that genuinely charms an enemy and converts him into a friend. Lewis noted in Chesterton's Father Brown a disarming humility that confounded the little cleric's sophisticated antagonists. The latter mistakenly thought their worldly knowledge superior to his moral integrity and knowledge of truth. And the humor of these short tales of a guileless detective priest depended, Lewis believed, "on the continual pricking of this bubble."[15] The mighty and proud are continually brought down by the meek and humble, and mostly in humorous fashion.

Humility necessarily reminds us of our feet of clay. It is thus an extremely important virtue for religious people who live with their heads in the heavens. The comedies of Aristophanes and Molière, for example, take those with hubris, who live in the rarified atmosphere of Cloud Cuckooland or are clothed in their own self-importance, and bring them back to earth as humiliated and naked clods. Humor provides the perspective for an honest and accurate understanding of the self, as supplied in this poem by Stephen Crane:

> *I stood upon a high place,*
> *And saw, below, many devils*
> *Running, leaping,*
> *And carousing in sin.*
> *One looked up, grinning,*
> *And said, "Comrade, Brother!"*[16]

For Lewis, the perspective that humility offers provides the seat for humor. In his preface to *The Screwtape Letters*, Lewis described Goethe's Faust, rather than the urbane devil Mephistopheles, as the one "who really exhibits the ruthless, sleepless, unsmiling concentration upon self which is the mark of Hell." This self-absorption is the opposite of humility and of humor: for humor involves a sense of proportion and a power of seeing yourself from the outside."[17]

Humor can aid in the prevention of such sins as pride. Screwtape warned Wormwood of the dangers of awakening his patient's sense of humor. Instead, he advised, draw his attention to the fact that he has become humble.

> Catch him at the moment when he is really poor in spirit and smuggle into his mind the gratifying reflection, "By jove! I'm being humble," and almost immediately pride—pride at his own humility—will appear. If he awakes to the danger and tries to smother this new form of pride, make him proud of his attempt— and so on, through as many stages as you please. But don't try this too long, for fear you awake his sense of humour and proportion, in which case he will merely laugh at you and go to bed.[18]

When we awaken to an awareness of our true condition before God, we discover the most ordinate response to our sinful state is a humble repentance. As true repentance from sin results in initial sadness (and not self-pity), it then breaks out in spontaneous gladness and mirth. Because our sins are forgiven, the proper response is joy. Humility accepts grace with wild, self-forgetful abandonment. Lewis believed that "we all sin by needlessly disobeying the apostolic injunction to 'rejoice' as much as by anything else. Humility, after the first shock, is a cheerful virtue."[19] Or, in the words of John Donne, "Religion is not a melancholy, the spirit of God is not a damper."[20] Rather, the Spirit of God comes to liberate us from the prisons of pride where we are held captive to our own self-importance.

Religious posturing needs its knees buckled, that we might fall on our faces with humility and gratitude. Pharisaical pride needs pricking and deflating before one can join the contrite publican in the glad company of God. Humility brings a good-humored perspective to remind us that when we think we see solemn truths and our own privileged calling in Scripture, we may be seeing "only the reflection of our own silly faces."[21] The shock of such a vision (more startling and fantastic than anything Ezekiel saw) should humble us and cause us to break forth in the humility of laughing at our too-familiar, proud, solemn, silly faces. Humility is the small door to the divine playground of fun. One must bow one's high and holy head to enter this kingdom prepared for children.

15

Gravity and Levity

This world is not a theatre, in which we can laugh; and we are not assembled together in order to burst into peals of laughter, but to weep for sins. . . . It is not God who gives us the chance to play, but the devil.
—Chrysostom

Play is not frivolous. Anyone playing at something has to be serious, even as children are never so serious as when they are at play. A child does not skip rope casually, but with serious concentration. It is to her as important as any other human activity; indeed, it is the most important task at hand. To learn social skills of sharing and cooperating, giving and delighting, children must play. Most cultures recognize how this ludic impulse brings balance to lives that very easily go askew.

Work, such as that of an author, Chesterton points out, may be laborious, but that does not necessarily mean it is important. He wrote that if "you publish a book tomorrow in twelve volumes (it would be just like you) on 'The Theory and Practice of European Architecture,' your work . . . is fundamentally frivolous. It is not serious as the work of a child piling one brick on the other is serious." Anyone "playing at anything has to be serious."[1]

Yet while play is a serious activity, it is still fun. When all attention is focused upon the object in play, as though one is consumed with a passion, then one thoroughly enjoys the activity. Chesterton thus believed that ideas could be made both popular and serious, entertaining and sincere. He once instructed young journalists to write an essay for a sober church publication and another for the comics, and then put them in the wrong envelopes. "I cannot see why convictions should look dull or why jokes should be insincere," he wrote in explaining the vision of his *G. K. Weekly*. "I should like a man to pick up this paper for amusement and find himself involved in an argument. I should like him to pursue it purely for the sake of argument and find himself pulled up short by a joke."[2]

Championing the cause for levity, Chesterton confessed that the chief vice of a collection of his essays was that

> so many of them are very serious; because I had no time to make them flippant. It is so easy to be solemn; it is so hard to be frivolous. Let any honest reader shut his eyes for a few moments, and approaching the secret tribunal of his soul, ask himself whether he would really rather be asked in the next two hours to write the front page of *The Times*, which is full of long leading articles, or the front page of *Tit-Bits*, which is full of short jokes. If the reader is the fine conscientious fellow I take him for, he will at once reply that he would rather on the spur of the moment write ten *Times* articles than one *Tit-Bits* joke. . . . So in these easy pages I keep myself on the whole on the level of *The Times*; it is only occasionally that I leap upwards almost to the level of *Tit-Bits*.[3]

Just as Mark Twain apologized for writing a long letter because he hadn't time to write a short one, so Chesterton recognized the creative challenge of cracking a joke over crafting an essay. Anyone can write a long-winded thesis; only the inspired can put truth in a jest or an apt comic parable. A problem arises when one assumes the solemn essay is of more consequence than the lively jest. When his critics rebuked him for spicing his arguments with wit and comic chestnuts, Chesterton retorted:

> Mr. McCabe thinks that I am not serious, but only funny, because [he] thinks that funny is the opposite of serious. Funny is the opposite of not funny, and of nothing else. . . . Whether a man chooses to tell the truth in long sentences or in short jokes is a problem analogous to

whether he chooses to tell the truth in French or German. Whether
a man preaches his gospel grotesquely or gravely is merely like the
question of whether he preaches it in prose or in verse. . . . The
truth is, as I have said, that in this sense the two qualities of fun and
seriousness have nothing whatever to do with each other, they are
no more comparable than black and triangular. Mr. Bernard Shaw
is funny and sincere. Mr. George Robey [a well-known music hall
comedian] is funny and not sincere. Mr. McCabe is sincere and not
funny. The average Cabinet Minister is not sincere and not funny.[4]

The contemporary notion that fun stands opposed to seriousness
stems, in part, from old Daniel Webster's definition. Webster warned
that fun usually "implies laughter or gaiety but may imply merely a
lack of serious or ulterior purpose; . . . play stresses the opposition to
earnest without implying any element of malice or mischief."[5]

But on this side of paradise, play is weighted down, not by seriousness, but by solemnity. Lewis believed that there was too much
solemnity and speaking in holy tones. "As everyone knows," he wrote,
"*gravis* means 'heavy.'" That which is grave is seen as something that
"carries weight," and possesses importance. "Lucretius, depreciating
Heraclitus, says he has a higher reputation among those Greeks who
are inanes than among those Greeks who are *gravis* and really want to
know the truth. The contrast is between 'empty; and 'heavy' Greeks
(an empty jug is lighter than a full one)."[6]

Lewis saw a similarity between such gravity and sadness. An original meaning of the Anglo-Saxon word *saed* (and Latin *satur*) meant full
(of food), gorged, replete. Lewis cites Chaucer's use in saying that "the
messenger drank sadly ale and wyn." This use, Lewis argued, could be
translated that he "'drank solidly'—settled down, as the sequel shows
(for he was soon 'sleeping like a pig'), to a solid, or uninterrupted, or
sound, or heavy, or serious evening's toping."[7] Anyone or anything that
is full is heavier than something empty. Being *saed* or full indicated a
great weight laid upon someone—thus associating the meanings of

heavy, grave, or solid with that of sad. Sad things were grave things, and if grave things were important things, then sad connoted important and serious things as opposed to light and happy things.

People who are wrapped up with their own proud and important selves "will not understand that a joke is a joke. Everything must be serious."[8] To be serious meant to be heavy, and heaviness has rarely, if ever, been a virtue. Lewis, opposing the notion that laughter and seriousness are necessarily antithetical, pointed to his friend Dyson, a religious man with an honestly merry laugh, and asked: "Have you observed that it is the most serious conversations which produce in their course the best laughter?"[9] Such confusion about the mutual exclusivity of the comic and the serious led Lewis to exclaim: "Oughtn't the word *serious* to have an embargo slapped on it?"[10]

Lewis pointed out that such words as *grave* and *sad*, influenced by the very nature of metaphor, find themselves acquiring such meaning as "grievous," the opposite of light, merry, or sportive. "Thus we find sad used to mean 'serious,' i.e., not joking. 'Speak you this with a sad brow?' are you in earnest? (*Much Ado About Nothing* 1.1.183). And what is serious will always be thought gloomy by some, and gloom may by litotes be called seriousness."[11] The litote as understatement—in which something is affirmed by a negative to the contrary (as in "not a bad-looking woman")—leads to the moot belief that gloom, heaviness, and solemnity are serious virtues. This is one prime error of perception about laughter that Lewis helps us to avoid. And herein he is "sadly"—or, solidly—indebted to a classic paragraph from Chesterton's *Orthodoxy*, on the gravitational pull of pride:

> Pride is the downward drag of all things into an easy solemnity. One "settles down" into a sort of selfish seriousness; but one has to rise to a gay self-forgetfulness. A man "falls" into a brown study, he reaches up to a blue sky. Seriousness is not a virtue. It would be a heresy, but a much more sensible heresy, to say that seriousness is a vice. It is really a natural trend or lapse into taking one's self gravely, because

it is the easiest thing to do. It is much easier to write a good *Times* leading article than a good joke in *Punch*. For solemnity flows out of man naturally; but laughter is a leap. It is easy to be heavy; hard to be light. Satan fell by the force of gravity.[12]

Lewis acknowledged his debt to this passage in his defense of *The Screwtape Letters*. "Whatever else we attribute to beings who sinned through pride, we must not attribute this [humor]. Satan, said Chesterton, fell through force of gravity." The devil took himself too seriously—even, we may say, too sadly. The picture of hell that Lewis envisioned was a "state where everyone is perpetually concerned about his own dignity and advancement, where everyone has a grievance, and where everyone lives the deadly serious passions of envy, self-importance, and resentment," much like a university faculty meeting.[13]

The error of the church, however, has mostly been to partake of this life too gravely and solemnly. May "God who made good laughter" forbid this tendency of ours, wrote Lewis. "It is one of the difficult and delightful subtleties of life that we must deeply acknowledge certain things to be serious and yet retain the power and will to treat them often as lightly as a game."[14]

Seriousness is important in its proper place. No one wishes the pharmacist to approach his work carelessly. A certain amount of gravity is necessary for our very existence. We may jump onto a spinning merry-go-round with careless merriment, but we are glad that the amusement ride's makers did not put it together with the same wild abandon. Leaping onto a swing and soaring into the azure skies is a game of freedom that depends on whether the ride was constructed seriously. We may soar on a child's swing for a lark. But we are glad that the builder did not make loose chains for a lark.

Lewis viewed the opposite of seriousness, not as humor, but as triviality. (The opposite of the comic is likewise, not the serious, but the tragic.) To treat someone or something trivially was to not take them seriously. To joke or laugh did not necessarily imply a lack of seriousness; in fact, Lewis believed that the merriest kind of merriment could occur only between people who took each other seriously. In this way play, like joy, "is the serious business of heaven." In Chaucer's "The Clerk's Tale," we hear women being laughingly advised to be as "light as leef on linde"; in other words, to be as free and flighty as the linden tree leaf. "And *light* in Middle English," Lewis reminds us, refers as "often to cheerfulness, frivolity, and nimbleness of movement, as to smallness of weight."[15]

Accused of making game of his own death, Chesterton responded: "It is absolutely useless and absurd to tell a man he must not joke about sacred subjects. It is useless and absurd for a simple reason: because there are no subjects that are not sacred subjects."[16] Every bush is potentially a burning bush as every man is a walking, though bruised, image of God. Our every act and word and laugh is done for God or away from God. Thus, we do unto God everything in its proper and ordinate fashion. In writing of things comic in Chaucer and Rabelais, Lewis admonished that we are not to munch whipped cream as though it were venison. Some things require a serious response and others require merriment.

Knowing that God Himself is more solid and trustworthy than anything in this ephemeral world gives birth to the daring adventure of faith. This life, observed Chesterton, "is much too important to be taken seriously." Ransom recognizes this paradox in the symbol of Perelandra's halo. "He knew now what the old painters were trying to represent when they invented the halo. Gaiety and gravity together."[17]

The balance of humor with the serious side of life is crucial. One should not fall into the deadly seriousness of hell; yet neither should one be flighty or flippant. George MacDonald's *The Light Princess* tells the story of a little girl who was cursed at her royal christening by the king's wicked sister, the aunt who had been left off the guest list. At the baptismal font, the atrocious aunt pronounced this malediction: "Light of spirit, by my charms, / Light of body every part, / Never weary human arms—/ Only crush thy parents' heart!"[18]

The witch had deprived the child of all her gravity. Like a dandelion seed, she could be caught up by a breeze and blown about. Thus she had to be tethered like a kite. Yet physical gravity was not all she lost. When an enemy had cut the king's general and all his troops to pieces, she laughed. When her mother cried, she laughed. The Light Princess had no emotional or spiritual gravity whatsoever. Only the sacrifice of a watery death by a loving prince could restore weight and solidity to the lightheaded, lighthearted princess. Levity needs a solid foundation.

Chesterton argued that only the serious person can be truly hilarious. Pointing to the Scriptures that promise "wine makes glad the heart of man," Chesterton added, "but only of the man who has a heart. The thing called high spirits is possible only to the spiritual."[19]

This alloy of gravity and levity impressed Lewis in his own work, *The Great Divorce* in particular. In response to Blake's satiric poem, "The Marriage of Heaven and Hell," Lewis used this book to show their irreconcilable separation. In heaven, the people and the landscape are seriously substantial, down to each blade of grass or each drop of rain. All is solid and thick and weighty. Yet, also, all is light. Free and spontaneous laughter rings out from all its denizens. Gentle, tinkling laughter and booming, explosive laughter can be heard in the valley of the shadow of life. The laughter of rejoicing, play, and humor abounds with divine fecundity.

Not so in hell, where self-importance is heavy but hollow. The laughter that exists there is cruel, flippant, sarcastic. When a woman is cheated out of her place in line for the bus trip to heaven, the crowd roars with mean laughter. No kindly or benign comic spirit dwells there.

16

Food and Drink

A feast is made for laughter, and wine maketh merry.
—KOHELETH, ECCLESIASTES 10:19 (KJV)

"Verily," Lewis muttered during his convalescence from an illness, "he that but looketh on a plate of ham and eggs to lust after it, hath already committed breakfast with it in his heart."[1] The fact has to be faced head on: C. S. Lewis liked to eat, and he liked to drink. He saw these victuals not as mere necessities but as good and glad gifts from God. He felt sorry for all those who could not enjoy them, including angels. Lewis wrote:

> The angels have not senses; their experience is purely intellectual and spiritual. That is why we know something about God which they don't. There are particular aspects of His love and joy which can be communicated to a created being only by sensuous experience. Something of God which the seraphim can never quite understand flows into us from the blue of sky, the taste of honey, the delicious embrace of water whether cold or hot, and even from sleep itself.[2]

The sensuous experiences are given for our delight, and for Lewis few experiences were more delightful or delicious than those of food and drink. Lewis suggested that if you ever happened to pass a café door when you were sweat-sodden, hungry, and footsore, "and heard the plates clink and the music play, with laughter," would you not, then, "run to [a] table and become its happy guest?" This habit certainly was not foreign to Lewis and his brother, Warnie, who, after a long walk one day, "ate our egg sandwiches and pork pies and drank our

bottled beer . . . behaving just as we would have done fifteen years earlier. 'Having eaten everything in sight, we are now finished.'"³ Eating
and drinking were ripe occasions for fun, and as such provided ample
opportunity for laughter.

One of Lewis's friends, J. R. R. Tolkien, created some heartwarm-
ing creatures called hobbits, who are characterized by their partaking
of much food, drink, and comfortable merrymaking. Indeed, Lewis
and his friends were very much like a fellowship of grown-up hobbits, who enjoyed "health, quiet, an easy chair, a full, but not too full,
stomach."⁴ Lewis acknowledged that whenever he broke bread with
friends, he "feasted on friendship and good talk (ranging from religion
to bawdy) and kindness and cheeriness all day long."⁵ Lewis especially
enjoyed true holidays such as Christmas, since they provided opportunities for "merry-making and hospitality"; and, he emphasized, "I
approve of merry-making."⁶

Lewis ate and drank heartily. The cork popping out of a bottle
was to him a "heart-cheering noise."⁷ Had Jesus walked in Britain
in the twentieth century, certain churchmen might have gasped to
see Him mingling with gluttonous and winebibbing sinners such as
Lewis and Chesterton. (One apocryphal story relates that Bob Jones,
Jr., after meeting Lewis, supposedly remarked, "He may smoke and
he may drink but I do declare the man's a Christian.")

Lewis and Chesterton drank wine and ale and some spirits, too, as
most of us know. And they did so without becoming drunkards. They
believed that wine is given by God to bring cheer and gladness to the
heart of His people. (Eccl. 10:19 reminds us, "A feast is made for laughter, and wine maketh merry" [KJV].) It is not only a blessed beverage but
also a sacramental element and a constant reminder of divine miracles:

> God creates the vine and teaches it to draw up water by its roots and
> with the aid of the sun, to turn that water into a juice which will
> ferment and take on certain qualities. Thus every year, from Noah's
> time till ours, God turns water into wine. That men fail to see. Either

like the Pagans they refer the process to some finite spirit, Bacchus or Dionysius: or else, like the moderns, they attribute real and ultimate causality to the chemical and other material phenomena which are all that our senses can discover in it. But when Christ at Cana makes water into wine, the mask is off. The miracle has only half its effect if it only convinces us that Christ is God: it will have its full effect if whenever we see a vineyard or drink a glass of wine we remember that here works He who sat at the wedding party in Cana.[8]

For Lewis, Christ's first miracle of converting water into wine at the wedding feast proclaims that "the God of all wine is present. The vine is one of the blessings sent by Yahweh: He is the reality behind the false god Bacchus."

Every year, as part of the Natural order, God makes wine. He does so by creating a vegetable organism that can turn water, soil, and sunlight into a juice which will, under proper conditions, become wine. Thus, in a certain sense, He constantly turns water into wine, for wine, like all drinks, is but water modified. Once, and in one year only, God, now incarnate, short circuits the process: makes wine in a moment: uses earthenware jars instead of vegetable fibres to hold the water. But uses them to do what He is always doing. The Miracle consists in the short cut; but the event to which it leads is the usual one. If the thing happened, then we know that what has come into Nature is no anti-Natural spirit, no God who loves tragedy and tears and fasting for their own sake (however He may permit or demand them for special purposes) but the God of Israel who has through all these centuries given us wine to gladden the heart of man.[9]

The problem with drinking wine lies with the two extremists: the teetotaler and the drunkard. As Chesterton argued, "The dipsomaniac and the abstainer are not only both mistaken, but they both make the same mistake. They both regard wine as a drug and not as drink."[10] In discussing "The Problem of Drink," Chesterton called it an "inverted form of fetish worship. . . . No sillier to say that a bottle is a god than to say that a bottle is a devil."[11] Wine is not the problem; yet, like all of God's gifts, it can be abused. Blaming wine is like "calling the practice of wife-beating the Problem of Pokers."[12] Nevertheless, wine itself (and beer) has become a problem for many people of God, a fact that has caused some groups of Christians (notably, American ones) to reject it completely. Chesterton blamed the problem in part on Muslims, pointing out that "alcohol" is an Arab invention. Lewis agreed. "Of course Our Lord never drank spirits (they had no distilled liquors) but of course the wine of the Bible was real fermented wine and alcoholic. The repeated references to the sin of drunkenness in the Bible, from Noah's first discovery of wine down to the warnings in St. Paul's epistles, make this perfectly plain."[13]

The divine wine is liquid play, fairies' drink, yet its boundaries must also be maintained and its rules obeyed. Chesterton wrote, "It is strange and weird that I cannot with safety drink ten bottles of champagne; but then the champagne itself is strange and weird, if you come to that. If I have drunk of the fairies' drink it is but just I should drink by the fairies' rules."[14] Aware of the hazards, Chesterton offered a rule for holy and healthy drinking: "Drink because you are happy, but never because you are miserable . . . drink when you would be happy without it, and you will be like the laughing peasants of Italy."[15] One should never drink beer or wine out of need, for this kind of rational drinking leads to death and hell. Chesterton advised two principles of communal pleasure and personal restraint. First, "Wine should be taken, not secretly but frankly and in fellowship as men in inns do dine." And, second, "We must thank God for beer and burgundy by not drinking too much of them."[16] As Pascal observed, "No wine, no wisdom; too much wine, the same."[17]

The wise, glad, and grateful embrace of both food and drink abound in Lewis's writings. The delight of eating, especially, occurs in one of Lewis's early poems. That lost soul, Dymer, seeing a table set before him, leaped for mirth: "He clapped his hands, his eye lit like a lover's. / He had a hunger in him that was worth ten cities. / Here was silver, glass and covers. / Cold peacock, prawns in aspic, eggs of plovers, / Raised pies that stood like castles, / Gleaming fishes and bright fruit / With broad leaves around the dishes."[18]

Lewis's *Chronicles of Narnia* also are packed with picnics, feasts, teas, banquets, snacks, homey dinners, British breakfasts, and meals in abundance. One cannot miss the delight and fun in virtually every meal in Narnia, from tea with Mr. Tumnus to the hearty, good home-cooking of freshwater trout and sticky, hot marmalade rolls at the Beavers'. When Narnia tastes the first fruits of her thaw from winter, who should appear but a jolly and ruddy Father Christmas, full of generous Christmas cheer and mirth and bringing food for everybody.

In Lewis's works, when no or little food is available, one expects an equal loss of enjoyment. Arriving in Narnia, the four children find that they have with them only two squashed lunches. Peter warns: "That'll be two lunches among four. This isn't going to be such fun."[19] In *Prince Caspian*, however, when Caspian begins "to sleep under the stars, to drink nothing but well water and to live chiefly on nuts and wild fruit," he finds "he had never enjoyed himself more."[20] Never had food tasted more savory than during these simple but ample meals in the wild. In *Voyage of the Dawn Treader*, Lewis even ventured to give his readers a glimpse into how (and what) a dragon eats. (Eustace as a dragon preferred his wild goat or swine raw, but he ate in private because his meals were a bit messy.)

Foods in Lewis's works are many and varied and described in vivid detail. On the magician's island, in *Voyage of the Dawn Treader*, omelets, strawberry ice, and cups of chocolate are served when the company is hungry—and "all hungry times are one o'clock." At dinner on the magic island, "everyone had by magic what everyone liked best to eat and drink."[21] Later, the crew comes upon a grand banquet at Aslan's table where food is set out, eaten, and renewed every day, an eternal refreshment of turkey, salmon, lobsters, ice puddings, pomegranates, peaches, grapes, and pineapples. In *That Hideous Strength*, the preparation for Ivy's husband, Tom, after his release from jail, centers upon cold pie and pickles, cheese, and a bottle of stout. Even on other planets Lewis served remarkable food. On Perelandra, for instance, Ransom stumbles across the yellow fruit of the bubble tree, which tastes "sharp, sweet, savoury, or voluptuous, creamy, or piercing."[22] It is, for any salivating reader who missed dinner, an enviable, sumptuous snack.

The "orgiastic and alarming pleasure" of these fruity gourds does not detract from the pleasure of plain food, however, which is "the delight of munching and being nourished, a 'sober certainty of waking bliss.'"[23] In fact, Lewis's readers can readily identify the good characters in his fiction because they are the ones who enjoy good, ordinary, plain food. When Edmund starts to go wrong in *The Lion, the Witch, and the Wardrobe*, he demonstrates this by getting hooked on the exotic, bewitching Turkish Delight that the White Witch gives him. On the other hand, in *That Hideous Strength*, we know that the tramp, mistaken by many for an evil magician, is not really evil but good because he simply wants a toasted cheese sandwich. In the same story, a sign of repentance in the erring Mark Studdock reveals itself when he "thought sometimes about Jane, and sometimes about bacon and eggs, and fried fish, and dark, fragrant streams of coffee, pouring into large cups."[24] And in *Out of the Silent Planet*, Ransom, nervously awaiting his meeting with the Oyarsa on the planet Malacandra, thinks to himself that he would like a cup of tea more than anything in the world. Later, on his return to earth, he barely survives a crash landing. His spacecraft explodes only minutes after he struggles out of it. Exhausted, he limps down a road, staggers into a pub, drags himself up to the bar and says, "A pint of bitter, please."

Eating and drinking are fun—and often funny—but for Christians these also are sacramental acts. Even outside of religious settings, the simple meal—the eating of bread and drinking of wine—carries with it a holy health. It quietly reminds us of grace, especially when a quiet grace is said over it. In a world full of poverty and hunger, being able to eat at all, let alone to enjoy eating, is providential, that is, an act of a gracious providence.

Indeed, our enjoyment of food and drink should go hand in hand with our thankfulness for them. In Lewis's works, this is as true on other planets as it is on Earth. On Perelandra, Ransom enjoys a serving of bubble fruit, a meal of nourishment and fun. But the experience is capped by thankfulness—and that is the last word on food and drink. After a riotously fun meal a million miles from home, "a man, or at least a man like Ransom, felt he ought to say grace over it; and so he presently did."[25] And that belch of the heart called laughter punctuates much of the grace we say in gratitude for the merry meals we take with our family and friends. A shared sandwich is as laugh inducing as a pie in the face. Wine and food can make a heart merry. Laughter is the ineffable prayer of those of a merry heart whose communion is a continual feast of delight (Prov. 15:15).

17

Adventures and Games

He that plays when he is a child will play when he is a man.
—John Wesley

C. S. Lewis didn't think much of a modern person's capacity (or lack of it) for adventure. The medieval man and woman seemed to him to have been bred with much more of an adventurous temper than their nineteenth- or twentieth-century counterparts. This was due, Lewis believed, to the differences in their perspective. "Historically as well as cosmically, medieval man stood at the foot of a stairway; looking up, he felt delight. The backward, like the upward, glance exhilarated him with a majestic spectacle, and humility was rewarded with the pleasures of admiration."[1] This breathtaking posture admitted him not only to all kinds of terrors, but to a world of thrills, challenges, games, and fun as well. Waiting around every bend, like an unexpected inn or perhaps a friendly highwayman, was a delightful surprise.

Lewis found all manner of delightful surprises in the history of literature. He tried to rouse the world to the startling oddness and wonder of life through literature by reintroducing two comic Italian poets who would splash cold, shivering, refreshing water on our dusty faces: Boiardo and Ariosto. The essence of Boiardo's *Orlando Innamorato* is speed and fun, a pell-mell pace of adventures with a wild and crazy carnival jollity.

> He invents a world in which though love and war are almost the sole occupations, yet a major character hardly ever has time to lose a life or a maidenhead, for always, at the critical moment, a strange knight, a swift ship, a bandersnatch, or a boojum breaks in and we

are caught up into another story. It is extremely enjoyable, but in a breathless way; it is rather like a ride on a switchback.[2]

Fun permeates Boiardo's episodes, as in a roller-coaster Punch and Judy show. For example, one of his knights encounters a Monty Pythonish character who is hard to kill because each of his limbs regenerates itself as soon as the knight cuts it off. Lewis compared the plucky resourcefulness of the knight—who solved the dilemma by quickly tossing the arms in the river after cutting them off—to Mickey Mouse.[3]

Boiardo's countryman, Ariosto, a "master of irony and of comic construction," spreads out "God's plenty," preaching the abundance of life available to any who would partake. Lewis said of this divine fullness of earthly adventure: "You can no more exhaust it than you can exhaust nature itself. When you are tired of Ariosto, you must be tired of the world."[4]

In his *Orlando Furioso*, Ariosto spins a literary form that is one of the oldest tricks in the book: the tall tale. Impudent boasts and inventive lies, such as belong to the comic marvels and adventures of Baron Münchausen or Paul Bunyan, inhabit this work. This is the kind of extravagant fun that charms men and women in their childhood. In one episode a thief, Brunel, comes upon a knight who obliviously is meditating—and he steals the knight's horse right from underneath him. Lewis teased that whenever you "feel that you can read no more adventures, at that very moment he begins another with something so ludicrous, so piquant, or so questionable in its exordium that you decide to read at least this one more. And then you are lost: you must go on till bedtime, and next morning you must begin again."[5]

The pleasure one finds in these preposterous adventures is not merely the pleasure of mockery that adults often find in fairy tales (such as those of Louis XIV or Parnell), but the pleasure of "great fun." This is whimsy at its wildest. "Even while you laugh at it, the old incantation works. Willy-nilly the fairies allure, the monsters alarm, the labyrinthine adventures draw you on." Lewis allowed only one English critic the possibility of doing "justice to this gallant, satiric, chivalrous, farcical, flamboyant poem: Mr. Chesterton should write a book on the Italian epic."[6]

In contrast to these two medieval poets, far too many "moderns," Lewis believed, live in a tiny, windowless universe. Imagination and the spirit of adventure have wilted so much in our day that the task of teachers and critics is not so much to cut down weeds as it is to nurture, water, and fertilize small sprouts. Eliot's vast wasteland spreads across our blank and empty minds. "Let us Awaken!" Lewis commanded, lest we become lulled into a final sleep. "Hardier spirits seek real danger and real fear for pleasure's sake," Lewis wrote. "A mountain climber once said to me, a climb is no fun unless there has been one moment at which you have sworn that if once you get down alive you will never go up a mountain again."[7]

An advocate of adventure, Lewis incorporated loads of it in his fiction. Many of his novels, in fact, are actually adventure stories. And Lewis's adventures are truly adventurous: desperate battles, daring quests, distant explorations—all accompanied, as they should be, by danger and its attendant fears. Some of the fears are exquisitely intense. In *The Magician's Nephew*, two children, Digory and Polly, arrive by magic in an in-between place between worlds. They discover that the various small ponds in the in-between place are actually entrances to new worlds. They step out of the pond that brought them to the in-between place and begin to walk around selecting others to try. Moments before they jump into a new pond, Polly pauses and says, "Stop! Aren't we going to mark this [the earth's] pool?"

> They stared at each other and turned quite white as they realized the dreadful thing that Digory had just been going to do. For there were any number of pools in the wood, and the pools were all alike and the trees were all alike, so that if they had once left behind the pool that leads to our own world without making some sort of landmark, the chances would have been a hundred to one against their ever finding it again.[8]

This kind of delicious danger spices Lewis's fictional adventures. In *Out of the Silent Planet*, Ransom, newly arrived on an unknown planet, flees in terror from a ghostly white, ten-foot-high specter called a "sorn." These surrealistic bogeymen were "stalky distortions of earthly bipeds . . . like something seen in one of those comic mirrors."[9] Later Ransom feels an old lift of the heart when he is forced to ride on the shoulders of one of them (they turn out to be friendly). The creatures still made him nervous, but "Ransom found something reassuring in the thought that the sorns were shepherds. Then he remembered that the Cyclops in Homer plied the same trade." Despite his fear, Ransom had fun. It was like riding on his father's back or on an elephant at the circus; he felt a sober and ecstatic sense of life "in unasked and unmeasured abundance. If there had been air enough in his lungs he would have laughed aloud."[10]

In the same book, one character, the walruslike hrossa of Malacandra, expresses a theory of the necessity of danger in adventure. The hrossa describes to Ransom the snapping black jaws of the killer hnakras (sharklike monsters) that inhabit the lakes. They are dangerous beasts, but the hrossa is philosophical about it. "I do not think the forest would be so bright, nor the water so warm, nor love so sweet," he says, "if there were no danger in the lakes."[11]

Chesterton's works, such as *The Ball and the Cross* and *The Man Who Was Thursday*, also explode with a fireworks blend of adventure, tall story, and delight. These literary romps are outrageous adventures in wonderland, bringing wonder home and finding home full of wonder. In his introduction to *Orthodoxy*, Chesterton proposed the romantic tale of an "English yachtsman who slightly miscalculated his course and discovered England under the impression that it was a new island in the South Seas." In doing so, he stumbled upon the amazing experience of finding this world astonishing and strange, and yet homey. A sense of curiosity and wonder intermingled with an awareness of intimacy and welcome.

Like Lewis, Chesterton could find adventure in the tamest, most familiar, of places. Why concern ourselves with trying to interview a gorgon or a griffin, he asked, creatures that do not exist, when one can "discover that the rhinoceros does exist and then take pleasure in the fact that he looks as if he didn't?"[12] Even turkeys appeared as occult and awful mystic apparitions to Chesterton because "God has never told us what a turkey means. And if you go and stare at a live turkey for an hour or two, you will find by the end of it that the enigma has rather increased than diminished."[13] All kinds of strange and delightful adventures await whoever will embrace them. And Chesterton detected in them a conspiracy cloaked in natural phenomena. "One elephant having a trunk is odd," he commented, "but all elephants having trunks looked like a plot."[14]

The health of sane men and women is strengthened by recognizing the world to be an odd and adventurous place. It is a place in which one might never have seen, never have been born into—for it is a place that might never have been itself. It is a place that was rescued from the wreck and chaos of existence; and all that is rescued, such as on Robinson Crusoe's island, is to be appreciated.

In Lewis's thinking, adventure came under the category of play. Games should have fallen into that category as well, but Lewis had some discouraging experiences with them in his childhood—experiences that discolored his view of games for the rest of his life. "I accepted games (quite a number of boys do) as one of the necessary evils of life, comparable to Income Tax or the Dentist." In Lewis's school days, "the organized and compulsory games had . . . banished the element of play from school life almost entirely. There was no time to play (in the proper sense of the word). The rivalry was too fierce, the prizes too glittering, the 'hell of failure' too severe."[15] When games become professional, they become serious and cease really to be games at all. To be truly and fully fun, games must be played for fun by amateurs. One is robbed of "all real play by making games compulsory."[16] When you think about it, it is really a shame. Here, at school, is young Lewis, a person who will give the world so much play and fun and who already possesses a heightened sense of both, but who by virtue of inadequate talents could not play at things that were designed for play. (And heaven help him if he should laugh at those who did play.) He later described the experience this way:

> If the reader will picture himself, unarmed, shut up for thirteen weeks on end, night and day, in a society of fanatical golfers—or, if he is a golfer himself, let him substitute fishermen, theosophists, bimetallists, Baconians, or German undergraduates with a taste for autobiography—who all carry revolvers and will probably shoot him if he ever seems to lose interest in their conversation, he will have an idea of my school life. Even the hardy Chowbok (in *Erewhon*) quailed at such a destiny. For games (and gallantry) were the only subjects, and I cared for neither. But I must seem to care for both, for a boy goes to a Public School precisely to be made a normal, sensible boy—a good mixer—to be taken out of himself; and eccentricity is severely penalized.[17]

After that experience, Lewis was able to detect this same warped "professionalization" in the use, for instance, of the word *hiking* and "its abuse for something so simple as going for a walk." To Lewis this tendency to formalize the language of play was indicative of the professional's "passion for making specialized and self-conscious stunts out of activities which have hitherto been as ordinary as shaving or playing with the kitten."[18]

In the same letter, Lewis decried the fact that the BBC now paid professionals to play for an audience "the same games we used to play for ourselves as children."[19] Fun, when mass-produced, is stripped of its vitality. Who knows? Soon there even may be a television channel devoted solely to playing games for us. We will be condemned merely to watch. A symptom of this malaise is that professionals rarely laugh in their games and amateurs frequently (so much so sometimes that they can't finish their game). In "The Perfect Game," Chesterton

described a contest of croquet with a man named Parkinson who took
the game too seriously:

> "Oh, Parkinson, Parkinson!" I cried, patting him affectionately on
> the head with a mallet, "how far you really are from the pure love
> of the sport—you who can play. It is only we who play badly who
> love the Game itself. You love glory; you love applause; you love the
> earthquake voice of victory; you do not love croquet. You do not
> love croquet until you love being beaten at croquet."[20]

Only amateurs enjoy their play, argued Chesterton. "Our play is
called amateurish; and we wear proudly the name of amateur, for amateurs is but the French for Lovers. We accept all adventures from our
Lady, the most disastrous or the most dreary."[21]

Scholar Peter Berger believes that when we surrender to our play
and let it remain simply that, we encounter a "signal of transcendence."
Play gives us a taste of eternal joy in the midst of the momentary. "In
playing," Berger suggests, "one steps out of one time into another."[22] We
all have had, in our childhood at least, the experience of being unconscious of time while we played some game for all we were worth. In
hours like these, consciousness evaporates and we are ushered into a
timeless and deathless world of delight. Games—the amateur kind—
and adventures are for smacking ourselves in the face, waking us up,
reminding us of the amazing, so-often-taken-for-granted miracle of our
existence. To be alive and to be laughing is itself an adventure and a
game created by a miracle of God—a miracle that is beyond our com-
prehension. Often, therefore, in the midst of our play a quiet voice
whispers to us; a still, small voice speaks our names. Did we really hear
it? We freeze in our footsteps, listening, like "children playing burglars
hush suddenly: was that a *real* footstep in the hall?"[23] Is someone else
out there? The game, which seemed so carefree and independent, has
another participant, another player of whom we were unaware.

The breathless adventure of life, an adventure in which all partake, is a safari, a hunt, except that in this cosmic adventure the tables are turned, the roles are reversed. We are not the hunters: We are the hunted. And it is not a familiar, civilized hunter who pursues us—not at all! It is Someone outside of our experience, outside, even, of our whole world. It is the Hound of Heaven Himself. We have slipped into an adventure of our own unmaking. We play the game of our lives, indeed, the game of life. And it is meant to be played by exuberant, daring, and fun-loving amateurs.

The laughter that results from our tiny adventures and play is one of liberation, one in which we feel God's pleasure in our lungs. Fun splashes a fresh liberation upon the gloom of our labors. It inhabits the Sabbath, or should, to bring rest and relief to those who live by the sweat of the brow or stress of the brain. It is a brief and fleeting respite in which God recreates His creatures through His gift of recreation.

The Christian can, as St. Aquinas argued, play and romp to the glory of God as much as he can work and eat to His glory. It is curious that of the Ten Commandments the one to honor and keep the Sabbath is the one with the most immediate benefit to us, yet it is the one we break most casually. Aquinas thus reminded us to be refreshed in our service to God. In a chapter from his commentary on Aristotle's *Nicomachean Ethics*, he observed that

> there is some good play, in as much as it is useful for human life. As man needs from time to time to rest and leave off bodily labours, so also his mind from time to time must relax from its intense concentration on serious pursuits: this comes about through play. Hence Aristotle says that man obtains in this life a kind of rest from his anxieties and preoccupations in playful conversation.[24]

For Lewis, playful conversation was a primary form of fun. He hated games in school because he was all thumbs. "Games allow for companionship with many excellent people who can be approached in no other way," Lewis wrote, but he himself was to games, "as the old proverb has it, like an ass to the harp." When Lewis was approached about going to study with a special tutor, he was asked, "Would he be happy with no companions of his age?" He responded in ecstatic relief:

> The mere thought "Never, never, never, shall I have to play games again" was enough to transport me. . . . My heart laughed. Happy without other boys? Happy without toothache, without chilblains, happy without pebbles in my shoes. . . . If you want to know how I felt, imagine your own feelings on waking one morning to find that income tax or unrequited love had vanished from the world.[25]

Christianity frees us to have fun with the rest of life once our first duties are done. In fact, Lewis acknowledged, "there may seem to be an almost comic discrepancy" between the ultimate issues of our lives and the immediate tasks God gives us, much as "a young priest finds himself involved in choir treats and a young subaltern in accounting for pots of jam . . . Happy work is best done by the man who takes his long-term plans somewhat lightly and works from moment to moment 'as to the Lord.'"[26] Placing our life under the infinite and inexorable claim of God's rule does not "exclude any of the ordinary human activities. St. Paul tells us to get on with our jobs. He even assumes that Christians may go to dinner parties, and what is more, dinner parties given by pagans. Our Lord attends a wedding and provides miraculous wine."[27]

It is not without significance that most comedies end with a wedding ceremony, for wedding parties are generally fun. Therefore, would it be so irreverent to imagine that at the wedding recorded in the Gospels—and very early in His ministry—Jesus, too, had fun? At the very least, by turning water into a most excellent wine, He made the party festive and cheery. This conclusion, one suspects, is unavoidable: it is difficult to believe that, as a fully human guest of the wedding, He did not liven it up.

Lewis saw health in mirth. Laughter, the Scriptures inform us, can make the heart glad and healthy. It could be therapeutic in its potential to liberate. Lewis once recommended to his introspective friend Arthur Greeves that instead of brooding he should "keep to work and sanity and open air—to the cheerful and the matter of fact side of things." On occasions that tend to draw forth the melancholy or depression of a soul, "a plunge into the cheery and homely world of 'good fellows' and women has something of the same wholesome effect as a romp with dogs or children."[28]

Play is crucial not only for health and sanity, but for courtesy and kindness. When the old English universities of Oxford and Cambridge were accused of being playgrounds for the governing class, Chesterton responded in bold, extravagant fashion: "Let there be a playground for the governing class. I would rather be ruled by men who know how to play than by men who do not know how to play. . . . [The playground is] a place for humanizing those who might otherwise be tyrants, or even experts."[29] Play makes one tolerably genial and jolly; it makes one fun. Without play one would be molded into a standard shape, a conformity of solemnity. Each person would lose those rough and boisterous angles, which, Chesterton suggested, might mean coming to look like Humpty Dumpty.

In celebrating and praising play, Chesterton argued that it might

> reasonably be maintained that the true object of all human life is play. Earth is a task garden; heaven is a playground. To be at last in such secure innocence that one can juggle the universe and the stars, to be so good that one can treat everything as a joke—that may be the real end and final holiday of human souls. When we are really holy we may regard the Universe as a lark.[30]

If all the world is a stage and we are merely players, we must rehearse our play; for we are being prepared for the playground of heaven. Our laughter here on earth is but a tune-up for the joyful hallelujahs of being in God's presence.

18

The Fun in Nature

The fields, the floods, the heavens, with one consent
Did seeme to laugh on me, and favour mine intent.
—EDMUND SPENSER

Nature, like each of us, is "a creature, a created thing, with its own particular tang or flavor."[1] She is a character both cruel and fair, baffling
and fun. But as one of God's temporal creatures, nature will go the
way of all of God's creatures: she will change, and not for the better. As
Chesterton observed: "If you leave a thing alone you leave it to a torrent
of change. If you leave a white post alone it will soon be a black post."[2]
(In another, more morbid analogy, Lewis once quipped that his "hand,
this hand now resting on the book, will one day be a skeleton's hand."[3])

Indeed, nature has gone wrong. Following the corruption of
Adam, she is doomed to decay and die. But after death, the church
looks forward to a resurrection, one in which nature will participate.
Before spring comes, she must suffer the winter. She who was baptized by floods must yet be purified by fire in order to be made new.
"She, like ourselves, is to be redeemed. She will be cured, but cured in
character: not tamed (Heaven forbid) nor sterilized. We shall still be
able to recognize our enemy, friend, play-fellow and foster-mother, so
perfected as not to be less, but more, herself. And that will be a merry
meeting."[4] Lewis wrote that all nature is "visibly emblematic of the joy
of Easter. . . . 'Nature herself—the very face of the earth now truly
renewed after its own manner of renewal—bids us Rejoice."[5]

The God of the Jews had a double character in His relation to
nature. As Charles Williams intoned, "This also is Thou, neither is this
Thou."[6] In *Miracles*, Lewis wrote:

On one hand He is the God of Nature, her glad Creator. It is He who sends rain into the furrows till the valleys stand so thick with corn that they laugh and sing. The trees of the wood rejoice before Him and His voice causes the young deer to bring forth their young. He is the God of wheat and wine and oil. In that respect He is constantly doing all the things that nature-gods do: He is Bacchus, Venus, Ceres all rolled into one.[7]

Nevertheless, we must not mistake Him for a nature-god, for He clearly is not. He does not die and revive annually like the old corn-king. Lewis warned: "He may give wine and fertility, but must not be worshipped with bacchanalian or aphrodisiac rites."[8] He is not part of nature, as its Soul or Spirit or Life-force; no, He is wholly beyond nature. He created nature—it is His creature. He is the transcendent Creator, Maker, and Controller, and He made nature good, as Genesis declares. Like His other creation (human beings), however, nature has gone bad, been spoiled and corrupted, or, as Lewis often phrased it, has become "bent."

But despite its inevitable decline, good persists in nature, as supernaturalists can see without ignoring the bad. For the time being, nature encompasses both the blessed imprint of God and the smudging that followed the Fall. "Come out, look back, and then you will see," beckoned Lewis, "this astonishing cataract of bears, babies, and bananas: this immoderate deluge of atoms, orchids, oranges, cancers, canaries, fleas, gases, tornadoes and toads."[9]

Nature is not ultimate reality. Yet neither is it a mere "stage set for the moral drama of men and women." Nature is full of concrete, individual determinate things, opaque facts like "flamingoes, German generals, lovers, sandwiches, pineapples, comets and kangaroos." And nature is not dull or humorless. When Chesterton experienced enjoyment in places that others called "dull as ditchwater," he mounted his soapbox and challenged the simile. "And, by the way, is ditchwater dull? Naturalists with microscopes have told me that it teems with quiet fun."[10]

While microscopic nature is teeming with "quiet fun," macro-scopic nature teems with riotous fun—with monkeys swinging from trees, kittens chasing their tails, and puppies chasing the kittens. In other words, it teems with animals, which are the most fun part of it. With a loyal affection for animals, Lewis was also a student of their behavior. He once recommended to his friend Dom Bede Griffiths a book on animal and bird behavior by Konrad Lorenz entitled *King Solomon's Ring*: "There are instincts I had never dreamed of: big with the promise of real morality. The wolf is a very different creature from what we imagine."[11] "Talking of beasts and birds," Lewis wrote to his friend Barfield,

> have you ever noticed this contrast? . . . When you read a scientific account of any animal's life you get an impression of laborious, incessant, almost rational economic activity (as if all animals were Germans), but when you study any animal you know, what at once strikes you is their cheerful fatuity, the pointlessness of nearly all they do. Say what you like, Barfield, the world is sillier and better fun than they make out.[12]

Lewis wrote that, as an example, he once saw "one young pig cross the field with a great big bundle of hay in its mouth and deliberately lay it down at the feet of an old pig. I could hardly believe my eyes. I'm sorry to say the old pig didn't take the slightest notice. Perhaps it couldn't believe its eyes either."[13]

Lewis's attitude toward animals seems at times to be elevated to the level of his view of humans. He believed, for example, a certain veterinarian practicing animal psychology to be a charlatan on the grounds that, in his opinion, neither humans nor animals deserved to be subject to psychology. "Psychological diagnoses even about human patients seem to me pretty phony. They must be even phonier when applied to animals. You can't put a cat on a couch and make it tell you its dreams or produce words by 'free association.'" But, Lewis concluded, "shrewd cats probably see through the analyst better than he'd see through them."[14]

A close relation of human to animal is reflected even in Scripture, where, for instance, Job recognizes that he is brother to the owl and cousin to the jackal. The prophetic gift (or satirical habit) for seeing humans as animals was also present in George MacDonald's character Curdie. The Princess tells Curdie that it is always what men do—in mind or body—that makes men become less than men, that is, beasts. The change, she says, begins in their palms. And they do not know what is happening, for "the nearer a man gets to being a beast the less he knows it."[15] (Ironically, in Orwell's *Animal Farm*, the more cruel, greedy, and wicked the pigs become, the more they become like men.) In "Eden's Courtesy," a poem connecting "beast and man," Lewis found such a natural love between the two that "children all desire an animal book."[16] In the poem, Lewis confesses that until he tames the sly fox, timorous hare, and lording lion in himself, he could find no peace. The wild animal kingdom formed Jungian archetypes of the brutes within his soul; animal and human were closely related.

In Narnia, the overly sensitive bulldog and its persnickety offenses taken might remind one of any number of people. In trying to ascertain whether Uncle Andrew is human or vegetable, a she-elephant (a pachyderm Cyrano de Bergerac) points to the holes in his face as possible eyes and mouth:

> "No nose, of course. . . . Very few of us have what could exactly be called a Nose." She squinted down the length of her trunk with pardonable pride. "I object to that remark very strongly," said the Bulldog.
>
> "The Elephant is quite right," said the Tapir.[17]

The bulldog is repeatedly offended. Challenging the elephant's proposition that smelling isn't everything, the bulldog asks: "If a fellow can't trust his nose, what is he to trust?" The elephant replies: "Well, his brains perhaps." Twice more the bulldog complains: "I object to that remark very strongly."[18] The bulldog's touchiness makes him a comic caricature of an overly sensitive British prig.

Along the same lines, the physiognomist G. B. Porta used to describe men's characters according to which animals their faces resembled. Lewis told the story of an unintentional prank pulled upon a fellow whose face, at the crucial moment, would have delighted Mr. Porta. The innocent victim was sitting next to the fireplace reading the football results when a match not fully extinguished was inadvertently flung into his open collar. Suddenly, as Lewis describes it, the man went "ape face."[19] His "body then rose in a vertical line from the fender, without apparent muscular effort, as though propelled by a powerful spring under his bottom . . . with a distension of the cheeks and a blowing noise, he exclaimed in a heightened voice: 'It isn't so bloody funny'" to the stifled guffaws of his usually placid colleagues. (I suspect that, to Lewis, a man so absorbed in sports scores seemed a bit of a trousered ape already, so that his face, in an emergency, merely conveyed his already ensconced character.)

Chesterton wrote, "Alone among the animals [man] is shaken with the beautiful madness called laughter; as if he had caught sight of some secret in the very shape of the universe hidden from the universe itself."[20] Chesterton's man in the cave was remarkably unique from the apes outside. The difference was the wit of man, both his rationality and his risibility. Lewis illustrated this in a friendly and sparkling dinner conversation with Rector Marett of Exeter College. Neville Coghill remembered that the rector threw out a snippet of newsy gossip as a gambit to Lewis:

> "I saw in the papers this morning that there is some scientist-fellah in Vienna, called Voronoff—some name like that—who has invented a way of splicing the glands of young apes onto old gentlemen, thereby renewing their generative powers! Remarkable, isn't it?"
>
> Lewis thought. "I would say 'unnatural.'"

"Come, come! 'Unnatural'! What do you mean, 'unnatural'?
Voronoff is a part of Nature, isn't he? What happens in Nature
must surely be natural? Speaking as a philosopher, don't you
know"—(Marett taught philosophy)—"I can attach no meaning
to your objection; I don't understand you!"

"I am sorry, Rector; but I think any philosopher from Aristotle
to—say—Jeremy Bentham, would have understood me."

"Oh, well, we've got beyond Bentham by now, I hope. If
Aristotle or he had known about Voronoff, they might have changed
their ideas. Think of the possibilities he opens up! You'll be an old
man yourself, one day."

"I would rather be an old man than a young monkey."[21]

No monkey could laugh at such wit. Even old, wrinkled Shift
would rather be an old, wrinkled man than the clever ape he is. We
even find in Aristotle (on the "Parts of Animal") the observation that
"man alone is affected by tickling is due firstly to the delicacy of his
skin, and secondly to his being the only animal that laughs."[22] Both
humans and animals are creatures of habit, expecting "new situations
to resemble old ones. It is a tendency which we share with animals; one
can see it working, often to very comic results, in our dogs and cats."[23]

Lewis found himself musing about the kind of animal he might
be becoming when he found it difficult to sleep (or not sleep) at night.
"Perhaps I am turning into a nocturnal animal. Bat? Wolf? Owl? Let's
hope it will be owl, the bird of wisdom (And I always was attracted
by mice!)."[24] When Lewis's natural strength was sapping and slipping,
he suggested the best way to cope with the mental debility and total
inertia was to submit to it entirely: "Pretend you are a dormouse and
even a turnip."[25] Lewis readily identified his spiritual state with various types of animals, such as in his poem "The Nativity":

> *Among the oxen (like an ox I'm slow)*
> *I see a glory in the stable grow*

Which, with the ox's dullness might at length
Give me an ox's strength.
Among the asses (stubborn I as they)
I see my Saviour where I looked for hay;
So may my beastlike folly learn at least
The patience of a beast.
Among the sheep (I like a sheep have strayed)
I watch the manger where my Lord is laid;
Oh that my baa-ing nature would win thence
Some wooly innocence![26]

Although Lewis had a great deal of fun with the similarities of animals to humans and vice versa, one thing he saw as hilariously absurd was the movement in the early 1960s in which American women tried to persuade President Kennedy to have animals properly clothed "in the interests of decency." Lewis found this idea fundamentally foulminded; nevertheless, it piqued his imagination. "What fun!" he wrote.

The elephant looks as if he wore trousers already, but terribly baggy ones. What he needs is braces. The Rhino seems to wear a suit much too big for him: can it be "taken in"? What sort of collars will giraffes wear? Will seals and otters have ordinary clothes or bathing suits? The hedgehog will wear his shirts out terribly quickly, I should think.[27]

Of smaller animals Lewis wrote that he "never knew a guinea-pig that took any notice of humans." However, amused at their fertile habits, he added that "they take plenty of one another." He supposed that if guinea pigs talked, they'd probably speak German. Hamsters he found the most amusing of small animals, but he still was fond of mice (as evidenced by Reepicheep in Narnia) in spite of Mickey Mouse, whose commercial nature he disliked. For Lewis, mice, like guinea pigs, had that most funny talent of multiplication. He wrote to

Sarah, his godchild: "When I last met your father and mother, mice were weighing rather heavily on their minds. I should think the population runs into millions by now."[28] He sent his love to Sarah's parents and—only at a distance—to the mice as well.

Creatures out of their natural element attained comic stature for Lewis. He incorporated this fish-out-of-water humor in his fiction. In *Out of the Silent Planet*, for instance, the hrossa on Mars laugh at the clumsy swimming of the human Ransom. In *The Last Battle*, when all the Narnians race toward the heart of the new Narnia, many of the animals are out of their element as they all swim up a glorious waterfall. "What looked funniest was the Dogs. . . . There was plenty of spluttering and sneezing among them; that was because they would keep on barking, and every time they barked they got their mouths and noses full of water."[29]

Just desserts also provide triumphant laughter when animals are involved. Few can resist the enjoyment in *Prince Caspian* of seeing a classroom of smug, stuffy, and conceited little brats in starched collars "get theirs." When Aslan and his festive friends liberate the boys' harassed schoolteacher, the boys flee in abject terror. And, Lewis wrote with a wry touch, "those particular little boys were never seen again, but there were a lot of very fine little pigs in that part of the country which had never been there before."[30]

Lewis's personal friends in the animal kingdom formed a broad company. As a boy he had a poor dog, Tim, "the most undisciplined, unaccomplished and dissipated-looking creature that ever went on four legs. He never exactly obeyed you; he sometimes agreed with you."[31] Later in Lewis's life, the canine Mr. Papworth limited his owner in their walks. "You can't go that way because there is a dog that fights: and you can't go that way because there are sheep and you have to keep him on the lead. In fact it is rather like Dick Swiveller's walks in London."[32]

The characters of dogs and cats were as real and as distinct to Lewis as those of humans. One of Lewis's cats liked being lifted up by her tail, "an operation which I can't imagine I should like if I were a cat." His wife Joy's Siamese "stepcat" struck Lewis as terribly conversational, even chatty. It "talks all the time and wants doors and windows to be opened for her 1,000 times an hour." Another cat, a ginger named Tom, whom Lewis called a "great Don Juan and a mighty hunter before the Lord," was quite elitist and snobbish in his relations to the point of being pharisaical. He would respond to others but not to Lewis himself. "He thinks I'm not quite socially up to his standards, and makes this very clear. No creature can give such a crushing 'snub' as a cat! He sometimes looks at the dog—a big Boxer puppy, very anxious to be friendly—in a way that makes it want to sink into the floor."[33]

In a philosophical discussion about cats and dogs, Lewis concluded that "both have consciences but the dog, being an honest, humble person, always has a bad one, but the cat is a Pharisee and always has a good one. When he sits and stares you out of countenance he is thanking God that he is not as these dogs, or these humans, or even as these other cats."[34]

Lewis's letters show an acute awareness of the fun that was evident in the behavior of animals. (It is a divine joke that Lewis should have become a Christian on the way to a zoo full of them.) In a letter to his godchild, Sarah, he described an old rabbit who lived near the college, a fearless and even greedy (but funny) creature: "A funny old man had a habit of giving a leaf to a rabbit. At first it was shy but then, by and by, it got rude and would stand up to grab it."[35] In another letter to Sarah, he wrote about drawing cats and included some sketches. "I can only draw a cat from the back view like this. I think it is rather cheating, don't you? because it does not show the face which is the difficult part to do. It is a funny thing that faces of people are easier to do than most animals' faces except perhaps elephants and owls."[36]

Animals are not comic in and of themselves, but only, as in Lewis's writings, when they are contrasted to human behavior. Biology alone is an insufficient base for comedy; it must include the uniquely human dimension. Peter Berger explained this idea that "animals become comic only when we view them anthropomorphically, that is, when we imbue them with human characteristics."[37] Thus, animals in the company of men and women supply an enormous measure of comedy as we see impressions of our neighbors in four-legged, furry creatures—and they, with democratic charity, see in us some fat and lazy beast. One of Lewis's poems, "Impenitence," which appeared in the British humor magazine *Punch*, highlighted the author's affinity for literary animals and anthropomorphic humor.

> All the world's wiseacres in arms against them
> Shan't detach my heart for a single moment
> From the man-like beasts of the earthy stories—Badger or Moly.
> Rat the oarsman, neat Mrs. Tiggy Winkle,
> Benjamin, pert Nutkin, or (ages older)
> Henryson's shrill Mouse, or the Mice the Frogs once
> Fought with in Homer.
> Not that I'm so craz'd as to think the creatures
> Do behave that way, nor at all deluded
> By some half-false sweetness of early childhood
> Sharply remembered.
> Look again. Look well at the beasts, the true ones.
> Can't you see? . . . cool primness of cats, or coney's
> Half indignant stare of amazement, mouse's
> Twinkling adroitness,
> Tipsy bear's rotundity, toad's complacence . . .
> Why! they all cry out to be used as symbols,
> Masks for Man, cartoons, parodies by Nature
> Formed to reveal us
> Each to each, not fiercely but in her gentlest
> Vein of household laughter. . . . [38]

The use of bestiary fit well into Lewis's indirect teaching methods. Animal imagery offers oblique and ironic ways of saying things.

Animals were not mere cartoon material for Lewis but veritable masks for the mass of humankind: They caught and reflected our nature upon a comic screen. Lewis could and often did see a resemblance to animals, especially to herds of animals, in children (in the manner of a gruff but gentle and bluffing W. C. Fields). Having recently met a friend for a walk, Lewis noted that "his children are now so numerous that one ceases to notice them individually any more than a scuffle of piglets in a field or a waddle of ducks. A few platoons of them accompanied us for about the first mile, but returned like tugs, when we were out of harbor."[39] Lewis could adopt the perspective of an animal cartoonist concerning his own behavior too. After a cyst had been lanced on the back of his neck, he compared the problem he had in not being able to get his "whole head and shoulder under water in my bath" to "getting down like a Hippo with only my nostrils out."[40]

In his reading, Lewis enjoyed "Brer Rabbit" and the animals of Beatrix Potter—animals that talked and behaved like humans but related to their worlds like real rabbits, endangered by and afraid of foxes and men. He enjoyed seeing things from the animals' points of view. In fact, he and Charles Williams once planned to write Bible stories about animals, from the animals' points of view. Lewis said he knew "small boys who'd be much improved by the same treatment" that the obnoxious boys who taunted Elisha got from the bears (the lads got eaten).[41] Collaboration by these two whimsical writers, however, would have included some surprises. They envisioned Bible stories "told by the animals concerned—the story of Jonah told by the whale or that of Elisha told by the two she-bears. The bears were to be convinced that God exists and is good by their sudden meal of children."[42] Lewis did suggest that if "the earthly lion could read the prophecy of that day when he shall eat hay like an ox, he would regard it as a description not of heaven, but of hell."[43] For that matter, we would also see the impertinence of the lamb in lying down with the lion (not inside the lion, as Chesterton quipped). Lewis wrote,

I think the lion, when he has ceased to be dangerous, will still be awful: indeed, that we shall then first see that of which the present fangs and claws are a clumsy, and satanically perverted, imitation. There will still be something like the shaking of a golden mane: and often the good Duke will say, "Let him roar again."[44]

Lewis obviously had a particular affinity for the lion, yet his interest in animals was democratic: He did not neglect the lowly. A notable example is his sympathy for the donkey, or the ass. In the story of one of Lewis's poems, "Donkeys' Delight," the human narrator tells how, by his own works, he sought love, art, and wisdom, only to be disappointed at each turn. In courtship, he was disappointed when a lighthearted sailor stole away his bright-haired prize; for the Muses, he sacrificed his dearest's blood and watched as favor went, carelessly, unfairly to a singing boy who passed that way. Seeking paradise through ascetic fasts and vigils, the poet yet again saw a reckless, feckless ne'er-do-well (who smelled of shag and gin) welcomed in before him. So, crushed by all the injustices of life, he stood in the chill of the great morning:

> *Aghast. Then at last—*
> *Oh, I was late learning—*
> *I repented, I entered*
> *Into the excellent joke,*
> *The absurdity. My burden*
> *Rolled off as I broke*
> *Into laughter; and soon after*
> *I had found my own level;*
> *With Balaam's Ass daily*
> *Out at grass I revel,*
> *Now playing, now braying*
> *Over the meadows of light*
> *Our soaring, creaking Gloria,*
> *Our donkey's delight.*[45]

By the force of his humility, Lewis's beast of burden—emptied and robbed of any creaturely merit—falls into grace and into happy grazing. Indeed, there is no animal better than the ass to show how humility, laid low before the stable, can rise in glory. The excellent joke of God's mercy generally comes to those fools and mules who have no other hope. For Lewis, the donkey is a favorite symbol of how God can use anyone, "as He made a donkey preach a good sermon to Balaam."[46]

In a letter to Sister Penelope, Lewis shared this comfort, writing that "God used an ass to convert the prophet; perhaps if we do our poor best we shall be allowed a stall near it in the celestial stable—rather like this." The remainder of the sheet is filled with an amusing drawing of the ass, flanked by a nun and a figure in a mortarboard, seated outside a stable in the radiance of the heavenly city.[47]

Although Lewis enjoyed the animal kingdom immensely, he still found it a strange mystery. Of their real purpose and destiny, "we remain ignorant. We know to some degree what angels and men are for. But what is a flea for, or a wild dog?"[48] His wonder about the animals' purpose did give way to one bit of playful speculation: Having been warned not to raise the question of animal immortality in a discussion of heaven and hell, he proceeded to respond to the jocular inquiry, "Where will you put all the mosquitoes?" with the answer that, if worse came to worst, "a heaven for mosquitoes and a hell for men could very conveniently be combined."[49]

19

Wild Play

A little Madness in the Spring
Is wholesome even for the King.
—EMILY DICKINSON

We have talked about the fun in nature and soon will be talking about the fun in culture. Fusing these two arenas of pay is the realm of myth. Myth adds social, psychological, and spiritual significance to the concrete realities of nature. In myth, blood, death, sex, and the seasons all take on meanings that transcend their mundane existence. Needless to say, for many church people this area of fun requires an apologist—for the church has long seen myth as being at war with truth, just as the Canaanites were at war with the Hebrews.

C. S. Lewis did not condemn mythologies out of hand or the pagan religions that spawned them, as some religious folk have often done. He wrote that one must not worry or be ashamed of "the mythical radiance resting on our theology" and neither should the fact that pagan rituals do indeed overlap with the Christian and Jewish experiences be cause for worry.[1] The elements that make up the myths of the world float about like pollen on a fertile spring day. Some of the blossoms from which they have come, in fact, are God's truths; therefore, Lewis believed, much of our heritage of fantastic and comic myths carries a hint or promise of truth. ("All truth is God's truth," as St. Augustine observed.) Indeed, the truths of God have permeated all of life, just as any light has a tendency to invade any darkness. Lewis acknowledged he had no way of judging whether a writer of myths was "illuminated" by the Holy Spirit, but he did affirm his belief that "God is the Father of lights—natural lights as well as spiritual lights (James 1:17)."[2]

In *The Golden Bough*, Sir James Frazer discusses one such well-lit myth: the myth of the dying god. Here is an example of how an element of truth can rest like an uncut diamond within a pagan myth. The myth of the dying god was one that hounded Lewis until he recognized that long after its promulgation in classical times (or before), the myth had become fact. At a point in history, "at the right time" (Rom. 5:6), God did come to earth, die for His people, and rise from the dead. The celebration in the Christian faith of this fact in history has its imitation and *Ersatz* duplication in other cultures that have not yet received the full truth. Yet because of the elements of truth in the myths of other cultures, Lewis found fun in many foreign festivals, particularly in those of mythology. He was not ignorant of the dangers and vices inherent in them, but he recognized the good that was there—the part that reflected God's truth. I suspect that, besides appreciating the truth in myth, Lewis simply enjoyed the fabulous elements in myth and, above all, the revelry. (One has to admit, the antics of Bacchus and old Silenus are, within bounds, rollicking good fun.)

Pre-Christian religious revelry is generally regarded as the origin of comedy, which endeared it to Lewis, admirer of comedy that he was. Harvest songs, carnival masquerades, and Dionysian celebrations marking spring and celebrating fecundity gave comedy its name. Comedy weds the Greek *komos* (festival, dance) and *oidos* (a singer) to bring forth many children of jubilation. After the labors of a long, hot summer comes the harvest; beyond the dark, cold experience of winter is the spring. Both seasons liberate the longing for play. And in both we find play going wonderfully wild (before they go excessively perverse) in Oktoberfest and Mardi Gras.[3] These celebrations bring people together to share their merriment and, in fact, to increase it by sharing. The celebration of God's goodness (or of the gods' favor) issues forth in a hymn of praise called laughter.

Yet as the Christian finds levity in pagan rituals, he or she is apt to sweep the comic out of his or her home altogether, brushing away any trace of leaven before the coming of a holy day. The obsessively immaculate and spiritual person wants no earthly dust to settle in her impeccably spotless home. Yet the Hebrew psalmists themselves celebrated the pleasures of nature without being devotees of the nature religions. With sensuous delight, they reveled in the fullness of the earth.

The Jews themselves were an ancient agricultural people who expressed a *joie de vivre* in the gifts of the rains and earth that brought forth, as Lewis noted, "wine to cheer man up and olive-oil to make his face shine—to make it look, as Homer says somewhere, like a peeled onion." Lewis described the Jews as having an overwhelming gratitude, even gusto, for embracing things that have no practical use. He pointed to Psalm 104 as an example, in which "we have not only the useful cattle, the cheering vine, and the nourishing corn. . . . We have springs where the wild asses quench their thirst (11), fir trees for the storks (17) . . . and even with a glance far out to sea, where no Jew willingly went, the great whales playing, enjoying themselves (26)."[4] The Jewish enjoyment of creation parallels and is paralleled by pagan pleasures in nature. There seems to be an appreciative and even jolly devotion to God's nature. The psalmist finds joyful fields and rejoicing trees offering such revelry "as a Pagan poet might have used to herald the coming of Dionysius."[5]

For his part, Lewis—like Spenser and others before him—did not try to divorce the similarities, but let moonlight fairies and elves play into the sunrise. Standing at the crossroads betwixt the old nature religions and the starved, secularized, and meaningless universe of the moderns, Lewis's sympathies were with the former. He would almost "sooner be a pagan suckled in a creed outworn."[6] Unlike religious puritans, he did not worry one iota over a revival of paganism. He laughed: "It is hard to have patience with those Jeremiahs, in Press or pulpit, who warn us that we are 'relapsing into Paganism.' It might be rather fun if we were. It would be pleasant to see some future Prime Minister trying to kill a large and lively milk-white bull in Westminster Hall."[7] Would that we could see Parliament "opened by the slaughtering of a garlanded white bull in the House of Lords or Cabinet Ministers leaving sandwiches in Hyde Park as an offering for the Druids."[8]

Lewis reminded us of the old, simple facts about pagan nature religions, in which "you actually got drunk in the temple of Bacchus. You actually committed fornication in the temple of Aphrodite."[9] The immorality was rooted in real experiences of the earth, perverted in the pursuit of pleasure, but nonetheless connected to something truly natural. Pagan fertility rites mingled a marvelous and dangerous blend of religion, sex, agriculture, drink, sacrifice, and buffoonery—especially buffoonery.[10] And in order to increase the fertility and productivity of the land, the community invoked goodwill through the impregnation of the earth, often through the virile magic of the phallus. But with unrestrained celebration (and drinking), the phallic songs of the Dionysian revels became comic and bawdy. Aristotle's *Poetics* (9:683b) identifies the origin of comedy in these "phallic songs." Some of the comic poets most probably did not take the gods too seriously—and neither did Lewis.

When Lewis looked at the barrenness of modern secularism, the tweed-coated, portly professor was almost tempted to join in the pulsating drumbeats, riotous songs, blood sacrifices, and divine orgies of Dionysius. "Almost," wrote Lewis, "but not, of course, quite."[11] The idea of romping on the high places was much more appealing than the thought of sitting through another college faculty meeting full of dull heretics.

Pagan mythologies, with their thick, dark mysteries, are tainted with too many obscenities and cruelties for a man like Lewis not to have had objections about them. But the wild celebrations of paganism contained at least one right thing: wild celebration. Where joy is full, celebration ought to be also. Lewis espoused neither pantheism nor drunken ecstasy, but he did invite into his fiction (because of their capacity for celebration) Bacchus, his Maenads, and his old tipsy buddy Silenus. (Bacchus is the Ismeno of a poem by Statius "who delays the invading army by his enchantments" and following whom is the duly expected old Silenus and his ass.)[12]

Bacchus, the rude and irrepressibly rascally Greek god of wine, puts in a festive and exuberant cameo in Lewis's children's books. In *Prince Caspian*, the country of Narnia has been rescued from the evil Telmarines, and its liberation is both political and mythological. A party begins. Soon the god of wine arrives, unleashing his wild vine, which grows with kudzu-like rapidity and license, animating everyone and everything with which it tangles. Bacchus brings wild play into Narnia, along with wild women (it is difficult, I suppose, to have the former without the latter). The god of wine is described as "a youth, dressed only in a fawn-skin, with vine-leaves wreathed in his curly hair." His face was almost too pretty for a boy, but he had a look of wildness and an aura of unsettling sexuality. And "there were a lot of girls with him, as wild as he. There was even, unexpectedly, someone on a donkey. And everybody was laughing: and everybody was shouting out 'Euan, euan, eu-oi-oi-oi.'"[13] This shout combined Bacchus's Greek surname, *Euan*, and the ritual frenzied utterance of goodness or joy—*eu or euoi*—heard during a bacchanalian feast. *Euoi* is carnivalesque and earthy joy. When the rude and irrepressible Bacchus was let loose, he ushered in a summer celebration in which "streams would run with wine instead of water and the whole forest would give itself up to jollification for weeks on end."[14] (Meanwhile, Silenus, Bacchus's old and enormously fat companion, keeps falling off his donkey, all the while calling out, "Time for refreshments!")

Bacchus asks Aslan whether this is a Romp, and then the game goes wonderfully madcap. It hops from Tag (or, "Tig," but you couldn't tell who was "It") to Blind Man's Bluff (where everyone seemed blind-folded) to Hunt the Slipper (in which no slipper seemed involved). After vine leaves climb over everything and on everyone, refreshments appear. From the vines sprout bunches of grapes, which everyone begins eating. And "you have never tasted such grapes. Really good grapes, firm and tight on the outside, but bursting into cool sweetness when you put them into your mouth."[15] The celebrants gobble down the grapes, and even with full mouths, their laughter and yodeling reach a crescendo until everyone flops down breathless from gaming and feasting.

Lewis once recognized something gloriously bacchanalian about his friend Owen Barfield. After a supper with Barfield and his other friend Harwood, the three went for a walk into the woods. "Barfield danced round in a field—with sublime lack of self-consciousness and wonderful vigor—for our amusement and that of three horses."[16] The whole Barfield family seemed to share this happy spontaneity. Lewis wrote in a letter to Arthur Greeves that the Barfields had been making wine from the vines growing on their cottage: "And next year when it is ready to drink we think of having a Bacchic festival. The adopted baby is to be the infant Bacchus. Harwood with his fat shiny face on the donkey, will be Silenus. B. and I Corybantes. Mrs. B. a Maenad. B. and I will write the poetry and she will compose a dance. You ought to come."[17]

Even the pagan mysteries of fertility, sex, and birth—and their connection to transcendent truths—are not far from Scripture. When angels announce that old, barren Sarah is to become pregnant by old, old Abraham, Sarah's response is laughter and disbelief ("Shall I have pleasure again, even though Abraham is as old as dirt?"—or something like that). Their son is named, appropriately, Laughter (Isaac).[18]

Lewis celebrated the frolicsome play that is natural for God's creation, citing Revelation 4:11: "Thou has created all things, and for thy pleasure they are and were created" (KJV). God, who created pleasure, gives its delights fully and freely. Even sexual pleasure is given for our fun. "Indeed," wrote Lewis, "as we read the frank erotic poetry of [the Song of Songs] and contrast it with the edifying headiness in our Bibles, it is easy to be moved to a smile, even a cynically knowing smile, as if the pious interpreters were feigning an absurd innocence."[19] Scotch poet David Lyndsay offers a historical insight in writing that "our first parents loved *par amors* in Eden, delighting in each *utheris bodies, soft and quhyte.*"[20]

As an educator, Lewis's professional specialty was medieval literature. Many of the mythical ideas and images he incorporated into his work came out of the literature of that period—literature full of references to classical and European folk mythology. Lewis heartily

believed there was good in these myths and that the goodness in them
teemed with fun. An example of this goodness in myth is in the works
of Edmund Spenser. In Spenser's *The Faerie Queene*, the princess Una
is about to be raped and ravaged when she is rescued not in this case by
a lion like Aslan, but by a zoo of woodland creatures, fauns, and satyrs.
Like Susan reacting to Bacchus, Una stands in dread of these wood-
gods, but is soon amazed to discover "jocundity and jollity" in them.

> *They all as glad, as birdes of joyous Prime [Spring]*
> *Thence lead her forth, about her dancing round,*
> *Shouting, and singing all a shepheards rhyme,*
> *And all the way their merry pipes they sound,*
> *That all the woods with doubled Eccho ring,*
> *And with their horned feet do weare the ground,*
> *Leaping like wanton kids in pleasant Spring.[21]*

Relieved, the chaste Una, as Lewis points out, "recognized the
essential innocence of the creatures." Lewis calls this episode in *The
Faerie Queene* a "scherzo movement" because "it shows good as fun, as
a romp," bringing relief and relaxation of tension through true merriment. For Lewis, Spenser's work is an example of how "good may be
portrayed as the ingenuous, more or less unconscious, unspoiled and
humble. It is often accompanied by gaiety and fun."[22]

Lewis faithfully captures and photographs the fun of goodness in
Spenser's mythologically flavored poetry. At the end of the story of St.
George and Una, the dragon is dying, the "last deadly smoke rising"
from the nostrils, and the trumpets are blaring a triumph. The young
and old all gather for a solemn, joyous speech. Girls, garlanded with fresh
flowers, danced in a row, playing sweet timbrels, honoring St. George:

And they are compared to Diana's nymphs, some wrestling, some
running, some bathing. And after them—no, before, for they push
in front—[Lewis, like an on-the-spot roving reporter, catches the

action as it happens with an intimacy of you-are-there] come the "fry" of children with "their wanton sports." Una is crowned, but "twixt earnest and twixt game." Next a crowd fearfully inspects the dragon, one anxious mother scolding her child for playing with the talons. It is a frankly comic, almost Chaucerian, interlude.[23]

Mythological goodness has rarely been so entertaining and delicious—with festal jocundity and jovial fecundity—as it is in Spenser. Many feet fast thumping the hollow ground keep beat with the merry sound of a jolly shepherd's pipe, with all "full merrily and making gladfull glee."[24] This merry image of goodness is expressed in a striking theme of jocundity in the seasons and the months: Spring with his ten thousand singing birds is "lusty," while autumn is "joyed in his plenteous store." Even more descriptive and distinctive are the months:

> April is "wanton as a kid"; June is "jolly." An October "full of merry glee," "tipsy with the wine that made him so frollick and so full of lust," is succeeded by a November who "took no small delight" in planting, and a December who made "merry feasting" gladdened by the memory of his Saviour's birth. As for May, Lord! how all creatures laugh, when her they spite, And leapt and daunc't as they had ravisht beene![25]

In Lewis's world of Narnia, the wild play inspired by Bacchus is kept in bounds by the person of goodness, Aslan. It is his wisdom and authority that command such lusty forces as Bacchus. In other words, the wild play and revelry of myth must be kept in bounds; it must always be subordinate to the truth and sovereignty of God. Lewis did not keep his faith in one pocket and his work in another. He brought them together and made sure the latter submitted to the former, and not vice versa. As I mentioned in the introduction to "Fun," Lewis understood that "there is no neutral ground in the universe: every square inch, every split second, is claimed by God and counterclaimed by Satan."[26] Myth is no exception. If it is to be approached, and Lewis felt there was much benefit in doing so, it must be done with discernment and under the protection of God.

In *Prince Caspian*, when Edmund saw Bacchus, he said, "There's a chap who might do anything—absolutely anything."[27] His sisters recognized the intoxicating and ecstatic possibilities as well. Susan, the elder sister who was fast approaching the fullness of puberty, confided in her younger sibling, Lucy: "I wouldn't have felt very safe with Bacchus and all his wild girls if we'd met them without Aslan." "I should think not," said Lucy.[28] Revelry of wine and comedy could easily and dangerously explode into a wicked riot or drunken orgy if a good, moral, and holy presence does not constrain it. For Lewis, this festival of laughter may be rampant, welcome, and liberal, provided God is given His first fruits of right obedience. A holy ethic must accompany a comic passion, at least for safety's sake.

Lewis's liking for Edmund Spenser was not simply literary, for this poet took from the pagans what was good and redeemed it. The piquant tastes of life and thought stimulated by Spenser are served fresh, spicy, and full of special quality. Lewis wrote that *The Faerie Queene* is "Spenser's Hymn to Life," and Lewis, who usually disliked hymns, joined in his song like a baritone in a barbershop quartet. "*The Faerie Queen* never loses a reader it has once gained. . . . Once you have become an inhabitant of its world, being tired of it is like being tired of London, or of life."[29] What it offers is a celebration of life in all its fertility, spontaneity, order, and jollity—in short, a world of fun.

Play, in both Spenser's and Lewis's works, is full of energy.[30] It is whole and hearty, full of laughter and health. It is full of goodness— in fact, goodness is its primary taste. In the worlds of Shakespeare and Milton, we find evil a dramatic, restless, and lawless energy. Sin is rebellious and defiant. In *The Faerie Queene*, as in Narnia and Perelandra, however, evil does not usually appear abounding or upsurging. Evil takes on passive forms of bad enchantments or narcotic sleep, of winter's stillness, or of dead cities and empty castles.

The anti-Aslan figure of the ape in *The Last Battle* is known for its sloth.

"Good places are full of figures in joyous motion . . . often a matter of knightly quests, of dances, revels, and love-making, of 'skipping like wanton kids,' of romping."[31] One can discover mirth, rest, and recreation in the good garden that God created, now weedy and wilted in many parts but still alive with the beauty of "the almost imperceptible wine, the darting fish, the rabbits playing in the grass, and the 'ravishing sweetness' of stringed instruments."[32] One hears this in the challenge of Ishmael in *Moby Dick*, upon discovering a group of spying porpoises: "If you yourself can withstand three cheers of beholding these vivacious fish, then heaven help ye; the spirit of godly gamesomeness is not in ye."[33]

From his early boyhood days, Lewis and his brother discovered goodness and beauty in their play. Together they would make a toy forest out of "the lid of biscuit tin . . . covered with moss and garnished with twigs and flowers."[34] This toy garden gave them a sense of nature as cool, dewy, fresh, and exuberant. Lewis's image of the happy garden brought him different pleasures, such as an appreciation for Milton ("making a toy garden as we made them when were children."[35]) and a source of rejuvenation, as he wrote to his brother about tending his sick father. "When my patient is settled up for the night I go out and walk in the garden. I enjoy enormously the cool air after the atmosphere of the sickroom. I also enjoy the frogs in the field at the bottom of the garden, and the mountains and the moon."[36]

In Spenser's gardens Lewis discovered a contrast of the full inactivity of evil and the fruitful energy of goodness. On his journey, Knight Guyon stumbles upon the Garden of Adonis and the Bower of Bliss, which confront each other as competing delights. In the Garden of Adonis are naked damsels who are graces "doing something worthwhile, namely dancing in a ring 'in order excellent.'"[37] When they realize they are discovered, they vanish with due modesty and chastity. Goodness and beauty exist in this joyous paradise, where Venus lives when she visits earth. It is a garden of fertility and procreation, where natural fruitfulness abounds. The good Venus here is a picture of fresh fecundity, and the spontaneous sexuality beams with goodness, life, and blessed fruit.

In the artificial Bower of Bliss, however, we find imitation ivy as a garden ornament. What makes it of abominably bad taste is that this vegetation is made of metal (like that at the NICE in *That Hideous Strength*). In the fountains and pools of the Bower are two naked young women ("names are obviously Cissie and Flossie," quipped Lewis) who giggle and frolic in their bath as seductive exhibitionists, adolescent versions of those sirens who would woo a man to his death. Here is a bathing pool situated for the benefit of passing voyeurs. There is the teasing promise of fun here, with a sort of cheap, nervous laughter, but this sweetness is just a touch off base, a bit bent. When we see Acrasia herself (her name means "without control"), she is a portrait of lust— "not of lust in action, but lust delayed, lust suspended." We picture in this the whole sexual nature diseased. "Arcrasia does nothing," Lewis wrote. She is merely

> discovered posed on a sofa of roses, leaning over her latest young male captive, wearing only a semi-transparent piece of lingerie, as though posing for an advertisement for some new pornographic film. She is there, like the cinema, only for eyes—greedy, hungry eyes. There is not a kiss or embrace in the island; only male prurience and female provocation.[38]

Spenser is asking us what is wrong with this picture. This fun is not only deadly dull, but deadly. The fun sensationalizes but does not satisfy. It titillates to the climax of drooling, but it does not gratify. It is play in its darker, twilight hours. For Spenser and Lewis, "evil is solemn, good is gay. . . . Evil imprisons, good sets free. Evil is tired, good is full of vigour. The one says, 'Let go, lie down, sleep, die; the other, All aboard! Kill the dragon, marry the girl, blow the pipes and beat the drum, let the dance begin.'"[39]

Fun, to Lewis, was like stepping into a good garden, usually an enchanted one. In the opening of *Romance of the Rose*, we stumble upon such a place "from whose walls sorrow flies far." As the door opens, Lewis observed that "all that is required of you is to swim with the tide, to wrap yourself in voluptuous idleness, and to gather rosebuds while you may."[40] The Gardens of Delight designed for play are scattered all about, but, fortunately for us children, they do have boundaries.

Merriment and merrymaking can go berserk. When pleasure and its attendant laughter become tyrants for reigning over reason and righteousness, it is time for a moral rebellion to set things right side up. The story of the foolish god Faunus, for example, appears as a comic interlude in Spenser's *Mutability Cantos*. He cannot control a danger-ous gift he is awarded. Wanting to see Diana naked, he enlists the help of one of the mistress's nymphs. He gets his wish, but "betrays himself by his inability to maintain a reverent silence in the presence of divine beauty."[41] Instead, his response is a guffaw:

> *There Faunus saw that pleased much his eye,*
> *And made his hart to tickle in his breast*
> *That for great joy of some-what he did spy,*
> *He could him not containe in silent rest;*
> *But breaking forth in laughter, loud protest*
> *His foolish thought. A foolish Faune indeed*
> *That couldst not hold they selfe so hidden blest,*
> *But wouldest needs thine owne conceit areed.*
> *[But had to express your own idea]*
> *Babblers unworthy been of so divine a meed.*[42]

Comedy needs control and discipline. It must not control the man or woman (or Faune) lest one respond to beauty, truth, or good-ness inappropriately. When the apostle Paul exhorts against jesting or coarse humor, the standard to which he appeals is that it is not fitting or appropriate. There is, as Koheleth the Preacher tells us, a proper time to laugh. And conversely, a time to refrain from laughing.

20

The Fun of Reading

You know, humor is an expression of skepticism, of this disparity between what we aspire after and what we achieve. The greatest humorists, like Cervantes and Rabelais and Gogol and Shakespeare too, have all been believers, contrary to what is often supposed, whereas materialists are very serious people indeed because if you believe only in man, then you must hold man in great veneration.
—MALCOLM MUGGERIDGE

C. S. Lewis's leisure and sense of fun were dominated by his enthusiasm for literature. This chapter is mainly a discussion of Lewis's opinions on comic literature and about what he enjoyed reading. As you might expect, it is a long chapter; Lewis read everything from Ovid to Bergson, from St. Augustine to the Brothers Grimm. "You can't get a cup of tea large enough or a book long enough to suit me," he remarked.[1]

Lewis's lifelong correspondence with his friend Arthur Greeves is chock-full of their shared passions and pleasures in reading. Lewis devoted considerable space in his personal letters to writing about new books he had discovered, their prices, their bindings, their illustrations. He even acknowledged that Greeves, also an avid bibliophile, might "laugh at my everlasting talk about buying books which I never really get." He knew his father laughed at him for being so serious about his pleasure in buying books, but, he rebutted, "a thing can't be properly enjoyed unless you take it in earnest." Nevertheless, Lewis joked with his friend Greeves about "how people would laugh if they could hear us smacking our lips over our 7d's and Everymans just as others gloat over rare folios and an *Editio princeps*." The two men simply loved books. They not only appreciated the prices of them, but the materials they were made of. On the occasion of the publication of Lewis's book *Allegory of Love*, he wrote to Greeves to tell him that the binding and the paper Clarendon Press was using would be "excellent, exquisite, and admirable." "In other words," Lewis wrote, "if you can't read it, you will enjoy looking at it, smelling it, and stroking it. If not a good book, it will be a good pet!"[2]

Lewis had a number of books that were his pets, books he read and reread. For Lewis, reading as fun was surpassed only by rereading old favorites. He confessed he probably did it too much but that it was "one of my greatest pleasures: indeed I can't imagine a man really enjoying a book and reading it only once."[3] As mentioned earlier, Lewis tested the "literary-ness" of an acquaintance or student not by asking the kind of book he read but "by asking whether he often re-reads the same story."[4] To the nonliterary person, a novel once read is like yesterday's newspaper; to the literary one, it is an old friend.

Lewis once said he did not know whether the pleasure of literature is "more like revenge, or buttered toast, or success or adoration, or relief from danger, or a good scratch."[5] In truth, it is like all of them, with the addition of its own proper particular pleasures, such as "entrée to the comic." Insomuch as literature helps us see with other eyes and laugh with other lungs, it takes us out of ourselves and into the lives of others—"to occupy for a while their seat in the great theatre, to use their spectacles and be made free of whatever insights, joys, terrors, wonders, or merriment those spectacles revealed." We become less provincial and judgmental once we have seen a few things through other eyes of God's diverse humanity. Lewis regretted only "that the brutes cannot write books. Very gladly would I learn what face things present to a mouse or a bee . . . more gladly still would I perceive the olfactory world . . . for a dog."[6] (I confess the same wonder only up to a point; there are some canine odors about which I am not at all curious.)

Literature exists for the delight and joy of the reader, with each kind of book inviting a particular kind of reading pleasure. Yet not everybody understands this, or wants to. Lewis laughed at students who approached all reading tasks as grave academic assignments. Literary Puritans and solemn intellectual critics may fail most lamentably in this, the worst approach to reading. One discovers the slow, sure incongruities of an author like Jane Austen, for example, only by sensibly recognizing the comic context or climate of her work. Of the solemn types who cannot read the weather vanes, Lewis wrote:

> They are too serious as men to be seriously receptive as readers. I have listened to an undergraduate's paper on Jane Austen from which if I had not read them, I should never have discovered that there was the least hint of comedy in her novels. After a lecture of my own I have been accompanied from Mill Lane to Magdalene by a young man protesting with real anguish and horror against my wounding, my vulgar, my irreverent suggestion that *The Miller's Tale* was written to make people laugh. And I have heard of another who finds *Twelfth Night* a penetrating study of the individual's relation to society. We are breeding up a race of young people who are as solemn as the brutes ("smiles from reason flow") . . . solemn men, but not serious readers.[7]

One discovers the slow, pawky incongruities in Jane Austen's work by adapting to the comic tone or context of her work. One learns to read more than the words themselves; one learns to read the *worlds* of the authors, stepping into these new countries with keen, eager, and attentive minds.

Our excursions into literature, much like dancing or other recreational games done for fun, are serious—and yet, Lewis argued, "to do them at all, we must somehow do them as if they were not. . . . It is a serious matter to choose wholesome recreations: but they would no longer be recreations if we pursued them seriously. . . . for a great deal (not all) of our literature was made to be read lightly, for entertainment. If we do not read it, in a sense, 'for fun,' and with our feet on the fender, we are not using it as it was meant to be used."[8] To those who accused literature of being mere escapism, Tolkien retorted with the challenge: "What kind of person is preoccupied with, most hostile to, the idea of escape?" The simple answer: jailers.[9]

The serious reader may be "as playful as Mercutio," but she reads wholeheartedly, opening herself to the work in hand. This reader surrenders to the world of the book, and she finds there fun, adventures, and ideas that she could not have produced on her own. Such total and humble receptivity means that the reader cannot, therefore, read every book or poem or fairy tale solemnly or gravely:

> For he will read "in the same spirit that the author writ." What is meant lightly he will take lightly; what is meant gravely, gravely. He will "laugh and shake in Rabelais's" easy chair while he reads Chaucer's *faiblaux* and respond with exquisite frivolity to *The Rape of the Lock*. He will enjoy a kickshaw as a kickshaw and a tragedy as a tragedy. He will never commit the error of trying to munch whipped cream as if it were venison.[10]

The right way to enjoy reading is not to approach it with preconceptions—particularly not solemn ones—but to see the author's intention. "If all or most readers, or such readers as he chiefly desires, laugh at a passage, and he is pleased with this result, then his intention was comic, or he intended to be comic."[11] The reader is summoned to discover enjoyment in the varieties of literary experiences, from Tolstoy's mammoth novel *War and Peace* (from which, Lewis observed, we have lost in most of the translations "the humor which is an important merit in the real book") to Grimm's fairy tales.[12] Rather than place the work on a procrustean bed, one must submit to the book itself; *it* must be the guide for one's reading of it.

Lewis found that stories like *The Wind in the Willows*, which offer us a kind of happiness, are full of the simplest and most satisfying things—the kind of fun given in food, sleep, exercise, friendship, the face of nature, even (in a sense) religion. That "simple but sustaining meal" of "bacon and broad beans and a macaroni pudding" which Rat gave to his friends has, I doubt not, helped down many a real nursery dinner. And in the same way the whole story, paradoxically enough, strengthens our relish for real life. This excursion into the preposterous sends us back with renewed pleasure to the actual.[13]

According to Lewis, one does not "despise real woods because he has read of enchanted woods; the reading makes all real woods a little enchanted."[14] In writing about how Tolkien's myth enables us to see our lives more clearly through the homely and happy story of hobbits, Lewis claimed Tolkien lowered the "veil of familiarity," so he could see anew what is so close it is hidden:

> The child enjoys his cold meat (otherwise dull to him) by pretend-ing it is buffalo, just killed with his bow and arrow. And the child is wise. The real meat comes back to him more savoury for having been dipped in a story; you might say that only then is it the real meat. If you are tired of the real landscape, look at it in a mirror. By putting bread, gold, horse, apple, or the very roads into a myth, we do not retreat from reality: we rediscover it.[15]

In reading Lewis, one finds that all wardrobes lead into Narnia. All tastes of taffy are temptations of Turkish Delight. Courtesy, cour-age, and charity are communicated in and through the characters of Narnia, so that a child can come out of this wonderland of words to know their meanings and be compelled to practice them. They can even *enjoy* the practice of them.

Reading can consume one totally, producing an experience of "joy or exhilaration . . . an overplus of robust and tranquil well-being in a total experience which contains both rapturous and painful elements." It enchants, as T. S. Eliot said: "Music heard so deeply that it is not heard at all." The magic carpet of reading kindles imaginative enjoyment that allows no one time to contemplate the weave of the carpet; one is simply flying. It is like that "schoolboy who reads a page of Milton by chance, for the first time, and then looks up and says, 'By gum!' not in the least knowing how the thing has worked, but only that new strength and width and brightness and zest have transformed his world."[16] We miss much of the joy of our own world when we refuse to be present in all worlds. Home is never so distinct and sharp and tangy as when one returns to it from a foreign port.

The way to enlarge one's pleasure and one's vision is to put on the armor of the knight rather than strip him of it. "I had much rather know what I should feel like if I adopted the beliefs of Lucretius than how Lucretius would have felt if he had never entertained them. The possible Lucretius in myself interests me more than the possible C. S. Lewis in Lucretius."[17] Lewis punctuated his proposal with a reference to G. K. Chesterton's "wholly admirable essay called *On Man: Heir of All the Ages*. An heir is one who inherits and 'any man who is cut off from the past . . . is a man most justly disinherited.' To enjoy our full humanity we ought, so far as is possible, to contain within us potentially at all times, and on occasion to actualize, all the modes and feelings through which man has passed." Thus, in reading Milton, Lewis explained how his own Christian faith was an advantage in understanding the great poet, as "What would you not give to have a real, live Epicurean at your elbow while reading Lucretius?"[18] Such is the reason that Lewis, like Hazlitt before him, wrote an essay, "On the Reading of Old Books." Our own worlds are too much with us, and we need to be healed of our temporal provincialism and chronological snobbery. To find renewed pleasure in this world, we would do well to see and be pleased with other worlds.

Lewis identified another wrong way of reading: the attitude of, "I've already read that." It has been said that the quality of one's literary taste is best determined not by what one reads, but by what one rereads. The act of rereading was for Lewis the mark of a true lover of books. On the other hand, a reader who eschews rereading because it lacks novelty confesses that novelty is the sum of his or her reasons to read. Even so, after a lengthy sabbatical a once-read book becomes novel (no pun intended) once more and can be read again as if it were new. As Lewis ruefully commented, "We have all known women who remembered a novel so dimly that they had to stand for half an hour in the library skimming through it before they were certain they had read it."[19]

The tradition of comic writers carried weight for Lewis, even if it was lightweight to others. Chaucer, Rabelais, and Sterne brought him low, even to the floor, with laughter. These authors brought balance back into the toil and drudgery of life and into all of life's truly serious concerns. Out of their own epochs they brought to ours an equilibrium, a recovery of the norm, a fresh perspective. Each era cries out for such new vision, and the vision they offered can be comic, light, and liberating. We discover from the Dark Ages, Chesterton noted, that "the meaning of Aquinas is that medievalism was always seeking a centre of gaiety."[20] The significance of these three authors for Lewis was that they pointed him to this center of gaiety and inspired him with comic vision. These men were churchmen and found their glad foundation on the doctrines of the church. Their comedy was rooted in the mixed soil of Christian orthodoxy and a true perspective of the heart of man. And part of that true perspective was the ability to stand outside one's work and view it with wry humility.

Writers like Chaucer and Rabelais infected Lewis with their humor through the disclaimer: the asides and warnings of their own works that prepared their readers or, at least, made direct contact and appeals to them. Chaucer began his *Canterbury Tales* by gathering his company of pilgrims in mirth and joy and set them toward Canterbury, telling good tales "for truly there's no mirth, nor comfort, none, / Riding the roads as dumb as a stone." Of his miller, drunk and foolish, Chaucer advises those who would not like his ribald tale of the cuckolded carpenter that they should "turn over page and choose another tale. . . . / Be then advised, and hold me free from blame; / Men should not be too serious at a game."[21]

Chaucer admirably combined doctrine with his comic purpose. Even though his tales supplied a paradise of jokes, Lewis read in him more gravity than in the flippant and coldly cynical Boccaccio. Boccaccio contemptuously scoffs at the religion of love, for to him women are as fickle as the wind and heartless. Yet where Boccaccio "dethrones the deity, Chaucer complains of the severity of the cult. It is the difference between an atheist and a man who humorously insists that he 'is not of religion.'"[22] Chaucer was, as Dryden observed, "a perpetual fountain of good sense."[23] A profound and cheerful sobriety undergirded his humor. And Lewis warned that in reading into Chaucer too much irony, slyness, and archness, "we praise him for his humour where he is really writing with 'ful devout corage.' The lungs of our generation are so very 'tickle o' the sere'"; yet still the most appropriate response to Chaucer is rip-roaring laughter.[24]

Lewis recognized that his own age was "quite abnormally sensitive to the funny side of sententiousness to possible hypocrisy, and to dullness. . . . We must face the fact that Chaucer's audience could listen with gravity and interest to edifying matter which would set a modern audience sleeping or sniggering. Chaucer 'had it both ways'"—he could teach and entertain. And "laughing to teach the truth, what hinders?"[25]

The comedy of a poet like Chaucer must be viewed in its historical context, tied to its time like a button or buckle on a uniform. It shines best when seen in its proper place, unless we are boorish jackdaws who pick up any pretty piece for our own amusement. Thus, Chaucer hoped that his bawdy tales would not be counted against him as "vileinye"—that is, rude peasant behavior; for there is instruction here as well as comedy. Lewis observes that in Troilus,

what is funny—and doubtless intended to be funny—is the contrast between love's victim and love's doctrinaire. . . . There is comedy, too, in the prolixity and pedantry of Pandarus—the ease with which he reels off . . . the doctrine of contraries, the rules of a lover's service, and the lover's guide to letter writing—as though he had learned them by heart, as very probably he had. Complacent instruction, when the instructor is willing and the pupil is not, is always funny and specially funny to Chaucer. But the intention of Pandarus is not comic—Pandarus would be less comic if it were— and the content of his instruction is not meant to be ridiculous.[26]

Earlier, Lewis pointed out that "what will be very funny if it is meant to be serious, may often be very feeble as deliberate joke." Thus, Pandarus is not reeling off flat jests. He is a true believer in the doctrines he speaks, even as Polonius spoke maxims and topoi to Laertes that were common wisdom but from the lips of a foolish, prattling old man. As with Polonius, it is not what Pandarus says "that is comic, on Chaucer's view: it is the importunity, the prolixity, the laughable union of garrulity and solemnity, with which he says it"—so much that Troilus cries out: "Let be thyne ole ensaumples I they preye."[27]

Although Chaucer exhibits "nothing of the renaissance frivolity," one would have to be a dull reader to "take all the doctrinal passages in Chaucer seriously: that the speeches of Chauntecleer and Pertelote and of the Wyf of Bath not only are funny by reason of their sententiousness and learning but are intended to be funny, and funny by that reason, is indisputable."[28]

Chaucer gave us the broad comic effect of Pandarus,

a loquacious and unscrupulous old uncle [who] talks solemn platitude at interminable length. For Chaucer, a textuel man talked excellent doctrine which we enjoy and by which we are edified: but at the same time we see that this "has its funny side." Ours is the crude joke of laughing at admitted rubbish: Chaucer's the much more lasting joke of laughing at "the funny side" of that which, even while we laugh, we admire.[29]

The Canterbury Tales was a veritable treasure chest of comedy-with-piety. "The Reeve's Tale was told because what happens in it is unusually and all but impossibly funny." The silly old landlord "rich gnof" in "The Miller's Tale" was "conceivably gullible" and thus more realistically funny. The *raison d'être* of these stories is that we should "laugh as we follow" them.[30]

Rabelais dug even deeper in the earth for the comedy of dung and very vulgar topics. Laughter bursts out everywhere with comic names scattered like seeds in the wind of a giant flatus. Of all this (and much wilder besides), Rabelais wrote to his readers:

> *Good friends, my readers, who peruse this book,*
> *Be not offended, whilst on it you look:*
> *Denude yourself of all deprav'd affection,*
> *For it contains no badness nor infection:*
> *'Tis true that it brings forth to you no birth*
> *Of any value, but in point of mirth;*
> *Thinking therefore how sorrow might your mind*
> *Consume, I could no apter subject find;*
> *One inch of joy surmounts of grief a span;*
> *Because to laugh is proper to the man.*[31]

To sit in his easy chair and rock with laughter with Rabelais was not an uncommon event for Lewis. The first time he finished the formidable task of reading *Gargantua and Pantagruel*, he found it "very long, very incoherent, and very, very stercoraceous." Before Queen Victoria's time, Rabelais's work was like a comic book. The "first surprise is that 1/4 of the book is perfectly serious propaganda in favor of humanist education."[32] Even in his coarse and gross giant tales, Rabelais is fat with the ease and leisure of laughter. He mockingly threatens his audience with "sulphur, fire, and bottomless pits, in case you do not firmly believe all that I shall relate to you in this present Chronicle."[33]

Rabelais's classical attack on the monks, hypocrites, and counterfeit saints knew no merry bounds of sense and nonsense. "Rabelais was also an inventor in the realm of Nonsense, a follower of Lucian, and a predecessor of Lewis Carroll."[34] "Oh, by the way," Lewis wrote, "don't miss the utterly unexpected influence of Rabelais on Kingsley's Water Babies," in spite of the latter's propriety.[35] Rabelais would ask his readers, those illustrious drinkers and gouty gentlemen, if they had seen the ancient cynic philosopher Diogenes, and then declare, "If you have seen him, you then had your eyes in your head, or I am very much out of my understanding and logical sense."[36]

In spite of all his rowdiness, however, Rabelais sat in his pew in church. When John in *The Pilgrim's Regress* shared dinner with Mr. Sensible, Lewis pointed out that "the port, which was one in a thousand and the best thing on that table, had once belonged to Rabelais, who in his turn had it as a present from old Mother Kirk when they were friends."[37] Yet his ridicule of us, his audience, is a superb jolting jest: "If you say to me, master, it would seem, that you are not very wise in writing to us these flimflam stories and pleasant fooleries; I answer you, that you are not much wiser to spend your time in reading them."[38]

Rabelais was willing to sell his dedication to the highest bidder. In turn, Laurence Sterne dedicated *Tristram Shandy* to the Right Honorable Mr. Pitt with mock modesty. His poor and helpless dedication

> is written in a bye corner of the kingdom, and in a retired thatched house, where I live in a constant endeavor to fence against the infirmities of ill health, and other evils of life, by mirth; being firmly persuaded that every time a man smiles—but much more so, when he laughs, it adds something to his Fragment of Life. . . . If I am ever told, it has made you smile; or can conceive it has beguiled you of one moment's pain—I shall think myself as happy as a minister of state.[39]

Sterne was indeed a minister of the state of comedy for Lewis. Lewis enjoyed his descriptions of Tully comforting his daughter by the

"Kosmetic delights of rhetoric and philosophy" or the parish bull of whom Mr. Shandy had a "high opinion" because he "went through the business with a grave face." Although Lewis found Tristram's humor somewhat amorphous, it worked like a literary laughing gas.[40] Tristram's discussion of wit and judgment, for example, combines philosophical discourse with the vulgar humor of bodily humiliation. "Wit and judgment in this world never go together," Tristram argues, "inasmuch as they are two operations differing from each other as wide as east from west—so says Locke—so are farting and hiccupping, say I."[41]

Tristram announces that this story of his life and opinions is likely to make some noise in the world, and taking in "all ranks, professions, and denominations of men whatever—[shall] be no less read than the *Pilgrim's Progress* itself—and in the end, prove the very thing which Montaigne dreaded his Essays should turn out, that is, a book for a parlor window."[42]

The practice of gentle, self-mocking humor and subtle (and broad) teasing of one's readers was not lost on C. S. Lewis. In one sermon to a group of seminarians, Lewis compared himself to a sheep bleating before future pastors of flocks, telling them only what one sheep can. Lewis, in fact, was a veritable wit when it came to self-effacing humor. As he lectured one audience on the inadequacy of an inner ring or elite coterie to satisfy one's deepest needs, he paused to point out this is what happens "when you invite a middle-aged moralist. . . ." The author of *The Screwtape Letters* mocked his own diabolical popularity in the same address, saying, "The Devil, I shall leave strictly alone. The association between him and me in the public mind has already gone quite as deep as I wish: in some quarters it has already reached the level of confusion if not identification."[43]

Laurence Sterne's *The Life and Opinions of Tristram Shandy* garnered high praise from Lewis, which he characterized with Chestertonian description, as the "maddest book . . . 'ever wrote.' . . . It gives you the impression of an escaped lunatic's conversation while chasing his hat on a windy May morning."[44] Lewis shared the wonders of *Tristram Shandy* with a country parson of eighty, retired (of course), an irreplaceable character who enthused over the work with him: "You feel snug when you read that—you get in among them all in that little parlor. And my uncle Toby—ah (a very parsonical, long-drawn, almost devotional a-a-ah), ah, a beautiful character. And the jokes—I'm sure I don't know how the rascal thought of it all—the rascal!"[45] *Tristram Shandy* was to Lewis an offering of good company and grand characters, like Uncle Toby, for his reading pleasure. Part of the pleasure of such company was that it brought together the conjunction of opposed minds, picturing an affection that stretches across "unbridgeable gulfs of intellect." Tristram's "Father and Uncle Toby never understand one another at all, and always loved one another."[46] Uncle Toby stands as an ideal character of good-humored long-suffering. He easily joins in the laugh against himself, and so defuses all malice. Even toward the most irritable of creatures, Uncle Toby endures more than any natural man could. To a fly that buzzed about his nose throughout dinner, he spoke: "Go, . . . go, poor devil, . . . get thee gone, why should I hurt thee? The world is surely wide enough to hold both thee and me."[47]

Obviously Lewis enjoyed things comic within the body of literature. A short list of his favorite readings (a long list would require a book of its own) shows a catholic and colorful range. Both Greeks and Romans had a minor comic influence on Lewis. He enjoyed the broad, farcical, mob-pleasing Old Comedy of Aristophanes (whose plays included both political lampoons of Socrates and silly sound effects, like the humorous "Be Be Be" noise of sheep). The Old Comedy wallowed in the mud, in Greek rustic scenes, full of lusty, bawdy, ribald, and crude jokes. Like *A Funny Thing Happened on the Way to the Forum*, the Old Comedy was in classical Greece the popular comedy of excess, pregnant with belly laughs and hilarity. The extravagant Old Comedy of Aristophanes' *The Birds* or *The Clouds* shone with sparkling, racy language, loony puns, extravagant characters, and even obscenity. Flatulence would smother the stage, and gross, outrageous scurrility was aimed at the lowest tastes.

The change from democracy to the republic ushered in the advent of a stricter era, where the highly moral and civilizing New Comedies replaced the songs and dances of the Old. Whereas Aristophanes and Plautus splashed about in raucous laughter, the New Comedy diluted laughter and dried it up. It even went so far as to disregard laughter. Lewis found the New Comedy of Roman playwrights such as Terence to be inferior. It contained a genial humor and called for "thoughtful laughter—but this only meant it never got the really good laughs. "Would your gentle humour," Lewis addressed Terence, "were allied with comic fire to match to the scenic pride of Greece."[48]

Terence's comedy was lacking by half. The half that was present and good was derived from Menander, a comedy that was romantic, civilized, polite, polished, and prim. Menander taught civilization a lesson of cheerful, blithe living. He was, to rework Quintilian's phrase, "a good man laughing well," but also softly. While Lewis appreciated both, he practiced a very tame comedy. He avoided characters such as libidinous old codgers, and refused to invent ribald and coarse situations where men and women lived wildly ("Greeking it up" it was called). Lewis may have been closer to Menander, but he was a closet Plautus.

He knew Cicero's rhetorical tactic, however—that "if you want people to weep by the end, make them laugh in the beginning." Lewis offered this bit of instruction as part of a congratulatory note to Milward on his ordination to the priesthood.[49] The reverse worked as well, and Lewis worked it to full advantage in his fiction, particularly in the death and resurrection scenes of *The Lion, the Witch, and the Wardrobe* and *The Last Battle*, and the quasi-personal dilemma of Digory trying to save his mother from death in *The Magician's Nephew*. Gently inducing tears or moist eyes from his vulnerable readers, he would turn the tables and offer a feast of joyous laughter and surprise. And in *The Horse and His Boy*, he even produced the ultimate ending of comedy: a marriage between two happily quarrelsome people.

Lewis also enjoyed the Tory authors Jonathan Swift and Alexander Pope and their contemporary Joseph Addison. Though both Tories regarded satire as a sacred weapon, Lewis pointed out that much of their work is brightened by their sheer *vis comica*. "Swift's 'favourite maxim was *vive la bagatelle*.'"[50] He championed the joke of trifles, of the small, unimportant things. We miss the point of *Gulliver* and much of Swift's work if they do not "sometimes make us 'laugh and shake in Rabelais' easy chair.' Even their love of filth, is, in my opinion," Lewis wrote, "much better understood by schoolboys than by psychoanalysts: if there is something sinister in it, there is also an element of high-spirited rowdiness." Yet one title on Lewis's list of all-time unfavorites was Jonathan Swift's "Argument against abolishing Christianity." Although as a child Lewis enjoyed *Gulliver* immensely, as an adult and a Christian he couldn't abide many of Swift's satirical essays. They were thinly disguised attempts to teach spurious philosophies—philosophies that approached the blasphemous and irreverent. To Lewis such attacks on nominal Christianity were like thunderclaps.[51]

Joseph Addison, on the other hand, gave Lewis a completely different type of reading. The editor of the *Spectator* sought "to enliven morality with wit, and to temper wit with morality," bringing a moral foundation for laughter. Lewis distinguished between the cheerfulness in the Whig character of Addison and the mirth of his Tory contemporaries Swift and Pope. Addison "preferred cheerfulness to Mirth. The latter I consider as an Act, the former as a Habit of the Mind."[52] In the May 17, 1712, issue of the *Spectator*, Addison himself divided the two: "Mirth is like a flash of lightning that breaks through a gloom of clouds, and glitters for a moment; cheerfulness keeps up a kind of daylight in the mind, and fills it with a steady and perpetual serenity." But as Chesterton's Father Brown once observed, "People like frequent laughter, but I don't think they like a permanent smile. Cheerfulness without humor is a very trying thing."[53] In the Tories, Lewis found more mirth, epigram, repartee, frolic, extravaganza, and even buffoonery. You may hear cheerful conversation at teatime with Addison, but you would hear hearty, rollicking, even nasty laughter from Pope and Swift.

Pope and Swift do not have Addison's habit of cheerfulness, but they build on his sense of humor a sense of wild zest and savage satire. For the Tories, every enemy, powerful or merely irritating, becomes a grotesque caricature. "All who have, in whatever fashion, incurred their ill will are knaves, scarecrows, whores, bugs, toads, bedlamites, yahoos: Addison himself a smooth Mephistopheles. It is good fun, but it is certainly not good sense: we laugh and disbelieve."[54]

In marked contrast appears the urbane, sly, and reasonable Addison, who is "infuriatingly sensible," and consequently more effective than the loud, brash satirists Swift and Pope. His is a steady breeze matched against the thunderclaps. Whereas the Tories urge us to attack something as we would a fortress, Addison tricks us into admiring it as a ruin. He defuses, disarms, and even debones his opponent, like a charitable Victorian bourgeois host carving the turkey with all the smug complacency and decorum of his position. He shows a "playful condescension towards women," and

> sings charms to ills that ask the knife. If it were at all times true that the Good is the enemy of the Best, it would be hard to defend Addison. His Rational Piety, his smiling indulgence to "the fair sex," his small idealisms about trade, certainly fall short of actual Christianity, and plain justice to women, and true political wisdom. They may even be obstacles to them; palliatives and anodynes that prolong the disease.[55]

There is little passion, iron, meat, or strong drink in Addison. Lewis called his essays "rather small beer . . . they do not stir the depths." Of his adversaries, Addison casually wrote that "Round-heads and Wooden-shoes are standing jokes." The dizzy heights and stirring volumes of the Tories dwarf and drown out Addison, but steadily he endures. When Pope and Swift fall, they descend into an abyss of invective, hatred, cruelty, and even silliness. Lewis summarized Addison's world, in contrast, as sensible and comfortable, "not one to live in at all times, but it is a good one to fall back into when the day's work is over and man's feet on the fender and his pipe in his mouth." Addison's style of wit and humor Lewis found restful. Addison gives us

some tranquil middle ground of quiet sentiments and pleasing melancholies and gentle humor to come between our restless ideal-ism and our equally restless dissipations . . . (Do not fierce idealists slip from failed political meetings and literacy movements plumb down to the cinema and the dance band?) . . . Addison is, above all else, comfortable. He is not on that account to be condemned. He is an admirable cure for the fidgets.[56]

Known for his work on the satirical publication the *Spectator*, Addison did add the cheerful feature of "Surprize" to prevailing theories on wit such as Locke's incongruity theory, significantly con-tributing not merely a suddenness to the incongruity, but a freshness as well. Hence, for Lewis, the surprise element offered a fresh sense of perspective, permitting one to laugh in recognition of a comic context, such as in reading Jane Austen. Thomas Macaulay described Addison as possessing "a mirth consistent with tender compassion for all that is frail, and with profound reverence for all that is sublime." Lewis saw this role of the good gentleman in contrast to the rough giants. From the springs of laughter, Addison drew cool, refreshing waters. Laughter would bob up as suddenly as jest could invade or intrude any moment or occasion. What was important was to keep the jest fitting, or—the word Addison and Lewis would use—*decens*, appropriate.

Lewis remembered R. L. Stevenson's *The Wrong Box* "with chuck-les."[57] He liked Mark Twain but refused to reread *A Connecticut Yankee in King Arthur's Court* because of its "vulgar ridicule" of what were, to Lewis, the sacred and beloved literary traditions of knights and medi-eval romance. Lewis wrote that *Gulliver's Travels* "in an unexpurgated and lavishly illustrated edition was one of my favorites, and I pored endlessly over an almost complete set of old Punches."[58]

Lewis also appreciated the work of Charles Lamb: "His letters are as good as his essays" and he has a "sense of natural gusto—peculiar strength in liking everything—at once sane and whimsical, sweet, and pungent in the same sentence."[59] Lewis thought Lamb's essay on the "Superannuated Man" fit his retired brother, Warnie, quite well. Fielding's *Tom Jones* was another favorite. Squire Weston, with his rural jokes was an exemplary type of bluff, honest, genial English character.[60]

Above all, Lewis cherished the novels of Jane Austen, and the virtuous bourgeois stories of Chaucer and Dickens, both of whom were "fond of high moral vulgarity and indecency for its own sake."[61] Lewis extolled the "exuberance, the elbow-room, the heart-easing quality" of these two—and of Cervantes—and felt that they were masters of a literary art that "flows best from men who treat their work as a kind of play."[62] He particularly hailed this quality in Dickens's work. He believed that a British boy, such as Lewis was when he first read Dickens, could actually feel the familiar world of Pickwick by being immersed in and drunk with "so much of the Dickensy world indirectly through quotation and talk and other orders. . . . Certainly what I enjoy is not the jokes simply as jokes . . . but something festive and friendly about D's whole world . . . a great deal of it [communicates] the charm of goodness—the goodness of Pickwick himself, and Wardle, and both Wellers."[63] One might, by the way, see the forerunners of Lewis and the Inklings in the scene in *Pickwick Papers* in which "Mr. Pickwick and his friends were agreed that whatever had so affected them at the party, it couldn't have been the wine."[64]

Jane Austen's characters were on a par with Dickens's in Lewis's appreciation. He extolled the "great hostess who always separates two guests when she sees them getting really interested in conversation."[65] Perhaps partly because of her "indifference to all the great political, social, and intellectual upheavals" of her age, Jane Austen towered in Lewis's estimation.[66] He described her as the daughter of Dr. Samuel Johnson, inheriting his "common sense, his morality, even much of his style." Lewis thought that her comedy approached burlesque, with her "heroines making mistakes both about themselves and about the world in which they live." Like Molière's comedies, deception clouded the hearts of her characters, but the cause of the deception lay within. Her plot, wrote Lewis, "is always a husband-hunt . . . indeed Miss Austen has but one plot."[67] And her interesting women often married preposterous men. In real life, despite their choices, we would continue to respect these women. Once, in the midst of critical reflections on Austen, Lewis woke himself up asking,

> Have I been treating the novels as though I had forgotten that they are, after all, comedies? . . . I trust not. The hard core of morality and even of religion seems to me to be just what makes good comedy possible. "Principles" or "seriousness" are essential to Jane Austen's art. Where there is no norm, nothing can be ridiculous, except for a brief moment of unbalanced provincialism in which we may laugh at the merely unfamiliar.[68]

Of George Meredith, the great comic author and theorist of wit, Lewis wrote: "I began to read the 'Egoist' and after five pages came to the conclusion that it was one of the worst books I had ever seen or heard of. I don't know how [one] can stand Meredith's affectation."[69] Lewis put his judgment even more bluntly, declaring, "There's a good deal of the ass about Meredith." His witty conversations were "much poorer than real life." But he did concede that *The Egoist* provided a rare example where the conception was so good "that even the fantastic faults can't kill it."[70]

Meredith's deepest fault, in Lewis's opinion, may have been his underlying Gnostic worldview. Meredith's comic spirit arose from the "humor of the mind." The test of true comedy was, for Meredith, that it would awaken thoughtful laughter. It was decent, rational, even neo-Platonic laughter, not the mixed laughter of most English comedy that wedded mind, heart, and belly. In his 1877 "Essay on Comedy," Meredith complained that "people are ready to surrender themselves to witty thumps on the back, breast, and sides; all except the head," which is where good comic writers, like Molière and Meredith himself, aimed.[71] Lewis, on the other hand, while agreeing on a reasonable foundation for our laughter, saw the comic spirit properly encompassing the whole human being. We are not merely imprisoned intellects awaiting sweet, ethereal release; we are funny bones, shaking bellies, snorting nostrils, and all the parts of flesh so possessed by a goodly, incarnational comic spirit. Comedy should make one laugh even more than it makes one think. Lewis summed up his opinion succinctly: "Meredith's worldly wisdom—well just stinks, there's no other word." Lewis found Shakespeare's comedies funny, however, in "that way you come round to things you used to hate."[72]

What Lewis disliked may be just as interesting to his fans as what he liked. To begin with, he often expressed, to the dismay of his friends, a marked distaste for the Restoration comedy of William Congreve and company. His friend Neville Coghill tried vainly to plead for Congreve. "Asserting that there was a place for the Mirabellian worldling, the gentleman of wit, who might seem an apostate from romance, but who had a secret vision of love, however elaborately disavowed; there was a place for poise, for reserve, for a polished contempt."[73]

William Makepeace Thackeray joins the popular authors whose works Lewis disliked. Lewis criticized what he called Thackeray's voice of "the world" and commented that "his supposedly 'good' women are revolting, jealous *pharisiennes*. The publicans and sinners will go in before Mrs. Pendennis or Lady Castlewood." Lewis thought Thackeray's Renaissance conception of goodness was charming, infantile, and idiotic—not necessarily in that order. "All his 'good' people are not only simple but simpletons."[74] Lewis found it funny "what horrid young men" one met in Thackeray's works; yet better to meet them in fiction than in real life.

Lewis embraced the instructive element in comic literature, provided that both the literature and the teaching were sound. There are those like Jane Austen whom Lewis found a "sound moralist . . . and not platitudinous, but subtle as well as firm." (Austen, along with Scott and Trollope, were Lewis's favorite authors when he was ill.) Citing compelling works such as Austen's, Lewis believed that "Art can teach (and much great art deliberately set out to do so) without all ceasing to be art." In H. G. Wells, however, Lewis saw good fantasy but bad teaching. He saw and objected to "the preaching passages in Thackeray not because I dislike sermons but because I dislike bad sermons." But good art and good doctrine were combined, in Lewis's opinion, in Bunyan, Chesterton, Tolstoy, Charles Williams, and Virgil.[75]

In the course of discussing Lewis's taste in books, I have as yet barely mentioned some of his favorite characters—Dickens's Pickwick and Austen's heroines. As a lover and creator of literature, Lewis was immersed in character and characters. He was a student of them, both in his reading and in his writing. He traced the development of the phrase "sense of humor" to an early association with sensitivity to character. "We hardly remember," he pointed out, "that this was originally an awareness of humours (idiosyncrasies) in our neighbors."[76] "Everybody knows," wrote Chesterton, "that humour, in the Latin sense of 'moisture,' was applied . . . as part of the old physiological theory, by which the characters of men varied according to the proportions of certain different secretions in the human body."[77] This early theory of personality took Socrates' four fundamental elements of nature: fire, air, water, and earth, and theorized that these elements, mixed in different proportions, produced distinctive characters. Hot and moist (fire and water) mixed together made blood, the sanguine temperament; cold and dry (air and earth) produced melancholy; hot and dry brought choler; and cold and moist combined for phlegm. The four humors blended in this way to constitute the temperament (temper) or complexion or "ruling passion" of a person. For example, a person with a predominance of blood would be sanguine, cheerful, and optimistic.

Hippocrates treated patients according to these liquids in the human body, checking their humidity of blood, phlegm, and yellow or black bile. The degree of wetness or humidity was their humor. In his *Lexicon* (1755), Dr. Johnson listed nine definitions of humor, tracing its meaning from the Hippocratic moistures to temper to caprice and jocularity. William Hazlitt saw nothing more powerfully humorous than "keeping in comic character," that is, being fully what one is in one's humors. For Hazlitt, the proverbial phlegm of Sancho Panza and the romantic gravity of Don Quixote exemplified this quality. And this is what made these celebrated persons such excellent comic characters.[78]

Etymological knowledge of this sort contributed to Lewis's sense of character and to his preferences in literary characters. Lewis saw in the "Squire's Tale" evidence that blood is "nature's friend"—that is, that it produces the best humor: sanguine. In sanguine characters, such as Falstaff, for example, Lewis believed that we find "pleasant things . . . what we should call merry . . . a sanguine man is plump, cheerful, and hopeful"—not unlike, one may note, Lewis himself.[79]

Lewis saw the overwhelmingly sanguine character in that cannily practical man, Uncle Pandarus. "Every one has met the modern equivalent of Pandarus. When you are in the hands of such a man you can travel first class through the length and breadth of England on a third-class ticket. . . . And all the time, he will be such good company that he can 'make you so to laugh at his folye, / That you for laugher wenen for to dye.'"[80] Chaucer wrote about Pandarus cheering up his niece Cressida: "And told his jokes, some new, some old recast, / And made her laugh till she was out of breath / And thought that she would laugh herself to death."[81]

Of such sanguine characters, the most cosmic and comic could be combined into one being: Jove. Here was a character who jovially invaded Lewis's own literary world. In *That Hideous Strength*, the descent of Jove on the company of St. Anne's came like a thunderbolt of laughter hurled from the heavens. An orgy of jests, jokes, and poetry overwhelmed the modest and even austere fellowship sitting in the Blue Room having a spot of tea when the gods arrived. From a sober, funereal atmosphere (or a legal one with the reading of a will,

which isn't too much different), the members suddenly were ushered
into the shadow of a playful Pentecost, an inverse Babel, where

> all began talking at once, each, not contentiously but delightedly,
> interrupting the others. A stranger coming into the kitchen would
> have thought they were drunk, not soddenly but gaily drunk: would
> have seen heads bent close together, eyes dancing, an excited wealth
> of gesture. What they said, none of the party could ever afterwards
> remember. Dimble maintained that they had been chiefly engaged
> in making puns. MacPhee denied that he had ever, even that night,
> made a pun, but all agreed that they had been extraordinarily witty.
> If not plays upon words, certainly plays upon thoughts, paradoxes,
> fancies, anecdotes, theories laughingly advanced yet (on consider-
> ation) well worth taking seriously, had flowed from them and over
> them with dazzling prodigality. . . . For never in her life had she
> heard such talk—such eloquence, such melody (song could have
> added nothing to it), such toppling structures of double meaning,
> such skyrockets of metaphor and allusion.[82]

Mars brings with him heroic thoughts about ways to die, and
even sweet Mother Dimble launches into what "might be a nice way
to die." While discussing their impending deaths, "suddenly all their
faces and voices were changed. They were laughing again, but it was a
different kind of laughter. Their love for one another became intense.
Each, looking on all the rest, thought, 'I'm lucky to be here. I could
die with these.'" And when Jove himself arrives, grand and noble
ceremonies commence with elegant, stately dancing. "Kingship and
power and festal pomp and courtesy shot from him as sparks fly from
an anvil. The pealing of bells, the blowing of trumpets, the spread-
ing out of banners"—all are faint early symbols of his person. His
unearthly presence combines terror and unquenchable laughter. One
feels he could either die or laugh before this awesome angel. "If you
had caught one breath of the air that came from him, you would have

felt yourself taller than before." Cripples would rise in stature; beggars would wear their rags magnanimously.[83]

So, too, in Narnia, Father Christmas arrives like Jove—not only funny and jolly looking, but also big, glad, and solemn, dispensing gifts and glee. For Lewis, the jovial character combined largesse of heart and humor with an overwhelming largeness of size and duty.

Some medieval thinkers associated the planets with characters. Saturn, for example, gave rise to "melancholy and a dozen other diseases of body and mind. Born under Saturn, you are qualified to become either a mope and a malcontent or a great contemplative." The king of planets, Jupiter, produces character "imperfectly expressed by the word 'jovial'—but *Kingly*, a King at peace, enthroned, taking his leisure, serene. The jovial character is cheerful, festive, yet temperate, tranquil, magnanimous."[84]

In a poem entitled "Le Roi S'Amuse," Lewis animated Jove with gazes, stares, sighs, and thoughts—and laughter, for the king amused himself with Creation: "Jove laughed. Like cloven-shafted Lightning, his laugher into brightness broke."[85]

His laughter woke Sylvan, Satyr, a spirited stallion, and a disrespectful squirrel—and a clanging raven and kangaroo. The world and man unfurled their banner and a reeling, carousing holiday began with frolic. "Jove laughed to see the abyss empeopled, his bliss imparted, the throng that was his and no longer he."[86]

In another poem, "The Planets," Jove's orbit rolls with a rippled radiance and moves with music. His realm is festal and filled with joy and jubilee. His rays ripen on isles "of wrath ended / And woes mended, of winter passed / And guilt forgiven, and good fortune," where "Jove is master; and of jocund revel, / Laughter of ladies." No care darkens nor wrath wrinkles his calm and kingly forehead; for "righteous power / And leisure and largess their loose splendours / Have wrapped around him—a rich mantle of ease and empire."[87] The mirth of Jove is like tin tinkling, a silvery sound very similar to the thunder Ransom hears on Perelandra, a "different *timbre* from terrestrial thunder, more resonance, and even, when distant, a kind of tinkling. It is the laugh, rather than the roar, of heaven."[88]

Lewis not only excavated laughter from Jupiter but exported laughter to it, through the ambassador that he was. In one of his introductory lectures on medieval studies, he was describing the characters of men born under planetary influences when he arrived at Jupiter and explained: "The Jovial character is cheerful, festive; those born under Jupiter are apt to be loud-voiced and red-faced—it is obvious under which planet I was born."[89]

A person's humor could be exaggerated to such a degree that he or she becomes an eccentric of a certain type. For the peculiar little whims or vanities of eccentrics, flowing from their humor, lead to funny characters, people who are laughed at for being out of balance in their humors. The fossilized meaning of a "sense of humor" must be excavated and shown to mean an "unspecified awareness" of our neighbors' characters.[90] The characters of comedy are derived from the principle of both Aristotle's *Poetics* and Horace's *De Arte* that art should imitate the general and not the individual type. Thus "lovers in comedy behave like real lovers—true to nature."[91]

The imitation of the general life keeps us close to the ordinary, the everyday, the recognizably real. Lewis highlighted one amusing scene from Henry Bradshaw's *Lyfe of St. Werburge* (1513), in which "Werburge's mother, though herself a saint, becomes a very human *grande dame* to put her daughter's upstart suitor in his place. . . . The passage is funny because it is true to nature, and it is true to nature because Bradshaw keeps his eye on the object."[92]

Real characters often carry innate incongruities. Lewis pointed out the contrast within historical persons, such as "the union in Socrates of silly and scabrous titters about Greek pederasty with the highest mystical fervor and the homeliest good sense; in Johnson, of profound gravity and melancholy with that love of fun and nonsense."[93] As characters approximate life, they become almost unbelievably funny. Lewis quoted Lord Chesterfield's observation that "you will often meet with characters in nature so extravagant a discreet poet would not venture to set them upon the stage."[94]

Writing to his American correspondent about a neighbor, Lewis commented: "Your elderly neighbor would be comic if the matters at issue were not so serious. She has an odd idea of how to cheer people up! Like having a visit from a ghoul. People in real life are often so preposterous that one would not dare to put them in a novel."[95] The story of life, Lewis wrote, is a story with humorous characters in it, "characters who make no claim to historical reality, but whom, none the less, we know as real people: Falstaff, Uncle Toby, Mr. Pickwick."[96]

Voltaire, in his high and impertinent way, explained that men in their leisure, "left to themselves, abandon themselves to their characters, and become ridiculous." But of all men and women, those most left to themselves are those isolated on the isle of Great Britain. These happy few are a band of peculiar English characters. And among these eccentrics is manifest the hilarious English mirth that makes merry old England merry. (One does not, by the way, ever think of Robin Hood and his "efficient" men.)

English humor is renowned for its cast of whimsical and erratic characters. (Even Thor, with his humorous courage, was for Lewis "something of a Yorkshireman."[97]) Indeed, there is nothing quite so British as a peculiar character. The English servant, for instance, is legendary for being simultaneously respectful and disrespectful. The humorous and faithful Sam Weller is as memorable in *The Pickwick Papers* as Mr. Pickwick. The British borrow their image of the servant from the old Greek and Roman comedy. The ancient comic idea of the typical slave was plainly not the "submissive, abject man who cringes and flatters"; on the contrary, the truly comic, albeit servile, character was "cheeky, shrewd, cunning, up to every trick, always with an eye to the main chance, determined to look after number one." Lewis compared this ancient idea of the typical slave with modern British waiters in the worst type of "posh" restaurants, being both alternately fawning and insolent. This kind of character Lewis found in the *Spectator*, in which Steele described a mistress and her maid as two who "shall quarrel and give each other very free [abusive] language."[98] The cheeky British servant has a bit of the mischievous leprechaun in him as well. And, as Chesterton put it, "There is something sinister about putting a leprechaun in the work house. The only solid comfort is that he certainly will not work."[99]

Chief among humorous British characters aligned to be the Irish leprechaun is the don, the English professor. When Lewis, a don himself, moved from Oxford to Cambridge, he discovered that the stories of famous Cambridge "characters" were the same as the stories of famous Oxonian characters. He met many of these characters himself—aged and great dons whom he described as "crusty, fruity, 'humourists' (in the old sense), fathomlessly learned, and amidst all their kindness (there's no perfect dish without some sharpness) merciless leg-pullers."[100] The real Oxford, Lewis wrote, "is a close corporation of jolly, untidy, lazy, good-for-nothing humourous old men."[101]

Lewis polished this character image of the don in his fiction. Ransom, a fellow of Cambridge, "dressed with that particular kind of shabbiness which marks a member of the intelligentsia on a holiday." Identifying himself as a don, Ransom explained that "a don in the middle of a long vacation is almost a non-existent creature. . . . College neither knows nor cares where he is, and certainly no one else does."[102]

The British character—servant, master, or otherwise—is aggressively engaging; he thrusts himself out of his book and into your heart. Once there, he proceeds to earnestly instruct you in what his author thinks you need to know. Kenneth Grahame's *The Wind in the Willows* appealed to Lewis in this way. After a meeting with Mr. Badger, "that extraordinary amalgam of high rank, coarse manners, gruffness, shyness and goodness," a child would have in his bones "knowledge of humanity and of English social history which it could not get in any other way."[103] Lewis felt that Grahame chose a toad for the central character deliberately, choosing the squatty amphibian over a stag, pigeon, lion, or any other animal. His choice "is based on the fact that the real toad's face has a grotesque resemblance to a certain kind of human face—a rather apoplectic face with a fatuous grin on it." The quasi-human expression is biologically fixed. The "toad cannot stop grinning because its 'grin' is not really a grin at all. Looking at the creature we thus see, isolated and fixed, an aspect of human vanity in its funniest and most pardonable form."[104] Grahame invents Mr. Toad in his "ultra-Johnsonian humor," the character based on his moisture. What we learn from a meeting of such characters, Lewis suggested, is to gain a certain kind of amusement in and kindness toward all those vain and odd characters we meet in real life who so look like the toad.

Lewis found in fictional communities a unity marked by a colorful variety in its membership. His enjoyment of a book like *The Wind in the Willows* stems, in part, from its characters and their significance: "A trio such as Rat, Mole, and Badger symbolizes the extreme differentiation of persons in harmonious union which we know intuitively to be our true refuge both from solitude and from the collective. The affection between such oddly matched couples as . . . Mr. Pickwick and Sam Weller, pleases in the same way."[105] By seeing such peculiar characters interact and care for one another, one learns to appreciate the odd ducks that are one's own neighbors.

Seeing and learning—these are the great gifts that books give to their readers. And if the books are good—and particularly if they are funny—they give us a great deal of pleasure as well. Reading gives us legitimate, innocent pleasures, and an enormous amount of them. The pleasure can become dangerous, however (as any pleasure could for Lewis), when used wrongly—"under conditions which involve a breach of the moral law."

There is a moral dimension to all human activity; every idea and action has consequences. And the pleasures of culture, like all pleasures, must be subject to that law or they become destructive. Lewis claimed that art and literature could only be healthy "when they are either (a) admittedly aiming at nothing but innocent recreation or (b) definitely the handmaidens of religious or at least moral truth. Dante is all right and Pickwick is all right. But the great serious religious art—art for art's sake—is all balderdash."[106] As Cardinal John Henry Newman recognized, the pleasures of culture "are excellent diversion from guilty pleasures. We may, therefore, enjoy them ourselves, and lawfully, even charitably, teach others to enjoy them."[107]

21

Wordplay

A jest breaks no bones.
—Samuel Johnson

"Why did I become a writer?" Lewis asked rhetorically. "Chiefly, I think, because my clumsiness or fingers prevented me from making things in any other way."[1]

Lewis began writing early, when just a boy. In a letter to an eight-year-old named Jonathan, Lewis commented, "I began to write when I was your age and it was the greatest fun. Do try!"[2] By the time he was sixteen, Lewis was giving advice on the craft to his friend Arthur Greeves. "The first essential point for a letter writer to master," he wrote to Greeves, "is that of making himself intellagible [*sic*] to his reader." The ink of writing, he announced, is "the great cure for all human ills," but it must be spilled in "practice, practice, practice. It doesn't matter what we write (at least this is my view) at our age, so long as we write continually as well as we can."[3]

Lewis warned Greeves, by the way, that humor was a dangerous genre to try, because there were already "so many funny books in the world that it seems a shame to make any more."[4] But, of course, Lewis would come into worldwide popularity in a funny book, *The Screwtape Letters*. Even from his first attempts, such as *Boxen*, Lewis's work was highlighted by comedy. Yet Lewis sought criticism from Greeves on his unsuccessful jokes and bad taste in his earlier *Pilgrim's Regress*. In this book he aimed at being "idiomatic and racy" and avoiding archaic and literary words.[5]

Lewis enjoyed writing articles, books, poetry, and letters. Remarkably, he answered every letter he received, setting aside his mornings to answer little girls and insane men. After the success of his books, he received correspondence from lunatics who signed their names "Jehovah," and from unhappily married women who sought romantic advice from a male Ann Landers or Dear Abby.

Lewis saw writing to and for children as serious business. Children, he believed, must be met as equals in areas "where we are their equals." They must neither be patronized nor placed on a pedestal; and they must never be regarded as a "lump of raw material," like an advertising group, to be shaped into a certain mold. Lewis wrote: "I will not say that a good story for children could never be written by someone in the Ministry of Education, for all things are possible. But I should lay very long odds against it."[6] A clever schoolboy's positive reaction to his reading is "most naturally expressed by parody or imitation." He has got it as it was written, and shows his delight by his copying.[7]

But for Lewis, writing was like a "lust" or "scratching when you itch." It "comes as a result of a very strong impulse and when it does come, I for one, must get it out."[8] But, he continued, "If I didn't enjoy writing I wouldn't continue to do it. Of all my books, there was only one I did not take pleasure in writing . . . *The Screwtape Letters*. They were dry and gritty going." Lewis described as fatiguing the process of reversal—making the good things "bad" and the bad "good" in order to accomplish, "That's what the devil would say."[9] Books like this one, Lewis said, do not trickle "out of one like a sigh or a tear or automatic writing."[10]

The primary rule of writing for Lewis was to make it interesting. The unforgivable sin of enjoyment is dullness: "To interest is the first duty of art."[11] Lewis's friend Dorothy Sayers, writing on "a great comic poet," Dante, complained: "Many people are steeped in Virgil, sodden with Aristotle, or Bible-ridden to the verge of mania, who yet cannot tell an after-dinner story without mislaying the point and making their audience 'yawn as though overcome by fever or sleep.'"[12]

What Lewis did enjoy writing (and reading) were fairy tales. He rebuked those who suggested that one loses or grows out of such juvenile tastes. "Am I to patronize sleep because children sleep sound? Or honey because children like it." To the charge of "Peter Pantheism," Lewis turned the tables over: "Arrested development consists not in refusing to lose old things but in failing to add new things." Growth occurs when new pleasures are added, not replaced. Lewis's enjoyment of Tolstoy, Trollope, and Jane Austen joined his delight in fairy tales. This was growth—or, if you will, enlargement. Yet to merely set aside one set of pleasures for a more sophisticated set is not growth, but mere change. In maturing, one finds more ways of understanding the text. Lewis pointed to the changes in one's comic recognition from the nursery to adulthood. *Alice in Wonderland*, he wrote, "is read gravely by children and with laughter by grown-ups; *The Hobbit*, on the other hand, will be funniest to its youngest readers."[13] The pleasures of stories—and the enjoyment of their illustrations (those of Beatrix Potter's *Tales* were the happiness of Lewis's childhood)—are universal. "The popularity of stories with a mystery in them . . . needs no explanation. It makes a great part of the philosopher's, the scientist's, or the scholar's happiness. Also of the gossip's."[14]

Lewis gave his own stories their appeal by inventing a portrait gallery of comic villains and odd characters. One of his favorite comic targets was the proud and arrogant person. Under Lewis's brush, he or she seldom failed to become a buffoon. Those who look down their noses at others end up seeing their own funny feet. Those who snicker over their shoulders into mirrored faces find that they have become the butt of their own jokes. They see their own comic end.

In *Out of the Silent Planet*, Lewis's scientist, Weston, (who later demonstrates the horrible end of human arrogance), unknowingly humiliates himself before the Oyarsa because he will not humble himself. Weston's pride literally blinds him. He refuses to accept the possibility that the Oyarsa exists, so that when he is confronted by the Malacandrian lord, Weston can't see him.

The assembled creatures of Malacandra are overcome with mirth at Weston's consequent ridiculous behavior. Looking around for an authority figure other than the Oyarsa, Weston chooses an elderly hrossa sleeping on the fringe of the assembly. Weston bellows at him in defiant baby talk ("Why you take our puff-bangs away? We very angry with you. You do all we say and we give you much pretty things. See! See! Pretty, pretty! See! See!"). Holding up brightly colored beads and trinkets, the intergalactic imperialist Weston tries first to bribe and then to intimidate the slumbering hrossa. But the hrossa slumbers and snores through the entire performance. The striking result of Weston's prideful ignorance is "a roar of sounds as human ears had never heard before—baying of *hrossa*, piping of *pfifltriggi*, booming of *sorns*—burst out and rent the silence of that august place, waking echoes from the distant mountains." Weston is startled, but boasts that he isn't afraid of their noise. Finally, the voice of Oyarsa informs him: "You must forgive my people, . . . but they are not roaring at you. They are only laughing."[15]

"But Weston did not know the Malacandrian word for laugh: indeed, it was not a word he understood very well in any language." When he repeats his foolish gestures and "Pretty, pretty" gibberish, the sound of laughter redoubles in volume. Only sheer exhaustion stops the great scientist's comic performance, "the most successful of its kind given on Malacandra." Finally, his colleague Devine orders Weston: "For God's sake stop making a buffoon of yourself, Weston."[16] Creatures, trying to help, give Weston fourteen cold douches—during which his toupee falls off and the creatures worry because they thought it was the top of his head.

Weston is not the only buffoon in Lewis's fiction. Similar episodes of making a fool of oneself occur in Narnia with Prince Rabadash and Uncle Andrew. Each tries, throughout his respective story, to assert his dignity or importance—and consequently each becomes undignified, important only as the butt of a joke. Prince Rabadash is the treacherous, hot-blooded, and proud Calormene of *The Horse and His Boy*. He launches a sneak attack on King Lune in neighboring Archenland, but when Rabadash and his invaders are finally defeated, suddenly there arises a great roar of laughter. The joke is that the brash but unfortunate Rabadash has gotten stuck on a castle wall hook, "like a piece of washing hung up to dry, with everyone laughing at him." Having always been taken seriously in Tashbaan, he can't stand looking ridiculous; so he threatens, curses, and postures. He "rolled his eyes and spread out his mouth into a horrible, long mirthless grin like a shark, and wagged his ears up and down (anyone can learn to do this if they take the trouble)." His expression and grimaces look more and more like a donkey's until, low and behold, Rabadash *is* a donkey. His screams of rage die away into a donkey's bray. "And everyone laughed louder and louder (because they couldn't help it) for now what had been Rabadash was simply and unmistakably, a donkey."[17]

The ironic justice Rabadash finds is one in which the punishment fits the crime. Acting a fool and making an ass out of himself, he becomes an ass, with long ears, a tail, and loud braying. It is a fantastic tale right out of Ovid's *Metamorphoses* or *Pinocchio*. The masks we wear, Lewis warned, we will become. Thus, we are to dress up like Christ, to put on love and become like Him. Justice will mete out to us the face that we deserve; mercy, however, as in Max Beerbohm's story, "The Happy Hypocrite," will transform us into beings of surprising beauty. Both promise laughter for those who seek God. In fact, Lewis found the Hebrew response to "judgment" surprising, as when the psalmist sings: "Let the field be joyful . . . all the trees of the wood shall rejoice before the Lord for He cometh, for He cometh to judge the earth." Judgment for the Jews was tantamount to justice, when all wrongs against the chosen people would be rectified. Thus judgment is, appropriately, as Lewis observed, "an occasion of universal rejoicing."[18] The Jewish "delight in the Law," which tastes like honey, excites the laughter of hope; for, sitting by the rivers of Babylon, the people believe that justice will flow and they shall laugh again in Zion. Out of justice will spring joy and laughter.

Aslan announces to Rabadash that justice would be mixed with mercy. "'You shall not always be an Ass.' At this of course the Donkey twitched its ears forward—and that also was so funny that everybody laughed all the more. They tried not to, but they tried in vain." The prince became known, behind his back, as Rabadash the Ridiculous. If you act stupidly, Lewis warns his readers, "you are very likely to be called 'a second Rabadash.'"[19]

Lewis's treatment of ectomorphic Uncle Andrew in *The Magician's Nephew* reflects this same type of ironic justice. A magician-scientist, Uncle Andrew cruelly uses innocent animals for his brutal experiments. His smile is cunning and even greedy, showing all his teeth, and he appears as a very tall and thin "pantomime demon coming up out of a trap-door." He thinks he will vindicate himself as a magician, developing commercial possibilities in a pristine Narnia: "Ho, ho! They laughed at my Magic. That fool of a sister of mine thinks I'm a lunatic. I wonder what they'll say now?" He sees the fertility of a newborn Narnia, where whatever is planted bursts forth with life—and he greedily sees himself as a new exploitative Columbus: "What is America to this?" Indeed, everything Lewis loathed of railroads and capitalist progress was encapsulated in this imperialistic and avaricious Uncle Andrew.[20]

In his ambition to make himself superior, Uncle Andrew refuses to submit himself to the joke of himself. Self-conceit squashes humility and self-humor. But in Lewis's hands, anyone who cannot humble himself to be the object of a joke will eventually become a joke himself. When Uncle Andrew closes his ears and mind to the speech of the Talking Animals, hearing only snarls and growls, he shuts off all communication. In return, the Animals do not understand him: the Rabbit believes he is a kind of large lettuce, and the Jackdaw suggests he is the "Second Joke." To which the Panther replied, if so, it is not as good and funny as the first. Trying to hide among the rhododendrons, he is noticed by a group of curious creatures who rush at him "with roars, barks, grunts, and various noises of cheerful interest." Their laughter is even more frightful to Uncle Andrew, for it sounds like "a horrid, bloodthirsty din of hungry and angry brutes."[21]

They try to figure out if he is animal, vegetable, or mineral. The

Warthog and a Bear think he is a tree. That, finally, is the consensus: he is a tree. Therefore, the Elephant orders that a hole should then be dug and the tree planted. Fortunately Andrew is planted right side up, but he does look dreadfully withered, so the Elephant waters him, squirting him with gallons. Finally, by the mercy of Aslan, he is rescued from the earth, "a miserable object in muddy clothes." The Talking Animals even beg to keep their strange pet whom they had christened "Brandy, because he made that noise so often." Uncle Andrew is a buffoon not only because he is as vain as a peacock, but also because after two drinks he foolishly imagines that Queen Jadis, "a dem fine woman, a dem fine woman," would fall in love with him. Queen Jadis could and would do nothing of the sort. Her self-centeredness makes Uncle Andrew look like a prima donna paper doll.[22]

Both Uncle Andrew and Queen Jadis exhibit a haughty flippancy over the moral law. Challenged about the rightness of witchcraft, Uncle Andrew responded with a chuckle: "It depends what you call wrong. People are so narrow minded." With a smooth but forced laugh, he dismisses the suggestion that he would suffer moral consequences for his cruelty. And just as Uncle Andrew believes that men like himself "who possess hidden wisdom, are freed from common rules," so, too, Queen Jadis tells the children that "what would be wrong for . . . any of the common people is not wrong in a great Queen such as I." Yet her pride is more treacherous than the silly vanity of Uncle Andrew (who feels himself a "devilish well preserved fellow for [his] age"), as she is more powerful and possesses less humor.[23]

The solemn and supercilious queen is used in Lewis's fiction as a symbol of gravity without levity. When Digory anticipates being told the stories and legends of Charn, she proves to be an unnerving guide to grisly facts, and not a good narrator. "'That is the door to the dungeons,' she would say, or 'That passage leads to the principal torture chambers.'"[24] Lewis's own dark, droll humor makes Queen Jadis ridiculous in her cold, insufferable cruelty. Her assertions of power and demands to be recognized as the Empress Jadis are met with good-humored common sense from ordinary people. "Ho! Hempress are you?" British citizens scoff. "Three cheers for the Hempress of Colney 'Atch," and mocking cheers turn into roars of laughter, for Colney Hatch was the name of a well-known London insane asylum at the turn of the century. Finally she recognizes that they were only making fun of her, and the harsh awakening does not humble her but stirs her anger and wrath.

Bruno Bettelheim, child psychologist and writer, suggested that fairy tales help children deal with fears not only of abandonment or growing up, but also of appearing funny or stupid and being made fun of. Lewis reflected those young fears of being a buffoon by showing good characters being teased. Bree calls Shasta a name ("potato sack") and chuckles at him. At Bree's taunting, Shasta turns red. But the mirth is reversed when Bree rolls on the turf, waving all four legs in the air. "Shasta burst out laughing and said, 'You do look funny when you're on your back!'" Self-consciously Bree worries about looking funny and tries to excuse his behavior as a "silly clownish trick I've learned from the dumb ones."[25] The awkwardness of both Shasta and Bree allows Lewis's young readers to watch embarrassment from a safe distance, but also to share in the slight pain of being laughed at. The freedom from one's folly comes from identifying oneself as a fool. A young reader's heart, and an old one's as well, needs no other proof: one can recognize one's own buffoonery in the face of all other buffoons.

Lewis went easier on characters whose pride was softened by extreme silliness, such as the Calormene princess, Lasaraleen, in *The Horse and His Boy*. Everything detestable about fashionable and frivolous females, Lewis invested in this spoiled bubblehead. She prattles on incessantly about inconsequential things and frequently breaks off into giggles. Her friend, the heroine of the story, remembers at one point that Lasaraleen "always had been a terrible giggler." Like a silly, clueless teenager (and valley girl) Lasaraleen always titters and gossips about clothes and parties and weddings and scandals. When she commands her slaves not to disclose the presence of her friend Aravis, who is hiding from the wicked king, she warns: "And anyone I catch talking about this young lady will be first beaten to death and then burned alive and after that kept on bread and water for six weeks. There."[26]

Lasaraleen exemplifies the trivial, which, for Lewis, was the opposite of serious. Her fussing about dresses and social events reveals an absence of gravity, without which levity cannot lift one into true delight. After suffering this fool not too gladly, Aravis "began to think travelling with Shasta [on the road] was really rather more fun than fashionable life in Tashbaan."[27]

Lewis's playful invention of characters is magnified when one examines some of his favorite literary characters. Some of Lewis's most outrageous and hilarious creatures were presumably modeled on the Monopods of Pliny's *Natural History*. These are the Dufflepuds, of *The Voyage of the Dawn Treader*. The Dufflepuds began as creatures who felt they were made so ugly (by a magician's "uglifying spell") that they made themselves invisible. They are harmless, dim-witted creatures that hop about like huge grasshoppers, fleas, or frogs. They follow their chief and cheer his every pronouncement, most of which are silly tautologies. They "agreed about everything. Indeed most of their remarks were the sort it would not be easy to disagree with: 'What I always say is, when a chap's hungry, he likes some victuals,' or 'Getting dark now; always does at night,' or even 'Ah, you've come over the water. Powerful wet stuff, ain't it?'"[28] These Duffers are so stupid (how stupid are they, you ask?) that they clean the plates and silverware before dinner so they won't have to be washed up afterward, and plant boiled potatoes so the harvest won't have to be cooked when it's dug up.

Lewis applied the kind of humor typically used in elephant or moron jokes to these imaginary creatures. When they are made visible by another magic spell, Lucy cannot help laughing at their appearance. "'Oh the funnies, the funnies,' cried Lucy, bursting into laughter."[29] The Magician joins her in laughter till tears run down his cheeks. Bobbing about like rubber balloons or paddling themselves in the water (their huge, single foot acted as a natural raft or boat), the Duffers cause the sailors of the Dawn Treader, leaning over the sides of the ship watching them, to laugh until their sides ache.

In Lewis's fiction only the stupidity of the giants in *The Silver Chair* exceeds that of the Dufflepuds. In a routine not unlike the mindless antics of the Three Stooges (or Lewis's nonrelation, Jerry), Jill catches a glimpse of the huge, lazy giants with great, stupid, puff-cheeked faces. When the giants quarreled,

> they stormed and jeered at one another in long meaningless words
> of about twenty syllables each. . . . They lammed each other on the
> head with great, clumsy stone hammers; but their skulls were so
> hard that the hammers bounced off again, and then the monster
> who had given the blow would drop his hammer and howl with
> pain because it had stung his fingers. But he was so stupid that he
> would do exactly the same thing a minute later.[30]

In addition to creating funny characters, Lewis enjoyed coming up with funny names for them. He rolled funny-sounding words around in his imagination like a lozenge on his tongue. A "very funny word" like *knickerbockers* could lead to a good name for a dwarf like Bickerknocker.[31]

The names of places also excited mirth in Lewis. On discussing the route of one of his walking tours, Lewis mentioned that he had passed through a place called "Shapely Bottom." Another curiously labeled land quickened him to ask: "Who would not make sacrifices to pass through a place called Cuckold's Green?" What a horrible fate it must have been to live there in the seventeenth century, Lewis imagined, when strangers would ask where you and your wife lived. "By the age of forty, one would be quite definitely tired of the joke."[32] Lewis also punned on two places in his first Narnian chronicle. The goat-footed Mr. Tumnus inquires about the Spare Oom and the War Drobe. The simple play on words (which probably paid homage to Elizabeth Nesbit's story, "The Aunt and Amabel," and a place called

"Bigwardrobeinspareroom") offers children an introduction to the wonderfully low art of punning.

When it came to comic names, Lewis inherited the habit of inventing good ones from sixteenth-century poetry, as well as from all comic literature and drama. Comic names such as "Slingthrifty Fleshmonger" or "Stygian puddle glum" abounded in the ironically called Drab Age of that century. An effervescent spirit of youth, high-spirited jokes, and comic monikers—and distrust of the potato—characterized this Drab Period, 1534–1593. A prattling, brisk, cheerful Williams Harrison, a writer of that period, provided a litany of names for strong beer as "a sort of mental carouse—Huffcap, Go-by-the-Wall, Mad Dog and Merry-go-down."[33] Not much different are their modern counterparts, Screwdrivers and Harvey Wallbangers. Some names from the Drab Period initially intended for characters, such as Spenser's Braggadocio, would evolve into the name of a trait.

In *Prince Caspian*, Lewis used names to indicate occupations. Moles, who were responsible for digging with their spades, had names like Lilygloves (a "funny old" fellow) and Clodsley Shovel (a name conjuring up a seventeenth-century British naval hero). A deadly dull Telmarine academic author is names Pulverulentus Siccus, a sly Latin equivalent of the words *dust, slow,* and *dry.* Lewis merrily mocked medieval scholars with the title of this pedant's text: *Grammatical Garden or the Arbour of Accidence pleasantlie open'd to Tender Wits.* A chatterbox squirrel is appropriately known as Patterwig, and the valiant but tiny mice as Reepicheep and Peepiceek.

The most fitting name of the whole book, however, is that of the red-haired wife of King Miraz, Prunaprismia. Lewis, who loathed prunes, may have latched onto the alliteration "Prunes and Prisms," made by one of Charles Dickens's characters, as the perfect name for this disagreeable Queen. (Dickens was a major inspiration in Lewis's fiction: Mrs. General in *Little Dorrit*, for example, is a model for Lewis's dwarf, Trumpkin, in her use of such expletives as "Horns and Halibuts" or "Tubs and tortoiseshells.") The comic matching of personality and name also pops up in the first line of *The Voyage of the Dawn Treader*. "There was a boy called Eustace Clarence Scrubb and he almost deserved it."[34] This twerpy little bully was the kind of boy who "liked animals, especially beetles, if they were dead and pinned on a card. He liked books if they were books of information and had pictures of grain elevators or of fat foreign children doing exercises in model schools."[35]

One of Lewis's favorite characters with a funny name was also one of his best comic inventions: Puddleglum. Puddleglum, of *The Silver Chair* fame, was a cartoon, hieroglyph of human nature. Puddleglum's name was most likely derived from a Drab Age character by John Studley, who used "a diction which, whether 'low' in his own day or not, cannot now be read without a smile—'frostyface,' 'topsy turvy,' and (for *Tacitae Stygis* in *Hippolytus* 625) 'Stygion puddle glum.'"[36] Many of Lewis's comic characters were drawn from the lower levels of social rank. Puddleglum, for instance, looked and sounded remarkably like Lewis's gardener. Puddleglum's character, however, seems also to have a touch about him of a University College don called Arthur Poynton—a don with whom Lewis shared tea and of whom Lewis was very fond. Lewis described him as "a very humorous old man who says the funniest things in a monotonous melancholy voice." When Lewis satirized real academic or pedantic people, he did so mostly with charity and affection. He sought a lovable comedy so "that even my worst enemies in college were really funny and odd rather than detestable."[37] Indeed, in his comic invention, Lewis realized that he need not go to fantastic caricature to find a comic cast; they were usually close to school and home.

Characters of fiction can give us a taste of reality, much like Spenser's Bercilak—half-boy, half-buffoon, an irresistible and rambunctious figure who is "as jolly as a Dickensian Christmas host."[38] They can take us back to old friends, aunts, dear queens, or queer deans. Such was Puddleglum, who inherited the glum character of Lewis's old gardener and sometime cook, Fred Paxford, who used to sing hymns out of tune while working in the yard. Lewis told Walter Hooper that Puddleglum was indeed modeled after Paxford, "an inwardly optimistic, outwardly pessimistic, dear, frustrating, shrewd, countryman of immense integrity." Like Lewis's father, Paxford was a uniquely stamped character. Responsible for buying groceries for the Kilns, Paxford was very frugal about buying sugar only a pound at a time, and "could not be coaxed into buying more." He explained: "Well, you never know when the end of the world will come and we don't want to be left with sugar on our hands."[39]

Puddleglum is more than Paxford; he is almost Kierkegaardian in his spindly look and brooding wit, a sort of metaphysical jester, even a bit of a Woody Allen persona. But he also bears a faint resemblance to Charles Williams. Lewis explained that in Williams, "the two sides [of his head] lived in a perpetual dance or lovers' quarrel of mutual mockery. In most minds, and in his, the lower mocks at the higher; but in his the higher also mocked at the lower."[40]

Williams's core of belief was wholly optimistic, while his feelings were quite skeptical and pessimistic. The things he believed "did not negate the feelings; they mocked them." He was unlike a Woody Allen whose mocking comedy would be a shadow of a despairing philosophy. Allen said, "Most of the time I don't have much fun; the rest of the time I don't have any fun at all"; or, "Whosoever shall not fall by the sword or by famine, shall fall by pestilence, so why bother shaving?"—revealing his belief in the comic futility of the universe. Williams would laugh at his own tendency to flay himself and despair. His creed in the dark world was one of exuberance and carnival, "a little like Spinoza's *hilaritas*, if Spinoza could have progressed from his geometrical method to dance his philosophy." Williams lived with a sense of light but grand adventure in the spiritual life, like David dancing before the ark."[41]

Puddleglum was himself full of an unconscious hilarity. His traveling companion acknowledges that "he may be a wet blanket, but he has plenty of pluck—and cheek."[42] Puddleglum's daily pessimism hid an eternal optimism. He could play an archetypal comic buffoon: the drunk. As Old Froggy, he takes the cup of liquor given by the giants and tests it like poison. With a drop too much, his speech becomes drunken and blurred—"Nothing frog with me. I'm a respecta-biggle. . . . Reshpeckobiggle." He also seems related to two of A. A. Milne's characters. He tests the bottle by degrees, much like Pooh tested the honey jar in the Heffalump Trap. And his obvious cousin is the pathetic Eeyore, the Donkey. While Puddleglum is not as pitiful, he is as pessimistic. If Puddleglum were not one of Aslan's creatures, he certainly would be one of Kafka's.

Yet Puddleglum maintains an obstinate fidelity against narcotic spells and enchantments. He is living proof that faith is more than American pluck and optimism. When the soft, silvery laughter of the Witch adopts arguments of logical positivism, suggesting to her under-ground prisoners that the sun is only a big lamp and Aslan the Lion is merely a cat (and surely, said the Queen, "I love cats"), it is Puddleglum who is obstinate in his unyielding belief in the reality of the Sun and Aslan and Narnia.

The comedy we encounter in the long-faced and sunken-cheeked Puddleglum is the exaggeration of a genuine character, the pessimist. In fact, the bleak communities of marshwiggles seem like Scandinavian families scripted by Ingmar Bergman. Puddleglum may be gay about eternal things but he expects the worst about his present life. When he is first awakened, he asks, "What is it? Is the King dead? Has an enemy landed in Narnia? Is it a flood? Or dragons?" Even his hospitality to Eustace and Jill is dampened by his belief in the inadequacy of his home and this world: "There you are. Best we can do. You'll lie cold and hard. Damp too, I shouldn't wonder. Won't sleep a wink, most likely; even if there isn't a thunderstorm or a flood or the wigwam doesn't fall down on top of us all, as I've known them to do. Must make the best of it."[43]

Describing their quest as bleak and hopeless, Puddleglum encour-ages the children not to lose heart, for he will accompany them:

> "I'm coming, sure and certain. I'm not going to lose an opportunity like this. It will do me good. They all say—I mean, the other wiggles

all say—that I'm too flighty; don't take life seriously enough. If they've said it once, they've said it a thousand times. 'Puddleglum,' they've said, 'you're altogether too full of bobance and bounce and high spirits. You've got to learn that life isn't all fricasseed frogs and eel pie. You want something to sober you down a bit.'"[44]

Puddleglum, whose very name conjures up depressing, wet images, believes himself to be quite zesty. In the middle of a desperate situation, he declares that his company must be

"gay. As if we hadn't a care in the world. Frolicsome. You two young-sters haven't always got very high spirits, I've noticed. You must watch me, and do as I do. I'll be gay. Like this"—and he assumed a ghastly grin. "And frolicsome"—and he cut a most mournful caper. "You'll soon get into it, if you keep your eyes on me. They think I'm a funny fellow already, you see."[45]

Meeting the sad Earthmen of the Underworld, Puddleglum thinks their glumness is just the kind of sport he needed. "If these chaps don't teach me to take a serious view of life, I don't know what will." When Puddleglum does say something that sounds positive (he responds to Prince Rilian's praise of the wicked Lady by saying, "Sounds like a very nice lady indeed") one can be certain he is being ironic, for he said this "in a voice which meant exactly the opposite."[46]

As a marshwiggle, Puddleglum is rooted in the earth and mud. The creature with feet of humus is a creature with a head of humor and humility. He is a true comic hero with his matter-of-fact faith as an antidote to cynicism and sentimentalism. Puddleglum's perception of himself as too flighty and the children's initial view of him as a wet blanket provide a comic incongruity. It is he who restores the comic sense of proportion and balance to a crazy, chaotic world.

Lewis, however, was not a gag writer of belly laughter. His humor was more thoughtful, dry, and whimsical. Chesterton could summon up the boffo (the laugh that kills) guffaws from his readers with his outrageous observations; Lewis would bring a knowing smile and a titter or two. But the lack of volume in the sound of laughter does not signify the lack of humor or comedy in his writings. He enjoyed the games and adventures of life and passed on his delight in this odd, round, funny planet and its peculiar earthlings. His writings were immersed in his own laughter in the fun and play of life.

Lewis did not force comedy. When asked whether Christian writers should attempt to be funny, Lewis replied: "No. I think that forced jocularities on spiritual subjects are an abomination and the attempts of some religious writers to be humorous are simply appalling."[47] Lewis rejected attempts to inject jokes into spiritual discussions as being unfitting. Such attempts are not at all the same thing as writing humorously. "Some people write heavily; some write lightly. I prefer the light approach because I believe there is a great deal of false reverence about." Solemnity should not smother our sacred activities; we have a freedom to find what is fitting. For example, Lewis explained, "I can say a prayer while washing my teeth but that does not mean I should wash my teeth in church."[48]

The teaching of Jesus Himself, Lewis argued, "in which there is no imperfection," provides a helpful example. His communication "is not given us in that cut-and-dried, fool-proof, systematic fashion we might have expected or desired.

> He wrote no book. We have only reported sayings, most of them uttered in answer to questions, shaped in some degree by their context. And when we have collected them all we cannot reduce them to a system. He preaches but He does not lecture. He uses paradox, proverb, exaggeration, parable, irony, even (I mean no irreverence) the "wisecrack." He utters maxims which, like popular proverbs, if rigorously taken, may seem to contradict one another. His teaching therefore cannot be grasped by the intellect alone, cannot be "got up" as if it were a "subject." If we try to do that with it, we shall find

Him the most elusive of teachers. He hardly ever gave a straight answer to a straight question. He will not be, in the way we want, "pinned down." The attempt is (again, I mean no irreverence) like trying to bottle a sunbeam.[49]

The playfulness of Christ in His dealings with disciples and Pharisees is communicated through His parables and stories, in His dialogues with a woman at the well, and in His open invitation for the little children to come to Him. They apparently found Him to be fun. And so He called all men and women to become like little children; to come to the wedding feast; to rejoice, for His kingdom was at hand. And Lewis was one large, round, awkward, overgrown little child, who, coming to the party thrown by God, brought his own playfulness and hearty laughter of divine fun.

Part 4

The Joke Proper

The size of man's understanding might be justly measured by his mirth.
—SAMUEL JOHNSON

Introduction
Lewis's Theory of Laughter

It is only believers in the
Fall of Man who can really appreciate how funny men are.
—Malcolm Muggeridge

Many theories compete to explain the singularly human phenomenon of laughter. Even the idea that it is a uniquely human experience has been debated. Albert Rapp views laughter as a "roar of triumph" from some primitive jungle duel.[1] Konrad Lorenz interprets laughter as a controlled form of aggression on a par with baring the teeth. C. S. Lewis, however, argued that the human response to and appreciation of a joke is unique in the animal world. Man is *homo risens*, the *zoion gelastikon*—the animal that laughs. For Lewis, as for his mentor G. K. Chesterton, the ability to make a joke—as one would make an argument or a picture—is a specifically human act. Chesterton explained: "It sounds like a truism to say that the most primitive man drew a picture of a monkey. But it sounds like a joke to say that the most intelligent monkey drew a picture of a man."[2]

The fact that "men make coarse jokes" was for Lewis evidence of the truth of Christian theology, particularly of the Fall:

> The coarse joke proclaims that we have here an animal which finds its own animality either objectionable or funny. Unless there had been a quarrel between the spirit and the organism I do not see how this could be: it is the very mark of the two not being "at home" together. But it is very difficult to imagine such a state of affairs as original—to suppose a creature which from the very first was half shocked and half tickled to death at the mere fact of being the creature it is. I do not perceive that dogs see anything funny about being dogs: I suspect that angels see nothing funny about being angels.[3]

Being wholly animal, like a dog, does not lead to an innate contradiction. Neither does being wholly spiritual, like an angel. Angels may take themselves lightly (and thus fly), but there is no record that they laugh. Joy and play may thrive in their realms, but there are few jokes, if any. We humans, however, are stuck between two worlds, a natural one and a supernatural one. It was God's great enterprise "to make an organism which is also a spirit; to make that terrible oxymoron a 'spiritual animal.'"[4] This discrepancy, this tension between flesh and spirit (or the human and the universe), provides raw material for the joke. The discrepancy is that the two things do not fit together. As Chesterton observed, "Christian optimism is based on the fact that we do not fit into this world."[5] For sociologist Peter Berger the joke and all humor become "signals of transcendence," evidence that we do belong to another reality. We hear of a rumor of angels that leads us to discover—or rediscover—the supernatural in our modern society.

When Lewis defined what he called the joke proper, he did it through an inverted explanation of his devil, Screwtape. It is this definition and its implications that will be examined in this section, for Lewis's description of the joke proper involves much more than Joe Miller's *Jokebook* or a monologue by a late-night stand-up comedian. The joke proper was a category for him that included not only puns and jests, but an explanation for all of life's incongruities, not the least of which is that curious, inscrutable realm of sex—but all this in good time. First, we will take a ride through the tunnel of theories, those explanations of joking that do so much to suck the air out of our laughter.

Of the three dominant theories explaining laughter (relief, superiority, and incongruity), Lewis leaned toward the last. Yet the principles of the other two offered him relevant insights as well. Each contains its own seeds of truth. The relief theory proposes a biological and physiological source of laughter, whereby we break free of psychological fetters and find relief from tension or release from inhibition. For Sigmund Freud, this meant escaping moral prohibitions by laughing at social taboos: death, sex, religion, aggression, authority, and so forth. In *Jokes and Their Relation to the Unconscious*, Freud argues that the libido struggles to break free of the superego until the energy used to suppress forbidden thoughts or feelings is finally liberated through either inno- cent or tendentious (hostile or obscene) laughter. The comic is due to an economy in the expenditure of thought; humor, an expenditure of feel- ing, in which the ego and pleasure principle triumph. Then, apparently, the energy used by the superego (or conscience) to repress the activity of the id is redirected and rechanneled by the joke into laughter. This laughter, however, is mostly negative, reusing energy used to repress taboos in the unconscious.

In Lewis's writing and in his life, one can find examples of bawdy humor that might provide data for earnest Freudian psychoanalysts, intent on unveiling some secret neurotic repressions. A bachelor don who married late in life (don't all such unmarried British dons harbor latent perversions for the suspicious psychiatrist?), Lewis might be seen as a man who sneaked sexual jokes behind the censor of his superego. Yet he had already peeled the onions of psychoanalysis, exposing the Sisyphean task of trying to explain away a phenomenon. The expla- nation offered by some psychoanalysis regarding "bodily shame . . . [is] not satisfactory. It refers us to primitive taboos and superstitions— as if these themselves were not obviously results of the thing to be explained."[6] Something larger than little-boy naughtiness lies behind our laughter. We do laugh at things we shouldn't, but this leads us to the more universal, moral dimensions of the larger fact that we do things we shouldn't. Lewis did not deny that jokes often are made for the purpose of avoiding the censors. There is a bit of the rebel and the maverick in all humanity, especially when it comes to authority.

Laughter also functions as an economic catharsis of nervous energy. Being freed from the burdens of life can offer an occasion for the spill- ing or leaking of laughter. Lewis gives an example, illustrating how this perspective can explain some laughter in Perelandra. On the way to the watery new world of that name, Ransom has tense expectations and uncertainties that crowd out all the delights of travel. He lands on one of Perelandra's floating islands and struggles, fearfully, to orient himself in this strange environment. As he loses his balance and starts to roll to and fro on the undulating surface of the floating island, he undergoes "a blessed relaxation of the strain in which he had been living since his arrival [which] dissolved him into weak laughter," and he got a "real schoolboy fit of the giggles."[7] Later, during a crucial moment in the destiny of the planet Perelandra, Ransom is tense with worry and anxiety. He discovers that even as a stone may determine the course of a river, he is entrusted to be that stone at a particularly critical moment. "Then came blessed relief. He suddenly realized that he did not know what he *could* do. He almost laughed with joy."[8] Indeed, the release from overweening responsibility—from exalted expectations, from a burdensome law—turns one over to the freedom of laughter. When one walks out of the prison of the self, the doors opening to true release, the formerly chained prisoner shouts and laughs with joy.

In Lewis's brief epilogue to *The Iliad*, "After Ten Years," the heroic and Olympian perspective on the war and its exquisite cause is brought down to the realities of time and the comedy of human nature. When Yellowhead first looks in a hut and sees Helen, the prize that launched a thousand ships and for which all the Greeks have been fighting those ten years, he is astonished. Flesh had gathered beneath her chin, her hair had grayed, and her eyes had wrinkled. The legendary Helen of Troy was an old woman.

> For this Patroclus and Achilles had died. If he appeared before the army leading this as his prize, as their prize, what could follow but universal curses or universal laughter? Inextinguishable laughter to the world's end. Then it darted into his mind that the Trojans must have known it for years. They must too have roared with laughter every time a Greek fell. Not only the Trojans, the gods too. They had known all along. . . . The bitter wind of derision blew in his face. All for nothing, all a folly and himself the prime fool.[9]

Not as close to the situation, Agamemnon threw back his head and laughed his fill. The surprise is nonetheless a shock that requires an emotional outburst—and laughter becomes most fitting, even if it is despairing, hollow, self-mocking laughter.

This human tendency to seek and find relief from the strain of life via the comic spirit was identified by Lord Shaftesbury, defender of wit and humor, as a proper means to promote true religious faith. In "An Essay on the Freedom of Wit and Humour," he wrote: "The natural free spirits of ingenious men, if imprisoned or controlled, will find out other ways of motion to relieve themselves in their constraint; and whether it be in burlesque, mimicry, or buffoonery, they will be glad at any rate to vent themselves, and be revenged on their constrainers."[10] Lewis aptly demonstrates in one passage of fiction Freud's notion that jokes are the means by which we outmaneuver and trick the censors, allowing taboo topics to be addressed. Lewis played impishly with the word *bitch* in a wickedly funny passage of one of his children's books. (If parents tumble upon Lewis's private joke in this book, they most insouciantly read on as if nothing had happened.) In *The Last Battle*, the dogs and children and all kinds of creatures romp farther up and farther toward new Narnia. The pagan Emeth was testifying about how Aslan had rescued him:

> "And this is the marvel of marvels, that he called me, Beloved, me who am but as a dog—"
>
> "Eh? What's that?" said one of the Dogs.
>
> "Sir," said Emeth. "It is but a fashion of speech which we have in Calormen."
>
> "Well, I can't say it's one I like very much," said the Dog.
>
> "He doesn't mean any harm," said an older Dog. "After all, *we* call our puppies *Boys*, when they don't behave properly."
>
> "So do we," said the first Dog. "Or, *girls*."
>
> "S-s-sh!" said the Old Dog. "That's not a nice word to use. Remember where you are."[11]

Lewis's oblique comic bit is a tough naughty, and the reference to girl dogs is properly illustrative of that aspect of relief theory seeking to explain why we laugh or snicker at outsmarting our own stupidity, as put forth by Freud and others.

The second major theory of laughter, the superiority theory, evolves out of the view that laughter is at base aggressive. According to this theory, laughter is used by the witty to gain a superior vantage point from which to deride and degrade others, either to keep them inferior or to attempt to rock them from their high positions. Plato lends some classical support to this contention by describing laughter as a "pain in the soul" that involves malice. In *The Republic* he pointed out that the proper object of laughter is human evil, egoism, and folly; and he warned that "persons of worth, even if only mortal men, must not be represented as overcome by laughter, and still less must such a representation of the gods be allowed."[12] Laughter must be aimed only at what is ridiculous or foolish. And what was most laughable to Plato was self-ignorance. One who does not obey the oracle at Delphi to "Know thyself" is properly ridiculous. People hold the common delusions of seeing themselves as richer, fairer, or better than they actually are, and to Plato/Socrates this was a ridiculous vice.

Yet, although we recognize this vice in others, we must not deride them, but rather take heed lest we become infected and fall as well. "In heavy laughter, too, we lose rational control of ourselves, and so become less than fully human."[13] To be fair to Plato's somewhat heavy theory of humor, we must remember the final moments of his *Symposium*, in which a bunch of drunken men—a physician, a poet, a lover, a philosopher (Socrates himself), a comic author (Aristophanes), and others—sit around drinking large quantities of wine and talking about love and comedy. As Socrates begins a discourse on the genius of comedy, the others "being drowsy, and not quite following the argument" drop off to sleep.[14] Aristophanes was first of all the sleepers to leave the brilliant philosopher prattling away on the values of comedy. Anyone talking and writing about comedy, however, should take heed lest even those who have an alert sense of humor should be bored and snore. Even now, some comic Eutychus has fallen into a blessed stupor in the reading of these words on comedy.

Plato, incidentally, had significant influence on Lewis. Lewis raved about Plato's writings passionately. "To die without having read the *Symposium* would be ridiculous; it would be like never having bathed in the sea, never having drunk wine, never having been in love."[15] Professor Kirke in Narnia persistently hammers on about Plato. Yet, unlike Plato, Lewis did not refuse admittance of clowns and buffoons in his republic.

Aristotle was kinder to comedy than to his teacher (he was kinder to everything in the natural and phenomenal world), although he also held to a version of the superiority theory. In the *Poetics*, he acknowledged that "comedy aims at representing man as worse, tragedy as better than in actual life. . . . Comedy is . . . an imitation of characters of a lower type. . . . It consists in some defect or ugliness which is not painful or destructive." As an example Aristotle offered the comic mask, which is "ugly and distorted but does not give pain."[16]

In Lewis's story, "Ministering Angels," one of the crew members, Dickson, discovers that the two utterly unappealing and ugly women were brought to Mars for the crew's sexual satisfaction. His face underwent "certain contortions, became very red; he applied his handkerchief and spluttered like a man trying to stifle a sneeze." With his back turned and his posture slightly stooped, "you could see his shoulders shaking." The Fat Woman runs over to comfort him, until the Captain corrects her misreading of the situation. "I think," said the Captain, "the young man is laughing, not crying."[17] The idea of a fat, seventy-year-old mustard-haired tart and a prim, sharp, thin feminist serving as "ministering angels" to the men abandoned on Mars was a comical absurdity. Yet it was in fact an absurdity recommended by a Dr. Richardson. He predicted in an article that after men land on Mars, we will have "to send some nice girls to Mars at regular intervals to relieve tensions and promote morale."[18]

When there is real pain or ugliness and not just the appearance of it, comedy bleeds into tragedy. "Only by being terrible do [certain attitudes] avoid being comic. If there were no broken treaties with Redskins, no extermination of the Tasmanians, no gas-chambers and no Belsens . . . the pomposity of both [attitudes of cultural superiority] would be roaring farce."[19] Lewis described one of his characters, Professor Filostrato, the great physiologist, as "fat to that degree which is comic on this stage, but the effect was not funny in real life."[20] Likewise, when Dickens put poor Jingles in prison in *Pickwick*, the comedy dies for Lewis. "The whole spirit in which we enjoy a comic rogue depends on leaving out any consideration of the consequences which his character would have in real life; bring that in, and every such character (say Falstaff) becomes tragic."[21]

A person thinking himself wiser, healthier, and more clever or virtuous than he is deserves ridicule. Author and humorist H. Allen Smith once observed that a humorist "is a fellow who realizes, first, that he is no better than anybody else, and second, that nobody else is either."[22] And, if need be, the humorist will allow others to see the comic mask they too frequently forget they themselves are wearing.

Thomas Hobbes holds the distinction of being one of the most articulate proponents of the superiority theory and of a base view of human nature. Of course, anyone who wrote in a work entitled *Leviathan* that the "human race is a collection of individuals in constant struggle for Power over each other, until ceasing in Death" is not going to offer a bright and chipper theory of laughter.[23] Consistent with his philosophical framework, Hobbes argued that laughter was "a sudden glory arising from some conception of some eminency in ourselves, by comparison with the infirmity of others, or with our own formerly."[24] That is, Hobbes saw laughter as a triumph over others, a surprising and sudden realization that "I am better than those other people or better than I used to be myself." Lewis showed this principle in literary action where the "Trojans 'Keckit all' (*risere*) [laughed] at the man thrown overboard in the boat race."[25] All were glad and giddy that some other guy was the victim.

The fact that we sometimes laugh when misfortune happens to someone else is no surprise. At its core the enjoyment of jokes of this type consisted, for Lewis, of the pleasure of watching without having to participate. "We certainly do not wish to be the cross-gartered Malvolio or Mr. Pickwick in the pond. We might conceivably say 'I wish I'd been there to see'; but this is only to wish ourselves as spectators—which we already are—in what we suppose to be a better seat."[26] Lewis admitted to enjoying several moments of vindictive Hobbesian laughter. On a walking tour together, he and his brother, Warnie, exalted in the happiness of being free from one of the major ills of their lives, that of being schoolboys and suffering under a master nicknamed Oldie. Taking an after-lunch rest in a beautiful outdoor setting, Lewis and his brother developed their "own version of *si geunesse saviat.*"

> If we could only have seen as far as this out of the hell of [Belsen, their school]. I felt a half-comic, half-savage pleasure (Hobbes's sudden glory) to think how by the mere laws of life we had completely won and Oldie had completely lost. For here were we, with our stomachs full of sandwiches, sitting in the sun and the wind, while he had been in hell these ten years.[27]

The idea that we laugh to feel superior or to make others inferior is only partly true. To laugh at the misfortune of friends suggests tinges of envy or meanness in our hearts, as children's laughter sometimes degrades and humiliates a playmate. In *Lost in the Cosmos*, Walker Percy suggests that much sorrow for our neighbor's misfortune is putative and mingled with a hint of suppressed satisfaction. But if there is cruelty and hatred in our laughter, that is because they were already in our hearts. The fact that laughter is "never far removed from derision," as Quintilian wrote, underscores the fact that the lungs are near the derisive heart. When *Orual* arrives to fight her enemy in *Till We Have Faces*, the men of Phars roar with laughter to discover that an ugly woman will fight their champion.[28] The laughers mock, flaunting what they see as their own superiority.

"In laughter we always find an unavowed intention to humiliate and consequently to correct our neighbor," wrote French philosopher Henri Bergson, in his 1909 classic *La Rire*.[29] Bergson, another persuasive proponent of the superiority theory cited frequently by Lewis, was the foremost patron of the *elan vital* and the philosophical apologist for the "animating life force" that George Bernard Shaw popularized. Attacking the determinist tendencies of the late nineteenth and early twentieth centuries, Bergson complained of those who would freeze the flux of life, of those who would make human nature into a machine. It was Bergson who showed Lewis what Goethe meant by *"des Lebens goldener Baum."*[30] He taught him how to enjoy a new, fresh sense of grand, exultant art, rather than merely abolishing old tastes, to "relish energy, fertility, and urgency; the resource, the triumphs, and even the insolence, of things that grow."[31] Bergson chased away from Lewis that old bogeyman of Schopenhauer's that the universe "might not have existed" by awakening the awareness of necessary existence. Things are. This one divine gift offered Lewis an idea of immense potency, and was instrumental in his pilgrimage toward the robust fact of divine existence.

Lewis's familiarity with Bergson, read first in a convalescent camp on Salisbury Plain, brought forth affection and disagreement. Reading Bergson in 1920, Lewis found "all sorts of things clearer which were baffling a year ago."[32] His familiarity with Bergson included *L'Évolution Creatice* (1907), in which life is defined as "force" or "deamon" and Bergson's *Le Rire*, in which Lewis found a fine analysis of Molière's *Le Misanthrope*.[33]

What Bergson brought into philosophy was a concept of the life force of nature that gave way to being religious, at least in those moments of rude health and cheerful brutality. Lewis believed that this

more modern form of nature religion would be the religion started, in a sense by Bergson [Henri Bergson] (1859–1941). His "nature religion" is particularly evident in his *Matière et Mémoire* (1896) and *L'Évolution Creatice* (1907) (but he repented and died Christian) and carried on in more popular form by Mr. Bernard Shaw.[34]

Lewis further wrote in an attack on the philosophy of creative evolutionism that "quasi-religious responses to the hypostatized abstraction Life are to be sought in Shaw or Wells or in a highly poetical philosopher such as Bergson, not in the papers or lectures of biologists."[35] Lewis found Shaw's myth of the life force in *Back to Methuselah* comically senile. It was "not the work of a prophet or pioneer ushering in a new reign. . . . Admirable fun, but not of a new epoch brought to birth."[36]

When one considers, as Pascal did, the awesome nature of the cosmos, Lewis argued, we discover that the Christian need not fear the giant universe and personal decay or imminent self-destruction. "It is the creative evolutionist, the Bergsonian or Shavian, or the communist, who should tremble when he looks up at the night sky. For he really is committed to a sinking ship." Elsewhere, Lewis indicated that the intelligentsia—men such as Maritain and Bergson—were coming over to Christianity.[37]

This mythology of creative evolution ("Life must not cease"), begun in Keats and Wagner, is merely "the religion of the Twentieth Century," but already it wanes.[38] The idea of the life force, Lewis argued, is "the greatest achievement of wishful thinking the world has ever seen. All the thrills of religion and none of the cost."[39] Lewis wrote sarcastically of Shaw's life force that "all pictures yet offered us of the superman are so unattractive that one might well vow celibacy at once to avoid the risk of begetting him."[40] (After a lecture on "Culture and Coming Peril," Chesterton was asked: "Is George Bernard Shaw a coming peril?" "Heavens, no," replied Chesterton, "he is a disappearing pleasure."[41])

For Bergson, comedy arose from "something mechanical encrusted on the living. We laugh every time a person gives us the impression of being a thing." The chief virtue of life was the freedom and flexibility of being alive. Therefore, the person who was fixed or unchanging or mechanical in his pride or in his office was potentially funny. Whenever anyone became inflexible, or *inelastic*, like a puppet or a clockwork machine, she became funny as a violation of free, living, human spontaneity. Like Freud, Bergson recognized the comic as a fundamental discrepancy. For him the discrepancy that existed was between the superior human organism and his mechanical universe. "A situation is invariably comic," wrote Bergson, "when it belongs simultaneously to two altogether independent series of events and is capable of being interpreted in two entirely different meanings at the same time."[42]

Several principles of comedy filtered down from Bergson to Lewis, particularly this notion of the mechanical encrusted on the living as the source of humor. Just as humans become funny when they act like robots, so machines will become funny when they act like creatures with their own wills and wiles. In *Surprised by Joy*, Lewis recorded that inanimate things resisted or opposed him. This led to a belief that the universe was evil, malevolent, or at least mischievous. There was "a settled expectation that everything would do what you did not want it to do. Whatever you wanted to remain straight, would bend; whatever you wanted to bend would fly back to the straight; all knots which you wished to be firm would become untied; all knots you wanted to untie would remain firm."[43] It was as if a hostile world conspired to do in a fellow (as in the film comedies of Buster Keaton and early Woody Allen) or that the world was actually inhabited by leprechauns and pixies.

People will continue laughing at the actual pain and misfortune of others, such as those who once amused themselves in bearbaiting, cockfighting, or public executions, or even those in the nineteenth century who diverted themselves by visiting insane asylums to taunt the inmates. Yet one is persuaded by the truth of this theory of the laughing superior more so when one is the victim rather than the perpetrator. The prophet Elisha, jeered at by forty-two boys for being an old baldhead, is in good company with all whose infirmities are laughed at. But in a violently comic reversal, Elisha, having the superior power to curse, called out two she-bears who mauled the mocking brats.

Suffering from the death of his wife, Joy, Lewis saw God as a cosmic sadist. "Fate (or whatever it is) delights to produce a great capacity and then frustrate it. Beethoven went deaf. By our standards a mean joke; the monkey trick of a spiteful imbecile."[44] Lewis once feared that the Cross was "a vile practical joke that succeeded."[45] Perhaps suffering and pain invite dark laughter, even the insane laughter of Kafka or Sartre. The bare act of laughing at the cruelty may give one a temporary advantage, to laugh at death with some tragic, heroic craziness.

Bergson's and Hobbes's explanations of the superiority theory were insufficient, however, to humorists Max Eastman, G. K. Chesterton, and James Beattie. Eastman questioned Bergson's notion of the presence of hostility in all laughter by asking whether babies felt derisive. With *ad hominem* wit, Eastman wondered if Bergson not only had never seen a baby, but whether he had ever been one. Chesterton challenged the theory along the same lines:

> It may well be questioned whether some of the explanations [of laughter] are not too crude even for the crudest origins; that they hardly apply even to the savage and certainly do not apply to the child. It has been suggested, for example, that all laughter had its origin in a sort of cruelty, in an exultation over the pain or ignominy of an enemy; but it is very hard even for the most imaginative psychologist to believe that when a baby bursts out laughing at the image of the cow jumping over the moon, he is really finding pleasure in the probability of the cow breaking her leg when she comes down again.[46]

James Beattie argued that if laughter flowed out of pride and a sense of superiority over others, then the rich, powerful, strong, and beautiful must spend their lives in paroxysms of laughter as they consider the poor, weak, feeble, and homely. And if we laugh because of a perceived eminency of our present state compared to ourselves formerly, we would continually break up into guffaws and merriment as we reflect upon our childhood and the absurdity of our dreams.

Beattie mocked Hobbes's ideas, suggesting that if wit is based on superiority, then "Sir Isaac Newton must have been the greatest wag of his time."[47] The weakness of the superiority theory is that it is more than just a superior perspective that evokes our laughter. Chesterton subverts the illogic of this explanation, observing,

> It is surely obvious that it is not merely at the fact of something being hurt that we laugh (as I trust we do) when a Prime Minister sits down on his hat. If that were so we should laugh whenever we saw a funeral. We do not laugh at the mere fact of something falling down; there is nothing humorous about leaves falling or the sun going down. When our house falls down we do not laugh. All the birds of the air might drop around us in a perpetual shower like hailstorm without arousing a smile.[48]

Because laughter is sometimes derisive does not mean that it always is. That the tongue is wicked is no surprise. But that bitter waters come out in our speech does not mean there is never any sweetness. Lewis agreed that while much laughter with our friends comes at their expense, much more is directed at the unexpected minor comedies that all our lives share, such as the story of melted butter and the mess it made on one of Lewis's walking tours. Lewis and his friends had packed breads, cheeses, and butter in their walking packs and suffered a tiring, windy, hot trek. Finally exhausted, they "crouched under a scrannel gorse bush wherever prickles and sheep dung left a space, and produced our scanty and squalid meal. The appearance of the butter faintly cheered us (all of us except the man among whose socks and pajamas it had travelled), but it was a sight that moved mirth, not appetite."[49]

The theory of incongruity best explains Lewis's view of laughter. Based on a view of human nature as being created in two original incongruous states, dust of the earth/the breath of God and male/female, laughter was a peculiarly human (and therefore, for Lewis, rational) phenomenon. He agreed with philosopher Arthur Schopenhauer, who wrote of laughter as involving an escape from the oppressive "Dame Reason." The fact that laughter springs from this escape was, for Lewis, a tribute to the ultimate authority of Reason: Only in juxtaposition to her can anything be incongruous and, therefore, funny. Nonsense is funny because we have sense. The topsy-turvy is comic because we usually stand topsy.

Several other philosophers have testified to this juxtaposition of unlikely ideas as a cause of the comic response. One particularly significant inspiration of Bergson's ideas regarding humor was Blaise Pascal, a firm apologist for the church, reason, and satire. Pascal noted in a passing thought that "nothing produces laughter more than a surprising disproportion between that which one expects and that which one sees."[50] He wrote that, for example, "two faces which resemble each other makes us laugh, when together, by their resemblance, though neither of them by itself makes us laugh."[51] Schopenhauer expanded on this quality: "The cause of laughter in every case is simply the sudden perception of the incongruity between a concept and the real objects which have been thought through in some relation, and laughter itself is just the expression of this incongruity."[52]

In 1819, the Unitarian William Hazlitt lectured on this same theme: incongruity as the basis of wit and humor. (One lecture, "On Reading Old Books," in which he attacked women for wanting books like fashions, seems to have been the model for Lewis's essay of the same title.) Categories of the laughable and the ludicrous arose from simple surprise and contrast between expectation and event and from the sudden, accidental incongruity of what was customary or desirable. Even those things that were contrary to sense and reason—the ridiculous things—were rooted in a recognizable departure from what they ought to be. Incongruity occurred when one idea disconnected from another, or one feeling was jostled against another. It was, essentially, seeing one thing from a second perspective. Incongruity lurks most everywhere, especially in the nature of human beings themselves. Hazlitt found the most substantial example of this comic incongruity in the corpulent character of Falstaff, "one who manures and nourishes his mind with jests as he does his body with sack and sugar. . . . [In Falstaff] we behold the fullness of spirit, of wit and humor bodily."[53] Falstaff, like all of us, is incongruity incarnate, for the human, wrote Hazlitt, "is the only animal that laughs and weeps, for he is the only animal that is struck with the difference between what things are, and what they ought to be."[54]

Hazlitt's comic muse operated on this premise to unveil to men and women the comedy (and tragedy) of their peculiar situation. "In a certain stage of society, men may be said to vegetate like trees, and to become rooted to the soil in which they grow. They have no idea of anything beyond themselves." Thus, lawyers know only lawyers; accountants know only accountants; and professors know only professors. The good comic writer will take advantage of this "mixed and solid mass of ignorance, folly, pride, and prejudice" to hold up a mirror to the nearsighted blokes. "The proper object of ridicule," Hazlitt taught, "is egotism." So the comic muse must unmask our self-centeredness and teach "us to see ourselves as others see us."[55] Rigidity is loosened, folly is instructed, and pride is humbled though the vehicle of laughter— laughter at our vices and ourselves. Our disguises have been penetrated by the eyes least likely to see through them—our own laughing eyes. What silliness was concealed ultimately will be made known; what folly was whispered in the cellar will be shouted from the housetop.

"Humor involves a sense of proportion and a power of seeing yourself from the outside," Lewis explained.[56] The hidden joke becomes clear and funny, when one has eyes to see and ears to hear the naked truth about oneself. The sudden revelation of the incongruity of the self, of its inherent schizophrenia, can overwhelm one with inexorable tragedy or blessed comedy. To see the painful crack in the soul may aggravate lamentations before waking laughter.

Incongruity shows that something is not right with this world. That we hold certain expectations of what is right, both logically and morally, can be seen in our response to things that are not quite right. We appeal to standards of rightness, propriety, appropriateness. And an unexpected contrast or a sudden division between what is normal and expected and what is actual can produce laughter. "Once accept the Christian doctrine that a man was originally a unity and that the present division is unnatural, [and] all the phenomena fall into place. It would be fantastic to suggest that the doctrine was devised to explain our enjoyment of a chapter in Rabelais. . . . It does so none the less."[57] We laugh, then, because we see the incongruity of what we were made to be and what we actually are.

Such recognition brings either despair or laughter. In contrast to his own existentialist despair, Kafka saw in Chesterton something supernaturally different. Lewis wrote: "Kafka himself had not only read Chesterton's novels but admired them. He is quoted as having said that 'he is so gay, one might almost believe he had found God.'"[58] Chesterton believed God had found him, and he saw God as the standard against which His creatures were not only pitiful, but hilarious.

> If you really ask yourself why we laugh at a man sitting down suddenly in the street you will discover that the reason is not only recondite, but ultimately religious. All the jokes about men sitting down on their hats are really theological jokes; they are concerned with the Dual Nature of Man. They refer to the primary paradox that man is superior to all the things around him and yet is at their mercy.[59]

Lewis believed the laughter that springs from the joke proper "turns on sudden perception of incongruity."[60] And here there are not sufficient categories to describe all the jocular varieties of comic incongruities that can be had. There are wit and wordplay, comic insult and banter, surprises, taboos, nonsense, bawdiness; human beings make jokes of so many things it is impossible to list them all. Even on Malacandra, Lewis's hero Ransom encountered three separate species, each of which had their own distinct variety of humor.

> He learned . . . of Malacandrian humour and of the noises that
> expressed it. . . . Apparently the comic spirit arose chiefly from the
> meeting of the different kinds of *hmau*. The jokes of all three were
> equally incomprehensible to him. He thought he could see differ-
> ences in kind—as that the *sorns* seldom got beyond irony, while the
> *hrossa* were extravagant and fantastic, and the *pfifltriggi* were sharp
> and excelled in abuse—but even when he understood all the words
> he could not see the points.[61]

In the chapters that follow we will browse through some of the many incongruities that C. S. Lewis saw as the source of good jokes. We will look first of all at wit because the laughter of incongruity most naturally found in Lewis took that form. I hope, however, that the following section does not dissect wit too much and leave the poor readers without laughter, or worse, witless. For under an etymological microscope, we will see some fascinating ideas but few funny germs. Let the reader be forewarned.

22

Wit and Wordplay

Wit's an unruly engine, wildly striking
Sometimes a friend, sometimes the engineer.
—George Herbert

A brief, diversionary word study must be made before we further explore the wit of C. S. Lewis. We do so at Lewis's advice, for he said, "If a man had time to study the history of one word only, *wit* would perhaps be the best word he could choose."[1] For Lewis the semanticist, this word bubbles over with several lively possible meanings, and if we assume it to mean only clever and quick repartee we are apt to misunderstand its older uses. But a study of wit's etymology is important to us for another reason: it provides the rational roots of Lewis's understanding of the joke proper.

The oldest sense of the word *wit* indicated the basic good sense common to all rational creatures. The Anglo-Saxon *wit* or *gewit* referred to mind, reason, and intelligence. "Rational creatures are those to whom God has given wit."[2] To lose one's wits was to become irrational. Hamlet, for example, could not give a wholesome or sane answer to Rosencrantz and Guildenstern because his "wit's diseased" (*Hamlet*, 3.2.330). In medieval psychology, "common wit" is common sense (*communis sensus*). Without it, one would be not just dull, but truly witless—without a mind.

The old psychology, with its Aristotelian heritage of classifying and categorizing, established five outward and five inward wits. The five outward wits are what we now recognize as the five senses. "The five inward wits were originally memory, estimation, fancy, imagination, and common wit (or common sense)." People differed from one another in these latter kinds of wits, each person's wit having its own cast, bent, or temper: one quick and another plodding, one solid and another showy, one ingenious and inventive and another accurate and retentive. While we speak today of having skeptical or credulous, creative or analytic "minds," one once spoke of wits as meaning "types of mind, or 'mentalities,' or the people who have them."[3] The minds, or types of wits, distinguished one person from another. If one type of wit shone above the others, it became the dominant and honored meaning for the word *wit*.

Wit has no small relation to the Latin word *ingenium*. In Cicero and Quintilian, *ingenium* clearly means something like "memory ability"—high intellectual activity, cleverness, and quickness to learn. Such characteristics were tools of the ancient rhetor's trade. In the courts, before the legislature, or during a ceremonial celebration, an orator was honored if he could invent and deliver a persuasive speech. *Ingenium*, then, "really means something more like 'talent' or even 'genius.'" Wit eventually came to mean this, as Shakespeare writing of "the wits of former days" refers to "those writers of talent or genius who flourished before his time." What was being discussed here was the quality of imagination. This wit was ingenious or imaginative, as in Dryden's maxim, "Great wits are sure to madness near allied."[4] Indeed, too much wit, too much imagination, and one was thought to be in danger of a dash of insanity. Such a case would be, as Chesterton diagnosed, what happens when an ambitiously logical man tries to comprehend the universe and fit the whole world under his hat: his head explodes.[5]

To the extent that we have traced it so far, *wit-ingenium* does not yet contain an idea of a joke or of anything funny. Lewis challenged a Professor Empson on this point, because the latter saw a witticism, in the contemporary sense, behind every use of the word *wit* in Pope's *Essay on Criticism*. The "patriarch wits" who survived a thousand years do not include only Aristophanes and Lucian, but also Homer, Sophocles, and Virgil. Lewis proved his point with an exegesis of Nicolas Boileau's famous couplet from *L'Art Poetique*: "Some have at first for wits, then poets passed, / Turn'd critics next, and proved plain fools at last."[6]

Lewis pointed out that the rhetorical structure here demands that each of the steps—from wits to poets, poets to critics, and finally critics to fools (and finally, as one wag said, to lawyers)—is a descent. The people involved are becoming worse and worse. Therefore, if "wits" meant merely jokesters, the meaning of the couplet would be ruined. Lewis asked Professor Empson if Pope's work (similar to Boileau's) does not "become plain when—but only when—we take *wit* as *wit-ingenium*? Some have at first passed for men of genius; then for authors (or literary craftsmen); then for critics; and finally have proved fools."[7] Thus, Lewis was able to show that, at least up until Pope's day, the word *wit* was as yet not associated with humor.

It was not until the second half of the seventeenth century that the contemporary meaning of wit came into wide use. The drift of the word's meaning toward its modern understanding is witnessed by an abundant and amusing amount of evidence—amusing, Lewis pointed out, because the change in meaning consists "almost entirely of disclaimers. Everyone starts telling us what the word does not mean; a sure proof that it is beginning to mean just that." Various authors warned against the many invented definitions of what wit was coming to mean. For instance, wit should not mean "*conceits*, things that sound like the knacks or toyes of ordinary *Epigrammatists*" (Davenport); "clenches (puns), quibbles, gingles, and such like trifles" (Flecknoe); and "the jerk or stink of an epigram nor the seeming contradiction of a poor antitheses . . . the jingle of a more poor paronomasia (Dryden)."[8]

Lewis also cited Shadwell's preface to *The Sullen Lovers*, attempting to correct his ignorant audience who believed "that all the Wit in Playes consisted in bringing two persons upon the Stage to break Jests, and to bob one another, which they call Repartie." Shadwell, Dryden, Davenport, and other critics sought vainly to stem the disintegration of wit's meaning into what Dryden in his "Defence of the Epilogue" called "the lowest and most groveling kind of wit." Yet Lewis showed that these zealous grammarians themselves used wit in the same way when their guard was down. In *Dramatic Poesy*, Dryden himself wrote: "As for comedy, repartee is one of its chief graces; the greatest pleasure of the audience is a chance of wit, kept up on both sides and swiftly managed." When Dryden was "out of school," he often talked and wrote like the "vulgar judges" he sought to rebuke, slipping in and out of the various meanings without noticing. Lewis observed that this sort of slipping in and out of various meanings for a word is a common human tendency. "You and I at nine o'clock any morning, poring over the penciled washing bill presented by our bedmakers, complain 'I can't read the last figure.' At ten, during a supervision, we mention a figure (of rhetoric). At our elevenses we say to a friend that the young woman who has just left the tap-room has a fine figure. So then."[9]

Lewis saw that Dryden, Pope, and others were fighting a losing battle in their attempt to make wit mean what they wanted it to mean, much like Humpty Dumpty in *Through the Looking Glass* tells Alice that she can make words mean what she wants them to mean. Nevertheless, their good grammatical intentions (the road to syntactical hell is paved with such) were turned away, happily, said Lewis, by the grander, broader, more democratic popular use of the common people. What Dryden defined as "propriety of thought and words" in his "The Author's Apology," and Pope, in his *Essay on Criticism*, specified as "True Wit" ("True Wit is Nature to advantage dress'd. / What oft was thought but ne'er so well express'd") became, despite their protests, more and more closely aligned in the public's mind with Cowley's view, that wit "depends on the unexpected thought which yokes together 'things by nature most unneighborly.'"[10]

For Lewis, the "dangerous sense" of any word is the meaning that lies uppermost in the popular mind: "Whenever we meet the word, our natural impulse will be to give it that sense. When this operation results in nonsense, of course, we see our mistake and try over again. But if it makes tolerable sense our tendency is to go merrily on. We are often deceived." This process is dangerous because it easily comes to

dominate how we interpret many words. For our purposes the dangerous sense of *wit* is "that sort of mental agility or gymnastic which uses
language as the principal equipment on its gymnasium." Wit stands
on stage in the ordinary small change of conversation in which puns,
epigrams, and distorted proverbs or quotations are all *witty*. Thus,
"Lady Dorothy Neville's protest to the cook ('you cannot serve cod
and salmon')" is a *witty* extension of Jesus's warning against trying to
serve God and mammon.[11]

This currently dominant sense of wit is closely knit to the oldest
sense of rationality and good sense. One's intelligence "impresses other
people most and is most talked about if he displays it in conversation.
But no way of displaying it in conversation will be so obvious or so
attractive to most hearers as repartee, epigram, and general dexterity.
Thus, in Shakespeare's *Much Ado About Nothing*, the lovers Benedick
and Beatrice "never meet but there's a skirmish of wit between them."[12]
The battle is both between their brains (wit, old sense) and their quick
and clever mental gymnastics (wit, dangerous sense). So, too, wit could
mean both being wise and being funny as in Falstaff's claim, "I am not
only witty in myself but the cause that wit is in other men."[13] Lewis
explains that "the wit displayed by the other men was, as the context
shows, the 'invention' of things that 'tend to laughter.'"[14] One shows
one's wit and intelligence by showing one's wittiness.

The happy ending for the word *wit* is that it is defined by what it is
in practice. In the *Spectator*, Addison wrote that wit is not merely "the
assemblage of ideas . . . where in can be found any resemblance or con-
gruity," because "every resemblance of ideas is not that which we call
wit, unless it be such an one that gives delight and surprise." Therefore,
what this etymological trail finally brings us to is Lewis's conception
of wit in its most useful senses: it now means "the unexpected, the
lively, the dexterous." If disliked, wit is liable to be called "cleverness"
or "fireworks"; if liked, "intelligence," "astuteness." In the patriarchal
European tradition this could lead to a castigation of the wicked wit of
the West. However, Lewis did note a "conception of wit as something

with a very wide range (from the *Nocturnall upon D. Lucies Day* to *The Importance of Being Earnest*), but also with a continuity within that range."[15] He allowed wit to be that rational faculty that enables us to relate seemingly disparate things so as to excite laughter or amuse. For Lewis, it is the foundation for the joke proper, because it grounds incongruity in rational understanding.

23

The Word Made Joke

The world has joked incessantly for over fifty centuries,
And every joke that's possible has long ago been made.
—W. S. GILBERT

Wit and the joke proper have their genesis in the art of speech. The word gives birth to wit. It not only permits but also encourages the free playful expression of ideas, of contradiction, and surprises. Perhaps nowhere in literature is there such ontological connection between speech and jokes than in Lewis's creation of Narnia. Aslan, the great lion, bestows the gift of speech upon his dumb creatures, ushering in the possibility of the joke:

> "Creatures, I give you yourselves," said the strong, happy voice of Aslan. . . . "I give you the woods, the fruits, the rivers. I give you the stars and I give you myself. The Dumb Beasts whom I have not chosen are yours also. Treat them gently and cherish them but do not go back to their ways lest you cease to be Talking Beasts. For out of them you were taken and into them you can return. Do not so." "No, Aslan, we won't, we won't," said everyone. But one perky Jackdaw added in a loud voice, "No fear!" and everyone else had finished just before he said it so that his words came out quite clear in a dead silence; and perhaps you have found out how awful that can be—say, at a party. The Jackdaw became so embarrassed that it hid its head under its wing as if it was going to sleep. And all the other animals began making various queer noises which are their way of laughing and which, of course, no one has ever heard in our world.[1]

When the jackdaw asks if he has just made the first joke of Narnia, the lion answers: "'No, little friend, you have not *made* the first joke; you have only been the first joke.' Then everyone laughed more than ever; but the Jackdaw didn't mind and laughed just as loud till the horse shook his head and the Jackdaw lost its balance and fell off, but remembered its wings (they were still new to it) before it reached the ground."[2]

Significantly, it is in this original state of innocence that the first joke arrives with speech. The humor comes with the "humanity" of the beasts and manifests itself with appropriate humility. (Of Lewis's own self-effacing humor, it may not be too much of a stretch to connect "Jack" Lewis with this Narnian jackdaw. In a letter to his friend, Arthur Greeves, Lewis reported on a memorable event of having tea at a little village inn, where he discovered "glory of glories—an old tame jackdaw hopping about our feet and asking for crumbs. He is called Jack and will answer to his name."[3])

As wit and intelligence are bestowed upon these creatures, so, too, arrive wittiness, jokes, and laughter. The new creation of Narnia roars and guffaws with innocence. No malice or mean mischief mars the participants of the jokes. In the Edenic Perelandra, there is a freedom of laughter, to laugh and to be laughed at. When the Green Lady first sees Ransom, or, as she calls him because of his half-tanned condition, "Piebald," she laughs like a child. She is puzzled when Ransom does not join in, and the next day she announces: "I was young yesterday . . . when I laughed at you. Now I know that the people in your world do not like to be laughed at."[4] Indeed, the sin of earth sours the self's ability to be laughed at. Pride protests against being an object of laughter. But not so of innocence, as the Jackdaw and the Green Lady illustrate.

In Lewis's writing and conversation, the exercise of wit is seen most clearly in the context of conversation, both real and fictional. Wit includes wordplay. Lewis's wordplay both inhabits and decorates his writings. The witty dwells in his playful works as well as in his more serious discussions. Puns, epigrams, proverbs, and many small witticisms crept into both. Take, for example, the following informal (and some would say degenerating) discussion. In it Lewis and his friends Kingsley Amis and Brian Aldiss discuss a book entitled *Flatland*. Lewis has just pointed out the pun in the name of the author of the work: "A. Square."

> **LEWIS:** But of course the word "square" hadn't the same sense then.
>
> **ALDISS:** It's like the poem by Francis Thompson that ends "She gave me tokens three, a look, a word of her winsome mouth, and a sweet wild raspberry"; there again the meaning has changed. It really was a wild raspberry in Thompson's day. (Laughter.)
>
> **LEWIS:** Or the lovely one about the Bishop of Exeter, who was giving the prizes at a girls' school. They did a performance of *A Midsummer Night's Dream*, and the poor man stood up afterwards and made a speech and said (piping voice): "I was very interested in your delightful performance, and among other things I was very interested in seeing for the first time in my life a female Bottom." (Guffaws.)[5]

This type of wordplay and double entendre delighted Lewis. Semantic ambiguity gives birth to all manner of wit. Lewis offered, for instance, the phrase "Freud's psychology." It might mean, he commented dryly, "either a subject of which we have all heard much or one which, some would say, has been examined too little."[6]

The difference between what a word means and what a speaker means when she uses it often results in incongruities, malapropisms, or double entendres. Lewis enjoyed telling the anecdote of the nature-loving woman who walked on a road "untouched by the hand of man."[7] Lewis always was quick to catch the incongruity and to freshen up old usages of language to humorous advantage. He could be especially mischievous toward Americans in this regard. On one occasion, after many cups of tea, an American visitor, Father Walter Hooper, asked Lewis to show him to "the bathroom." "Lewis rose and led him to the bathroom, threw towels on the floor, and politely closed the door. A tub there was in the room, but nowhere was there a toilet. 'Well, sir, that will break you of those silly euphemisms,' roared Lewis with laughter."[8] Martin Moynihan compares Lewis with Chesterton in the ability to repossess or reappropriate an old phrase or image "to fresh advantage."

> I experienced something of this in the war: The *reeking tubes* you saw them reek. In this respect too, Lewis reminds me of what is told of Chesterton. You would see G.K.C. smile, then make a quick sketch; then look at the sketch he'd made—then smile again, indeed shake with suppressed laughter.[9]

If jokes and puns are weapons, they are only snowballs used to surprise, and perhaps wet, an enemy. For this reason Chesterton defended the human habit of punning. He complained that "many moderns suffer from the disease of the suppressed pun."

> I for one greatly prefer the sort of frivolity that is thrown to the surface like froth to the sort of frivolity that festers under the surface like slime. To pelt an enemy with a foolish pun or two will never do him any grave injustice; the firework is obviously a firework and not a deadly fire. It may be playing to the gallery, but even the gallery knows it is only playing.[10]

For his part, Lewis appreciated the play on words in a pun, but most especially when it was unintentional. Because words can mean several things at once, it is the context that provides an insulating power against the ambiguity of a word or phrase. The normal expectation of meaning is disrupted by comic semantic chaos. A "sudden transition from one meaning to the other," wrote Lewis, "would affect most speakers like a pun."[11]

What seems to me certain is that in ordinary language the sense of
a word is governed by the context and this sense normally excludes
all others from the mind. When we see the notice "Wines and
Spirits" we do not think about angels, devils, ghosts and fairies—
nor about the "spirits" of the older medical theory. . . . The proof of
this is that the sudden intrusion of any irrelevant sense—in other
words the voluntary or involuntary pun—is funny. It is funny
because it is unexpected. There is a semantic explosion because
the two meanings rush together from a great distance; one of
them was not in our consciousness at all till that moment. If it had
been, there would be no denotation. This comes out very clearly
in those numerous stories which decorum forbids me to recall (in
print); stories where some august person such as a headmistress or
a bishop, on a platform, gravely uses a word in one sense, blissfully
forgetful of some other and very unsuitable sense—producing a
ludicrous indecency. It will usually be found that the audience,
like the speaker, had till then quite forgotten it, too. For the shouts
of open, or the sibilations of suppressed, laughter do not usually
begin at once but after several seconds. The obscene intruder, the
uninvited semantic guest, has taken that time to come up from the
depths where he lay asleep, off duty.[12]

The intentional pun, to Lewis, was a simple intellectual game,
something he saw as a mere linguistic play upon the "homophonic status
of different uses of a word." Arthur Greeves's misuse of "bare" for "bear"
amused Lewis, who commented that his passage "I find it more difficult
to bare myself lovingly toward my neighbors" drew an unsurpassable
picture of Greeves "baring himself 'lovingly.'"[13] In his *Studies on Words*,
Lewis pointed out the comic potential of dual meanings: "If you said
'Jeremy Taylor can boast the longest sentence of any writer' and someone replied 'Poor Wilde had a longer one,' this would be a pure pun."[14]
     Lewis argued for the "half-punning antithesis of sense and sensi-
bility . . . preserved the title of Jane Austen's novel," as the root of sense

evolved into two meanings. For example, in Henry Fielding's novel, it is hard to maintain that "Sophia by being 'sensible and tender' where Tom Jones was concerned showed her good sense."[15]

Often puns are not necessarily funny, but perhaps only witty. Lewis cited "an old Greek semi-pun on *soma* and *sama* that the body is the soul's tomb."[16] One would not slap one's knee as much as stop and reflect on the relation. Lewis explained the workings of such wit in a letter: "I was maintaining yesterday that when a bifurcation of meaning is sufficiently old and wide, the resulting senses often enter the linguistic consciousness of each new generation as mere homophones, and their reunion has the explosion of a pun."[17] Lewis's protagonist in *Perelandra* reflects upon his name and his predicament: "To connect the name Ransom (from Ranolf's son) with the act of ransoming would have been for him a mere pun."[18]

In a similar way, literalisms may also produce a comic picture. If we were to regard all language as exact and precise, we would find ourselves stumbling into a wonderland of humor. Children often stumble into it. Lewis recalled that as a child he "evolved the theory that a candlestick was so called 'because it makes the candle stick up!'"[19] The metaphorical quality of language leads to this type of mischievous playfulness in communication. To take a metaphor literally is to invite laughter. As Lewis pointed out, when in the course of an argument a man says, "I follow you," he "does not mean he is walking behind you along a road."[20]

Like animals, some people tend to take everything literally—and a joke is symbolic. "You will have noticed that most dogs cannot understand *pointing*. You point to a bit of food on the floor: the dog, instead of looking at the floor, sniffs at your finger. A finger is a finger to him, and that is all. His world is all fact and no meaning."[21] The doglike mind cannot take in a joke. (And Lewis was not above being doggy-minded.) In a letter to a large American family of children on the birth of their new baby sister, Lewis wrote that he had never seen a picture of a baby shower before, and joked: "I had to put up my umbrella to look at it."[22]

The literal phrase can also provide a double meaning in an ambiguous context. In *The Last Battle* Lewis put a bittersweet double entendre in the mouths of Eustace and Jill when they arrive unexpectedly back in Narnia. Magically they feel: "This is really Narnia at last."[23] And it was. This was Narnia at last: they had finally returned, and they had returned during its final days.

It is a politician's or an evangelist's *façon de parler* to speak in hyperbole. Or, as Lewis wrote about the human habit of communicating with hyperbole: "Such is the human passion for exaggeration that even the *world*, on occasion, will not satisfy it." We speak of having a world of fun, or of a young man thinking the world of a young woman. Chaucer's Troilus doubts the hyperbole by declaring, "I'd like it better than this world twice over, than two such worlds." Even Johnson, in writing that he had "undeceived the world about the ghost story," means he "undeceived" a few hundred people. "The hyperbole talks of some men as if they were all men." Hyperbole of language extends comic imagination, such as in phrases like a villainous house of fleas or a villainous smell.[24]

People often do not literally mean what they are saying, which, consequently, makes the literal interpretation of it funny. Chesterton pointed out that much of the "theological" profanity we hear falls in this category.

I have known some people of very modern views driven by their distress to the use of theological terms to which they attached no doctrinal significance, merely because a drawer was jammed tight and they could not pull it out. A friend of mine was particularly afflicted in this way. Every day his drawer was jammed, and every day in consequence it was something else that rhymes to it. But I pointed out to him that this sense of wrong was really subjective and relative; it rested entirely upon the assumption that the drawer could, should, and would come out easily. "But if," I said, "you picture to yourself that you are pulling against some powerful and oppressive enemy, the struggle will become merely exciting and not exasperating. Imagine that you are tugging up a lifeboat out of the sea. Imagine that you are roping up a fellow-creature out of an Alpine crevasse. Imagine even that you are a boy again and engaged in a tug-of-war between French and English." Shortly after saying this I left him; but I have no doubt my words bore the best possible fruit. I have no doubt that every day of his life he hangs on to the handle of that drawer with a flushed face and eyes bright with battle, uttering encouraging shouts to himself, and seeming to hear all around him the roar of an applauding ring.[25]

Chesterton's essay points out the impotence of modern language, one of the symptoms of which, unfortunately, is an increasing scarcity of real wit. In its place we have the idle swear word, repeated over and over whatever the situation, until it is meaningless. The theological words among them, like *damn* or *hell*, have lost much of their eschatological and Christian significance since the absence of religion as a primary force in many lives has long ago emptied such words of their power. There is some humor yet to be found in their use, however, since "the man who says 'Damn that chair!' does not really wish that it should first be endowed with an immortal soul and then sent to eternal perdition."[26] Inflation of language has taken such words and made them mere spontaneous hyperboles of a heated temper. "Those who have no belief in damnation—and some who have—now damn inanimate objects which would on any view be ineligible for it," Lewis pointed out.[27] Such theological cursings are so common and so little understood by their users that they cease to be profane.

Their use is overshadowed, anyway, in this post-Freudian age by sexual curses. Instead of damning others and consigning them to everlasting fire, we now order them to perform an incredibly acrobatic sexual act, often requiring that they do it to themselves. This has taken the place of wit, of creative repartee today, much to our loss.

Comic Techniques and Topics

It is the business of a comic poet to paint the vices and follies of human kind.
—WILLIAM CONGREVE

Linguistic joking parades a throng of comic bits and techniques other than the well-known swarms of puns and literalisms. A clear indication of what Lewis thought was comic rises out of what his fictional characters laugh at (and, at the same time, we understand what kinds of characters they are by what they find laughable). All of Lewis's characters laugh—in Narnia and on Malacandra and Perelandra, in purgatory, in heaven, and on earth.

Perhaps the characters who laugh most are children. In this respect the things Narnian children laugh at differ little from what actual children laugh at. One obvious source of laughter spins off of physical appearance. In *The Lion, the Witch, and the Wardrobe*, when Edmund first meets the odd-looking, white-bearded, old professor, for instance, he tries to stifle his laughter. He pretends to blow his nose to hide the fact that he's giggling at the sight of the strange old man. The contrast of abnormal-sized people (anyone over five feet six, for example) to normal-sized people (I stand a good five feet five) is a sure cause of laughter, such as if a dwarf groom were to marry a giant bride. (Need I say it? My wife is five feet ten.) Lewis appreciated this type of comedy too. Odd sizes or unfamiliar appearances that strike one as foreign can elicit laughter. In the creation of Narnia, the Jackdaw suggests that the human Uncle Andrew and the children might be the second joke, as they appeared incongruous to this fresh, ripe new world of Talking Beasts.

The good giants in Narnia stand in comic contrast to the tiny things in that land—whether small mice like Reepicheep, or Lucy's handkerchief (or Lucy mistaken for a handkerchief!), or even the giants' own tiny brains. As Mr. Tumnus, the faun, confided, he never knew a giant that was very clever.

Narnian mice, long whiskered and long tailed, are dashing, martial creatures, but their size invites laughter. Prince Caspian has to try hard not to laugh when he first meets these brave but minuscule subjects, because the thought comes to him that all the mice "could very easily be put in a washing basket and carried home on one's back." At the same time, King Peter will not send Reepicheep the mouse out as a marshal in combat, although he bravely volunteers, because he is so small and, consequently, laughable. An awesome centaur is sent instead, because "no one ever laughed at a Centaur."[1]

The practice of making jokes of physical appearance is ancient. Aristotle's notion that the comic is actually a species of the ugly is constrained by limits: Something is comic only if it has the mere appearance of ugliness or pain, but not if these qualities are actual. True deformity and true ugliness are not comic because they are too real and painful. In Lewis's fiction, good characters usually do not joke meanly about others or demean them with cruel humor.

This distinction is maintained in Lewis's fiction, in which only the characters who are wicked laugh at true deformity or another's pain. In Lewis's *Till We Have Faces*, the King cruelly abuses Orual, the eldest of his three daughters, because of her ugliness. He calls her "curdface" and shouts murderous jokes like "don't come here to sour the morning drink for the men." Asked whether his daughter should be veiled when a new queen is coming, the King replies: "'Need you ask?' . . . with one of his great laughs, jerking his thumb in [Orual's] direction. 'Do you think I want my queen frightened out of her senses? Veils of course. And good thick veils too.'"[2]

Often only a thin line separates comedy from becoming wrong, frightful, or painful. Lewis's fictional characters know this. The eldest of the Pevensie children, Peter, tells his siblings that stories, jokes, and jolly-good hoaxes can be made up for fun, as long as they are not taken too far. Jill Pole finds she can easily laugh at danger or fears if they are safely distanced. She finds it easy to laugh at acrophobia until she stands upon a dizzying precipice. She decided to "jolly well get away from that horrible edge and never laugh at anyone for not liking heights again."[3]

Lewis knew what was a joke and what wasn't. In a hotel dining room once, Lewis unexpectedly found an ally in his loathing of prunes—a six-year-old at another table. "Sympathy was instantaneous. Neither of us thought it was funny. We both knew that prunes are far too nasty to be funny."[4]

When Prince Corin taunts a prisoner in *The Horse and His Boy*, his wise father rebukes him for being unjust. In that same book, however, while Corin was visiting a foreign enemy country, "a boy in the street made a beastly joke about Queen Susan."[5] Corin righteously defended her honor by knocking him down.

Large ears or a fat paunch or a long nose or a wiggle, on the other hand, are not serious sources of suffering. An Aristotelian example of the ugly pops up in the Underland in Lewis's *The Silver Chair*, in which Puddleglum, not exactly a pretty face himself, and his fellow adventurer capture a very ugly creature. "A most miserable little gnome, only about three feet long . . . [with] little pink eyes, and a mouth and chin so large and round that its face looked like that of a pigmy hippopotamus. If they had not been in such a tight place, they would have burst into laughter at the sight of it."[6]

Round, as the gnome is round, is also frequently a funny characteristic, particularly fat and round. It may or may not be a psychological fact that fat people are funnier or merrier than thin people, but it is a social perception. Endomorphic people, like Father Christmas, are seen as laughing more often and being jollier than ectomorphic people, like Dickens's Scrooge. Lewis freely bestows mirth on his small and chubby characters. Doctor Cornelius was a small, fat man, whose "voice was grave and his eyes were merry so that, until you got to know him really well, it was hard to know when he was joking and when he was serious."[7] Trumpkin, in the same story, is a fat little dwarf, who is hale and hearty and—somewhat like Lewis, perhaps—has a "bare head which was bald and extremely large, [and] shone like a gigantic billiard ball."[8] Trumpkin's donkey is a very fat little beast, too, that waddles as much as it trots. In Shasta's thinking, his newfound father, King Lune, is "the jolliest, fat, apple-cheeked twinkling-eyed King you could imagine."[9] In *Out of the Silent Planet*, Unwin (aka Ransom) delights in the hrossa children, the roly-poly cubs of the hrossa. Like puppies "they were jolly little things."[10] Even the Steward of Puritania was "an old man with a red, round face, who was very kind and full of jokes."[11]

The bulgy bears in Narnia are a variation on the theme of rotundity. They are not only funny for being so roly-poly, but also because they are clumsy, perpetually sleepy, hungry, and like to suck their paws in public (akin to humans who like to lick salt off their fingers in public). The comic laziness of the bears, wanting to sit at feasts, punctuates one of Lewis's observations: "Notice how often the actors in a comedy sit whereas those in a tragedy usually stand."[12]

Bears are the object of laughter in what is known as the Third Joke in the creation story of Narnia. One of the bears, criticizing the human Uncle Andrew who had just fainted, smugly announced: "'An Animal wouldn't just roll over like that. We're animals and we don't roll over. We stand up. Like this.' He rose to his hind legs, took a step backward, tripped over a low branch and fell flat on his back."[13] The overbearing, bumbling creature performs his own slapstick pratfall, his huffiness humbled into good humor.

The Shakespearean comic motif of mistaken identities is worked into *That Hideous Strength*, when the identities of a common tramp and ancient magician, Merlin, are confused. This time-honored device appears again in *The Horse and His Boy* at the first meeting of Shasta and his twin, Corin. Seeing their resemblance, Corin suggests: "I say: we ought to be able to get some fun out of this being mistaken for one another."[14]

Lewis seemed also to chuckle at slight senility and at the

eccentricities of those growing older. The failings of old codgers succeed as comic material. Confronted with two tousled human children, the dwarf Trumpkin is too old to be tactful: "[He] put his mouth close to the Owl's head and, no doubt, intended to whisper: but, like other deaf people, he wasn't a very good judge of his own voice, and both children heard him say, 'See that they're properly washed.'"[15]

In the same vein, errors of understanding or writing, among those without the excuse of senility, provide snickers as well. When Aslan warns that an evil had already entered the newly born Narnia, the innocent creatures misunderstand the term. "What did he say had entered the world?—A Neevil—What's a Neevil?"[16] Such puns that play on two different meanings of one sound could also appear as accidents in print. For example, Lewis's brother once sent him "a delicious printer's error in a description of a revivalist meeting in the Midlands: 'At the conclusion of the exercises, a large *crow* remained in the hall, singing *Abide with Me*.'"[17] Regarding errors of the pen, Lewis had to correct a correspondent's reading of his handwriting. He explained he had written about "*Greek*, not *great*, plays and about having a *bathe* rather than a *battle*."[18]

In addition to misunderstandings, the British are notoriously legendary for their practice of understatement. Where the French, Italian, and even American comedy would be broad, loud, and fast, the British comic would quietly, whimsically, slip on by one's consciousness. A classic example of understatement occurs in the opening of *The Lion, the Witch, and the Wardrobe*. Writing of old Professor Digory Kirke, Lewis explained that "he had no wife and he lived in a very large house with a housekeeper called Mrs. Macready and three servants. (Their names were Ivy, Margaret and Betty, but they do not come into the story much.)" Lewis passes on without so much as a twinkle in his eye, but he has pulled our legs. These three servants do not come into the story much because they never appear again.

British authors and poets could kindle wry smiles by a deliberate lack of emphasis. Lewis pointed to John Donne's seventy-ninth sermon, wherein the poet-preacher "rather comically passes favorable judgment on the style of the Omnipotent, assuring us that 'the Holy Ghost is an eloquent author.'"[19]

Proverbs offer condensed wit, brief gusts of humor. Cornered in a dangerous predicament, Swallowpad the Raven muses, "Easily in but not easily out, as the lobster said in the lobster pot!" The succinct Narnian saying contrasts with the coarser maxim of the enemy. The Tisroc tells his princely son not to kick the obsequious Vizier too much, "for as a costly jewel retains its value even if hidden in a dunghill, so old age and discretion are to be respected even in the vile persons of our subjects."[20] And in *Till We Have Faces*, the King mocks the proverbial wisdom of his Greek counselor with a pungent saying: "You'll tell me next that the best way to cure a man's headache is to cut off his head."[21]

"Suddenness is not without its comic effect," Lewis observed.[22] When improbable events occur, they carry a comic quality of being unexpected, of being a surprise. This is partly why births (and perhaps marriages) are comedies. Lewis recommended that one "think of the countless human acts, acts of copulation, spread over millennia, that led to the birth of Plato, Attila, or Napoleon," and of the begettings of Scripture that show an astonishing and amusing line of preparation for the Messiah.[23] The improbability of any person's existence is much more incredible, Lewis pointed out, than Mr. So-and-so winning the lottery.

> When you consider the immense number of meetings and fertile unions between ancestors which were necessary in order that you should be born, you perceive that it was once immensely improbable that such a person as you should come to exist: but once you are here, the report of your existence is not in the least credible.[24]

As the old joke goes, against the millions of sperms that raced to the egg, *you* won. The fact of one's birth is the comic consequence of a divinely planned lottery.

The value of comic repetition is that a phrase or word or look becomes new, fresh, and imbued with a different, and layered, significance each time it is repeated. Lewis cited the comic repetition of Molière as an example. His work

> doesn't, like Shirley, give us endless change of language and leave us exactly where we were—but takes the very same words—as he takes the misanthrope's "je ne dis pas cela" . . . and uses them over and over again and yet, at each repetition gives them a new force. . . . The funniness consists in his bobbing up irresistibly after each suppression, only to be suppressed again. The identical phrase develops a new *vis comica* in each new context.[25]

Shirley in *The Lady of Pleasure* would have invented variations on a theme—turning "round and round on the same spot like a dog that cannot make up its mind to lie down."[26] Lewis recognizes the possibilities of repetition as a comic device in that it not only reiterates a gag, drilling its presence into the audience, but it also builds upon its previous life, multiplying the joke against itself. At least four times in bracketed avuncular asides in *The Lion, the Witch, and the Wardrobe*, he cautioned children who were tempted to go into magical wardrobes "not to close the door behind them." While the repetition makes his practical point, it also concocts the character of a protective bachelor author.

As Eustace, Jill, and Puddleglum descend into the bowels of the Underland, a gloomy Earthman repeatedly intones a liturgy that many sink down into the deep realm, *and few return to the sunlit lands.*[27] Even Puddleglum sees the monotonous spokesman as a chap of one idea, harping on and on into the realm of the ridiculous. After the cataclysmic destruction at Edgestow, people unrelievedly shared their testimonies (often exaggerated) of how they escaped the chaos. The catchphrase "No, I *don't* want to hear how you got out of Edgestow" in the end became a joke.

In Lewis's worlds, those who are able to laugh at themselves will enjoy the laughter with others. On the other hand, those who live in strict control of themselves (and often others) are particularly primed for a fall from dignity. In *Prince Caspian*, such a happy disaster happens to Miss Prizzle, a Mrs. Grundy-type schoolmarm (and a cousin of sorts to Oscar Wilde's governess, Miss Prism), and her disciplined and dull history class. She regards a student's report of a lion talking as nonsense and orders two demerit marks for her. Nonsense, however, overtakes her and her class of "mostly dumpy, prim little girls with fat legs."[28] Such just desserts provide a source of triumphant jokes in Lewis's fiction.

Comic topics for Lewis included the avoidable ignorance of schoolboys and scholars, such as those who believe a new biology or new astronomy will "make a man stop hitting his daughter."[29] The ignorance of a stupid husband may result in his being cheated, but, wrote Lewis, as "cuckolds have often been ridiculed . . . it seems very hard that they should be thus scolded as well."[30] Lewis laughed as well at the ignorance of some anti-Darwinian theologies that argued that God created the fossils to deceive people.[31]

The Green Lady on Perelandra laughs at Piebald Ransom for speaking not loudly but so often. "I laughed, Piebald, because you were wondering, as I was, about this law which Maleldil has made for one world and not for another. And you had nothing to say about it and yet made the nothing up into words."[32]

Lewis's people not only laugh at others when they are stupid, however, they also laugh at what they don't want to believe or understand even when it is the truth. Caspian explained that where he had come from "the people who laughed at Aslan would have laughed at stories about talking beasts and Dwarfs."[33] If these stories were true, it would mean changing the way one lived. When the pilgrim, John, hears that there is no landlord and is persuaded of "the vastness and impudence and simplicity of the fraud which had been practiced over him," he began to laugh with relief till he was almost shaken to pieces.[34] The fool in his heart laughs at the idea of God, but it is a short-lived laughter.

Joking about another's ignorance or lack of sense depends upon the relations of the joke's participants. Among equals, such a jest provides for friendly bantering and an affectionate combat. It is a more delicate and strategic matter between those of different ranks. For example, a superior must never use humor to demean or demoralize his or her charges. The good King Lune tells his son not to scoff at the captured scoundrel, Rabadash: "Never taunt a man save when he is stronger than you: then, as you please."[35] Among equals, like a husband and wife, however, good-natured taunts can be a sign and a way of showing affection. Lewis impishly recorded that Princess Aravis and Prince Cor had many quarrels, but "they always made it up again: so that years later, when they were grown up they were so used to quarreling and making it up again that they got married so as to go on doing it more conveniently."[36] Mingled with measures of mutual love and respect, playful teasing can indeed indicate a secure relationship. In *Prince Caspian*, when Edmund continues to tease Trumpkin, calling him "Our Dear Little Friend," or "D.L.F." for short, Susan reproves him. "'That's all right, lass,' said Trumpkin with a chuckle. 'A jibe won't raise a blister.'"[37]

Of course one expects brothers and sisters to trade barbs and insults. In *Prince Caspian*, when the children are lost, Edmund mocks the female: "That's the worst of girls. . . . They never can carry a map in their heads." To which the indomitable Lucy responds to the chauvinist male: "That's because our heads have something inside them."[38] Male-female repartee also sparkles between Jill and the bewitched Prince Rilian in *The Silver Chair*. Thinking himself a knight, Prince Rilian is held captive by a serpentine lady whom he is soon to wed. "'Where I come from,' said Jill, 'they don't think much of men who are bossed about by their wives.' 'Shalt think otherwise when thou hast a man of thine own, I warrant you,' said the Knight, apparently thinking this very funny."[39]

Such whimsical—and romantic—bantering occurs also in *Voyage of the Dawn Treader* at Aslan's Table where Caspian and his crew have found three noble Narnian lords asleep. A great and beautiful lady explains the sleepers' enchantment, to which Prince Caspian responds:

> "In the world from which my friends come" (here he nodded at Eustace and the Pevensies) "they have a story of a prince or a king coming to a castle where all the people lay in an enchanted sleep. In that story he could not dissolve the enchantment until he had kissed the princess."
>
> "But here," said the girl, "it is different. Here he cannot kiss the princess till he has dissolved the enchantment."
>
> "Then," said Caspian, "in the name of Aslan, show me how to set about that work at once."[40]

The curious way of a man with a maid is too wonderful for understanding in any world. And too comic in its transparency.

Education, or lack of it, often qualifies for similar roasting from Lewis, a university don. When Mr. Beaver exclaims at a dramatic moment: "It isn't *her!*" the author pauses to comment, "this was bad grammar of course, but that is how beavers talk when they are excited."[41] Dr. Cornelius must also correct the speech of his young student, Prince Caspian: "*Whom*, not *who*, your Highness. . . . Perhaps it is time to turn from History to Grammar."[42] This type of ignorance, the type that is unavoidable, is fair game for jokes. Lucy laughs at Mr. Tumnus because he doesn't understand her when she tells him where she's from. She explains she came from Narnia through the wardrobe in the spare room. Mr. Tumnus exclaims later: "Daughter of Eve from the far land of Spare Oom where eternal summer reigns about eternal city of War Drobe, how would it be if you came and had tea with me?"[43] Mr. Tumnus regrets that he didn't study his geography harder when he was a little faun. If he had he might have known of these strange countries. The Narnian's ignorance of the children's world, however, is equaled initially by the children's ignorance of Narnia. When the children find out about the wicked queen in Narnia, Mr. Beaver laughs with a great laugh at their naïve suggestion that the White Queen might turn Aslan into a stone. "What a simple thing to say," Mr. Beaver exclaims.[44]

Ever the teacher called to stomp out invincible ignorance, Lewis would instruct children on a variety of topics in his personal letters to them. To one young boy writing poetry, Lewis pointed out that his proposed meter was "far too rollicking and comic for any original poem in so solemn a metre as the Virgilian hexameter." It was fit only for words like: "A pound of that cheese and an ounce of the butter / Aeneas replied with his usual stutter."[45]

In comic technique, Lewis saw the proper use for English hexameter to be for comic purposes. The Italian meter, *ottava rima*, the stanza that rhymes *abab abcc*, he found to be a "beautifully light, rapid medium excellently adapted for describing a breathless chase on horseback or telling an amusing anecdote with a dash of impropriety in it."[46]

Lewis confessed that his preference in humor included "drollery, whimsicality, the kind of humor that borders on the fantastic."[47] The droll brought forth out of Lewis his delight in jesters, fools, buffoons, and all sorts of fun and farce. He particularly enjoyed the jester whose antics or jests took one off guard. For example, Thomas More's "drollery requires the grave tone and even the drudging pace of his sentences: it is irresistibly comic because the funniest things are said with a straight face."[48] Lewis's character Puddleglum fits this straight-faced description. Even his logic is droll and waggish, as when he responds to Jill's declaration that "we've got to start by finding a ruined city." Puddleglum answered: "Got to start by *finding* it, have we? . . . Not allowed to start by looking for it, I suppose?"[49]

Likewise, in *The Screwtape Letters*, one can almost hear the droll drawl in his voice as Screwtape solemnly recommends that his blundering nephew, Wormwood, read "a little booklet, just issued, on the new House of Correction for Incompetent Tempters. It is profusely illustrated, and you will not find a dull page in it."[50]

Much of Screwtape's humor, in fact, arises out of his solemnity. In this, Lewis acknowledged his debt to Stephen McKenna's *Confessions of a Well-Meaning Woman*, from which he borrowed a "moral inversion—the blacks all white and the whites all black—and the humor which comes of speaking through a totally humorless *persona*."[51]

In Lewis's undergraduate days, a senior tutor named Farquharson gave Lewis a personal experience of such drollery. On one occasion he glided up to Lewis

> with an *air* (not a gesture, an air) that would have suggested an embrace rather than a handshake: then, laying one hand on my shoulder, he wrung my hand with the other, cooing in refined military voice, "My dear fellow, this is very good of you." (He knew perfectly well that I had come on business and hadn't any choice but to come.)[52]

There was something unpredictable and something of a lark in this tutor. Lewis could not tell when "Fark" was pulling his leg a bit. As a prank, Fark would put "himself down on the list as lecturing on Heraclitus every summer term for years. I am the only person who ever volunteered to go," wrote Lewis, "and he said it was off *that* year: also the surviving fragments of Heraclitus occupy about two pages!"[53] Fark's droll manner would become, every now and then, a bit serious and deferential.

> [Then] out would come some extremely indecent story: without a tremor of this gravity. But only a minute later the egg would suddenly crack and he would go off into great chunks of laughter—the sort of "Ha-Ha-Ha" with long intervals between which one imagines Johnson laughing. When I left he told me about how much I'd helped him. I said I hadn't known anything at all about the points he'd raised. He said, "It was the stimulus of my presence" . . . and left me wondering whether he went back to chuckle at me.[54]

Lewis rehearsed a comparably amusing style, even in his mammoth *English Literature of the Sixteenth Century*, which was part of the *Oxford History of English Language*—abbreviated as O-HEL by Lewis and friends and an apt choice for charade games. In this literary criticism, Lewis practiced a humor modeled on his own description of Richard Hooker's drollery. Hooker, Lewis wrote,

> has plenty of humor, almost a mischievous humor, but not of this kind that could appear in quotation; the point depends not on the verbal but the argumentative context. Indeed very few of Hooker's beauties can be picked like flowers and taken home: you must enjoy them where they grow—as you enjoy a twenty-acre field of ripe wheat.[55]

Lewis exhibited a similar quiet drollery, though more quotable. In the same work, for example, he wrote that "the narrator of the 1595 voyage on which Drake and Hawkins both died often has matter which no one could make dull, but he brings it nearer to dullness than one would have thought possible."[56] It seems the nature of the Englishman to downplay or understate the facts of a matter, much like Chesterton's description of an Englishman "always saying, 'My house is not damp' at the moment when his house is on fire."[57] Lewis also noted the amusing contradictions within *Pilgrim's Progress* when Bunyan's "long conversation . . . which Christian and Hopeful conduct 'to prevent drowsiness in this place' . . . will not prevent drowsiness on the part of many readers. Worse still is the dialogue with Mr. Talkative."[58]

Whimsy appears in the fanciful correspondence between Lewis and Owen Barfield on the subject of the legal problems of Sir Tristram and King Mark. Sparked by a casual remark of Lewis regarding how the whole affair of Tristram and Iseult might be viewed by solicitors, Barfield and Barfield, Solicitors, filed a petition, dated 14 June 503, suing for divorce on grounds of adultery, to Messrs. Inkling and Inkling.

A response indicated Blaise and Merlin denied any misconduct during the voyage. A hearing was set for the 19 of June and an appeal made to precedent in the case of *Arthur v. Lancelot*. Barfield and Barfield wrote Lewis (aka Bleyse) with a special request that he keep his wizard, Merlin, chained: "May we add, without offence, that we should like to be assured that your junior partner is also thoroughly seised of this point."[59]

Master Bleyse indicated he could not promise to corral Merlin, for it was "not in our power to let hym to doon his wil for hee is of ful maisterful mood and passing orgulous." Merlin was so enraged against Bleyse for having the solicitors' letters that "he sodenlie by his crafts transformed me in the likeness and feature of an Asse." Only because he was his "old scholemast," did he restore his form, "yet imparfaitlie for I know not by what negligence he hath left me with the unnatural eares and hoofs of that beast." Whether a "lyke peril" would come to the Barfields, he could not answer.[60]

The words of Lewis are wrapped in whimsy, full of romantic and fantastic ideas and creatures. Medieval legal wranglings, talking animals, and travel into a woman's mind are curious inventions, even rum and capricious ones. But their absurdities are drawn from quaint facts. If there were lawyers representing Tristram and Mark they would surely wrangle. And who has not imagined that their pet poodle can communicate about television commercials as well as chow time? And though it may be preposterous that a man could ever understand a woman's mind, much less travel in it, it is the quixotic fancy of a young man that it might be possible.

With Owen Barfield, Lewis was at his whimsical best at invention. Together they produced a silly shorthand philosophy for *Oxford Magazine*, entitled "Abecedarium Philosophicum." This capricious piece of doggerel verse expanded all the letters of the alphabet into delightfully waggish poems of absurd philosophical reductions. Barfield and Lewis did not attempt to curb their doggerel wit. Two letters will illustrate: "B is for Bergson who said: 'It's a crime! / They've been and forgotten that Time is Time!' / D is for Descartes who said: 'God shouldn't be / So complete if he weren't. So he is Q.E.D.'"[61]

Whimsical humor easily and unpredictably mutates into the fantastic and extravagant. Anything fanciful that extends beyond the Aristotelian norm becomes excessive and even a part of the species of the ugly. Cyrano's nose becomes comic because it protrudes like a ship being launched from the port of a face. It is wonderfully extravagant—that is, one is so full of wonder as to the grand length (and height and breadth) of the nose that one stares, gawks, and titters. "If it bleeds, it is the Red Sea."

Such extravagant humor was, for Lewis, a broad extension of the normal, something totally unexpected. One cannot fathom its silliness. Yet the preposterousness of any conceit is the point of the humor. The extravagance, paradox, and surprise of John Donne's impudent wit on "Woman's Constancy," in which the poet treats the faithlessness of woman playfully, is essential to its enjoyment. "If you are not enjoying these you are not enjoying what Donne intended."[62]

The extravagance and rollicking nonsense of sixteenth-century comic poetry, Lewis found more aligned with Edward Lear and Lewis Carroll (and Rabelais, Aristophanes, and Lucian) than with Chaucer and Dickens. A wild nonsense touches the indecent and the blasphemous innocently enough. Two specimens from the Bannatyne anthology (1568), No. CCXXX and CXCVII, illustrate the good-natured delight of the poets, writing with lively twinkles in their eyes. The first tells how the first Highlander was created. God and St. Peter had gone for a walk when they discovered an unsavory object on their path. St. Peter jokingly challenged God to create something from it. "One stir of the almighty 'Pykit staff' and 'vp start a helandman, blak as ony draff.' Questioned about his plans, the new creature announced he would be a cattle-thief. God laughed heartily, but even while He was doing so (it is like Mercury and Apollo in Horace's ode) the Highlander had contrived to steal his pen-knife."[63]

In "Kynd Kittok," a disreputable good dame died of thirst. On her way to a burlesque heaven, she stopped at an ale house for the night. The next morning she arrived at the gate, "hungover," as it were, but managed to sneak by St. Peter: "which was the worse for him since, during her seven years' residence as Our Lady's hen-wife, she 'held him in strife.' The end of the poem leaves her once more outside the gate and permanently established at that same neighboring ale house, where future travellers, we are told, will find it worth their while to call on her."[64]

In both poems, we hear the enormous sound of God laughing. In seeing Kynd Kittok steal into heaven without St. Peter noticing, "God lukit and . . . lewch His hairt sair" (He looked and laughed His heart sore). The apparent free use of "blasphemy," Lewis wrote, "is not intended to move ironical smiles, nor the indecency to move prurient titters; what both want from the audience is a hearty guffaw."[65] (The use of St. Peter and the saints continues today in the comedy of the religious. When one annoying voter told a Roman Catholic candidate that he wouldn't "vote for him even if he were St. Peter," the candidate responded: "If I were St. Peter, you wouldn't belong to my district.")

The comic supernaturalism is funny for its extravagance. The poems are boldly preposterous and hilarious. They do not mock or demean God as much as make Him the Father of the good joke. In *Mere Christianity*, Lewis looked at the extravagant claims of Christ, which placed Him beyond the possibility of being a mere man. "The claim to forgive sins . . . unless the speaker is God, this is really so preposterous as to be Comic. . . . Asinine fatuity is the kindest description we could give of his conduct."[66] Like a man who forgave you for stepping on other people's toes is Christ who forgives you for all sins. The claim is so extravagant and silly for a normal good man that, unless that man is God, it is comic and blasphemous. But if the man is God, then this comic extravagance becomes divine comedy.

Unexpected events or ideas give birth to comedy in Lewis's work as they did in his life. When Lewis accidentally took about sixty prisoners in the First World War ("that is, discovered to my great relief that the crowd of field-gray figures who suddenly appeared from nowhere, all had their hands up"), he saw it as a joke on the level of Falstaff taking Sir Colville of the Dale.[67] An echo of this tale occurs with Prince

Cor— in *The Horse and His Boy*: Emerging from the battle, laughing at his bandaged hand, he confesses, "If you want to know the truth, it isn't a proper wound at all. I only took the skin off my knuckles, just as any clumsy fool might do without going near a battle."[68]

Such nonsense was an early acquaintance of Lewis's. He remembered the day during World War I when he met "the great goddess Nonsense" (apparently it was love at first sight). He was traveling for fifteen hours on a troop train in a small and freezing compartment with three other officers.

> There was no heating; for light we brought our own candles; for sanitation there were the windows. . . . In the tunnel just outside Rouen . . . there was a sudden wrenching and grating noise and one of our doors dropped off bodily into the dark. We sat with chattering teeth till the next stop, where the officer commanding the train came bustling up and demanded what we had done with our door. "It came off, sir," said we. "Don't talk nonsense," said he, "it wouldn't have come off if there hadn't been some horseplay!"—as if nothing were more natural than that four officers (being, of course, provided with screwdrivers) should begin a night journey in midwinter by removing the door of their carriage.[69]

Some jokes that often seem like silly nonsense, Lewis claimed, may make the best sense. "Would you think I was joking if I said that you can put a clock back, and that if the clock is wrong it is often a very sensible thing to do?"[70] For Lewis, the modern world mixed and confused sense and nonsense. People were often inconsistent in their thinking. Lewis understood those who denied miracles altogether, but saw those who believed other miracles and "drew the line" at the Virgin Birth to be ridiculous. He wrote, "Is it that they think they see in this miracle a slur upon sexual intercourse (though they might just as well see in the feeding of the five thousand an insult to bakers) and that sexual intercourse is the one thing still venerated in this unvenerating age?"[71]

"Those who call for Nonsense will find that it comes," Lewis warned.[72] To the charge of his own dabbling in nonsense about the devil, Lewis responded:

> I know someone will ask me, "Do you really mean, at this time of day, to re-introduce our old friend the devil—hoofs and horns and all?" Well, what the time of day has to do with it I do not know. And I am not particular about the hoofs and horns. But in other respects my answer is "Yes, I do." I do not claim to know anything about his personal appearance. If anyone really wants to know him better I would say to that person, "Don't worry. If you really want to, you will. Whether you'll like it when you do is another question."[73]

Strategizing on the best ways to use jokes or humor, Screwtape recommended a specially promising tactic for the English,

> who take their "sense of Humor" so seriously that a deficiency in this sense is almost the only deficiency at which they feel shame. Humor is for them the all-consoling and (mark this) the all-excusing, grace of life. Hence it is invaluable as a means of destroying shame. If a man simply lets others pay for him, he is "mean"; if he boasts of it in a jocular manner and twits his fellows with having been scored off, he is no longer "mean" but a comical fellow. Mere cowardice is shameful; cowardice boasted of with humorous exaggerations and grotesque gestures can be passed off as funny. Cruelty is shameful—unless the cruel man can represent it as a practical joke. A thousand bawdy, or even blasphemous, jokes do not help towards a man's damnation so much as his discovery that almost anything he wants to do can be done, not only without the disapproval but with the admiration of his fellows, if only it can get itself treated as a Joke. And this temptation can be almost entirely hidden from your patient by that English seriousness about Humor. Any suggestion that there might be too much of it can be represented as "Puritanical" or as betraying a "lack of humour."[74]

The English sense of humor is, ironically, often treated more solemnly than other more charitable virtues (that can mutate into vices). Yet the English are not the sole carriers of the diseased laughter; humanity itself suffers an epidemic of flippancy. The corroding laughter of irony undercuts for the sake of undercutting, attacking traditionally cherished beliefs and values in a fit of unrelenting put-downs. Such laughter, which implies that all belief is false and futile, denies all but the art of denial and debunking, of destruction and deconstruction. Its only belief is in dark laughter and put-down. It sticks on the human face a perpetual smirk at whatever is good, lovely, true, or right. But challenge this smug mockery and you may find a very morally impassioned, solemn reaction of comic self-righteousness.

In the *Screwtape* passage, Lewis argued that wit and humor can cloak what is right. They can fog or camouflage the moral thing to do. This doesn't mean, however, that the joke is not funny. The fact that it is funny diverts our attention away from the fact of its being wrong. Chesterton emphasized the same point in writing about a boy, who, as a prank, painted a statue of a foreign general a vivid red.

> When some trick of this sort is played, the newspapers opposed to it always describe it as a "senseless joke." What is the good of saying that? Every joke is a senseless joke. A joke is by its nature a protest against sense. It is no good attacking nonsense for being successfully nonsensical. Of course it is nonsensical to paint a celebrated Italian General a bright red; it is as nonsensical as "Alice in Wonderland." It is also, in my opinion, very nearly as funny. But the real answer to the affair is not to say that it is not funny, but to point out that it is wrong to spoil statues which belong to other people.[75]

Laughter, as Quintilian pointed out, "costs too much when purchased by the sacrifice of decency" and goodness. An excess of laughter at goodness can subvert that goodness.

What jokes need is a court of justice. The jester may cause hilarity in the judge, but that should not excuse him from stealing the judge's wig. The court jester may offer as his exhibit his sense of humor, but that must not obstruct the judge's sense of justice. What is needed, exhorted Chesterton, is "some sharp and definite moral law, capable of resisting the counter-attraction . . . of humor." Otherwise we may find ourselves at the chaotic mercy of unprincipled fools, clowns, and wits. "Every burglar who burgles in really humorous attitudes will burgle as much as he likes."[76]

This is not to say that the crime may not be as funny as bad cheese and musical beans. But to say that is, more importantly, to acknowledge that the joke may be as wrong as bad deeds and immoral deans. In 1869, W. H. Lyttleton warned that not everyone could be "trusted with much freedom of jesting; it is only good men, and all of us only so far as we are good."

Excessive laughter is not only irritating, but also dangerous. In fact, much mischief is done when limiting the Aristotelian virtue of moderation or temperance to drink or food. It applies to all other aspects of life as well.

> A man who makes gold . . . the centre of his life, or a woman who
> devotes all her thoughts to clothes or bridge or her dog, is being
> just as "intemperate" as someone who gets drunk every evening.
> Of course it does not show on the outside so easily; bridge-mania
> or golf-mania do not make you fall down in the idle of the road.
> But God is not deceived by externals.[77]

The person who laughs too easily, quickly, and continually may become desensitized to that which deserves pity, remorse, compassion, or mercy instead of mirth or jesting. Gluttons of hilarity may ruin good laughter. Then one is no longer drunk with the Spirit of love, but drunk with jokes.

25

Taboo Humor

Those who know God is with them even in death also know
that death itself is not to be taken too seriously.
—George Bernard Shaw

In a limited and tame fashion, Lewis participated in what might be perceived as black comedy or gallows humor—a comedy that deals with things ultimate in a temporal sense. Lewis was able to joke about death—seemingly a morbid practice—because he knew it wasn't a last thing. Death and sickness were commas in life, horrible and miserable commas, but still only pauses before the exclamation point of resurrection. Thus, while death might haunt with existential pain, it could, in an eternal perspective, be mocked and laughed at. Peter Berger pointed to the powerful testimony of French writer David Rousset who endured execrable suffering in a Nazi concentration camp. He recognized "that the comic was an objective fact that was there and could be perceived as such, no matter how great the inner terror and anguish of the mind perceiving it."[1]

Lewis found the comic relief in *Hamlet* to be the "strangest comic relief ever written—comic relief beside an open grave, with a further discussion of suicide, a detailed inquiry into the rate of decomposition, a few clutches of skulls, and then 'Alas! poor Yorick.'"[2] When Hamlet takes the jester Yorick's skull to Ophelia's chamber (to see if she will laugh at that), it is comic relief of the gallows humor kind.

Robert E. Harvard remembered the darkness surrounding the news of early September when Hitler had just invaded Poland and war was imminent. At a dinner where depression and doom hung like heavy curtains, Harvard recalled Lewis trying to lift the gloom by saying:

"Well, at any rate, we now have less chance of dying of Cancer."[3] Such an attitude found its way into his fiction as well.

On the day in which Ransom was to battle to the death, he wakes to find sweet fruit gourds to eat, and he thought whimsically: "A good breakfast on the morning you're hanged."[4] Wrestling against the demonic Weston in turbulent waters, he sports with the prospect of death for himself and his evil adversary: "Buck up Weston. It's only death, all said and done. We should have to die some day, you know. . . . As for drowning—well, a bayonet wound, or cancer, would be worse."[5]

Lewis found it difficult to "keep from laughing" when he found "people worrying about future destruction of some kind or other. Didn't they know they were going to die anyway? Apparently not."[6] He continually met young people whose fear of the Bomb gave them excuse for "poisoning every pleasure and evading every duty in the present. Didn't they know that, Bomb or no Bomb, all men die (many in horrible ways)? There's no good moping and sulking about it."[7] Lewis identified a central problem as the fact that "the stock response to death has become uncertain. I have heard a man say that the only 'amusing' thing that happened while he was in the hospital was the death of a patient in the same ward."[8]

Times of death do usher in opportunities for bizarre and outrageous humor. Upon the death of his father, Lewis and his relatives visited the undertakers. The occasion had an "insane air of diabolical farce." "A superior person led us into an inner room and enquired if we wanted a 'suite of coffins'—sounded like the offer of some scaly booking clerk at an hotel in Hell." The undertaker would drum a coffin and remark: "That's a coffin I'm always very fond of." To which Lewis's Uncle Bill, a notorious bore, provided welcome relief by intoning: "What's been used, before, huh?"[9]

The timing of this morbid humor is crucial. It best appears in the midst of crisis. Laughter enables those suffering to gain a perspective on their pain. William Dunbar's religious comic poetry gave men humorous perspective on dark and terrible things, such as devils, in which men "believed and doubtless trembled." But, observed Lewis, men also laughed at what they feared. One such bit concerned a devil disguised as St. Francis. The devil urged Dunbar to join the friars, but Dunbar responded that he would rather be a bishop. The devil disappeared with "stink and fyrie smoke." Much of the macabre humor of the sixteenth-century Howleglass takes place on the hero's bier and in his coffin. "No moral question is involved in our liking or loathing for this book; [it] depends on the strength of man's stomach."[10]

Gallows humor also deals with the fearful and forbidden. It breaks the taboo of talking about death or mutilation by laughing at it. As Lewis observed:

> The mixture of farce and terror would be incredible if we did not remember that boys joked most about flogging under Keate, and men joked most about gallows under the old penal code. It is apparently when terrors are over that they become too terrible to laugh at; while they are regnant they are too terrible to be taken with unrelieved gravity. There is nothing funny about Hitler now.[11]

Before his conversion, Lewis joked with his friend Greeves about various taboo topics such as whippings, sadism, and masochism. He suggested inventing new slogans such as, "Decapitation each night / Teaches you to spell right."[12]

Lewis acknowledged that some of the comic parts of Thomas Deloney are "too violent for the tastes of my generation; I can hardly regard burying a man alive (even if he were a 'massing priest') as a 'mad pranke.'"[13]

Yet not too violent was this poem by Lewis:

> *All things (e.g., a camel's journey through*
> *A needle's eye) are possible, it's true.*
> *But picture how the camel feels, squeezed out*
> *In one long bloody thread from tail to snout.*[14]

Dark humor did descend like the night upon Lewis during his season of suffering, grief, and bereavement over the death of his wife, Joy. How can people say they are "not afraid of God because I know He is good"? Lewis wrote. "Have they never been to the dentist?"[15] A candid but cold bitterness ekes out of Lewis's pen, even in his reflections on God. Lewis had lost his mother, his father, and his wife to cancer. Now he asked:

> Is God a clown who whips away your bowl of soup one moment
> in order, next moment, to replace it with another bowl of the same
> soup? Even nature isn't such a clown as that. She never plays exactly
> the same tune twice. . . . I am more afraid that we are really rats in
> a trap. Or worse still, rats in a laboratory. . . . Supposing the truth
> were "God always vivisects"?[16]

Lewis, an ardent antivivisectionist, was deeply fond of every sort of animal. Those who experimented with the little creatures were villains, along the lines of Uncle Andrew in *The Magician's Nephew*. Yet Lewis could mix a gruesome horror with wickedly funny scenes to stress his opposition. Uncle Andrew admits that his earlier magic experiments "were all failures. I tried them on guinea-pigs. Some of them only died. Some exploded like little bombs."[17] It was a "jolly cruel thing to do," as Digory exclaimed. Such cruelty carries a perverse comedy when the idea, however obscene, is funny even while the fact is not.

In his angry and painful reactions to death, Lewis turned his hurt wit to see God as continually "preparing the next torture" for life. God became the "Cosmic Sadist, the spiteful imbecile."[18] Yet, as in the psalms of complaint, the poet finds an answer before his wailings and invective overwhelm him. Inquiring as to why he allowed such filth and nonsense to visit his mind, he saw his own heart's reflection.

All that stuff about the Cosmic Sadist was . . . of hatred. I was getting from it the only pleasure a man in anguish can get; the pleasure of hitting back . . . mere abuse; "telling God what I thought of Him" . . . what I thought would offend Him (and His worshippers) most. That sort of thing is never said without some pleasure. Get it "off your chest." You feel better for a moment.[19]

In hearts of darkness, laughter helps, but only as an aspirin. It does not heal; it only helps to hold the hurt and injustice and horror at bay for a moment. Gallows humor fills, however temporarily, the void of understanding in the wake of death. It is only a bandage—but sometimes a bandage can help us until the physician arrives.

The bright eternal truth puts the dark temporal fact into a comic perspective. Lewis asked how it might have been if "when I served in the first world war, I and some German had killed each other simultaneously and found ourselves together a moment after death. I cannot imagine that either of us would have felt any resentment or even any embarrassment. I think we might have laughed over it."[20]

Certain things are recognizably ridiculous and worthy of being a joke. A lawyer with his shirt hanging out his zipper is a worthy source of laughter (if he is not your lawyer). Death and taxes can be funny when neither has come to collect. It is the joke that discovers the incongruity even in the darkest of times. Yet it is not so much that a joke arouses funny feelings in the self, but that the joke *is* funny. It is something in the nature of the funeral director that is comic. He buries dust in the earth that shall yet be remade in a gloriously new body. Around the secret taboos of death and decay, the mortician puts on a gloomy face, not recognizing he is the farmer who plants the seed of eternal life. To laugh at the joke is to respond ordinately to the double nature of a thing. Even to see the joke about death as funny is a gift that is given to the Christian community of life.

Chesterton warned that the joke belongs to the democracy; if we abolish the joke from the people, we abolish the community of humor.

> By the wholesome tradition of mankind, a joke was a thing meant
> to amuse men; a joke which did not amuse them was a failure, just
> as a fire which did not warm them was a failure. But we have seen
> the process of secrecy and aristocracy introduced even into jokes. If
> a joke falls flat, a small school of aesthetes only ask us to notice the
> wild grace of its falling and its perfect flatness after its fall. The old
> idea that the joke was not good enough for the company has been
> superseded by the new aristocratic idea that the company was not
> worthy of the joke. They have introduced an almost insane indi-
> vidualism into that one form of intercourse which is specially and
> uproariously communal. They have made even levities into secrets.
> They have made laughter lonelier than tears.[21]

The shared laughter of the Christian community offers a perspective that helps to transcend real pain, suffering, and chaos. It takes on
taboos as topics of life that must be freed from the tombs. It opens the
dark closets of insane individualism and exposes the private tremblings
and titterings to the blazing light of spiritual truth. With its own consuming moral fire, it purges evil with irony. If torture and cruelty
make one laugh, then why not tighten the screws? If dead-baby jokes
bring only a roar of laughter and not outrage from the mob, why not
kill the kids, or at least continue to abort them? (In a sort of Swiftian
modest proposal, babies could be put back onto the breakfast table!)

A moral and rational foundation reminds us what is right and
good. With such a foundation, one can laugh at dark and gallows
humor—but only in the light. Some of the sick comedy of our times
remembers health; some is a mere pleasure in perversity and disease.
Yet the response is not merely to shout down the bad joke, to cut down
the jungles of twisted jokes, but to shout out the good joke, to irrigate
the parched and starved souls with hearty comedy. If one is to awaken

audiences from the slumber of cold vulgarity, obscenity, and cruelty, one must awaken them into a sunshine of splendid hilarity. The right defense against mean humor and false sentiments is to inculcate good comedy and just sentiments. If one demon is chased out and no good, holy and happy spirit settles into that heart, seven more diabolical laughters will repossess.

One cannot keep the human lungs from laughter. Yet one can seek to fill those lungs with clean, fresh comedy rather than polluted and poisonous air.

26

The Vernacular and the Vulgar

I am sitting in the smallest room of my house.
I have your letter before me. It will soon be behind me.
—Voltaire

When one recognizes, as Chesterton pointed out, that the joke belongs with all humanity, one realizes that the joke is thus costumed in the garb of ordinary people. It dresses in the vernacular and the vulgar. It clothes itself in language that is common and often coarse.

A seminarian should be given a test of translating his theology into the vernacular, Lewis suggested in an essay on "Christian Apologetics." The problem of the vernacular, however, is that for the sophisticated it is too vulgar. Lewis learned early, at the knees of his nurse "Lizzie Endicott," that goodness was not removed from peasantry, from the low and common. "From before I can remember I had understood that certain jokes could be shared with Lizzie which were impossible in the drawing room; and also that Lizzie was, as nearly as a human can be, simply good[1]"

Lewis was accused by Dr. Pittenger of condescending to offensive images in writing on theological topics. Lewis's image of the Trinity as a cube, for example—wherein six squares make one cube as three Persons make one Godhead—struck Pittenger as offensive because of its vulgarity. Lewis thought this complaint warranted no apology.

Suppose the image is vulgar. If it gets across to the unbeliever what the unbeliever desperately needs to know, the vulgarity must be endured.

Indeed the image's very vulgarity may be an advantage; for there is much sense in the reasons advanced by Aquinas . . . for preferring to present divine truths *sub figuris vilium corporum* (under the figures of vile bodies). (*Summa Theologica*, Qu. I, Art 9 *ad tertium*).[2]

There have been people who thought maypoles, Canterbury pilgrimages, and Olympic Games vulgar. And, declared Chesterton, they were vulgar. Let's not deceive ourselves. "If by vulgarity we mean coarseness of speech, rowdiness of behavior, gossip, horseplay, and some heavy drinking, vulgarity there always was wherever there was joy, wherever there was faith in gods. Wherever you have belief you will have hilarity, wherever you have hilarity you will have some dangers."[3]

A choleric correspondent also criticized Chesterton for treating a serious subject with ordinary examples. Truth is truth whatever figures one uses, he responded, probably with gusto. "It is an equally awful truth that four and four make eight, whether you reckon the thing out in eight onions or eight angels, or eight bricks or eight bishops, or eight minor poets or eight pigs." If God did create all things, one could consider the fact of his existence by studying noses or smelling nosegays. Chesterton believed that the more serious the discussion, the more grotesque and even comic the terms should be. "For a subject is really solemn and important in so far as it applies to the whole cosmos. . . . So far as a thing is universal it is serious. And so far as a thing is universal it is full of comic things."[4] Small, isolated things, like Stalin or microbes, are tragic. Such small, isolated things can endanger you.

Only the large things, like the solar system, can be comic. A charitable heart can be comic because it is large. "The germs are serious, because they kill you. But the stars are funny, because they give birth to life and life gives birth to fun." Chesterton argued that

if you have, let us say, a theory about man, and if you can prove it by talking about Plato and George Washington, your theory may be a quite frivolous thing. But if you can prove it by talking about the butler or the postman, then it is serious, because it is universal. So far from it being irreverent to use silly metaphors on serious questions, it is one's duty to use silly metaphors on serious questions. It is the test of one's seriousness. It is the test of a responsible religion or theory whether it can take examples from pots and pans and boots and butter-tubs. It is the test of a good philosophy whether you can defend it grotesquely. *It is the test of a good religion whether you can joke about it.*[5]

The problem in joking about one's religion is the misperception that the sacred is solemn and the holy is humorless. Lewis addressed the Christian Holy Scriptures on the subject of their humor. Responding to a letter inquiring about the apparent absence of humor in the Scriptures, Lewis wrote that he thought

there may be *some* humor. Matt. IX.12 (People who are well don't need doctors) could well be said in a way that wd. be v. funny to everyone present except the Pharisees. So might Matt. XVII.25. And in Mark X.30—quickly slipping in "tribulations" among all the assets—that cd. be funny too. And of course the Parable of the Unjust Steward (its comic element is well brought out in Dorothy Sayers's excellent *Man Born to Be King*).[6]

Lewis praised Sayers's plays as works of art that could make real things real, even as others accused them "of irreverence and vulgarity and blasphemy," the same accusations brought against the Lord Himself.[7]

"If there were more humor, should we (modern Occidentals) see it? I've been much struck in conversation with a Jewess by the extent to which the Jews see humor in the O.T. where we don't. Humor varies so much from culture to culture." The book of Jonah, with its grotesque events, for example, offers a "distinct, though of course edifying vein of typically Jewish humour."[8]

How much wd. be recorded? We know (John XXI.25) that we have only a tiny fraction of what Our Lord said. Wd the Evangelists, anxious to get across what was vitally necessary, *include* it? They told us nothing about His appearance, clothes, physical habits—none of what a modern biographer would put in.[9]

Lewis did notice the incongruity in the Gospel of St. Mark during the transcendent moment on the Mount of Transfiguration. The writer observed during this very holy event that their garments were so radiant, "no laundry could make it so white."[10]

Such thoughts, no doubt, were influenced by his marriage to Joy, "a Jewess by blood," as mentioned above. In a letter to Dom Bede Griffiths, Lewis expressed one of Joy's views on the "Semitic genius": "That we Goyim misread much of the O.T. because we start with the assumption that its sacred character excludes *humor*. That no-one who knew the Jewish ethos from inside would fail to see the fully accepted comic element in Abraham's dialogue with God (Genesis XVIII) or in Jonah."[11]

Lewis began his use of the comic to discuss philosophical ideas early in life. In his correspondence with Arthur Greeves, Lewis returned to the argument that sentiment should not

be confined to that sphere of human nature where it is delightful—viz. art. That is almost as sensible as to say that trousers are delightful only because they are a part of human clothes: therefore they ought to be worn, not only on the legs, but every where else. Do you maintain that it is a highly commendable and philosophical act to wear trousers, say, on your head?[12]

Greeve's response to his sixteen-year-old friend's common and ridiculous imagery brought forth another outburst:

And because I choose trousers for an example you say that it is "very funny." Moi, I didn't know trousers were funny. If you do, I picture your progress from the tram to the office something thus: "Hullo! Good lord, there's a fellow with trousers over there! And's another. Ha-Ha—Oh this is too screaming. Look-one-two-three-more"— and you collapse in a fit of uncontrollable merriment.[13]

Because the image was funny, the discussion of the idea continued. The humorous and grotesque imagery drawn from the ordinary speech of men and women captures the imagination, attention, and reflection much more than vague abstractions. It is not without wisdom that Jesus spoke to the multitudes about sheep and goats, lost coins and lost sons, wine and virgins, even thieves and plucked-out eyes.

Lewis fought those who wanted to replace vernacular, "anthropomorphic" mental pictures of God with abstract, impersonal ones. When a person claims to believe in a great spiritual force and not in a personal God, Lewis responded that we have only substituted images about "winds and tides and electricity and gravitation" for living images. When another says that they believe "we are all parts of one great Being which moves and works through us all" (a Tillichian model), Lewis argues that "he has merely exchanged the image of a fatherly and royal-looking man for the image of some widely extended gas or fluid."[14]

> To say that He is "re-absorbed" into the Noumenal is better than to say He "ascended" into Heaven, only if the picture of something dissolving in warm fluid, or being sucked into a throat, is less misleading than the picture of a bird, or a balloon, going up. . . . To call God a "Force" (that is, something like a wind or a dynamo) is as metaphorical as to call Him a Father or a King.[15]

By refusing to communicate in real and concrete and vulgar images, we may even convey something bizarre, as the girl who was "brought up to regard God as a perfect 'substance'; in later life she realized that this had actually led her to think of Him as something like a vast tapioca pudding. (To make matters worse, she disliked tapioca.)"[16]

Not only did Lewis argue passionately that we should translate our theology into the vernacular, but he practiced his own advice so much that he was accused of various degrees of vulgarity, even of allowing humor to sit with holiness. For example, on illustrating the Incarnation, Lewis wrote that if you want to get the hang of God's becoming man, "think how you would like to become a slug or a crab."[17]

Falsely pious people may often adopt solemn postures and speak religious platitudes to show their spirituality. But, warned Lewis, "there is no good trying to be more spiritual than God. God never meant man to be a purely spiritual creature. That is why He uses material things like bread and wine to put the new life into us. We may think this rather crude and unspiritual. God does not: He invented eating. He likes matter. He invented it."[18]

And God did not consult us, Lewis teased, when he invented something so odd and vulgar as sex. God's workings are wonderfully ordinary and surprising at the same time: "I should never have seen any connection between a particular physical pleasure and the appearance of a new human in the world."[19] The fact that God not only invented pleasures but also expected His creatures to enjoy them was an insult to Screwtape. God, the Almighty Hedonist, doesn't have "the least inkling of that high and austere mystery to which we rise in the Miserific Vision. He's vulgar, Wormwood. He has a bourgeois mind. He has filled His world full of pleasures."[20]

Chesterton added a final reason for why we should

defend grotesquely what we believe seriously. It is that all grotesqueness is itself intimately related to seriousness. Unless a thing is dignified, it cannot be undignified. Why is it funny that a man should sit down suddenly in the street? There is only one possible or intelligent reason: that man is the image of God. It is not funny that anything else should fall down; only that a man should fall down. No one sees anything funny in a tree falling down. No one sees a delicate absurdity in a stone falling down. No man stops in the road and roars with laughter at the sight of the snow coming down. The fall of thunderbolts is treated with some gravity. The fall of roofs and high buildings is taken seriously. It is only when a man tumbles down that we laugh. Why do we laugh? Because it is a grave religious matter: it is the Fall of Man. Only man can be absurd: for only man can be dignified.[21]

When we give up our dignity and humble ourselves, we can speak clearly and gladly with our fellow human beings. We speak not to the lawyers and Pharisees, but to the vulgar people, the happy, common people, to each other. Lewis saw critics who attacked this popular and common approach as being like the musical snobs who would "look down their nose at Verdi and talk about 'the cheapness of his thematic material.' What they really mean is that Verdi could write tunes and they can't."[22]

The democracy, on the other hand, observed Chesterton, condescends to joke only about truly solemn matters, like marriage, the origin of life, or bad cheese. "Bad cheese is funny," he wrote, "because it is . . . the type of the transition or transgression across a great mystical boundary. Bad cheese symbolizes the change from the inorganic to the organic. Bad cheese symbolizes the startling prodigy of matter taking on vitality. It symbolizes the origin of life itself." Like bad cheese, such a matter of consequence as marriage, which also symbolizes the origin of a new flesh and life, is funny. "Thus, for instance, the democracy jokes about marriage, because marriage is a part of mankind. But the democracy would never deign to joke about Free Love, because Free Love is a piece of priggishness."[23]

In our dual nature, we discover, as Lewis put it, that "most of us have a dash of prudery or prurience and many among us of both."[24] We find ourselves communicating about all things coarse and vulgar. Even holding Norse creation myths in high esteem, Lewis saw the possibility of indulging "in a cheap laugh at their crudity," where a giant gives birth to a son and a daughter from his armpit.[25] Chesterton enjoyed prescribing a diet of beans to a variety of stuffy men with stuffy modern ideas. Their ideas would then be aired with a most fitting dignity.

One legendary (and perhaps apocryphal) moment in the Chesterton-Shaw public debates was when Shaw thumped Chesterton on his overripe belly and teased: "What are you going to name it when it's born, Gilbert?" To which Chesterton replied: "If it is a boy I shall call him John; if a girl, I shall name her Mary; but if it's gas I shall call it George Bernard Shaw." And it was Chesterton who challenged the incomparable Max, Sir Max Beerbohm, satirist of English life, London's elitist man-about-town, and outspoken critic of mass vulgarity, on his understanding of true vulgar humor.

I believe firmly in the value of all vulgar notions, especially of vulgar jokes. When once you have got hold of a vulgar joke, you may be certain that you have got hold of a subtle and spiritual idea. The men who made the joke saw something deep which they could not express except by something silly and emphatic. They saw something delicate that they could only express by something indelicate. I remember that Mr. Max Beerbohm (who has every merit except democracy) attempted to analyze the jokes at which the mob laughs. He divided them into three sections: jokes about bodily humiliation, jokes about things foreign, and jokes about bad cheese. Mr. Max Beerbohm thought he understood the first two forms; but I am not sure that he did. In order to understand the vulgar humor it is not enough to be humorous. One must also be vulgar, as I am.[26]

Lewis recognized that he could not effectively use the emotional approach of calling people to Jesus, but he was charitable to those tub-thumpers and evangelists who were so called. He defended reformer Hugh Latimer against those who would call his "straight talkism" or "high-pressure Christianity" charlatanism. Lewis, with a touch of drollery, described Latimer "as importunate as Hazlitt. He would have made a fine broadcaster." (This came from a BBC story.) In defense of such direct evangelism smacking of the vulgar, Lewis quoted General Booth's reply to Kipling: "Young feller, if I thought I could win one more soul to the Lord by playing the tambourine with my toes, I'd—I'd learn how."[27] The Eternal Word became common flesh to communicate with us on our vulgar level. We may find it ridiculous that God should speak through such unclean lips, but God has shown us that He can communicate through any instrument. "Balaam's ass, you remember, preached a very effective sermon in the midst of his 'hee-haws.'"[28]

Lewis pointed out that his argument about the unnatural division in human nature is not

> in the least affected by the value-judgments we make about ghost stories of coarse humor. You may hold that both are bad. You may hold that both, though they result (like clothes) from the Fall, are (like clothes) the proper way to deal with the Fall once it has occurred: that while perfected and recreated Man will no longer experience that kind of laughter . . . yet here and now . . . not to see the joke is to be less than human. But either way the fact bears witness to our present maladjustment.[29]

The maladjustment is clearly evident in the Scottish humor of extravagance, such as the joke of a dwarf having an ancestry of giants. Through a magnifying glass, we get a Rabelaisian or Swiftian image of an overgrown human body, with every hair and mole and wart and odor exaggerated a hundred times. The jokes become too obvious and large to miss. That is why, Lewis pointed out, "giants, in this kind of literature, are chronically flatulent."[30] They disclose in public, and the open air of the marketplace, the hilarious private secrets of every man's and every woman's body.

For anyone who has seriously contemplated his or her own body one must conclude with a touch of wonder ("What is man that Thou hast created him?"), despair ("dust to dust, ashes to ashes"), or the praise of laughter. A meal of bad cheese will bring one to one's knees in any of those attitudes. Lewis once wrote to Arthur Greeves in a postscript: "Can meditation be combined with emptying of the bowels? What a saving of time, especially for a constipated man like you."[31] (With a friend like Lewis, who needed bad cheese?)

Bad cheese smells funny, because we have sniffed good cheese. We laugh at coarse and indecent humor because it showcases the abnormal, contrasted against the normal. Arguing that a *Tao*, a universal moral law exists, Lewis pointed to the Greeks.

> It is untrue to say that the Greeks thought sexual perversion innocent. The continual tittering of Plato is really more evidential than the stern prohibition of Aristotle. Men titter thus only about what they regard as, at least, a peccadillo: the jokes about drunkenness in Pickwick, far from proving that the nineteenth-century English thought it innocent, prove the reverse.[32]

Incongruity and its wild offspring sink their roots into a foundation of rationality, even if it is a reasonable universe gone berserk. On writing of the one branch of satire, Chesterton proclaimed, "Satire may be anarchaic [*sic*], but it presupposes an admitted superiority in certain things over others, it proposes a standard. One of the main conditions of its appeal through satire [is] the appeal to sense."[33] George Bernard Shaw thought otherwise. Reviewing Meredith's "Essay on Comedy," Shaw defined comedy as the "fine art of disillusion . . . For after all the function of comedy . . . is nothing less than the destruction of old-established morals."[34] But for Chesterton and Lewis, comedy should function to reaffirm and establish what is good, right, and moral.

27

The Oldest Joke

Lord, grant me chastity . . . but not yet.
—St. Augustine

"The fact that we have bodies," Lewis pointed out, "is the oldest joke there is."[1] So old, in fact, that jokes about the body were already ancient in the days of classical Greece. Aristophanes' clown in *The Frogs* referred to jokes about the body when he asked: "Shall I crack any of those old jokes, master, at which the audience never fails to laugh?" The body, Lewis pointed out, is "the parent of three-quarters of the world's jokes."

> Remove the standard of decency in the written word, and one of two results must follow. Either you can never laugh again at most of Aristophanes, Chaucer or Rabelais, the joke having partly depended on the fact that what is mentioned is unmentionable, or, horrid thought, the oral *fableaux* as we have all heard it in the taproom (not by any means always vile or prurient, but often full of humour and traditional art) will be replaced and killed by written, professional *fableaux*: just as the parlour games we played for ourselves fifty years ago are now played for us by professionals "on the air." The smoking-room story is the last and least of folk-arts but the only one we have left.[2]

The authorless tradition of passing on ballads, stories, and even devotional pieces mouth to mouth has almost vanished, except in the ribald joke. Vulgar and lowbrow, such humor begins as popular entertainment. It delights and tickles the common people. Ovid was scribbled on the walls of Pompeii. Molière found "the best judge of his work in the old woman who never failed to laugh in the same place as the audience—the audience he wrote to please."[3] This is vulgarity in its happy, common, human sense. Humanity smiles when someone like Grove, anticipating Donne's poem, wishes "that 'Jove would him convert' into a 'black flea' in his lady's bed. But in what sense!" laughed Lewis.[4] The obsession with modern cleanliness has rendered Donne's flea disgusting, Lewis wrote, and in doing so, "has also rendered it comic."[5]

Of three general views of the body, Lewis opted for that expressed by St. Francis, stuck between an ascetic pessimist and nudist optimist. The little monk called his body "Brother Ass." "*Ass* is exquisitely right," declared Lewis, "because no one in his senses can either revere or hate a donkey. It is a useful, sturdy, obstinate, patient, lovable and infuriating beast; deserving now the stick and now a carrot. . . . So the body. There's no living with it till we recognise that one of its functions in our lives is to play the part of buffoon."[6] This view of the body's function is reflected in Lewis's fiction where even the hero is often a clown. When Ransom arrives in Perelandra, he is shocked to discover that, to the natives, he looks ridiculous. "Certainly his legs presented an odd spectacle, for one was brownish-red (like the flanks of a Titian satyr) and the other was white—by comparison, almost a leprous white," due to being exposed to sunrays on one-half of his body. When the Lady of the planet first sees him she points. For a second, Ransom

> thought she was going to cry. Instead she burst into laughter—peal upon peal of laughter till her whole body shook with it, till she bent almost double with her hands resting on her knees, still laughing and repeatedly pointing at him. The animals like our own dogs in similar circumstances, dimly understood that there was merriment afoot; all manner of gamboling, wing-clapping, snorting, and standing upon hind legs began to be displayed. And still the Green Lady laughed.[7]

Ransom finally does recognize how ridiculous he looks when the Green Lady names him Piebald. He recognizes he is the joke, knowing "his body to be a little ugly and a little ridiculous." Later, as he scrambles over the island, he wishes—with Lewis's full amused sympathy, I'm certain—"I'd give a good deal to have a pair of trousers on."[8]

In contrast to cheerfully ribald humor, indecorous or tasteless vulgarity centers on biological functions, what Chesterton would include in bodily humiliation—primarily reproductive and excretory functions. One old rabbi, expounding on Ruth's covering Boaz's feet on the threshing floor, toyed with the interpretation that "covering the feet" is a euphemism for covering the genitals. The old rabbi said that Hebrew words often have three meanings—one of which is always obscene. Lewis likewise reminded us, seemingly as often as a mother, that sex, food, and drink contribute to vulgar humor. This comic quirk sets us apart from the animals and angels as well. No cherubim finds custard in his beard funny. No cow giggles nervously in watching the bull approach her. No chicken laughs when another hen steps in its chicken dung. Dogs don't smirk and joke about the local lamppost or fire hydrant. Woodpeckers don't do "knock, knock" jokes. And penguins don't titter when a honeymoon couple returns from an isolated iceberg. The cuckoos don't perform comic plays on fellow cuckolds. Only man and woman acknowledge the hilarious possibilities of the body and its ways.

Lewis himself tipped his hat to a modest bit of vulgarity in *The Four Loves*. In illustrating how need-pleasures abruptly lose their attraction once they are used, he wrote: "If you will forgive me for citing the most extreme instance of all, have there not for most of us been moments (in a strange town) when the sight of the word GENTLEMEN over a door has roused a joy almost worthy of celebration in verse?"[9] Here laughter is easy, earthy, common, and, above or below all, vulgar. Screwtape didn't foresee much potential for temptation in this "indecent or bawdy humor, which, though much relied upon by second-rate tempters, is often disappointing in its results."[10] Such laughter acknowledges a moral and social standard and confesses, tactfully, how much we have strayed from it.

Chesterton cited jokes about bodily humiliation as one of Beerbohm's three categories of vulgar humor (the other being jokes about foreigners and jokes about bad cheese). Not only can a body fall down on its brother ass, but it can do all kinds of humorous and humbling tricks. A classification of the various noises it can make would exhaust a catalog of onomatopoeia. Even simply studying the sounds of kissing, Kierkegaard discovered a symphony of smacking, booming, hissing, hollow, and squeaky noises.[11] Kissing, of course, is not generally repulsive (at least not to those involved); but something about Kierkegaard's catalog of its onomatopoeic noises distances us from the reality of a kiss and makes it sound disgusting. Lewis believed that common swear words, obscenities, work on the same principle: "It is the words, not the things, that are obscene. That is, they are words long consecrated (or desecrated) to insult, derision, and buffoonery."[12]

Investigating the historical use of four-letter words, Lewis opened the glossary of Skeat's Chaucer. Most obscenities were used for comic or abusive reasons. He discovered the normal contexts for selected words were the realms of farce and abuse. For example:

> *Ers* (*nates vel annus*)—Occurs twice in Miller's Tale where context is slapstick farce and in the Summoner's Tale where the teller is insulting friars as sharply as he can.
>
> *Fart*—Always in slapstick farce as Miller's & Summoner's Tales.
>
> *Queynte* (*bele chose*)—In farce Miller's Tale and in the mouth of the Wife of Bath.[13]

None of the evidence Lewis unearthed indicated serious use of four-letter words without belly laughter or snarls of hatred. Four-letter words do not occur in erotic poetry or prose. "Our ancestors were sometimes shamelessly frank about the kinds of pleasure they demanded from certain kinds of literature." Thus we find four-letter words and obscenities "too gross to move desire, / Like heaps of Fuel do but choak the Fire." They are not aphrodisiacs but rather the untamed vocabulary of farce or spite: "Either innocent, or loaded with the very opposite evil to that which prudes suspect—with a gnostic or Swiftian contempt for the body."[14]

Even in Latin, several four-letter contenders are not sued in any pornography. When used anatomically, words like *penis* and *cunnus* appear in the harsh and jeering satires of Juvenal and Horace. Ovid, the real pornographer, has occasion to use such common words, but avoids them as not in keeping with his purpose. "It was surely significant that the great comedian [the Greek Aristophanes] gave one a four-letter word about once in every twenty lines," and commentators, Lewis noted, could usually show him unnoticed instances of breaking wind or other indecencies.[15]

On at least two occasions in the Narnian chronicles Lewis suggested unmentionable things. Having been jilted by Queen Susan, Rabadash storms about "with many descriptions of Queen Susan which would not look at all nice in print."[16] When Eustace returns to his shipmates as a dragon, he scares everyone dreadfully, "some of the sailors with ejaculations I will not put down in writing."[17] Certain language is not appropriate for polite society or young readers, even if it can be heard on television or in pubs.

Lewis, a man once described as "for a jig or a tale of bawdry!" enjoyed the hearty indecencies lurking behind the rustic jokes of the Scottish humor in which exaggerated dialect and peasant manners winked at a frisky bawdiness. The rustics, meeting in "Secreit Place" show some of this fun peasant earthiness: "Quothe he 'My claver, / My curledoddy, my hony soppis, my sweit possody, / Be not o'er bustious to your billie.'"[18]

Even more so, wrote Lewis, the "very comic title 'Robin's Jock come to wow our Jynny' indicates the sort of humor (and a very good sort too) which we are invited to enjoy."[19]

Lewis did not, however, understand fully those types of dull clowns (on a low intellectual and less pious level than their ordinary neighbor) who seemed "to think they have achieved either a voluptuous or comic effect—I am not sure which intended—by chalking up a single indecent word on a wall."[20] Nevertheless he set forth certain distinctions among types of vulgarity:

> VULGARITY. Usually means obscenity or "smut." There are bad confusions (and not only in uneducated minds) between: (a) The obscene or lascivious: what is calculated to provoke lust. (b) The indecorous: what offends against good taste or propriety. (c) The vulgar proper: what is socially "low." "Good" people tend to think (b) as sinful as (a) with the result that others feel (a) to be just as innocent as (b).[21]

Lewis found examples of the second category of the vulgar—the indecorous or indelicate—in the oddest places. He expressed surprise that one man, F. K., objected to the Annunciation on the ground that it was "*indelicate.* This leaves one gasping." Lewis responded:

> One goes on reacting against the conventional modern reaction against nineteenth century prudery and then suddenly one is held up by a thing like this. . . . The Middle Ages had a different way with these things. . . . In one of the Miracle Plays, Joseph is introduced as the typical comic jealous husband, and enters saying, "This is what comes of marrying a young woman."[22]

For such things that offend against taste or decorum, Lewis advised that we not tack on a prohibition that claims: "Thus saith the Lord."[23]

Lewis pointed out that in Jean de Meun's *Romance of the Rose,* Reason, referring very explicitly to certain physiological facts, is accused of being indecent. In her defense, Reason claims she has "learned her manner of speech from God."[24] One may sketch the human body with ease; if one then is to name the parts, one finds that scientific jargon or slang must be used. Our language is humorously cautious about private parts or, as the British say, the "naughty bits." The courtly lover in *Romance* is as "embarrassed as Gulliver was among the horses, and can only plead that if God made the things, at least He did not make the *names* by which Reason refers to them. A modern reader is reminded of Shaw's dictum—'it is impossible to explain decency without being indecent!'"[25]

Lewis clarified the irony of this passage by pointing out that the "spirit of polite adultery should be genuinely shocked by the unrepentant grossness of the divine Wisdom—should wish, like Milton's enemies to speak more cleanly than God—is a conception as profound as it is piquant."[26] Or, in other words, God identifies sinful acts in blunt language.

This peculiar situation I found paralleled in my own classroom, where a mature woman was more righteously offended by the flatulence in Chaucer's "Miller's Tale" than by the adultery. Being fallen creatures, Lewis noticed, we "tend to resent offenses against our taste, at least as much as, or even more than, offenses against our conscience or reason." We often want to inflict the same kind of condemnation on obscene or indecent jokes, which have "afflicted us like a bad smell," that we inflict on those who speak heresy or blasphemy. "This tendency is easily observed among children; friendship wavers when you discover that a hitherto trusted playmate actually *likes* prunes. But even for adults, it is 'sweet, sweet, sweet poison' to feel able to imply 'thus saith the Lord' at the end of every expression of our pet aversions."[27]

As words are wont to do, they take on a life of their own and change. Thus, language meant solely to offend or hurt does so "strangely little." This can be seen clearly, Lewis says, "when we catch a word 'just on the turn.'"

> *Bitch* is one. Till recently—and still in the proper contexts—this accused a woman of one particular fault and appealed, with some success, to our contempt by calling up an image of the she-dog's

comical and indecorous behavior when she is in heat. But it is now increasingly used of any woman whom the speaker, for whatever reason, is annoyed with—the female driver who is in front of him, or a female magistrate whom he thinks unjust. Clearly the word is far more wounding in its narrower usage.[28]

Sexual intercourse is good; our language, on the other hand, tends to smudge and dirty its beauty. Lewis explains that our "old human reticence about some of our bodily functions has bred such mystery and prurience." One way to unclothe this mystery is to be bawdy. For Lewis, if they belong anywhere, indecencies belong in comic works. Paradoxically, the presence of lewd comedy may actually protect the noble purpose of a work. Chaucer's *Parlement of Fowls*, which Lewis borrowed as a model for his parliament of owls in *The Silver Chair*, is a moral poem of high courtly sentiment containing much vulgar humor. But the humor neither ridicules nor subverts the impact of the poem. In fact, argued Lewis, it "would almost be better to miss every joke in Chaucer than to believe that the Goose and the Duck are his spokesmen, and the Turtle and the Eagles his butt."[29] The interruption of laughter within the serious debate punctuates the vital significance of the issue at hand. The inclusion of such language is an internal line of defense for the poem.

> [It] protects itself against the laughter of the vulgar—that is, of all of us in certain moods—by allowing laughter and cynicism and their place *inside* the poem; as some politicians hold that the only way to make a revolutionary safe is to give him a seat in Parliament. The Duck and Goose have their seats in Chaucer's Parlement for the same reason.[30]

Chaucer, observed Lewis, mingled hearty and realistic comedy with beauty and delight in this "supremely happy and radiant work." The beauty shines more brightly, however, because Chaucer allows the ugly (in Aristotle's sense) to sit beside it.

The appearance of such figures in a poem does not mean that the main tendency of the work is satiric: it almost means the opposite. . . . The comic figures in a medieval love poem are a cautionary concession—a libation made to the god of lewd laughter precisely because he is not the god whom we are chiefly serving—a sop to Silenus and Priapus lest they should trouble our lofty hymns to Cupid. When this has been understood (and not till then) we may, indeed, safely admit that Chaucer has sympathy with the Goose and the Duck. So had every knight and dame among his listeners. There would be no need to make a concession to the "lewd" point of view if it were not present in the minds of all. Chaucer and his audience knew, better than some know now, that human life is not simple.[31]

Most of us have a closet taste for the vulgar, unless education or society irons it out of us. Shakespeare kept the mob laughing with his coarse clowns. Among the Elizabethans, Lewis demonstrated that "belly laughter or graphic abuse could be supplied by almost everyone."[32] That one concedes a role in the play to the vulgar clown means neither that you let him dominate the entire drama nor that you permit him to intrude at inappropriate times. The French critics resented and attacked Racine (with "delicious reproaches") for allowing the comic to intrude in certain scenes of his *Adromaque*. It was an offense against decorum. Even though such intrusions are the essence of vulgar comedy, Lewis lectured that there is not only a time and place, but also a style that is proper for the comic interruption.

If one can allow comedy and satire in great, lofty works (and Lewis allowed it), cannot one excuse the wrong kind of comedy at the wrong time? As an example, Lewis cited the "hackneyed and heavy-handed type" of tavern comedy that occurs in John Dryden's heroic *Alexander's Feast*:

That Alexander in his cups should resemble exactly the first drunken braggart whom you may meet in a railway refreshment room, appears to Mr. Eliot to add "a delicate flavour." But what is there delicate about it? Indelicacy, in the sense of grossness and crudity of apprehension . . . is surely the essence of it. It does not seem to have crossed Dryden's mind that when Alexander got drunk he may have behaved like a drunk gentleman or a drunk scholar and not like an "old soldier." No: this is not a subtle or delicate joke. If it is to be defended at all, it must be defended as a "good plain joke." As such, Mr. Eliot apparently likes it, and I do not: and this is of very little consequence. . . . The joke may be good or bad in itself. Let us suppose that it is good;—the question remains whether even a good joke, of this tavern type, really contributes to the total effect of the ode.[33]

Lewis questioned whether Dryden was concerned with the integrity of his work, whether the comic material actually contributed to the goodness. Even worse for Lewis was Dryden's tragic and "heroic" story of *Sigismonda and Guiscardo*. "This old poet goes out of his way to insert at the beginning of his story a ribald picture of his heroine as the lascivious widow of conventional comedy. . . . Dryden winks and titters to his readers over time-honored salacities." Lewis found such lewdness most inappropriate for beginning a tragic story, shaping the sublime with the mold of the ridiculous. This, Lewis charged, is poetic blasphemy, where a poet sells his birthright and destroys his worthy art for a pot of comic porridge, "if only he can win in return one guffaw from the youngest and most graceless of his audience."[34]

Lewis defended this position against those partisans of Dryden, who would accuse him of being enslaved to some Victorian canon of solemnity as the essence of poetry and of judging Dryden by an alien standard:

I have no quarrel with comic or cynical or even ribald poetry. I have no quarrel with Wycherley, I admire Congreve, I delight in Prior and still more in Don Juan. I delight in Dryden himself when he is content to talk bawdy in season. . . . But in these fables—Dryden . . .

lost the game by rules of his own choosing . . . being rather a boor, a gross, vulgar, provincial, misunderstanding mind.[35]

The time to laugh asserts a certain season for comedy, even vulgar comedy. However, vulgarity forgets or neglects—even intentionally—to obey its own propriety. There are rules even for vulgarity to be funny, or to fall as mere dung to attract flies.

In studying ancient comic poetry, Lewis tapped into literary earthen vessels, full of vulgarities and obscenities. But their presence worked to show rules, even though *via negative*. He established that a

rule of decorum exists to avoid clashes or shocks to organized sensibility: but it was an early discovery that an occasional defiance of the rule, resulting in a shock can give pleasure; a pleasure rich in . . . comic possibilities. Indeed one of the purposes for which the rule exists is that it may sometimes be broken. Thus taking "decorum" in its narrower sense to mean a standard of decency in our references to bodily functions, it is clear that *all indecent humor depends on that standard of decency*: the mention of certain things becomes funny only after we have agreed that they are unmentionable.[36]

Derek Brewer offered a trivial example of Lewis's practical and humorous awareness of such rules of decency:

[Lewis] once said that he could not for many years properly enjoy the poetic phrase "the chambers of the sun" because of the all-too-literal image evoked for him by the word *chamber*, i.e., the old-fashioned euphemism for chamber pot. In compensation he was able to appreciate the description by one of his pupils (not me) of the institution of courtly love as a "vast medieval erection."[37]

From here one can slip to the vulgar in its morally bad sense, where it really is a term of moral reproof. "It is low hearts, and not low brows that are vulgar. . . . It is a fatal, unconscious welcome held out to the lower when the lower has offered to usurp the place of the higher, 'a downward appetite to mix with mud.'" Lewis thus criticized Chapman's translation of Homer where "a suggestion of senile eroticism, old men in heat, looking at the beauty of the Queen: is foisted upon the work and cheapens it."[38]

The old "Kaleyard" and "eldritch" (fairy) kinds of Scottish comic poetry dealt with the humors of the people—Lewis's third level of vulgar humor, that which is socially low and coarse. We find the common "humours of a 'bank holiday crowd,' quarrels and riots in which the extreme pugnacity of both sexes is neutralized by their lack of skill and courage." This poetry is not merely confused and vulgar poetry as much as poetry about confusion and vulgarity. It is later in Skelton's courageous portrayal of an inn run by a "dirty ole ale wife" with all female customers, that we gather more "foul words, foul breath, and foul sights in plenty."[39] For those who view the "gentler sex" as the civilizing saviors of mankind [sic], here is evidence to the contrary, where a crude picture of thirsty old trots shows not only that all is alive, but that all is ugly as well.

Sir John Harington (the inventor of the "john") invented similar comic images (his phrasing, Lewis told us with something of a snicker, has "the vividness of a clown's red nose. We read of old trots in the wrinkles of whose face 'ye may hide false dice and play at cheerypit in the dint of their cheekes'"[40]). With Sir John, we step into coprophilous humor (no novelty here) modeled on that of Rabelais. This kind of humor is relegated to the lowbrow.

In an essay on highbrow and lowbrow, Lewis sought to pinpoint the difference in kinds of literature. First he examined the distinction between comic and serious literature, between *The Decameron, The Canterbury Tales, The Furioso, Pickwick, The Marriage of Figaro*, and the entertaining novels of Sir Walter Scott on one hand and the *Divine Comedy* and *War and Peace* on the other. "In one sense," he opined, "*serious* is simply the opposite of comic. But if *serious* means 'worthy of serious consideration,' then a gay song by Prior may be more serious than some of the most lugubrious items in our hymnbooks. What is more, a pure *divertisement* may be more serious than a long, well-documented tendentious, ethical, or sociological novel"—not to mention "research" by Americans.[41]

As such, Ariosto's *Furioso* is a light, fun work, but the author did not take it lightly. Part of Ariosto's greatness lay in his ability to combine tragic and even religious elements with "his licentiousness, his mockery, and his wonderful comic invention."[42] He can transport us to moods of gravity and sadness as well as ribaldry and burlesque. Lewis's own *Screwtape Letters* is a light work, but it was the most difficult of all his works to write and carries serious moral instruction to its readers.

We cannot contrast simply between the comic and the serious, Lewis noted, for then the stories in our *Parish Magazine* would be labeled highbrow and *Le Misanthrope* as lowbrow. Neither would one use a classification of being momentous, for Molière's play, though comic, would fit the bill; Oscar Wilde's *Importance of Being Earnest* would fall short.

Lewis suspected, with amusement, that difficulty might turn out to be "the real criterion of Literature, Good Books, or classics—if a comedy which was mere commercial art as long as everyone could see the jokes became aesthetic and spiritual as soon as you needed commentators to explain them."[43]

Thus, Rabelais and Chaucer, with their jokes about sex and flatulence, now become highbrow. Lewis mocked the social kidnapping of the good, plain man, who through the subtle, numbing forces of educational brainwashing is made into "a pathetically willing and bewildered university student [who] will sometimes praise the great works which he has dutifully read and not enjoyed, for the excellence of their style. *He has missed the jokes in the comedy.*"[44]

English literature is packed with ribald mirth. The *Howleglass* and the *Hundred Merry Tales* are collections of practical jokes and humorous stories. The author's motive in the first is "to make the readers laugh at hoaxes," and that involves much coprophilous humor about excrement. The second is a good anthology that includes stories that in an austere setting broke Lewis himself into laughter. He wrote: "In any story one happens not to have read before, the point comes like a thunderclap, and even such a drudge as a literary historian, reading on a hard chair in a library, will probably laugh aloud." Lewis found the moral attached to each of the imperturbably grave and droll stories to be "the funniest part of all." For example, when a "woman is told a cuckold's hat is a good charm against a disease infecting her pigs, [she] tries to borrow one from insulted neighbors." Rejected by all, she resolves to make sure she can have one of her own by next year. The moral appended is: "It is more wysdome for a man to trust more to his owne store than to his neyghbours genteelness."[45]

Chaucer was able to be comically vulgar without being obscene because obscene humor and vulgar humor are not synonymous. Though both may be funny, the former has morally degrading qualities. It appeals to the prurient within us all. With subtle tongue-in-cheek, Lewis acknowledged his own sexual vulnerability when writing about John Donne's "pornographic poem," *Elegy XIX*. He described it as "descriptive, not dyslogistic, intended to arouse the appetite it describes, to affect not only the imagination but the nervous system of the reader. And I may as well say at once—but who would willingly claim to be a judge in such matters?—that it seems to me to be very nearly perfect in its kind."[46] Like former President Jimmy Carter confessing "lust in his heart," Lewis here becomes transparently—and comically—human. So, too, did Malcolm Muggeridge make his own soul naked in an autobiographical aside quoting St. Augustine: "There's nothing so powerful, he said when he was a Bishop, in drawing the spirit of man downwards as the caresses of a woman." Muggeridge wrote, "[Augustine] was speaking from experience and I, for what it's worth, endorse his opinion."[47]

Lewis used these suggestive inserts for subtle comic tension. This kind of wit does not attempt to incite vulgarity or depravity. But there are those obscene acts and writings that do undermine virtue, and many of them have to do with a sexual solemnity whose object aimed at is "four bare legs in a bed."[48] In *The Four Loves*, Lewis discussed the kind of man who says he wants a woman. It is a lie, he says, for this man does not want the woman but merely the sexual experience for which a woman happens to be the necessary apparatus. He wants "it," not her.

Lewis would maintain, however, that obscenity as humor was not as deadly as obscenity as solemnity. He lashed out at the earnestness of D. H. Lawrence, who suggested that "today, human beings [have] evolved and cultured far beyond the taboos . . . inherent in our culture." "The evocative power of the so-called obscene words must have been very dangerous to the dim-witted, obscure, violent natures of the Middle Ages, and perhaps is still too strong for slow-minded, half-evolved lower natures to-day."[49]

The use of filth and obscenity to convey a realistic atmosphere was to Lewis "a symptom, a sign of a culture that has lost its faith. Moral collapse follows upon spiritual collapse."[50] For Lewis, the fact that something was true to life was a poor excuse for using it in art and literature. "To the objection 'This is obscene' or 'This is depraved' . . . the reply 'This occurs in real life' seems . . . sufficient."[51] "Lawrence says that 'in life' we 'have got to live or we are nothing.'" But, responded Lewis, this is silly and captious because "'to live' means 'to have or lead (or both) the sort of life that Lawrence values.'"[52] Thus, Lewis attacked the false actuality of Lawrence's literature. To describe in *Sons and Lovers* a young couple copulating in the woods, not fretting about themselves, is for Lawrence a glad, rich illustration of being one with every grass-blade and being carried away by life. Lewis mocked this superficial sexual sense of life. Why is our unity with grass and trees illustrated by "copulation any more (or less) than by nutrition, excretion, or death?" Lewis wondered. Are young people, being passionately carried away by life, concerned with fertility, or have they prudently taken contraceptive measure, so as to flow with life "just so far as is convenient and no further"? "In cold logic, the fact that there was a great deal of organic life

besides that of the two lovers in the wood is the most absurd argument
for not 'fretting about themselves'; as they would have discovered if that
other organic life had included a plentiful supply of adders, mosquitoes,
or poison-ivy."[53] Chesterton satirized this literary tendency of viewing
humanity of needing to return to the naturalism and erotic primitivism
of the man and woman in the cave. "When the realist of the sex novel
writes, 'Red sparks danced in Dagmar Doubledick's brain; he felt the
spirit of the cave-man rising within him,' the novelist's readers would
be very much disappointed if Dagmar only went off and drew large
pictures of cows on the drawing-room wall."[54]

Against Lawrence and his ilk, Lewis fought this tendency to treat
sex too solemnly and reverently. "Religions buzz about us like bees. A
serious sex worship—quite different from the cheery lechery endemic
in our species—is one of them."[55] Lewis satirized the obscene obses-
sions of (mostly) men who are enslaved to their sexual impulses. "If
a healthy young man indulged his sexual appetite whenever he felt
inclined, and if each act produced a baby, then in ten years he might
easily populate a small village. This appetite is in ludicrous and preposterous excess of its function."[56] One of the things in modern life that
Lewis thought most insanely and sadly obscene was that one could get
a "large audience together for a strip-tease act—that is, to watch a girl
undress on the stage." He invented a parody of this sexual appetite by
comparing it to another normal appetite gone berserk.

> Now suppose you came to a country where you could fill a theatre
> by simply bringing a covered plate on to the stage and then slowly
> lifting the cover so as to let every one see, just before the lights went
> out, that it contained a mutton chop or a bit of bacon, would you
> not think that in that country something had gone wrong with the
> appetite for food? . . . There is nothing to be ashamed of in enjoying
> your food: there would be everything to be ashamed of if half the
> world made food the main interest of their lives and spent their time
> looking at pictures of food and dribbling and smacking their lips.[57]

In a comic Bergsonian fashion, men allow themselves to become uncontrollable sex machines, throwing away morality, rationality, and self-control. Too many exponents of modern culture, seemed, to Lewis, "to be 'impudent' in the etymological sense. They lack *pudor*, they have no shyness where men ought to be shy. They handle the most precious and fragile things with the roughness of an auctioneer and talk of our most intensely solid and fugitive experiences as if they were selling us a Hoover."[58] Jokes may obtrude or invade into situations in which they are not fitting, convenient, or *decens*. Thus, the apostle Paul speaks in his epistle to the Ephesians(5:4) of the indecency or inappropriateness of coarse humor for those certain seasons where thanksgiving, praise, and encouragement are more fitting. There is a time for everything, and everything must be in its right and proper season.

More than the silly jesting, it is the serious and blasphemous nonsense we must battle. Of the vile things often said about our holy ancestors, Lewis argued, there are several things which we must *not* say. In a sordid anti-God paper, Lewis read a taunt that "we Christians believe in a God who committed adultery with the wife of a Jewish Carpenter." Such mockery is not only blasphemous but misinformed. For God is the Father of us all. The other mistake one must not say is that our ancestors "'believed in miracles because they did not know the Laws of Nature.' This is nonsense. When St. Joseph discovered that his bride was pregnant, he was 'minded to put her away.' He knew enough biology for that."[59] And they were probably more frank about biological matters than a modern liberated populace.

In jokes about sex, Lewis's devil (and Lewis's imagination—though the two are not synonymous) divided the human participants into two classes. "There are some to whom 'no passion is as serious as lust' and for whom an indecent story ceases to produce lasciviousness precisely in so far as it becomes funny."[60] A sense of humor can awaken one out of an erotic enchantment; it can break the bonds of obsession. At the wrong moment, Lewis wrote, laughter is "fatal to sensuality." Thus Ovid and Byron "keep their sensuality tolerable (when they do) by being comic and ironical."⁶¹ Bawdy humor ought to be "outrageous and extravagant" but should avoid the cruel or pornographic. But others joke about sex simply as an opportunity to dabble in their lusts; joking is a pretext for prurience. Screwtape informed Wormwood that humans are pretty clearly split into these two types over indecent humor. The second involves those "in whom laughter and lust are excited at the same moment and by the same things."

> The first sort joke about sex because it gives rise to many incongruities; the second cultivate incongruities because they afford a pretext for talking about sex. If your man is of the first type, bawdy humor will not help you—I shall never forget the hours which I wasted (hours to me of unbearable tedium) with one of my early patients in bars and smoking rooms before I learned this rule. Find out which group the patient belongs to—and see that he does *not* find out.⁶²

Lewis, most likely, belonged to the first group. His brother, Warnie, wrote in a memoir of his brother's "liking for beer and bawdy late-night talk" during any one of his Thursday "Beer and Beowulf" celebrations at the Bird and the Baby (the Eagle and the Child).⁶³ Roger Lancelyn Green described Lewis just as Lewis characterized his friend Neville Coghill: "He spoke much 'ribaldry' but never 'vilenger.'"⁶⁴ Bawdy stories for Lewis did not mean dirty stories containing smut or blasphemy. When such stories were "told in his presence, he did not disguise his annoyance." But as sex was something of a hilarious incongruity to Lewis, he could easily poke fun at it or at himself. Green remembered "offering him a hard-boiled egg when we stopped for refreshments in a railway buffet on the way from Oxford to Cambridge, and he refused it, saying: 'No, no, I mustn't. It's supposed to be an aphrodisiac. Of course it's all right for you as a married man—but I have to be careful.'"⁶⁵

That which is calculated to blaspheme, to provoke lust, or to promote the cruel or pornographic is fully wrong. In contrast, being simply outrageous and extravagant is what bawdy humor is all about. Lewis concluded that "within those limits I think it is a good and wholesome *genre*; though I can't help feeling sorry that it should be the *only* living folk-art left to us."[66] Such was Lewis's theory. As to his practice, biographer Roger Lancelyn Green recalled only one bawdy joke that Lewis told, and that was to a male gathering of the Inklings at their favorite pub, the Bird and the Baby. Green said that Lewis apologized profusely if anyone found anything objectionable about it, but "he felt it was so funny as to cancel out any such possibility." As Lewis told it,

there was a new waiter being instructed in a hotel by an old waiter as to his duties who finished up, "And the most important thing, my boy, is tact."

"How do you mean—tact?" asked the new waiter.

"Well, I'll give you an example," said the old waiter. "A few days ago I went up to the bathroom to leave a fresh cake of soap— and there was a lad in the bath, who had forgotten to lock the door. So I said: 'A fresh cake of soap, sir'—and went straight out as if nothing were wrong."

A week or two later the two waiters were again talking, and the old waiter said: "And how are you getting on—particularly in the matter of tact?"

"Oh, splendidly," answered the young waiter. "I'll give you an example. A few mornings ago I took a tray of tea into the bridal suite, and there were the bride and bridegroom in bed together. . . . So I put down the tray by the bed and said as I turned to go: 'Your early morning tea, gentlemen.'"[67]

28

Falling from Frauendienst

It is better to live in a corner of a roof,
Than in a house shared with a contentious woman.
—Proverbs 25:24

There is little doubt that for Lewis women were funny. Whether it was because, as some modern critics claim, he was a chauvinistic bachelor most of his life or simply because, as I believe, he was a man and found women to be amazingly foreign (like the French), he saw an abundant measure of humor about the female.

Some things are funny for the very reason that they are foreign and unfamiliar. Indeed, to Chesterton, there is a subtle and spiritual idea in the fact that we laugh at foreigners:

> It concerns the almost torturing truth of a thing being like oneself and yet not like oneself. Nobody laughs at what is entirely foreign; nobody laughs at a palm tree. But it is funny to see the familiar image of God disguised behind the black beard of a Frenchman or the black face of a Negro. There is nothing funny in the sounds that are wholly inhuman, the howling of wild beasts or of the wind. But if a man begins to talk like oneself, but all the syllables come out different, then if one is a man one feels inclined to laugh, though if one is a gentleman one resists the inclination.[1]

To Lewis, even more than to Chesterton, woman was an enigma wrapped in a riddle surrounded by a conundrum—all of which, like Mother Russia, made her foreign and thereby funny. In part, he was infected with the *vis comica* of all men, from Adam to Ovid to Addison to Oxford's new residents. The cheerful chauvinism and underlying charity of Chesterton, a happily married man, was especially contagious to such a well-confirmed bachelor as Lewis.

When played on the comic stage, the war between men and women has no serious casualties. The pride of both may be punctured, but that is no great loss. In *The Magician's Nephew*, Polly and Digory argue incessantly and taunt each other, accusing the other of acting "just like a boy" or "just like a girl." The stereotypes are comic, partly because they are so familiar.

Lewis juggled these vivid types with predictable ease. Once, under medication for some pain, he suffered strange dreams. One in particular focused on purgatory and had the effect of extending his male-female distinctions. Lewis "envisioned a great big kitchen in which things are always going wrong—milk boiling over, crockery getting smashed, toast burning, animals stealing. That was purgatory, he knew, because the women had to learn to sit still and mind their own business; because the men have to learn to jump up and do something about it." In a letter to Mrs. Neylan he further explained: "I am a man, therefore lazy; you are a woman, therefore probably a fidget."[2]

Lewis mocked what might have been a bit of his own chauvinism in *That Hideous Strength*, when Mother Dimble, a traditional but fiercely independent female, explains that men could be induced to do housework, but it would most probably make them grumpy. The wisdom of Mother Dimble on the nature of man even included Ransom, the Director. She acknowledged his limitations: he may be a wise man, but he is "still a man and an unmarried man at that."[3] Lewis's sly playfulness with the topic can also be seen on the bookshelf of Mr. Tumnus, the faun in *The Lion, the Witch, and the Wardrobe*. Such mysteries as *Is Man a Myth?* stand beside such a curious volume for an old bachelor (even a faun) entitled, *Nymphs and Their Ways*. One can imagine its counterpart in Oxford, sitting untouched on Lewis's shelf, entitled *Women and Their Ways*—certainly a mystery for a bachelor.

But for Lewis, a man, humor was located in the feminine. What makes women funny is intimately connected to the question of what makes them worthy of being worshiped. Lewis was significantly informed of the medieval practice of *Frauendienst*, the devout worship and service of ladies. In this age, a growing reverence for women and an imagination that idealized love brought an intense gravity to romance. And when something like courtly love takes itself too seriously, it is time for the onslaught of comedy. Should the fat cows of Bashan become sacred, the butcher may sharpen his axe with a grin.

Jean de Meun was a traditional satirist. Like Ovid, the *Concilium*, and Andreas Capellanus before him, he chose what Lewis considered to be necessary ingredients for tasty, saucy satire.

> The subjects of his satire are, in the main, two: women and churchmen. It will be noticed that neither of these is a novel subject for satire. How should they be? *Whatever claims reverence risks ridicule.* As long as there is any religion we shall laugh at parsons; and if we still (though much less frequently than our grandfathers) make fun of women, that is because the last traces of *Frauendienst* are not yet wholly lost.[4]

Satires and jokes about women and clergy are commonplace throughout history. Whenever the clergy or religious evangelists puff themselves up, they become fair game as stuffed piñatas to be struck and emptied of all their prized delights. Langland's invention of Piers, the honest Ploughman, a character once as familiar as Father Christmas, Uncle Sam, or John Bull, stands satirically against various "estates." Where his satire falls heaviest, Lewis pointed out, is "where we should expect it to fall—on idle beggars, hypocritical churchmen, and oppressors."[5] But the comedy about women (most writers were men) dominates all estates as the choice topic, though great wits like Aristophanes, in *Lysistrata*, could swipe at his own gender's preference for sexual favors over war and the women's strategic knowledge of the fact. Ovid ridicules gullible women as well as those lounge lizards who would buy how-to-pick-up-women books from a local kiosk. Chaucer introduces the image of the wife of Bath, who boasts a voracious sexual appetite and confesses how she had to "send unobedient husbands to Jesus."[6] The secret to her Canterbury tale was the simple fact that what women want most of life is ruling over their husbands and lovers.

No double standard of the sexes existed in Lewis's appreciation of comedy. Ovid's ironical instructions to men were matched by the preposterous advice of the *Roman's* Vekke to Bialacoil, where women are told "how to fleece their lovers, how to deceive their husbands, how to 'make up' and so forth." The history of comedy between the sexes favors one side, then the other. The twelfth-century *Concilium in Monte Romarie* is the French poet's *Jeu-d'esprit* in a flippant version of *Frauendienst*. The erotic religion with its tittering nuns parodies the medieval church wherein "Doctor Ovid's Rule instead of the evangelist's was read." The elaborate Ovidian joke of the Concilium "operated upon . . . the medieval taste for humorous blasphemy [and] brought Ovid's smirking into the nunnery." The nuns publicly make confession of the "practick part of the Amatory Art," and clerics are recommended over knights as objects of cloistered amours.[7]

Lewis confessed he could laugh at the funny passages of the good moralist Gower, "in which the faithless husband gives his wife an account of his day's sport" and at John Donne's extravagant and playful conceits about the faithlessness of woman.[8] One ideal woman in Shakespeare—Venus herself—falls into uproarious comedy because of the poet's invention of her as a larger-than-life beloved. Appearing in Shakespeare's sonnet, Venus fares poorly as an aggressive, oversexed woman. Lewis could not conceive why Shakespeare made Venus

> not only so emphatically older but even so much larger than the unfortunate young man. She is so large [How large is she?] that she can throw the horse's rein over one arm and tuck the "tender boy" under the other. . . . She threatens to "smother" Adonis with kisses. The word "smother," combined with these images of female bulk

and strength is fatal: I am irresistibly reminded of some unfortunate child's efforts to escape the voluminous embraces of an effusive female relative.[9]

With comic self-disclosure, Lewis echoed elsewhere that Venus "knows her own art so badly that she threatens, almost in her first words, to 'smother' him with kisses. Certain horrible interviews with voluminous female relatives in one's early childhood inevitably recur to the mind."[10] But in the power of female appetites, Lewis identified another appropriate poet. "If female spiders, whose grooms (I am told) do 'coldly furnish forth the marriage tables,' wrote love-poetry, it would be like Marlowe's."[11]

The image of the mammoth female reinforced Lewis's dread of the dominance of the female. Speaking as a bachelor don, he said that as far as he could see, even a woman who wants to be head of her own house does not usually admire the same state of things when she finds it going on next door. "She is much more likely to say 'Poor Mr. X! Why he allows that appalling woman to boss him about the way she does is more than I can imagine.'"[12] "Both sexes must be told 'Mind your own business' but in two different senses—men are more likely to hand over to others what they ought to do themselves, and women are more likely to do themselves what others wish they would leave alone."[13]

Chesterton added mothers-in-law and feminists to the list of comic female topics. He noted about the former that

it is not the least true that mothers-in-law are as a class oppressive and intolerable; most of them are both devoted and useful. All the mothers-in-law I have ever had were admirable. Yet the legend of the comic papers is profoundly true. It draws attention to the fact that it is much harder to be a nice mother-in-law than to be nice in any other conceivable relation of life. . . . The same is true of the perpetual jokes in comic papers about shrewish wives and henpecked husbands. It is all a frantic exaggeration, but it is an exaggeration of a truth; whereas all the modern mouthings about oppressed women are the exaggerations of a falsehood. If you read even the best of the intellectuals of today you will find them saying that in the mass of the democracy the woman is the chattel of her lord, like his bath or his bed. But if you read the comic literature of the democracy you will find that the lord hides under the bed to escape from the wrath of his chattel. This is not the fact, but is much nearer the truth. Every man who is married knows quite well, not only that he does not regard his wife as a chattel, but that no man can conceivably ever have done so. The joke stands for an ultimate truth, and that is a subtle truth . . . that, even if the man is the head of the house, he knows he is the figure-head.[14]

If a man ever wears a crown as head of a home, Lewis wrote, it is only a paper crown or a crown of thorns.

Chesterton relished that horrible tale of the brothers Grimm, "The Boy Who Could Not Shudder." In this excellent, shocking joke, the young male hero is not frightened a whit by severed heads and legs falling down the chimney and walking about. He "slapped bogies on the back and asked the devils to drink with him." What was most fearful about all these scary wonders, wrote Chesterton, was the young man's own absence of fear. However, the hero was "at last taught to shudder by taking a wife, who threw a pail of cold water over him." In that one sentence, concluded Chesterton, "there is more of the real meaning of marriage than in all the books about sex that cover Europe and America."[15]

Chesterton offered the New Woman or the suffragette as fodder for the comic papers and as additional evidence that the common joke is truer than the fact. The early feminist was caricatured in the popular papers as "an ugly woman, fat, in spectacles, with bulging clothes, and generally falling off a bicycle." Chesterton conceded this is plainly not factual. Many such women are extraordinarily good-looking and dress well. "Yet the popular instinct was right. For . . . in this movement . . .

there was an element of indifference to female dignity, of a quite new willingness of women to be grotesque." Thus the stately woman of art and culture is turned into a comic shrew or slob. "The healthy and vulgar masses were conscious of a hidden enemy to their traditions who has now come out into the daylight, that the scriptures might be fulfilled. For the two things that a healthy person hates most between heaven and hell are a woman who is not dignified and a man who is."[16]

Humor pops into view when a person is not what he or she should be. Thus, both Lewis and Chesterton, as traditional chauvinists, believed that men and women have particular and proper places in the scheme of the universe. When a churchman was not truly pious or when a woman was not truly dignified, there was opportunity for satire and humor. Lewis, for example, found a student laughable because of his inexcusable ignorance. "Ignorance is laughable because it could be avoided."[17] When anyone neglects his (or her) expected role or duty, he (or she) becomes potentially comic.

The New Woman was a suitable object for humor and satire. Lewis's studies in Medieval and Renaissance literature impressed a particular belief upon him. Dignity and modesty were natural to a woman. Some aroma of Thomas Rymer's thought lingers on in Lewis:

> "If a woman has got any accidental historical impudence" (i.e., immodesty, *impudicitia*) "she must no longer stalk in Tragedy . . . but must rub off and pack down with the carriers into the *Provence* of comedy." She is proper in comedy (no doubt) because its corrective function is precisely to pillory aberrations from general nature.[18]

The impudent woman was a grotesque anomaly to Lewis. Discussing his nightmare fears in his autobiography, Lewis revealed he was terrorized by bad dreams about specters and insects. The second scared him more. "To this day I would rather meet a ghost than a tarantula." He saw in the anthill and the beehive "two things that some of us most dread for our own species—the dominance of the female

THE JOKE PROPER

and the dominance of the collective."[19] (Lewis discovered later that a "real objective curiosity"—like a scientific study of insects—could chase away such phobias; one wonders if an objective interest in strong women—perhaps in his marriage—rid him of this phobia. Love does conquer fear.)

In the thirteenth-century English version of *Sawles Warde*, Wit, the husband (the author's equivalent for *animus*) is given a silly wife called Wil. "It is she who sets the whole *familia* wrong if she is not carefully watched."[20] One can suspect this wayward image comes in part from Plato, who clearly said in *Timaeus* (42b) that "the souls of wicked men may be reincarnated as women, and if that doesn't cure them, finally as beasts."[21]

Not a small man, Lewis nevertheless commented in several places on large women. In Spenser's *Faerie Queene*, he finds the "amazon Radigund who enslaves men and sets them to female tasks" representing a form of insubordination in the hierarchy of things: the "monstrous regiment of women."[22] Britomart is her opposite, wholly strong but feminine in the role of knight errant. There is nothing of the virago or feminist in her. "Radigund, on the contrary, is a real feminist . . . revenging herself on all mankind because one man Bellodant rejected her love."[23]

"Can the humor here be intentional?" Lewis asked, then answers: "I think it is. Radigund is to Spenser both a horrible and a grotesquely comic figure." There is indisputable burlesque when the knight Artegull strikes her with a huge blow that "had she not it warded warily, / It had depriv'd her mother of a daughter."[24] Lewis copied such a grotesque caricature in *That Hideous Strength*. Fairy Hardcastle, a name right out of a union of Spenser and Freud, is one harsh, cigar-smoking, tough woman—a parody of Chesterton's New Woman.

Relations between the sexes have their own comic history, much of it based on female dominance. David Lyndsey enjoys "flyting" or scolding the ambitious counselors surrounding the royal throne in his "Complaynt to the King." He boasts, with humor, of the service he has rendered to the king, "concluding with a joke asking for loan, to be repaid 'when churchmen yearn for no dignity / Nor wives no sovereignty.'"[25] It will be an eternal loan.

In dealing with royalty, Lewis also recorded a merry impudence in a poem by William Dunbar. "Being sure of the queen's favor, Dunbar tells the king that he is praying for 'your Grace, baith nicht and day'; but what he prays is that the king should become . . . a hen-pecked husband." And another comic poem, "The Dumb Wife," about the unintended consequences of healing a mute spouse "tells amusingly how a husband by means of a spell learned from 'ane greit grim man' cured his dumb wife and how bitterly he regretted it."[26]

Lewis explained that much of the source of this kind of humor comes from the incongruity of the ideal and the real. In ages where women became objects of wholehearted reverence, they also became objects of hearty ridicule. Cynical periods follow idealistic periods. Even in Northrop Frye's categories, the Winter of satire and irony follow the noble but tragic grandeur of Autumn and the Fall of humanity. "'Cynicism' and 'idealism' about women," wrote Lewis, "are twin fruits on the same branch—are the positive and negative poles of a single theory."[27] Ridicule arises to tweak those who would worship women in *Frauendienst*, pretending that such love is the whole of life, that it is not. All that rises must fall; that which is lifted up and exalted will be brought low. The pedestal upon which men set women, or the platform that women (or men) mount, will both crumble, by satire and humor, if not by hubris.

29

Sex and Marriage

Marriage has many pains, but celibacy has no pleasures.
—SAMUEL JOHNSON

Incongruity is one of the chief sources of humor, which is why marriage is such a good source of jokes. In this way, beyond the mandate for procreation, the incongruous companionship of man and woman brings a delicious added value to marriage: comedy.

Lewis, for one, found laughter virile and frisky in marriage. I suspect that he derived much of his view of marriage as such an incarnate incongruity from Chesterton's jolly opinions of "what is wrong with the world":

> If Americans can be divorced for "incompatibility of temper" I cannot conceive why they are not all divorced. I have known many happy marriages, but never a compatible one. The whole aim of marriage is to fight through and survive the instant when incompatibility becomes unquestionable. For a man and a woman, as such, are incompatible.[1]

The Chestertons were the very model of the image of incongruity—one tiny and seemingly frail, the other gigantic and overwhelmingly hearty. But for Lewis, as for Chesterton, the fundamental joke inherent in marriage is that God split His image into two: male and female—so divinely similar, apparently in His eyes, yet so frustratingly different in their own. Nevertheless, Lewis wrote, citing Origen, "it is the married couple, united in the relation called one flesh, that is the *Imago Dei*."[2]

Lewis believed, like Milton, that beauty resides in the female. It is a comedy of errors (and one of humility on the woman's part) that would even bring them together. In *Paradise Lost*, Milton describes a scene in which Eve

> sees herself in a pool of water, and falls in love with her own reflection. Then God makes her look up, and she sees Adam. And that sight is a disappointment—he is not as interesting as herself—but divinely guided, Eve gets over his difficult *pons asinorum* and lives to learn that being in love with Adam is more inexhaustible, more fruitful, and even better fun than being in love with herself.[3]

Lewis incorporated this same temptation in the Green Lady's vanity in *Perelandra*. "The beauty of the female is the root of the joy to the female as well as to the male." Yet to "desire the desiring of her own beauty is the vanity of Lilith, but to desire the enjoying of her own beauty is the obedience of Eve, and to both it is in the lover that the beloved tastes her own delightfulness."[4] Lewis once saw this Lilithian desire to be admired as the basis for the incredible "idea of female beauty [as] the erotic stimulus for women as well as men . . . i.e., a lascivious man thinks about women's bodies, a lascivious woman thinks about her own. What a world we live in!"[5]

Ransom, in speaking with a rational Malacandrian creature called Kanakaberaka, says that people on earth must work hard digging in their mines. "They are kept at it because they are given no food if they stop." Ransom asks:

> "Does no one keep your people at their work, Kanakaberaka?" "Our females," said the *pfifltrigg* with a piping noise which was apparently his equivalent for a laugh. "Are your females of more account among you than those of the other *hnau* among them?" "Very greatly. The *sorns* make least account of females and we make most."[6]

The *pfifltriggi* possess the most abusive and teasing sense of humor, as can be seen in blaming their women for making them work. They joke more about their mates because they take them more seriously than any of the other Marian species. But the overarching fact is they joke about each other: The female mocks the male even as the male mocks the female. Even crusty old Milton defended the

> non-sexual element in marriage! His argument is (a) St. Augustine was wrong in thinking God's only purpose in giving Adam a female, instead of a male, companion, was copulation. For (b) there is a "peculiar comfort" in the society of man and woman "beside (i.e. in addition to, apart from) the genial bed"; and (c) we know from Scripture that something analogous to "play" or "slackening the cords" occurs even in God. That is why the Song of Songs describes a thousand raptures . . . far on the hither side of carnal enjoyment.[7]

To Lewis the carnal delights of nuptial ecstasy were fertile with comic possibilities. Writing on Christian marriage, he demythologized the intense romantic notion of being in love.

> If the old fairy-tale ending "They lived happily ever after" is taken to mean "They felt for the next fifty years exactly as they felt the day before they were married," then it says what probably never was nor ever could be true, and would be highly undesirable if it were. Who could bear to live in that excitement for even five years?[8]

One would either die of exhaustion, become a militant celibate, or go merrily insane.

The heavenly origin of the institution of marriage is played out on earth where the dual nature of human beings, who are both the image of God and the product of dust, adds that element of the joke to the process. As Lewis wrote:

I can hardly help regarding it as one of God's jokes that a passion so soaring, so apparently transcendent, as Eros, should thus be linked in incongruous symbiosis with a bodily appetite which, like any other appetite, tactlessly reveals its connection with such mundane factors as weather, health, diet, circulation, and digestion. In Eros at times we seem to be flying; Venus gives us the sudden twitch that reminds us we are really captive balloons. It is a continual demonstration of the truth that we are composite creatures, rational animals, akin on one side to the angels, on the other to tom-cats. It is a bad thing not to be able to take a joke. Worse, not to take a divine joke; made, I grant you, at our expense, but also (who doubts it?) for our endless benefit.[9]

Lewis's own late-blooming sexuality in a May-December marriage gave him opportunity to appreciate the joke, laughing at himself as he merrily enacted Castiglione's observation that "even old men . . . can still be lovers in their proper mode."[10] The happy absurdity of having a honeymoon in a country hotel when he was in his fifties tickled Lewis. "I'm such a confirmed old bachelor that I couldn't help feeling I was being rather naughty (Staying with a woman at a hotel! Just like people in the newspapers!)"[11]

Lewis's merriment derived in part from the clear perception that the marriage bed is a bed of laughter. He often chuckled over his good fortune, that what had passed him by in his early years as a bachelor was given to him at a more mature, ripe, and hilarious age. I have little doubt that Lewis, married on March 21, 1957, and publishing *The Four Loves* in 1958, put theory into practice. As with wrinkled and sagging Abraham and Sarah, laughter could be heard within the tent.

But Lewis's jokes about marriage were born out of a high and sacramental belief about its nature. He played upon its light comedies because he believed in its gravity. Through characters like Mark and Jane Studdock in *That Hideous Strength*, he attached the frigid, modern perversions of this blissful state for the purpose of bringing the couple home again, back to the marriage bed. To the Studdocks, initially, marriage was a prison, "a door out of a world of comradeship and laughter into solitary confinement."[12] The differences of men and women were self-evident; the sexes were foreigners to each other, living in different worlds. Lewis expressed some of these differences humorously through the words of Mother Dimble, an experienced wife, who says to Jane: "Jane, that's the third time you've yawned. You're dropping asleep and I've talked your head off. It comes of being married thirty years. Husbands were made to be talked to."[13]

All the women at St. Anne's, where Mother Dimble lives, laugh at the obstructive and skeptical nature of their resident bachelor, MacPhee. Even Ransom, the Director of their community, teases this hyperrational man, for whom logic smothers emotion: "Heaven forbid," Ransom laughed, "that I should claim to know what goes on in the two halves of your head, MacPhee, much less how you connect them." MacPhee's rude and untamed nature needs civilizing, and Lewis seemed to suggest that marriage is the proper arena for taming his passionate and querulous nature. At one point, when MacPhee and Miss Ironwood are engaged in one of their many arguments, the Director threatens: "If you two quarrel much more, I think I'll make you marry one another."[14]

For humor to thrive in a marriage, humility must arrive first. Separated first by their own selfishness and then by cataclysmic events, the Studdocks finally seek to reunite. As Mark Studdock makes his way back to Jane, he is struck by his own fault in the previous failure of his marriage. As he drags himself, exhausted, through the ruins of Edgestow, he makes some painful admissions.

> Inch by inch, all the lout and clown and clod-hopper in him was revealed to his own reluctant inspection; the coarse, male boor with horny hands and hobnailed shoes and beefsteak jaw, not rushing in—for that can be carried off—but blundering, sauntering, stumping in where great lovers, knights and poets would have feared to tread. . . . How had he dared?[15]

Confronted by his own careless stupidity and selfishness, Mark understands that he has been a loud-voiced intruder in the garden of his marriage. His wife, Jane, must also descend the ladder of humility. She must go down, that she might accept him. For her part, as she heads for home, Jane walks past the "liquid light and supernatural warmth of the garden and west lawn, past the see-saw, the greenhouse, and the piggeries . . . going down to the Lodge," where her husband waits. Inside there are "sweet smells, bright fire with food and wine and a rich bed," but she hesitates at the latchkey. Here, in the inaction of Jane's doubts, Lewis showed the action of wedded humility and humor; for here, at the crossroad of the restoration of her marriage, Jane "noticed that the window, the bedroom window, was open. Clothes were piled on a chair inside the room so carelessly that they lay over the sill: the sleeve of a shirt—Mark's shirt—even hung over down the outside wall. And in all this damp too. How exactly like Mark! Obviously it was high time she went in."[16]

Lewis painted a certain regal solemnity into the Studdock's reunion, but, overall, never let consequential things like the marriage bed take too grave an importance or become too seriously earnest. The importance is not being earnest in the bedroom. On the contrary, Lewis believed, too many moderns had been encouraged to take sex "too seriously; at any rate, with a wrong kind of seriousness. All my life a ludicrous and portentous solemnization of sex has been going on."[17] Psychologists like Freud, Kraft-Ebbing, and Havelock Ellis and most media advertisements approach the whole subject with the rapt intensity of those who seek to establish, or restore, a religion of sex. Lewis could imagine some young couples so intent on performing its rites correctly that they are continually consulting the complete works of some sex psychologist, which they have spread out all around their bed. Sex is serious, Lewis acknowledged, just as eating and drinking are serious. But all become equally ridiculous when they are venerated. It is the gourmet or connoisseur bringing a bluebook to the dinner table who best supplies the raw material for caricature. Men and women who behave like animals determined to make sure their species survives are fair game for satire. Thus, we must not approach our sexual appetite as if we were in church or in heat. We must beware taking this sensory pleasure too gravely. "God who made good laughter forbid. It is one of the difficult and delightful subtleties of life that we must deeply acknowledge certain things to be serious and yet retain the power and will to treat them often as lightly as a game."[18]

For an age that is too serious about sex, said Lewis, the antidote was good old-fashioned bawdy humor. "Cheery old Ovid, who never either ignored a mole-hill or made a mountain of it, would be more to the point. We have reached the stage at which nothing is more needed than a roar of old-fashioned laughter."[19] Indeed, in *The Allegory of Love*, Lewis carried us back to Ovid. This impish poet wrote an instructional composition on the art of seduction for the gleeful amusement of a society who understood his irony well.

> The very design of the Art of Love presupposes an audience to whom love is one of the minor peccadilloes of life, and the joke consists of treating it seriously—in writing a treatise, with rules and exampled *en regle* for the nice conduct of illicit loves. It is funny, as the ritual solemnity of old gentlemen over their wine is funny. Food, drink and sex are the oldest jokes in the world; and one familiar form of the joke is to be very serious about them. From this attitude the whole tone of the *Ars Amatoria* flows. In the first place Ovid naturally introduces the God Amor with an affectation of religious awe—just as he would have introduced Bacchus if he had written an ironic *Art of Getting Drunk*. . . . In the second place, being thus mockingly serious about the appetite, he is of necessity mockingly serious about the woman. . . . No one who has caught the spirit of the author will misunderstand this. The conduct which Ovid recommends is felt to be shameful and absurd, and that is precisely why he recommends it—partly as a comic confession of the depths to which this ridiculous appetite may bring a man.[20]

Lewis appreciated Ovid as a cheery old reprobate and his worldly-wise advice. "When he writes 'If you would be loved, be lovable' only meant 'If you want to attract the girls, you must be attractive.'"[21] In his comic masterpiece, Ovid—having been mockingly serious about the uncontrolled appetite is now "mockingly serious about the woman"—tells his readers: "Don't visit her on her birthday; it costs too much."[22]

The proper function of comedy about the sexes was to enable men and women to view sex in a more realistic way. If we take Venus too seriously, Lewis predicted, we will find ourselves the victims of a comic prank. As a goddess, she is "a mocking, mischievous spirit, far more elf than deity, and makes game of us."

> When all external circumstances are fittest for her service she will leave one or both the lovers totally indisposed for it. When every overt act is impossible and even glances cannot be exchanged—in trains, in shops, and at interminable parties—she will assail them with all her force. A hour later, when time and place agree, she will have mysteriously withdrawn; perhaps from only one of them. What a pother this must raise—what resentments, self-pities, suspicions, wounded vanities and all the current chatter about "frustration"— in those who have deified her! But sensible lovers laugh. It is all part of the game; a game of catch-as-catch-can, and the escapes and tumbles and head-on collisions are to be treated as a romp.[23]

Wise lovers will recognize this reign of comedy, play, and buffoonery over their bodies and their lovemaking. The king and queen become their own jesters in their private chamber. Even the jester may be Don Juan in his own small kingdom. "The highest does not stand without the lowest," Lewis emphasized. "Thus in old comedies the lyric loves of the hero and heroine are at once parodied and corroborated by some much more earthy affair between a Touchstone and an Audrey or a valet and a chambermaid."[24]

Lewis thus appreciated sex as a source for jokes. And the place

where men and women find the most fertile opportunity to laugh
and joke about the subject is, of course, in the marriage bed. Lewis
brought the holiness of the marriage bed together with its humor in
That Hideous Strength. When Jane Studdock, for instance, is drawn
to a fellowship of believers at St. Anne's and joins Mrs. Dimble in the
daily tasks of airing the house and making beds, such simple labors
stir her literary memory. She starts thinking about

> age old superstitions, jokes, sentimentalities about bridal beds and
> marriage bowers. . . . [Jane seemed to] join hands with some solemn
> yet roguish company of busy old women who had been tucking
> young lovers into beds since the world began with an incongru-
> ous mixture of nods and winks, and blessings and tears—quite
> impossible old women in ruffs and wimples who would be mak-
> ing Shakespearian jokes about cod-pieces and cuckoldry at one
> moment and kneeling devoutly at altars the next.[25]

Lewis very likely drew this humor of old matrons from the familiar
type of humor of all parents and of old uncles, aunts, and grandparents. The raillery and chuckling banter of Chaucer's Pandarus and
Cryseide give us a vintage taste. This avuncular humor was like

> the old gentlemen who joked about christenings at marriages in the
> nineteenth century [who] were no doubt being gross and common-
> sensible of the expense of the devout emotions felt by the bridal
> pair. . . . But you must not suppose that these same old gentle-
> men repudiated the monogamic idealism and romanticism of their
> period, or would have been anything but outraged at a serious
> attack upon it. . . . They eat their cake and have it too, like rational
> creatures. If romantic love were not venerated, who but a simpleton
> would poke fun at it? And so it is with Pandarus, [who] can tease the
> lovers' prudency or laugh away their fears, "She will not bite you,"
> as he says to Troilus.[26]

In all matters of sex, comic relief pops up like a child's Jack-in-the-Box in the midst of a formal dinner. In Shakespeare, for instance, while Romeo and Juliet wail and moan in sublime poetry, Mercutio is making bawdy jokes. The gravity of our sexual appetite requires a balancing levity that will keep it from becoming a suicidal love pact. We forget the playfulness and the promise of humor in sex and marriage when we forget that all our members are products of a heavy Fall. We must admit, and laugh at the fact, that our fallen naked bodies are a clumsy, comic means to dance out our desires' delight. That the awkward things ever achieve the glad grandeur of a physical and spiritual union is a surprise that surpasses all understanding.

To submit to the countless jokes of Eros and Venus is to enjoy them fully for what they offer. Even in times of misery or poverty or pain, they may be God's instruments of grace and laughter. Lewis, who was no stranger to the agony and anxiety of watching his beloved die, wrote the following:

> Even when the circumstances of the two lovers are so tragic that no bystander could keep back his tears, they themselves—in want, in hospital wards, on visitors' days in jail—will sometimes be surprised by a merriment which strikes the onlooker (but not them) as unbearably pathetic. Nothing is falser than the idea that mockery is necessarily hostile.[27]

Lovers faithfully tease and laugh at each other. There is a close relationship between the high esteem that one sex gives the other and the resultant comic teasing. It is the sign of a secure love, that lovers will playfully imitate and mock each other. And, Lewis suggested, lovers are always laughing at each other "until they have a baby to laugh at."[28] The fruit of laughter will be the fertile seed of another blessed, hilarious laughter. In *Till We Have Faces*, even in the midst of a life of suffering, Orual delights in looking after her new baby sister, Psyche. Orual passed from the worst anguish of her life "into the beginning of all my joys, I think I laughed more in those days than in all my life before. And I laughed because she was always laughing. She laughed before the third month."[29]

Such humor fit Lewis's idea that "it is not for nothing that every language and literature in the world is full of jokes about sex." Many of them may be dull or disgusting, and nearly all of them are old; but we must insist that they embody an attitude to Venus that in the long run endangers the Christian life far less than a reverential gravity.

> We must not attempt to find an absolute in the flesh. Banish play and laughter from the bed of love and you may let in a false goddess. She will be even falser than the Aphrodite of the Greeks, for they, even while they worshipped her, knew that she was "laughter-loving." The mass of the people are perfectly right in their conviction that Venus is a partly comic spirit.[30]

Too many treacly, heartbreaking love songs along the lines of Romeo and Juliet need to be replaced with the comic opera of Papageno and Papagena.

But in sex and marriage, as in any other topic, there is a fine line between appreciating its humor and profaning its blessedness, between grateful laughter at its incongruities and arrogant mockery. Lewis openly criticized the latter, pornography and obscenity, and, therefore, was accused of being against sex. He denied it. He had been against the perversion of her gifts, but never against foam-born Venus or golden Aphrodite. "I never breathed a word against you. If I object to boys who steal nectarines, must I be supposed to disapprove of nectarines in general? Or even of boys in general?"[31] What he did object to was the abuse of something good—to God's gift of sexuality being cheapened and ruined by being misused. And obscenity, like thievery, stole the good and left emptiness behind.

Lewis argued that, historically, the Christian has had a redemptive perspective on sexuality, one that enables us to laugh at what's funny and cherish what's sacred. He pointed out that "Christianity, by its insistence on compassion and on the sanctity of the human body, had a tendency to soften or abash the more extreme brutalities and flippancies of the ancient world in all departments of human life, and therefore also in sexual matters."[32]

Lewis tried to show how fitting sexual humor could be, once men and women are freed by Christ, in the farcical finale of *That Hideous Strength*. When the goddess Venus descends on the community at St. Anne's, all manner of love and lovemaking breaks forth in glorious, fertile comedy. Like a Shakespearean comedy, all manner of couples began to unite at the end. Mr. Bultitude, the resident bear, waits as the future Mrs. Bultitude refreshes herself, bobbing up and down, lifting her legs in a funny way as though trying to dance, and getting mixed up in a string of onions and a plum pudding. Bears seemed quite modest when it came to lovemaking, Lewis thought. "Perhaps they neither marry nor are given in marriage, but gather their young from the flowers as Virgil thought the bees did. It would explain why the bear's whelp has to be 'licked into shape.'"[33] Lewis's own Mr. Bultitude in *That Hideous Strength* is warm, bumbling, friendly, and, when his beloved appears, very modest. The Jackdaw flies away with his Jill as hedgehogs, mice, and an excited mare and her stallion all grunt, squeak, and whinny in revelry on such a delicious night. ("*So geht es in Snutzeputzhausel Da singen und tanzen die Mausel!*") "This," the old Scottish bachelor MacPhee says with great emphasis, "is becoming indecent." "On the contrary," says Ransom, "decent in the old sense, *decens*, fitting, is just what it is. Venus herself is over St. Anne's."[34]

MacPhee still wants to draw the curtains, as elephants begin their mating dance, like a minuet of merry giants. "You seem to forget," he retorts, "there are ladies present." To which the resident spinster Grace Ironwood counters: "There will be nothing unfit for anyone to see." She orders the curtains drawn wider.

Rather than obscene smirking or prudery among the company, there is a joyous celebration of things as they were created. "Man is no longer isolated," Ransom announces. "We are now as we ought to be—between the angels who are our elder brothers and the beasts who are our jesters, servants, and playfellows."[35] Obscenity is erased by delight. That laughter joins goodness is indicated by one minor, anonymous Scottish poet who poetically (and literally) spoke of passion for a real woman. In *The Kingis Quair*, we are reminded that

> Aphrodite even in her first appearance, when all the future is dark and the present unsatisfied, is still the golden, the laughter-loving goddess. Such is the reward of his literalism, his Scotch fidelity to the hard fact. And this fidelity has another, perhaps a stranger result. As love-longing becomes more cheerful it also becomes more moral. His Aphrodite loves laughter, but she is a temperate, nay a christened, Aphrodite.[36]

To follow this goddess in her laughter and her loving may be for some the beginning of a pilgrimage into goodness.

After exuberant courtships, even the animals are as private as human lovers, wandering off to their own boudoirs. But they model the bold freedom and natural goodness of enjoying the sexual act. There is no embarrassment, only humility and expectation. Jane Studdock is told that her estranged husband, Mark, is waiting for her back at the Lodge (where she unknowingly had prepared her own chamber bed), and she demurs: "Am I a bear or a hedgehog?" Ransom answers her: "More—but not less. Go in obedience and you will find love."[37] When the decent arrives, the indecent must depart. Seen in their divine places, the objects of obscenity are redeemed, washed, perfumed. They become occasions for beauty and glory, and for blessed and fertile human comedy.

Part 5

Satire and Flippancy

Mock on, mock on, Voltaire, Rousseau:
Mock on, mock on: 'tis all in vain!
You throw the sand against the wind,
And the wind blows it back again.
—WILLIAM BLAKE

For where God built a church, there the
Devil would also build a chapel . . .
Thus is the Devil ever God's ape.
—MARTIN LUTHER

Introduction

It's hard not to write satire.
—Juvenal

On the border between wit and flippancy lies the dangerous realm of satire. Whenever wit aims at striking you sharply in the face rather than slapping you heartily on the back, it falls into satire. Whenever flippancy applies itself to the surgical removal of the cancers of hypocrisy, heresy, and other human vices, it rises into satire. One laughs aloud at good wit and chuckles, perhaps, at clever flippancy; but the laughter that satire evokes (if laughter does occur) teeters between a shocked snort and cynical chuckle.

Satire appeals to a different sense than the rounder, funnier types of humor, like fun and jokes. The latter appeals to our comic sense, the funny bone that vibrates at the sight or sound of sudden incongruities. But satire appeals to our common sense, that part of our minds that distinguishes sense from nonsense and finds the contrast ridiculous. Common sense is the foundation of satire because it is the recognition of common sense that forms the "accepted background . . . against which figures can be made to look comic and sprawling like caricatures."[1]

Like the joke, satiric laughter arises out of the unexpected and the incongruous, which means that one must first conceive of the expected and congruent. If there is no norm, then nothing will appear abnormal and worth satirizing. If chaos or lunacy reigns, there is no role for the jester; rather one looks desperately for a judge. But if reason rules, comedy may run wild. Laughter is a green tree that must die without its roots in rationality, and, in that sense, satire is like an argument: Both require a reasonable foundation. Lewis, then, could find quarreling, as well as jesting, funny.[2] Chesterton circled and cornered this idea: "A lunatic is not startling to himself, because he is quite serious; that is what makes him a lunatic. A man who thinks he is a poached egg is to himself as plain as a poached egg. . . . It is only sanity that can see even a wild poetry in insanity."[3]

The nature of the universe, Lewis argued, cannot really be alien to reason. A mindless, irrational nature cannot be the mother of reason, for the irrational cannot give birth to the rational. Lewis argued: "It is as if cabbages, in addition to resulting *from* the laws of botany also gave lectures in that subject; or as if, when I knocked my pipe, the ashes arranged themselves into letters which read: We are the ashes of a knocked-out pipe." Laughter still protects the universe with reason as well. It deters passion from taking over, for "once passion takes part in the game, the human reason, unassisted by Grace, has about as much chance of retaining its hold on truths as a snowflake has of retaining its consistency in the mouth of a blast furnace."[4]

In *The Pilgrim's Regress*, John is rescued from the giant's dungeon and the spirit of the age by Virgin Reason. Her riddles and parables confound the giant, whose realm falls apart without a reasonable foundation. It is Reason that frees John to laugh at the illusions and skeptical disbelief under which he was held captive.

Those who would be skeptical of human thought must be skeptical even of the skeptical thought of the moment—"just as the man who warns the newcomer 'Don't trust anyone in this office' always expects you to trust him at that moment."[5] Much of Lewis's (and Chesterton's) satire is directed against modern thought and modern things. On psychoanalysis and economics explaining away the validity of thought, he wrote: "Thus the Freudian proves that all thoughts are merely due to complexes except the thoughts which constitute this proof itself. The Marxist proves that all thoughts result from class conditioning—except the thought he is thinking when he says this."[6] If a person's mind is skeptical and open on the ultimate foundations of theoretical or practical reason, Lewis quipped, "Let his mouth at least be shut."[7]

Reason may be the ground for satire, wit, and humor, but, like every aspect of life, it, too, has a natural tendency to go wrong. Like everything tainted by original sin, it needs balance and proportion (and ultimately redemption) lest it also become an object for satire. Those who try to fit an understanding of all the world in their heads will most likely find their heads exploding. Great secular wits and other naturalists trying to comprehend all mysteries of life may fall into a witless madness. "Their incessant calculation of their own brains and other people's brains is a dangerous trade," warned Chesterton. "A flippant person might answer that a hatter is mad because he has to measure the human head."[8]

Lewis and Chesterton saw nothing irrational in exercising powers other than our reason, and even suggested that mirth be allowed to air reason out. Lewis cited a conversation from Jane Austen's *Pride and Prejudice* as an apt illustration of this interplay:

> "I should like Balls infinitely better," said Caroline Bingley, "if they were carried on in a different manner. . . . It would surely be much more rational if conversation instead of dancing made the order of the day." "Much more rational, I dare say," replied her brother, "but it would not be near so much like a Ball."[9]

As reason is the basis for recognizing the laughable and the absurd as deviation from the normative standards, so is laughter the pit for tripping and trapping a tyrannical, oppressive Dame Reason—and a balm for healing a sick and enflamed reason. When Reason tries to organize and regulate all of life, laughter catches the Dame being hoisted by her own petard. The world may be reasonable, but it is not to be imprisoned by Reason.

In *The Abolition of Man*, Lewis decried the loss of rationality and an objective sense of morality in modern education. Reason rules the appetites by means of the "spirited element." "The head rules the belly through the chest—the seat . . . of Magnanimity, of emotions organized by trained habit into stable sentiments. The Chest—Magnanimity—Sentiment—these are the indispensable liaison officers between cerebral man and visceral man."[10] Those who would take away the teaching and practice of the natural law would produce what may be called "Men without Chests." Claiming to be intellectuals, these debunkers of traditional values show not an "excess of thought" but a "defect of fertile and generous emotion . . . Their heads are no bigger than the ordinary: it is the atrophy of the chest beneath that makes them seem so."[11]

To be without a set of moral laws is also to be soon without a basis for comedy. To be without chests is to be without the healthy lungs that give us hearty laughter, or to let all laughter descend to the belly and below. If rationality is no more than instinct, what amount of attention will be paid if one discovers that "my impulse to serve posterity is just the same kind of thing as my fondness for cheese"?[12]

Lewis satirized this condition in both apologetic and fictive works. "The man without a moral code, like the animal, is free from moral problems. The man who has not learned to count is free from mathematical problems. A man asleep is free from all problems." He didn't deny the possibility of people at some times being in an ethical vacuum—of obeying no ethical system. "But most of those who are in that state are by no means engaged in deciding what system they shall adopt, for such men do not often propose to adopt any. They are often concerned with getting out of gaols or asylums."[13]

An ethical system points to an ideal and points to the fact that we do not attain that ideal. Lewis identified these two facts as the foundation of all clear thinking: "First, that human beings, all over the earth, have this curious idea that they ought to behave in a certain way, and cannot really get rid of it. Secondly, that they do not in fact behave that way."[14]

This discrepancy shouts of our human predicament. When we deny or ignore it, we lose all sense of what the universe and we are about. The ingenuous and witless act of thinking we are good, fine, nice people misses the terrible crisis in the core of our being. "Yes, thank you, we enjoy God and all is well." Lewis suggested we need to be shocked out of our complacency to recognize how deep and critical the problem really is.

Does one "care for" or "enjoy" the Sermon on the Mount? I suppose no one "cares for" it. Who can like being knocked flat on his face by a sledgehammer? I can hardly imagine a more deadly spiritual condition than that of the man who can read that passage with tranquil pleasure. This is indeed to be "at ease in Zion" (Amos vi. 1.). Such a man is not yet ripe for the Bible; he had better start by learning sense from Islam: "The heaven and the earth and all between, thinkest thou I made them in jest?"[15]

Everything demands a proper or ordinate response. A roaring cataract calls for a sense of sublimity. A decaying corpse invites a sense of the numinous. A sight of a tall woman and a short man walking hand in hand offers objective data for a sense of humor. The feebleminded notion that all is well with ourselves deserves a long-needled shot of satire if we hope for a cure for our feeble minds.

Chesterton warns that it is a grave error to underestimate this kind of wit as something trivial: "For certain purposes of satire it can truly be the sword of the spirit, and the satirist bears not the sword in vain. But it is essential to wit that he should bear the sword with ease; that for the wit the weapon should be light if the blow be heavy."[16]

Even the light blow of irony, like satire, requires a norm. "Unless there is something about which the author is never ironical, there can be no true irony in the work. 'Total irony'—irony about everything frustrates itself and becomes insipid."[17] A salad of all onions would overwhelm the taste buds, but as Sydney Smith put it in his *Recipe for Salad*: "Let onion atoms lurk within the bowl / And, half-suspected, animate the whole." The presence of a subtle hint of anise may do more to undo a reader's mind than a Swiftian deluge of garlic. In *Sir Gibbie*, George MacDonald spelled out the irony of a character who was "sorely troubled with what is, by huge discourtesy, called a bad conscience—being in reality a conscience doing its duty so well that it makes the whole house uncomfortable."[18]

Irony can be found in many aspects of life. For example, Lewis poses a question that points out the curious relations of cause and effect in romance: "As for the lady who consents to marry you—are you sure she had not decided to do so already? Your proposal, you know, might have been the result, not the cause of her decision."[19]

Mark Studdock encounters the irony of his writing profession when, as author of an authoritative article on vagrancy, he actually meets and experiences a genuine tramp, a vagrant.

In *After Ten Years*, Agamemnon laughs at Yellowbeard and his wife. "You don't know how to handle women," he said. "When a man does know, there's never any trouble. Look at me now. Ever heard of Clytemnestra giving me any trouble? She knows better." The irony of the king's speech occurs when he returns home and his wife kills him. Boast not, lest ye fall into irony. Such, too, is the irony of Screwtape's Hell. "The justice of Hell is purely realistic, and concerned with results. Bring us back food, or be food yourself." Such an instructive declaration to Wormwood comes from his "increasingly and ravenously affectionate uncle."[20]

When Eustace and Jill are told that they will be the special guests for the giants' autumn feast, the underlying meaning is menacing and morbid. The irony darkens when the evil Green Lady sends "the two fair Southern children for the autumn feast" in the giants' city of Harfong. The giants smile in sinister ways, for the chief ingredient of the autumn feast is man: "This elegant little biped . . . long valued as a delicacy."[21] The invitation to be the central part of the feast means simply that they are to be the feast, being the primary ingredients for a human stew. Such is the double entendre of *How to Serve Man*, which is a cookbook rather than a manual on courtesy and etiquette.

The irony of people receiving what they ask for is humorously drawn out in *The Last Battle*. Shift, the ape, is seen as a fool. But a dwarf sees the ironic justice (and relishes it) of this ape who didn't believe in Tash getting more than he bargained for when Tash the demon-god came. "'Ho, ho, ho!' chuckled the Dwarf, rubbing its hairy hands together. 'It will be a surprise for the Ape. People shouldn't call for demons unless they really mean what they say.'"[22]

The grim humor of irony to criticize by praise is exhibited in Lewis's poetry. The actual meaning is expressed in terms that convey the opposite meaning:

> She was beautifully, delicately made
> So small, so unafraid,
> Till the bombs came.
> Bombs are the same,
> Beautifully, delicately made.[23]

Orual complains against the seemingly ironic injustice of the gods: They expect humans to know what to do, but they only hover and hint. They "will not show themselves openly and tell us what they would have us do." They draw near only in dreams and oracles and become "dead silent when we question them and then glide back and whisper (words we cannot understand) in our ears when we most wish to be free of them. . . . What is all this but cat-and-mouse play, blindman's bluff, and mere jugglery?"[24] The irony of Orual's complaint turns on her own deafness and blindness. How can the gods meet us face-to-face until we have faces? We must wait to receive the ability to receive, to see, and to hear even before we understand the ways of the gods.

Lewis defended the Christian faith with wit and humor as much as with discursive apologetics. The feather disarmed an opponent as effectively as the rapier. It tickled and caught one off guard, allowing truth to surprise the opponent unaware, and, in a sense, to pierce defenses more easily than could a battling adversary engaged in hand-to-hand combat.

One early tactic of Lewis was to allow truth to descend from any source, from classic mythology to Balaam's ass. His jolly freedom to accept evidence from any quarter assuredly threw adversaries off balance. Knowing his own solid foundation, he was willing to let others stand on whatever sands they wished, only to discover that whatever

rock was beneath was merely a hidden part of orthodoxy. Thus, for
Lewis, a

> Christian who understands his own religion laughs when unbe-
> lievers expect to trouble him by the assertion that Jesus uttered no
> command which had not been anticipated by the Rabbis—few,
> indeed, which cannot be paralleled in classical, ancient Egyptian,
> Ninevite, Babylonian, or Chinese texts. We have long recognized
> that truth with rejoicing.[25]

All religions and philosophies held hints or traces of the one
true and complete faith. Lewis cited Hooker's belief that "all kinds
of knowledge, all good arts, sciences, and the disciplines come from
the Father of lights and are 'as so many sparkles resembling the bright
fountain from which they rise.'"[26] God is the Father of all lights—
natural lights as well as spiritual lights, scintillating, comic lights as
well as steady, solemn ones.

Lewis, in fact, was concerned over those who deny or neglect the
natural for absorption in the supernatural lights. When Deguileville's
fourteenth-century homiletic poem, *Pelerinage*, attacked *Romance of
the Rose*, it was more concerned to preach a sermon against nature
(using the allegorical method of pulpits) than to delight its audience.
In it, an allegorical Grace Dieu overthrows Nature (and then human
reason), described at her first entry as "a mere bustling and scolding
old woman. The comic effect . . . is almost certainly intended, for the
homiletic tradition by no means excludes buffoonery."[27]

Lewis criticized such a tendency, writing that he was "inclined to
distrust that species of respect for the spiritual order which bases itself
on contempt for the natural." And Lewis would be especially suspicious of anyone who would portray Venus not as young and beautiful
but "old and crone-like and masked, riding on a sow," as someone
removed from the truths behind the Song of Songs. He found such
ideas more pagan than Christian. He was more inclined to recognize

Nature and her virtues as expressions of God's revelation. Alanus, in his *Anticlaudianus*, wanting to unite goodness, had Natura call for her virtuous sisters: "Concord and Youth, Honesty, Prudence, Good Faith, Nobility, Virtue, Reason who is the measure of good, and Laughter [Risus] who clears the clouds of the mind."[28] These natural allies, like Virtue in *The Pilgrim's Progress*, are not saviors but friends. They are, if one will, Godsent humanistic helpers and companions on the road to goodness. They will not get one through the gates of Jerusalem, but for their part they will point to what Jerusalem is all about.

A knowledge of such virtues and moral truths was for Lewis one of two basic facts of human experience. The first, as has been simply stated, is we know that we ought to live in a certain way. The second fact is also clear to all honest people: that we do not in fact live that way. None of us lives up to the standard we acknowledge.

Lewis's definition of a practicing Christian was one who was seeking a perfect imitation of and obedience to the life of Christ; "Not in an idiotic sense—it doesn't mean that every Christian should grow a beard, or be a bachelor, or become a travelling preacher. It means that every single act and feeling, every experience, whether pleasant or unpleasant, must be referred to God."[29] God does not want us to become nice people but wants us to be recreated in His Spirit as new men and new women, to be lifted from our natural lives to an abundant life in and through Jesus Christ.

When asked the question, "What are we to make of Jesus Christ?" Lewis almost laughs: "This is a question which has, in a sense, a frantically comic side. For the real question is not what are we to make of Christ, but what is He to make of us? The picture of a fly sitting deciding what it is going to make of an elephant has comic elements about it."[30]

Lewis set the claims of Christ beside other religious leaders and suggested a comic meeting of the minds. It was as if one (other than Steve Allen) asked Buddha, Socrates, Confucius, and Mohammed: "Are you God?" Buddha would probably respond, "My son, you are

still in the vale of illusion." Socrates would have laughed heartily at
you. Confucius might reply (like a fortune cookie): "Remarks which
are not in accordance with nature are in bad taste," and Mohammed
would have screamed, "Rent his clothes and then cut your head off."[31]
Christ's claim to be God, however, places Him *Aut Deus aut malus
homo*, either God or a bad man (or, as Lewis parroting Chesterton
writes elsewhere, a complete lunatic on the level of a man who thinks
he is a poached egg).[32]

Laughter allows one to sneak theology in the back door, past dis-
approving and stern dragons, to communicate truth and goodness
past watchdogs of political and ideological correctness. Mathews, a
convert to the Christian faith, wrote Lewis a letter:

> My mother says I have waited too long to thank you for having
> turned me into a reasoning and fairly lovable Christian. It seems
> I was quite the simpering little demon before reading *Screwtape*,
> etc., and she wants you to know how grateful she is to you for hav-
> ing taken me off her hands (spiritually speaking). She claims you
> accomplished this by speaking to my sense of humor (the logical
> approach to most young demons, I tell her) and that, with your
> help, I literally laughed my way out of the darkness (which is bet-
> ter, I feel, than groping around in the cloisters with God with a
> Knapsack on one's back, and a look of smug piety on one's face).[33]

Satire's ostensible purpose is, as a good public relations firm would
advertise, to function as a social corrective, a comic form that cuts
through pride, prejudice, and errors like a knife cuts through butter. It
does not aim at laughter as much as it does at exposing fraud and folly.
It is supposed to cauterize wounds without killing the patient, but, of
course, it also adds salt and injury to open sores. The purgatory pain
is, or rather could be, cleansing and healing—after an often brutal and
bloody surgery, as in the verbal wars of Roman Catholics and their
reformers in the sixteenth century.

30

A Storehouse of Satire

*Satire is a sort of glass, wherein beholders do generally
discover everybody's face but their own.*
—JONATHAN SWIFT

One great surprise to those who have not studied the religious con-
flicts of the sixteenth-century Reformation is the familiar presence of
humor and satire. Medieval pulpits admitted the excellences of comic
style regularly, and religious battles were brightly colored with comic
literary banners. The conflict twixt Papists and Protestants summoned forth the weapons of satire and humor on both sides. And
Lewis, who believed passionately in the unity of Christian orthodoxy,
not only permitted one segment of the faithful to mock and satirize
the faults and excesses of another, but he seemed to relish the comic
taunting that occurred within the family of God. Each member could
justifiably satirize and purge its enemy and its brother.

The saintly and ascetic Roman Sir Thomas More was famed for his
witty and abusive sense of humor. His friend Erasmus praised More's
passion for jokes, suggesting that one might even suspect that "he had
been born for them." In 1516, More's *Utopia* arrived. "Erasmus speaks
of it as if it were primarily a comic book. . . . More himself in later life
classes it and *The Praise of Folly* together as books fitter to be burned
than translated in an age prone to misconstruction."[1] Its real place,
Lewis argued, is not, as modern readers see it, as a serious philosophical or political treatise, but as a work of satire and imaginary invention.
Tongue-in-cheek, Lewis wrote: "It is, of course, possible that More's
sixteenth-century readers, and More himself, were mistaken." The
modern reader takes grandly serious what was bubble blowing for

More. "And here we have to do with one who, as the Messenger told him in the *Dialogue*, 'used to look so sadly' when he jested that many were deceived."[2] Lewis suspected, with good reason, that *Utopia* works best as a "satiric glass" in which we should see our own face and avarice, rather than a tract of practical advice.

> On my view . . . it becomes intelligible and delightful as soon as we take it for what it is—a holiday work, a spontaneous overflow of intellectual high spirits, a revel of debate, paradox, comedy and (above all) of invention, which starts many hares and kills none. It was written by More the translator of Lucian and friend of Erasmus, not More the chancellor or the ascetic. Its place on our shelves is close to *Gulliver* and *Erewhon*, within reasonable distance of Rabelais, a long way from the *Republic* or *New Worlds for Old*.[3]

His imaginative geography and politics are wonderfully satiric inventions. He makes imaginary maps for fun and sheer pleasure. "That is what readers whose interests are rigidly political do not understand"—but anyone who has ever made up an imaginary world (like Lewis's own Boxen or Narnia) or a satiric hoax will understand fully. Even in a horror book on purgatory, *Supplication of Souls*, More does not desert his humor, but uses it in all its dark and macabre power. With the howls of graphic physical torture come "peals of harsh laughter—of devils, whose company is more horrible and tormenting than the pain itself."[4] It is enough to persuade one to become a convert.

More possesses an armory of comic and slapstick weapons. His use of low comedy, with old medieval jokes (many stale) about women— like the lady who stopped her husband's lecture on astronomy or the woman who talked in church—are merry, refreshing, and persuasive in his confutations. Lewis argued that More was our "first great cockney humorist, the literary ancestor of Martin Marprelate and Nashe," because he knew how to play to the gallery. More could be scurrilous in his humor. He was not "more scurrilous, only more amusingly scurrilous, than many of our older controversialists."[5] Father Cuthbert noted a mental resemblance between More and Chesterton and "could well imagine them sitting together making jokes, some of them very good and some of them very bad."[6]

In such references to heretics who "have as much shame in their face as a shotten herring hath shrimps in her tail" or to "lowsy Luther" and his "abominable bichery," we see More's ability to appeal to the common and vulgar with the gusto of "hard-hitting, racy, street-corner abuse." Lewis had no quarrel with comic abuse in his polemical writings. "It is when he is being serious that his abusiveness becomes a literary fault. . . . He cannot denounce like a prophet; he can only scold and grumble like a father in an old-fashioned comedy."[7]

In his comic and grotesque style, More writes well. When he tries to be a solemn or merely scurrilous essayist, he becomes heavy and stodgy. It is humor that kept him effective. His homely, good phrases ("every finger shall be a thumb," "fume, fret, frot, and foam") and merry tales make for excellent vernacular communication. Lewis noted: "Nearly all that is best in More is comic or close to comedy."[8]

In writing of More's sanctity, Lewis observed that "he lived and died like a saint, and that is a better thing than to write like one, but it is not the same thing; and More does not write like a saint." Rather he writes for a common citizen of Tudor London. Whatever heights of wisdom and goodness More rose to, he remained "unmistakably rooted in a world of fat, burgher laughter, contentedly acclaiming well-seasoned jokes about shrewish wives or knavish servants, contemptuous of airs and graces and of what it thinks unnecessary subtleties."[9] And to the droll humor, the satiric and fictional invention, and the imaginative fertility of More's mind, Lewis himself was not to be less but more indebted.

From William Tyndale, on the other hand, Lewis took more theology than writing style. "In one quality, he is obviously inferior to his great antagonist [More]: that is, in humour." The great Reformer dismissed, unflinchingly, "fables of love and wantonness and of ribauldry, as filthy as hart can thinke." (This, as Lewis pointed out, oddly included Robin Hood.) Yet even in a diatribe against asceticism and Ovid's false chastity (in his filthy book on the remedy against love), Tyndale attacked the vile, Manichaean tendencies of medieval thinking against the goodness of womankind and marriage. He was as scurrilous as More but only occasionally used humor. Lewis cited one example (probably the only one) where Tyndale ventures a joke (to Lewis's thinking) so good that, however More detested the application, his "lips must have twitched when he read it. Tyndale has been attacking the doctrine that we can profit by the superfluous merits of the religious orders; and ends with the advice 'If thy wife geve thee nine words for three, go to the Charterhouse and bye of their silence.'"[10]

Lewis felt the primary difference between the two to be a brooding melancholy in More, even amid the fatness of his jokes. In Tyndale's severities, there is a lighter, more joyous and lyric quality, "something like laughter, that laughter which he speaks of as coming 'from the low bottom of the heart.'"[11]

Tyndale's Scottish Ally John Knox inherited some of the ferocious and boisterous humor of his Scottish forefathers. Knox describes the assassination of Cardinal Beaton "down to the last grim detail of packing the corpse in salt ('the wether was hote'). . . . 'These things we wreat mearelie: but we wold that the reader should observe Goddis just judgementis.'" Lewis commented that Knox was "apparently afraid lest the fun of the thing might lead us to forget that even an assassination may have its serious side."[12]

Mr. H. W. Brown once asked Lewis if it were true that "Christianity (especially the Protestant forms) tends to produce a gloomy, joyless condition of society which is like a pain in the neck to most people." Lewis answered:

As to the distinction between Protestant and other forms of Christianity, it is very difficult to answer. I find by reading about the sixteenth century, that people like Sir Thomas More, for whom

I have a great respect, always regarded Martin Luther's doctrines not as gloomy thinking, but as wishful thinking. . . . [Having] never lived in a completely non-Christian society nor a completely Christian one . . . [I find it difficult to answer.] I think there is about the same amount of fun and gloom in all periods. The poems, novels, letters, etc. of every period all seem to show that.[13]

Lewis found the nineteenth-century fictional Puritan to be a false image. For example, "Dickens's Mrs. Clennam, trying to expiate her early sin by a long life of voluntary gloom, was doing exactly what the first Protestants would have forbidden her to do." She smacked "too much of papistical and ascetic expiation," of too much fasting and puny, ridiculous efforts to set herself right. Faith, not works, is the heart of the Puritans.

Some of the stock gags in the commercial theater of Shakespeare were grounded in this tension between faith and works. "The real reason why any reference to faith and works (or merit) is sure of a response in the theatre is that this topic touches men's pockets: one of the seats of laughter."[14] Those who emphasize the priority of works as the best kind of charity are usually those who want the money. On the other hand, those who stress faith (usually a tightfisted landlord or usurer) would refuse to see the relevance of money in the practice of their faith. Jibes were easily recognized as referring to either the penurious faith of the Puritans or the greedy, indulgence-selling Romans.

The first doctrines of the radical Puritans were not of labor and fear but of joy and hope, and relief and buoyancy characterized their lives. For Thomas More, Protestants were not too grim, but too giddy and glad to be true—"dronke of the new must of lewd lightnes of minde and vayne gladness of harte." This lightness is evident even in the *Institutes* of the severe Swiss John Calvin, who wrote that when God created food, "He intended not only the supplying of our necessities but delight and merriment (*hilaritas*)."[15] But that was as light as Calvin got.

When one examines the quarrel between the Puritans and Papists, one discovers (surprisingly at odds with popular imagery) that the Romans were more rigorous and the Puritans more liberal. For example, Lewis wrote:

> On many questions and specially in view of the marriage bed, the Puritans were the indulgent party, if we may w/o disrespect so use the name of a great Roman Catholic, a great writer, and a great man, they were much more Chestertonian than their adversaries. The idea that a Puritan was a repressed and repressive person would have astonished Sir Thomas More and Luther about equally.[16]

As we have mentioned, More viewed Puritans to the contrary as erring in the "direction of fantastic optimism," as those who "loved no Lenten fast."[17]

The Puritans were not a sour, precise company attacking a merry olde Catholic England. The Puritans—emphasizing a purity of theology and polity, and not primarily chastity—were seen as "young, fierce, progressive intellectuals—very fashionable and up to date." As they were not teetotalers, their special aversion was bishops, not beer. Their creed was revolutionary, progressive, and humanistic. "In reality the puritans and the humanists were quite often the same people," both joining to burn scholastic, medieval, and popish books in Oxford in 1550. The humanists or classicists were characterized by a new hatred of medieval things like romance, Latin, chivalry, fairies, and scholasticism. They prided themselves on the purity of Ciceronian Greek and an avoidance of the simple, rustic, low, or ugly. "That is how," Lewis pointed out, "the humanists came to create a new literary quality—vulgarity." One could comically "catch a humanist using a word, that Heaven forbid, Cicero did not use."[18] The humanist's tendency toward classical sophistication and urbanity and the emphasis away from low and vulgar things (including comedy) was then shared with the Puritan, who was thus infected with the image of the proper and hypocritical Mrs. Grundy.

At the outset, however, we see a closer resemblance to Luther's *Table Talk*, where "we are at once struck by the geniality. . . . If Luther is right, we have waked from nightmare into sunshine" and into a celebration of marriage, food, drink, and women. More, on the other hand, "hardly ever mentions a woman save to ridicule her."[19] When one hears Martin Luther recommending that "it is pleasing to the dear God whenever thou rejoices or laughest from the bottom of thy heart," one receives a raucous, even carnival, sound of laughter.[20]

Throughout history, the thrust and parry of satire demonstrates how the divine virtue of justice was administered to bring low the high and mighty. The apologist who uses satire to cut and expose may be closer to a surgeon than a swordsman. Lewis once described himself as a "doctor of death" operating on those cancerous philosophies and the deadly Zeitgeist of life force optimists like Bergson and Shaw.[21] But Lewis was a words-warrior too. The little man who wields the mighty satiric pen can become Jack the Giant killer. And when he does, his first duty, as Lewis saw it, is to probe his own society with his pen—to impale his own and his contemporaries' faults on the sword of satire.

> It seems to me of practical importance that the analytical and critical bent of our age should not be expended entirely on our ancestors and that confusions should sometimes be exposed while they are still potent. *It is more dangerous to tread on the corns of a live giant than to cut off the head of a dead one: but it is more useful and better fun.*[22]

As will be shown, Lewis tilted his lance at the live giants not a few times in his personal and critical writings.

The conditions of a sick society not only invite satire but also seem to demand it. Looking at the hypocrisy and avarice of the medieval church, Lyndsey aptly satirized monks and friars as birds of prey. In 1588, when the church and its bishops controlled the press, "Martin Marprelate" published his raucous satires such as *Oh read over D. John Bridges*. Lewis expressed no sympathy with those who, with prim mouths, were outraged at Martin "Bad-Prelate" for "introducing scurrility into theological debate, for debate was precisely what the bishops had suppressed. Those who refuse to let their opponents dispute have no right to complain if they hear instead lewd catcalls in the street; in a sense, it is what they have chosen."[23]

Grave and solemn members of Martin's own party disowned him primarily for the kind of common weapon he chose for his satire. His methods were hardly intended to convert a critical inquirer. He justified his choice of battling in a "racy, fleering, cockney manner": "The most part of men could not be gotten to read anything in the defence of one and against the other. I bethought me therefore of a way whereby men might be drawn to both." His catalog of old and new devices provides an arsenal for satirists of any age, such as Steven Colbert or John Stewart. He suggested inventing novel, high-falutin' language or feigned mispronunciations (*Confocation house, Paltripolitans, dissimblation*), and imitating inarticulate noises (*Ha, Ha, Ha* or *Tse-tse-tse*) to offset one's opponent. In his practice of apologetics, Lewis himself seemed to copy Martin's recommendations for "interruptions or encouragements from voices in the margin ('Now I pray the good martin speake out') and again replies to these voices ('Why sauceboxes, must you be prattling?')."[24] Martin simultaneously promises and threatens to publish other books for the clergy that they might hear of "good sport." This novel and rowdy guerrilla style in various controversies, these loud jeerings and raillery, are known as a special offshoot of satire called *flyting*.

Sixteenth-century England encouraged this bellicose kind of abusive satire. Flyting was a primarily Scottish practice of scolding or quarreling with angry words, which could easily become a verbal brawl. Traditional flyting was mostly a personal attack on all "estates" in government, aristocracy, clergy, and the *hoi polloi*. For example,

Robert Greene's lively sixteenth-century satire on various professions took on prissy tailors "eating their pease with their needels pointes, one by one."[25]

Lewis found the opening of Alexander Montgomerie's poetic attack against Polwart irresistible. The 1597 work was called, simply and clearly, "Flyting." "Polwart, ye peip like a mouse amongst thornes; Na cunning ye keip; Polwart, ye peip. Ye luik like a sheipe [if] ye had two hornes; Polwart, ye peip like a mouse amongst thornes" [peip = squeak].[26]

Mean and vicious words are thrown like poisoned darts. In fact, satire is often thought to be derived from the notion of throwing. Before battles among ancient peoples, the satirist was sent out first. Believing enthusiastically in the magic of the word, where, as Kenneth Burke points out, the word was the act, curses were thrown at the enemy like a barrage of arrows. Examples occur not only in Homer but in the Old Testament as well. Before wielding his sword, Goliath taunts the Israelites and little David, whom he threatens to feed to the birds. Elijah mocks the prophets of Baal in their contest. Words, especially abusive words, have the power not only to demoralize but also to destroy. They carry their own efficacy and power.

Satire speaks with such stings and arrows to wound the enemy. When it is done with wit and humor, it becomes a splendid art. Two favorites of Lewis stand out as masters of comic flyting: William Dunbar and Thomas Nashe.

Dunbar's satiric poems are laced with a streak of comic meanness. He, like a medieval shock jock, composed

typical squibs on some episode that had amused the court for a day . . . on a "rag" in the queen's apartments which seemed funny to the participants though its humours have long since faded . . . on the death of the cheery old reprobate Andrew Kennedy, whose testament in shameless, reeling, goliardic vein does a man's heart good to the present day.[27]

In his *Complaint to the King*, Dunbar exhibits a goblin energy.
With rollicking gusto he slaughters a set of unworthy rivals for secur-
ing a promotion he missed, calling them "these driveling, shuffling,
puff-cheeked, club-faced hashbalds, haggar-balds, and mandrakes."
The bright colors and extravagance of his language lend noticeable
force to his abusive play. His couplets of advice to those who live in this
unfair world are touched with a light insouciance: "Be mirry, Man,
and tak nocht for in mynde / The wauering of this wrechit world of
sorrow. / Man, pleis they Maker and be mirry / And sett nocht by this
warld a chirry."[28]

Lewis warns those who would read Dunbar: "If you like half-
tones and nuances you will not like Dunbar; he will deafen you." His
other work does not flyte as much as flaunt his wild and noisy fun
making. The wanton whoops of boisterous laughter come through in
Dunbar's most celebrated satire: *The Twa Maritt Wemen and the Wedo*
(two married women and the widow). The poem sets up its audience for a serious love allegory with idyllic romance wafting through
the air. However, Dunbar plays a practical joke on any settled expectations for a romance poem on two married women and a widow.
"Instead of romance, a sheerly preposterous poem bursts upon them,
with almost unparalleled grossness of the things the three women
say . . . piling audacity on audacity."

We are cautioned to correct our modern, refined expectations of
connecting "extreme indecency with technical coarseness of form and
with low social rank." (This, Lewis chides, we get from the classical
humanists.) We must readjust our own tastes and "think ourselves
back into a world where great professional poets, to the entertainment
of great lords and ladies, lavished their skill on humors now confined
to the preparatory school or the barrack-room." Lewis does not judge
whether we have improved. Lewis advised of this unrestrained and
coarse barracks atmosphere of horseplay: "If you cannot relish a romp
you had best leave this extravaganza alone; for it offers you no other
kind of pleasure."[29]

On Thomas Nashe, Lewis wrote that "the very qualities which we should blame in an ordinary conversationalist are the life and soul of Nashe. He is unfair, illogical, violent, extravagant, coarse: but then that is the joke."[30]

This Elizabethan pamphleteer was an impudent word juggler "who can keep a crowd spellbound by sheer virtuosity." Nashe is not a little offensive (as is, Britisher Lewis noted, Mark Twain when he writes of King Arthur) because he is bold, sassy, and abusive; yet he is a most original satirist of the uncultured, unrefined, *literary sansculottisme*—those, literally, without breeches. He was a supreme master of lower class, cheap-jack, and gutter-snipe elements, with an irrepressible relish for roguery. These techniques require their own sort of genius. Yet, Lewis wrote, he added "something quite different: comic inkhorn terms, burlesque rodomontade, gigantic hyperbole, Rabelaisian monstrosity." Nashe claims his style "is no otherwise puft up than any mans should be that writes with any spirite." Such a style is preferred to that "demure soft *mediocre genus* that is like wine and water mixed together, but give me pure wine of itself, and that begets blood and heates the brains thorowly."[31]

Lewis, who himself valued the vernacular and enjoyed a touch of the vulgar, praised Nashe's hearty extravagance, which was "happily married to the colloquial." Where Nashe's "predecessors had talked merely like Shakespeare's rogues, Nashe talked like Falstaff. Or, to put it the right way round, when Falstaff promises that his cudgel shall hang like a meteor over the horns of Mr. Ford, he owes something to Nashe."[32]

Lewis described Nashe's *The Terrors of the Night*—a fun, skeptical work for chasing away night-fears—as a sort of grotesque literary art comparable to the paintings of Hieronymus Bosch. In contrast to the man who dreams merrily, "like a boy new breetcht, who leapes and daunceth for joy his paine is past," Nashe draws a legion of hideous minor devils like a dark, comic company in an old carnival freak show. These nightmarish devils, "of whom infinite millions will hang swarming about a worm-eaten nose" or "entrench themselves in the wrinkles of a hag," are comic, argued Lewis, "only if you see them in a flash and from exactly the right angle. Move a hair's breadth, dwell on them a second too long, and they become disturbing."[33]

Nashe exploits this grotesque material for comic effect. Lewis borrowed from a Chestertonian image in saying that Nashe "rides the nightmare, not the nightmare him, though his seat is not always secure. Hence he is closer to Mr. Thurber's pictures than to Picasso's. He is a great American humorist."[34] His triumphant comic impudence, Lewis suggested, was bequeathed to American rather than British descendants.

Nashe's comic flyting hit a pinnacle of ridicule when it took flight against one Gabriel Harvey. The sparring between these two adversaries was quite uneven—for Nashe not only had more wit and humor, but a recklessness that was enjoyably unpredictable. Enjoyable, that is, only if you were an ally of Nashe. It is like

> when a half drunk street-corner humorist decides to make a respectable person . . . ridiculous, it is useless for the respectable person to show that the charges brought against him are untrue—that he does not beat his wife, is not a cinema star in disguise, is not wearing a false nose. The more eagerly he refutes them, the louder the spectators laugh. When the butt is anyone so unamiable, so grotesque, as Gabriel Harvey, we enjoy the fun with (almost) a clear conscience.[35]

Nashe flytes Harvey, undressing him with ease and nonchalance. He invents and flings satirical names at the man, conferring "a grievous immortality: Gilgilis Hobberdehoy, Braggadochio Glorioso, Timothy Tiptoes, Gerboduck Huddleduddle." Lewis emphasized Nashe's witty dominance in this duel: "Poor Harvey may writhe at allusions to his father the ropemaker; the more fool he, says Nashe, for 'had I a Ropemaker to my father . . . I would fourthwith have writ I praise of Ropemakers and prov'd it by sound sillogistry to be one of the 7 liberal sciences.' He would have, too."[36]

The abusive and grotesque in Nashe's satires are ridges that lead down into very different valleys: into the comic or into the cruel and sadistic. It is Nashe's low and common humor that enables him to descend, mostly, into the former. Gabriel Harvey, however, is stuck in a hole. His flyting seems merely to be retaliation for personal offenses. He is, noted Lewis, "completely overmatched by Nashe in comic abuse and what is fun to the adversary is death to him." What is also dead and absent in Harvey's flyting is the leavening comic touch. He exhibits, instead, a "hard sanctimony." He "gloats and jeers" over one man for dying in poverty and another (Marlowe), "as far as we can make out, for dying at all." Such humorless abuses, Lewis complained, were "revolting to nineteenth-century taste, as they are to mine."[37]

Lewis found a similar difficulty with Thomas Cartwright, whom he dubbed the "puritan" of popular tradition and satire. Cartwright's flyting takes off where Harvey's stopped. He wrote to correct not only great offenses and crimes but also "the smaller faultes of lying and uncomely jesting," in a style devoid of any bright patch of play. He ridicules his opponents "with great resentment, using direct insult, innuendo, taunts, and irony, but all these with hardly any humor. Hatred so massive as his, so completely reconciled to the conscience, leaves no room for fun."[38]

To argue that truth and morality are at stake does not give one the privilege of slashing and humiliating the one in error. Lewis included such mockery in a list of sins to the mind and body: massacres, theft, floggings, rape, lynching, insult, and odious hypocrisy that "smells to heaven."[39]

Such flyting results in laughter only from those who hate and wish to laugh at their enemies. The object of ridicule and abuse becomes like "the man in the 'Dark Night of the Flesh,'" a composite type that Lewis drew from the Psalms. He is

> in everyone else's eyes extremely funny; the stock joke of that whole
> school or hut or office. They can't see him without laughing; they

make faces at him (22:7). The drunks work his name into their comic songs (69:12). He is a "by-word" (44:15). Unfortunately all this laughter is not exactly honest, spontaneous laughter such as a man with some oddity of voice or face might learn to bear and even, in the end, to join in. These mockers do not laugh *although* it hurts him nor even without caring whether it hurts or not; they laugh *because* it will hurt. Any humiliation or miscarriage of his is jam to them; they crow over him when he's down—"when my foot slipped, they rejoiced greatly against me" (38:16).[40]

Such humiliation transforms satire into invidious sarcasm, like a witch turning a prince into a toad, weasel, or lawyer. It becomes mere abuse. But abusive language, without the tang of wit or humor, loses its potency to do more than stab. Personal jeering becomes a splenetic scream. Certain terms of abuse, like *swine, villain, cad,* and *knave,* are used to make "the enemy odious or contemptible by asserting he was like somebody or something he already disliked or looked down on." Lewis invented a parody of a syllogism: "Pigs (or servants or my juniors) are contemptible—John is like a pig (or servant or adolescent)—therefore John is contemptible." But this is all outdated, Lewis conceded: "It would have been far more wounding to be called swine when the word still carried some whiff of the sty and some echo of the grunt; far more wounding to be called a villain when this conjured up an image of the unwashed, malodorous, ineducable, gross, belching, close-fisted and surly boor. Now, who cares?"[41] The key to apt satire is to find what is odious in one's age and pin it on the dastardly victim/villain.

Lewis found the satires of the Elizabethan nineties a weary lot. They denounced directly, without subtlety or wit, and threw epithets around like hot Irish potatoes. "Nothing is easier, or less interesting, than to proclaim with raucous conviction that whores are unchaste, misers ungenerous, and hypocrites insincere: and the raucous passes with equal ease into the falsetto."[42]

John Donne blundered into a confusion of *satira* with *satyros*, concluding that "the one should be as shaggy and 'salvage' as the other." In his satires, however, this resulted in a "complete absence of the cheerful normality which is in Horace, or that occasional grandeur which, in Juvenal, relieves the monotony of vituperation." Thus, in Donne, we descend into "objects of contempt and disgust," to what Aristotle would recognize as real pain and the authentically ugly. We do not find the appearance of real pain mixed with the ludicrous when we "enjoy" Donne's menu of satirical topics: "coffins, 'itchie lust,' catamites, dearth, pestilence, a condemned wretch 'at Barre,' vomit, excrement, botches, pox, 'carted whores.' Instead of a norm against which the immediate object of satire stands out, we have vistas opening on corruption in every direction."[43] Satire has been undone by Donne's reign of the ugly and wretched.

Two other moralizing—and demoralizing—satirists appeared in the Elizabethan press: John Hall, who boasted (without grounds but with the published *Toothless Satires* [1597]) that he was the first English satirist; and John Marston, one nemesis worthy of his opponent's unworthiness. Hall's concern was with satire more than the objects for satire. He championed obscurity in "modern satire," so much so that Marston ridiculed him for "giving us Sphinxian riddles wrapped in such pitchy clouds as would have amazed Oedipus." Hall does use irony instead of vituperation quite admirably, at least once. In reply to his critic "Labeo," Hall "recants, admits that 'in so righteous age' he ought never to have been a satirist, and proceeds to praise his contemporaries for all the virtues they notoriously lacked." And though the following couplet does lack rich humor, it does attract one of the most deserving targets for flyting: the legal estate. "Wo to the weale where manie lawiers bee, / For there is sure much store of maladie."[44]

The best Lewis allowed from Marston is a caveat for any budding satirists: "Authors in Marston's position do not always realize that it is useless to say your work was a joke if your work is not, in fact, at all funny."[45] These men were moralists who generally practiced a humorless and witless form of satire, often merely caustic comments or bludgeon invective.

The tendency of satire toward this loudmouthed, self-righteous invective professed an ethical motive. The real motive was generally personal and sarcastic. One wise and witty man, however, attacked these censorious moralists and mocking Pharisees. Samuel Rowlands reproved other satirists as "preachers turned gamekeepers." Alone of the Elizabethan satirists, Rowlands was crowned by Lewis as having

> grasped the fact that it is useless to attack knaves unless you enter-
> tain readers, that neither moral purpose not personal malice will do
> instead of comic power. With him satire ceases to shout and learns to
> chuckle, and by dropping the shrill moral pretensions of his prede-
> cessors he becomes far more amusing and certainly no less moral.[46]

In his *Letting of Humours Blood in the Head Vein* (1600), Rowlands puts satire back on track; he takes the whips out of the hands of the flyting floggers. His satire, while never great, is nevertheless for Lewis recommendably "sane, readable, and often funny." In the grand tall-tale tradition of Baron Münchausen, he pokes fun at a lying impostor: "Heele tell you of a tree that he doth know / Upon the which rapiers and Daggers grow / As good as Fleetstreete hath in any shoppe, / Which being ripe doune into scabbards droppe."[47]

Satire should be handled as a weapon, but, as Pope and Swift believed (and practiced), a "sacred weapon" and a holy sword.[48] Lewis acknowledged the Gregorian view of culture itself as a weapon: "And a weapon is essentially a thing we lay aside as soon as we safely can."[49] But it can remain handy, for giants have many and large corns.

Lewis didn't always appreciate the art of satire, however. In a letter to his brother, he conceded that though some of Rabelais's satire was, to use a good old word, "sly," nevertheless, "satire tends always to bore me."[50] Later in life, though, Lewis learned to appreciate satire more, especially when the author prunes or masters his material—not using the satire as a megaphone to stammer or shout out his own hatred, but as a work of art that speaks for itself. Thus he preferred George Orwell's *Animal Farm* over Orwell's less effective and inferior *1984*. Lewis wrote on *Animal Farm*: "Wit and humour (absent from the longer work) are employed with devastating effect. The great sentence 'All animals are equal but some are more equal than others' bites deeper than the whole of *1984*."[51]

Lewis distinguished satire as a literary kind from the satiric, an element occurring in almost any composition. In almost any novel some character will make a satiric remark at one time or another; that does not make the work a satire. In satire as a literary type, every remark is satiric. Satire is the language with which the entire work is veiled. A variety of these types of literary satires exist. Great vernacular works like *Animal Farm*, *Candide*, *Gulliver*, *The Duncaid*, *The Rape of the Lock*, and *Hudibras* belong to a family of fantastic or mock-heroic narratives. Their "true ancestors," Lewis commented, "are Rabelais, Cervantes, the *Apocolocyntosis*, Lucian, and *The Frogs and Mice*," rather than the *Satira* of the Romans.[52]

These were satirists who could laugh at foibles without losing their balance or their souls. Rabelais was supreme in being the kind who "enjoys himself, and then enjoys his enemy. In this sense he loves his enemy, and by a kind of exaggeration of Christianity he loves his enemy the more he becomes an enemy." Rabelais would laugh because he was happy. Swift, on the other hand, laughed against his unhappiness. He was, wrote Chesterton, inflamed by "some intolerable sense of wrong. He is maddened by the sense of men being maddened; his tongue becomes an unruly member, and testifies against all mankind."[53]

But the best, and most honorable, type of satirist was the man or woman who rose "superior to his victim in the only serious sense which superiority can bear, in that of pitying the sinner and respecting the man even while he satirizes both."[54] Here is the one who can rescue the person if not correct the wrong.

Satire generally seeks to be redemptive and beneficial; yet its attack on a sick society can cross the bounds of goodness. The means can become worse than the end. The contrast between the satires of the Roman authors Horace and Juvenal suggests how desperate and sharp the art may become. Writing sermons (conversation pieces) in the golden age of Roman politics (15 BC), Horace used gentle sarcasm in chiding the follies and foibles of the Augustians, as in his fable of the city and country mice. His sword is like a rapier, light and quick and mild, such as in poking fun at aging men:

> *Why all these questions that worry and weary us?*
> *Let's drop the serious role for a while.*
> *Youth, with smooth cheeks, will be laughing behind us;*
> *Age will not mind us; the cynic—he'll smile.*
> *Come, for the gray hairs already are fretting us;*
> *Girls are forgetting us. Lord, how we've got!*
> *Come, let's convince them our blood is—well, red yet.*
> *We are not dead yet. Let's show them we're not!*

Horace's delicate swordplay is fun—yet his satire breathes in the free air of a prospering Rome. Not so for Juvenal. He takes up his broadaxe in AD 115 under Domitian, by which time subtlety had become insufficient. Avarice, perversion, and vice had reached an apex, and Juvenal proclaimed it "impossible not to write satire" in such an age.[55]

The corruption of the wealthy deserved nothing better than his bitter and scathing invective. Even on such an apparently insignificant subject as a rich woman's cosmetics, Juvenal draws blood. Describing the lady's use of ointments, creams, tonics, and donkey milk to preserve her complexion, he writes viciously: "Is that a face or an ulcer?"[56]

Juvenal believed his satire was the drastic and hostile action required to shake the complacency of a very decadent world. Lewis argued similarly that the satires of Juvenal's Roman predecessors, Lucian and Statius, "are vehicles whereby to express . . . sincere reaction to the terrible period in which they lived. No honest man's comment on that age could be made in plain terms."[57]

Lewis noted that in Juvenal's age, when the sickness of the social soul was unto death, satire "could safely deal only with those criminals who were already dead or disgraced" and as such had "little commerce with laughter."[58] In such desperate times, satire descends into a style of *de-rision*, a reversal of laughter, a removal of laughter from the arena of wit in order to awake righteous indignation. Yet satire is sharpest and most piercing when it slices into is subject and cauterizes the sore with a searing smile. Laughter keeps the doctor from despairing over her own hopeless diagnosis.

31

The Sword of Satire

Satire was for Lewis a weapon—a bright and shining sword to be wielded in the honorable service of bright and shining Reason. It would be wrong, however, to wield such a deadly weapon in anything but a deadly battle. A man who uses a sword when a soupspoon or butter knife would do is a dangerous and unwelcome man. Often in Lewis's writing, his satiric weapon is nothing larger than a penknife. He carves off small pieces of hypocrisy for sport and fun, not for blood. Lewis praised those "great wits who had written paradoxes in praise of trifles or evils—Synesius on Baldness, Erasmus of Folly, de Mornay of Death, de la Noue of Imprisonment," and Nashe on red herrings.[1]

Somewhat akin in spirit to Nashe's comic invention of the Pope's dinner and the coronation of King Herring, Lewis claimed (tongue-in-cheek) to have unearthed a lost chapter from the work of Herodotus. This chapter, he maintained, commented on a curious Roman holiday called Xmas. Celebrated in Niatirb, Xmas is a season when "every citizen is obliged to send to each of his friends and relations a square piece of hard paper stamped with a picture. . . .

> The pictures represent birds sitting on branches, or trees with a dark green prickly leaf, or else men in such garments as the Niatirbians believe that their ancestors wore two hundred years ago riding in coaches such as their ancestors used, or houses with snow on their roofs. . . . They buy as gifts for one another such things as no man

ever bought for himself . . . all kinds of trumpery . . . being useless and ridiculous.[2]

Herodotus went on to explain how the Xmas rush distracts minds from sacred things. "And we indeed are glad that men should make merry at Crissmas; but in Exmas there is no merriment left. . . . The *Rush* is a racket (strangely an instrument for the barbarian game of tennis)." The Herodotus fragment discovered by Professor Lewis ends with an image of the day after Xmas when the people "are very grave, being internally disordered by the supper and the drinking and reckoning how much they have spent on gifts and on the wine."[3]

Lewis indicated his preference for fierce satire over flippancy, which he called the "characteristically Oxonian plague. For there is a bottomless urbanity that can be very boring."[4] His practice of rugged and intense satire ranged from the explicitly apologetic to the indirect fictional attack. *That Hideous Strength* (being derived from Lyndsay's phrase describing the tower of Babel's "schaddow of that hidduous strength"[5]) is *The Abolition of Man*, veiled only slightly. He took science fiction as a vehicle for satire in the way that "nearly all the most pungent American criticism of the American way of life takes this form."[6]

The first book of the series, *Out of the Silent Planet*, is an attack on something Lewis called *scientism*,

> a certain outlook on the world which is casually connected with the popularization of the sciences . . . the belief that the supreme moral end is the perpetuation of our own species, and that this is to be pursued even if, in the process of being fitted for survival, our species has to be stripped of all those things for which we value it—of pity, of happiness, and of freedom.[7]

It was against the outlooks on life and ethics of Shaw, Stapledon, and Professor Haldane that Lewis wrote his satiric fantasies. These men could be described, as Lewis's trilogy character Oyarsa described others, as being "wounded in the brain."[8] In another character in the trilogy, the physicist Weston, Lewis created a "Buffoon-villain image of the 'metabiological' heresy."[9] Weston was not unlike Marxist biochemist J. B. S. Haldane, whose ideas of emergent evolution in other possible worlds became a clear target for Lewis's arrows. This "mad but loquacious scientist" wanted to colonize the planets. If human society were to progress, he argued, such action was necessary, regardless of the moral consequences. Likewise, for Weston a great inscrutable life force poured up "into us from the dark bases of being." This life force could prompt anything in the name of progress: murder, international treachery, or even "print lies as serious research in a scientific periodical."[10]

Weston's pal Devine may have also been based on a real person to whose philosophy Lewis was intensely opposed—Cambridge philosopher T. D. Weldon, who sought to squeeze money out of scholarship. In Lewis's books, Devine profanes anything venerable, all for the prospect of making a quick fortune. In drawing this caricature, Lewis questioned whether "it was credible that such a gas-bag could ever have invented a mouse-trap, let alone a space-ship. But then, I wanted farce as well as fantasy."[11]

The central objects of satire in *That Hideous Strength* are "not scientists but *officials*. If anyone ought to feel himself libeled by this book it is not the scientist but the civil servant: and, next to the civil servant, certain philosophers. Frost is the mouthpiece of Professor Waddington's ethical theories: by which I do not, of course, mean that Professor Waddington in real life is a man like Frost."[12] The solemn sincerity of such men concerned Lewis. He told several friends that he'd "sooner live among people who cheat at cards than among people who are earnest about not cheating at lards. [Laughter]."[13]

Lewis's fear of the tyranny and disciplined cruelty of power in the hands of a few sanitized types was explained away by Professor Haldane as Lewis's unconscious motivation to escape the loss of social and personal position by social change. Lewis replied that it "would be hard for me to welcome a change which might consign me to a concentration camp."[14] But the motive game is an unprofitable ploy in understanding this issue, wrote Lewis, because the professor might equally welcome the change that would place him in a high rank of power.

The merits of each view should be studied over their motives, Lewis argued. In his view, Lewis believed that "no man or group of men is good enough to be trusted with uncontrolled power over others." Especially one cannot trust those with high (and spiritual) pretentions. Religious governments are worst of all; for as they "hear from God," they must act in obedience to the voice or vision that commands them to train or torture their victims. Thus, argued Lewis, if we must have a tyrant, let it be a robber baron rather than an inquisitor. Those who terrorize and hurt other citizens, and do it from a passionate sense of righteousness to purify and indoctrinate society, are more dangerous than those who do it for selfish and carnal reasons. The secret police, like Miss Fairy Hardcastle, bring out another insidious public danger, sadism. She is, wrote Lewis, the common factor in all revolutions; and, as she says, "you won't get anyone to do her job well unless they get some kick out of it."[15]

Lewis also attacked friendship with the "World," not merely the attraction and temptation of money and possessions, but an attitude of worldliness. "The most 'worldly' society I have ever lived in is that of schoolboys: most worldly in the cruelty and arrogance of the strong, the toadyism and mutual treachery of the weak, and the unqualified snobbery of both." Men will stoop to base and mean acts to share in the superiority of an "inner ring." In this sense, Lewis's satire was against those who seek power and are corrupted by it. The world can be more unjust and horrible when the religious Moloch, and not the secular Mammon, sits on the throne. Lewis cited Aristotle's maxim that "Men do not become tyrants in order to keep warm." The heights that human ambition craves are dizzying and intoxicating. It is a tower as high as Babel from which the power elite want to watch and manipulate. Under the guise of requiring desperate but necessary and politically correct remedies for the desperate diseases of society, every kind of abomination arises. "Hitler, the Machiavellian Prince, the Inquisition, the Witch Doctor, all claim to be necessary."[16]

Lewis based his science-fiction romance on the supposal that "under modern conditions any effective invitation to Hell will certainly appear in the guise of scientific planning—as Hitler's regime in fact did."[17] Lewis mapped the route of his scientific planners as parallel to the path of Hogarth's rake—a "progress" into the gutter, asylum, and grave.

Lewis attacked the collective and "the Party" and such abstract ideas of human relations in both right and left camps; for there the personal and individual rights are obscured by a higher worship, a worship of the impersonal and demonic—a worship that abolishes the wonderfully peculiar and eccentric aspects of person. When revolutionaries claim to be obeying some greater law of justice and in turn abrogate the moral law to achieve their ends, they are actually obeying their vices. At this point, there is a devaluation of language in which "kill" is replaced by "liquidate," or people become "undesirable social units," or "suicide" becomes "dying with dignity." Even in teaching a child how to write, Lewis advised using concrete language. "If you mean 'More people died' don't say 'Mortality rose.'"[18] "The uneducated man never makes this mistake," Chesterton observed. "He states the simple fact that he sees a German drinking beer: he does not say 'There is a Teuton consuming alcohol.'"[19]

The fantasies of Lewis's science-fiction trilogy are satires against such things—fables for communicating Lewis's beliefs and values. Lewis believed satire could be a proper vehicle for persuading a skeptical audience; it is a way to persuade reasonable people, wary of direct, hard-sell tactics, through the back door of their imaginations.

The misuse of language in Lewis's fiction is also employed to elicit laughter. Pompous, pedantic speech is prime material for parody or satire. Of the two ministering angels in Lewis's short story, the thin feminist one, like some deconstructionist academics, requires her own interpreters. Clearing her throat, she announces:

"Anyone who has been following World-Opinion-Trend on the problems arising out of the psychological welfare aspect of interplanetary communication will be conscious of the growing agreement that such a remarkable advance inevitably demands of us far-reaching ideological adjustments. Psychologists are now well aware that a forcible inhibition of powerful biological urges over a protracted period is likely to have unforeseeable results. The pioneers of space travel are exposed to this danger. It would be enlightened if a supposed ethicality were allowed to stand in the way of their protection. We must therefore nerve ourselves to face the view that immorality, as it has hitherto been called, must no longer be regarded as unethical—"

"I don't understand that," said the Monk.

"She means," said the Captain, who was a good linguist, "that what you call fornication must no longer be regarded as immoral."

"That's right, dearie," said the Fat Woman to Dickson, "she only means a poor boy needs a woman now and then. It's only natural."

"What was required, therefore," continued the Thin Woman, "was a band of devoted females who would take the first step. This would expose them, no doubt, to obloquy from many ignorant persons. They would be sustained by the consciousness that they were performing an indispensable function in the history of human progress."

"She means you're to have tarts, duckie," said the Fat Woman to Dickson.[20]

Lewis's love of language led him to satirize both pseudo-scientists and journalists in *That Hideous Strength*. The evasive and imprecise speech of the members of the N.I.C.E. is indicative of this thinking. Fuzzy or foggy communication (can one say obscure, abstruse obfuscation?) is born out of fuzzy or foggy understanding. Wither, for example, uses language to confuse, mislead, and deceive. When he pretends to forget names, we see how little he values humans. This pretense is a first step in the abolition of man. Lewis believed the best test of understanding was the ability to explain a thing to a scoutmaster or cleaning woman. If one could not translate an idea into the vernacular, it could be assumed that one did not really understand it oneself.

The abuse of language in *That Hideous Strength* builds up to its own Tower of Babel. The climactic banquet of Belbury brings down the curse of Babel upon the celebrants. Language is unmade, and humans are reduced to mere brutes. The scene is an operatic bouffe, a battalion of Mrs. Malaprops gone berserk. It begins with the token public administrator, Jules, babbling on in a typically dull after-dinner speech. In the midst of the low rumbles of unattended assent and obligatory laughter, Jules blunders with the phrase: "as gross an anachronism as to trust to Calvary for salvation in a modern war." Unaware of his error of Calvary for cavalry, Jules gibbers on: "The madrigore of verjuice must be talthibianised." Mad speech and chaotic spoonerisms run wild and descend into an abyss of linguistic hysteria. Everyone sounds wise and coherent to his own ears, but everyone utters total nonsense. When someone tries to hush Jules, he blurts: "Eh? Blotcher bulldo?"

Trying to restore sanity and order, the Deputy Director rises and addresses the guests: "Tidies and fugleman—I sheer foor that we all—ermost steeply rebut the defensible, though I trust, lavatory, Aspasia which gleans to have selected our redeemed inspector this deceiving. It would—ah—be shark, very shark, from anyone's debenture." Losing control, he shouts "Bundlemen, Bundlemen."[21]

The clamor sounds like the noise of a crowded restaurant in a foreign country to Mark. Then in the midst of the chaos of cries and confused epithets came the noise of terror as wild beasts—wolf, tiger, snake, elephant—from the animal laboratories (with a tip of the tail/tale to the Island of Dr. Moreau) attack the babbling idiotic villains. Lewis inserts his moral: "They that have despised the word of God, from them shall the word of man also be taken away."[22] The same sermon is given repeatedly in Narnia, especially at the Creation, where the Talking Beasts are warned that they may become dumb once again by disobedience. Lewis's satire reveals that the powerful stand and shout only on a platform of sand.

Lewis had little respect for journalists. He agreed with Chesterton, a journalist himself, who described the craft as largely consisting of "saying 'Lord Jones Dead' to people who never knew Lord Jones was alive." At least, Chesterton bragged, being a journalist was a job one could do lying in bed, which could not be said for whale harpooners.[23] One sister remembered Lewis saying, "Whereas Zacchaeus could not see Jesus for the press, we today often cannot see Him for the Press with a capital P!"[24] What is also sad, Lewis said through one character, is that the "educated reader can't stop reading the high-brow weeklies whatever they do. He can't. He's been conditioned." Mark Studdock, writer, joins a wicked conspiracy in the morally moot role as a journalist. Writing specious articles was "a kind of joke. . . . He was writing with his tongue in his cheek—a phrase that somehow comforted him by making the whole thing appear like a practical joke."[25]

Journalism, with a touch of sociology, twists language for political purposes for the N.I.C.E. (This acronym is itself ironic, standing for the National Institute for Co-ordinated Experiments, which is anything but nice.) Experiments on human criminals are called "re-education of the mal-adjusted" even as torture is known as "scientific examination." (Lewis hated all kinds of examinations: academic, medicinal, and military.)

The journalist is a villain who tells lies; yet, we participate in his wickedness with a tolerant laugh or a shrug. "Not one of us hesitates to eat with him, drink with him, joke with him, shake his hand, and what is worse, very few of us refrain from reading what he writes."[26] And what we do read daily, Lewis teased, "with unwearied relish, how, in some place he has never seen, under circumstances which never become quite clear, someone he doesn't know has married, rescued, robbed, raped or murdered someone else he doesn't know."[27]

Echoing Kierkegaard's belief that if his daughter were to become a prostitute he could hope for her salvation, but if his son were to become a journalist all hope would be abandoned, Lewis pined, "That journalists can be saved is a doctrine, if not contrary to, yet certainly above, reason!"[28]

American journalists seemed to him quite silly. Lewis laughed at an American periodical that would pay him generously on various subjects because they viewed him an "unaccountably paradoxical dog." To satisfy them, Lewis would only "recall, as well as I can, what my mother used to say on the subject, eke it out with a few similar thoughts of my own, and so produce what would have been strict orthodoxy in about 1900. And this seems to them outrageously paradoxical, avant-garde stuff."[29]

His poem "Odora Canum Vis" was a sly "defense" of modern biographers and critics, but applies to journalists as well: "Come now, don't be too eager to condemn / Our little smut-hounds if they wag their tails / (Or shake like jellies as the tails wag them) / The moment the least whiff of sex assails / Their quivering snouts. / Such conduct after all, / Though comic, is in them quite natural."[30]

As those who never tasted wine will overvalue beer, Lewis argued, so this smut-hound, knowing "neither God, hunger, thought, nor battle, must / Of course hold disproportioned views on lust." He invited such writers to play their part and pick their victim: "Fetch . . . Slaver, snuff, defile and lick."[31]

Lewis attacked the "Modern" journalistic education of his principal character Mark Studdock, "a glib examinee in subjects that require no exact knowledge." Without a classical (or even genuinely scientific) education, he becomes a man without a chest, without the values that form the foundation of high human moral tradition.

In *The Chronicles of Narnia*, Professor Digory Kirk frequently wonders aloud, "What did these modern schools teach anyway?" The British educational system was becoming hostile to real intellectual life. It neglected what was important and, Lewis felt, cruelly subjected students to games and "programmes" when solitude would have been preferred. Lewis saw modern society crowded with "busybodies, self-appointed masters of ceremonies, whose life is devoted to destroying solitude wherever solitude still exists. . . . If an Augustine . . . should be born in the modern world, the leads of a youth organization would soon cure him." So, too, if a "Wordsworth were born today he would be 'cured' before he was twelve," Lewis complained.[32]

Children of modern model schools might turn out too much like Eustace Clarence Scrubbs, who called his parents by their first names, Harold and Alberta. Lewis caricatured such "up-to-date and advanced" parents as the kind of people who represented his own peeves. "They were vegetarians, non-smokers and teetotalers and wore a special kind of underclothes." Such modern and speciously progressive notions did not attract Lewis's respect; in fact, Lewis opposed the idea that progress meant growth. When King Caspian orders a corrupt governor to restore justice and freedom to his island, the governor gasped: "But that would be putting the clock back. . . . Have you no idea of progress, of development?" "I have seen them both in an egg," said Caspian. "We call it *going bad* in Narnia."[33]

Progressive education, for Lewis, wrongly centered on exports and imports and governments and drains rather than on logic, rhetoric, and dragons (i.e., imaginative literature). The school that Eustace and Jill Pole attend is such a school. It is also coeducational, Lewis wrote, disparagingly, "what used to be called a 'mixed' school; some said it was not nearly so mixed as the minds of the people who ran it. These people had the idea that boys and girls should be allowed to do what they liked. And unfortunately what ten or fifteen of the biggest boys and girls liked best was bullying the others." ("It is one of the great tragedies of life," a character in Preston Sturges's film *The Palm Beach Story* remarks, "that the people most in need of a beating up are always of enormous size.") Experiment House was the kind of school in which Bibles were not encouraged. Lessons in survival were. "Owing to the curious methods of teaching at Experiment House, one did not learn much French or Math or Latin or things of that sort; but one did learn a lot about getting away quickly and quietly when They were looking for one."[34] Lewis's own experiences in avoiding "Them" echo especially—from a distance of time—within these pages.

Lewis's satirical commentary on the administrators of Experiment House (and perhaps on all academic administrators) is summed up in the fate of the Head. Having seen the glory and power of Aslan, the Head behaves like a raving lunatic. Investigators do not see the lion (he has gone back to Narnia); they see only a blithering crazy woman. An inquiry into the Experiment House brings down her house of cards, just as an investigation into Lewis's own Wynard School certified that headmaster Reverend Capron had been a bit of a batty ogre. "After that, the Head's friends saw that the Head was no use as a Head, so they got her made an Inspector to interfere with other Heads. And when they found she wasn't much good even at that, they got her into Parliament where she lived happily ever after."[35] Even in fiction, the truth of the Peter Principle thrives. If your boss is a tyrant, try to get him or her into politics.

Lewis also teased the American way. In a letter to an American girl, he congratulated her on her good grade in Latin and then wrote: "What a droll idea in Florida, to give credits not for what you know but for hours spent in a classroom! Rather like judging the condition of an animal not by its weight or shape but by the amount of food that had been offered it!"[36]

Dymer was the model of well-engineered, modern youth, programmed by efficient Boards of Education. "He passed through every test, / Was vaccinated, numbered, washed and dressed, / Proctored, inspected, whipt, examined weekly, / And for some nineteen years he bore it meekly."[37]

One moment in spring, however, undid all the refining and molding of Dymer's soul. Amusingly, Lewis placed the unexpected, rude awakening in "lecture-time one April morning." Alas, wrote Lewis, "who ever learned to censor the spring days?" Dymer was drowsy under the solemn and gloomy drone of the lecturer's voice. The events that followed could be any schoolboy's dream as Lewis liberated Dymer's soul from the bonds of the dull Academy—with laughter!

> *He yawned, and voluptuous laziness*
> *Tingled down all his spine and loosed his kneed,*
> *Slow-drawn, like an invisible caress.*
> *He laughed—The lecturer stopped like one that sees*
> *A Ghost, then frowned and murmured, "Silence, please."*
> *That moment saw the soul of Dymer hang in the balance—*
> *Louder then his laughter rang.*[38]

To the unbelieving and dazed awe of his fellow students, Dymer rose and guffawed heartily. Then with a lazy swing of his right arm, "he struck the lecturer's head. The old man tittered, lurched, and dropped down dead." Dymer escapes the prison classroom and runs into a field and river, stripping away all clothes "to play with bare toes dabbling in cold river clay."[39]

A young man like Dymer can go quite mad if confined too long. This explosive scream of laughter is a rebellion against the madness of the masters who would hold their victims down and quiet. When the peasants rise against their tyrants, they rise with wild hearts leaping and laughing, even if tragedy might follow.

Shift, a clever, ugly, and wrinkled Ape, represents another mirror of contemporary humankind, those who see themselves as Nietzschean super-persons. For Lewis, he is a very modern (and therefore very mean) creature. He puts down the meek donkey, Puzzle. "You know," he tells his servant, "thinking isn't your strong point." He declares himself an evolutionary miracle. "I hear some of you are saying I'm an Ape. Well, I'm not. I'm a Man. If I look like an Ape, that's because I'm so very old: hundreds and hundreds of years old."[40] He tells the other animals they are so stupid that Aslan can't be bothered talking to them.

Ironically, the Ape (calling himself the "most sapient Mouthpiece of Aslan") represents the undesirable area of modern progress. He promises not only that oranges and bananas will pour into Narnia, but "roads and big cities and schools and offices," and then showing the logical extension of the loss of freedom that such modern conveniences provide, the Ape continues his list "and whips and muzzles and saddles and cages and kennels and prisons—Oh, everything."[41]

In *Mother Hubbard's Tale*, Lewis found Edmund Spenser returning to the Renard tradition of satire. "Spenser, looking round on a great variety of evils (sturdy vagabonds disguised as old soldiers, idle parsons, dishonest and venal patrons, frivolity and unmanliness at court, and the insolence of upstarts in office) invents as their cause the ubiquitous activities of an Ape and a Fox. His poem is thus a satire on nearly all 'estates.'"[42] The similarity to Lewis's Ape and Ass in *The Last Battle* is not merely coincidental (especially when one notes the Ape's approach to the sleeping Lion). Shift and Puzzle are responsible for many of the ills that befall Narnia at its end. As residue of a fallen human nature, these two characters are ripe subjects for satire. Shift inheres the vices of Sloth and Greed, while poor Puzzle is merely stupid.

Lewis's "Evolutionary Hymn" is a sardonic psalm to the notion of evolutionary progress, which promises to lead us "up the future's endless stair."

> *Chop us, change us, prod us, weed us.*
> *For stagnation is despair.*
> *Groping, guessing, yet progressing,*
> *Lead us nobody knows where.*
> *Wrong or justice in the present,*
> *Joy or sorrow, what are they*
> *While there's always jam to-morrow*
> *While we tread the onward way?*
> *Never knowing where we're going,*
> *We can never go astray.*[43]

A great deal of Lewis's satire, and his tendency toward sarcasm, is connected with his deep aversion to all things modern. At one point in his life Lewis confessed to being "conscious of a partly pathological hostility to what is fashionable."[44] He set himself against his own generation, a dinosaur amiably but deliberately trudging through the Harrod's Department Store of ideas, the proverbial bull in the china shop of modern culture.

His campaign for tradition over modern perspectives was vigorously run on many fronts. Tradition offered a solid rock foundation, while the modernist provided only the shifting sands of fashion. Suppose a dog were trying to form a conception of human life and was plunged into human life from its simple canine experience: "A reverent dog would be shocked. A modernist dog, distrusting the whole experience, would ask to be taken to the vet."[45]

In *The Pilgrim's Regress* he slashed at the many intellectual and theological movements of the postwar period, including surrealism, materialism, and the silly poetry and gibberish literature of the "Lunatic twenties." In Lewis's hands, one fictional "high brow" recited grunts like "Globol obol oogle ogle global gloogle gloo," and made "a vulgar noise such as children make in their nurseries." Later, on rereading this work of his, Lewis faulted it as well for "needless obscurity and an uncharitable temper" and repented for what he now saw was a sweet "bitterness of certain pages of this book."[46]

Nevertheless, much of Lewis's satire is an acute and wily attack against modern thought and modern things. Lewis, in fact, was renowned for this aversion to all things modern, from railroads to cosmetics. One short lyric, owing something to Ovid, slashed at a woman's obsession with makeup: "Lady, a better sculptor far / Chiselled those curves you smudge and mar, / And God did more than lipstick can / To justify your mouth to man."[47]

For Lewis, the nadir of the modern female was embodied in his emancipated policewoman, Fairy Hardcastle (*That Hideous Strength*), with her smudge of lipstick and long black cheroot dangling unlit between her teeth. She finds male prudery an amusing diversion and out-shocks bawdy men with her smoking-room stories. (It is rumored that Elizabeth Anscombe was the model for this tough woman: True or not, Lewis's dislike of any "modern" woman is legendary.) In the character of Screwtape proposing a toast, Lewis mocked the prayer of a young female human who uttered: "'Oh, God, make me a normal twentieth-century girl!' Thanks to our labours," Screwtape promises, "this will mean increasingly, 'Make me a minx, a moron, and a parasite.'"[48]

Satire incorporates sarcasm and even flippancy to purge its audience. It is an unflattering mirror; it works as a microscope that forces the reader to place himself or herself on the slide and be examined. When Lewis entered the Shoddy Lands of a woman's mind, he found it cluttered with all manner of modern paraphernalia but empty of substance. The landscape of Peggy's mind was featureless and nondescript. Her mental universe was vague, dull, and gray. Trees and people were indistinct smudges. The few things that stood out distinctly were women's clothes, shoes, and jewelry.

Her view of her own body, cosmetically made over to copy advertisement images, struck the narrator as repulsive and horrible. A gigantic human shape, ghastly female and obscenely "modern," wore a "wisp of some brightly colored stuff round its hips and another round its breasts." When her two-piece swimsuit was removed, this gigantic Peggy looked at her tanned, brown body. "But round her hips, and again round her breasts, where the coverings had been, there were two bands of dead white which looked by contrast like leprosy." The narrator was sickened and saddened by the shabbiness of this woman's mind, which saw life only in relation or use to her own swollen self-image. Yet the author brings his satire home, setting it in front of himself and his readers like a full-figure mirror. "Suppose this sort of thing were to become common? And how if, some other time, I were not the explorer but the explored?"[49]

A special correspondent for the *London Times*, covering a Classical Association conference, once reported Lewis's fame for resisting modern movements. He wrote that "in spite of the unlikely hour (immediately after breakfast), the hilarity of Professor C. S. Lewis, in his most mischievous mood, proved irresistible this morning when he delivered . . . a withering attack on modern translations of the classics."[50]

Lewis's dislike of the modern poetry worms its way into his dream in *The Great Divorce*. Catching the bus to heaven, a young tousle-headed poet sits down beside him, confiding in Lewis the dreamer a sort of aesthetic superiority over the rest of the passengers. But with a shudder, Lewis sees him produce a "thick wad of typewritten paper."[51] Lewis mutters various excuses; he cannot escape the poets of the age, even on a bus trip to heaven.

Lewis called the "modern poet" a "lively oxymoron."[52] His disagreements with T. S. Eliot resulted in a tart response to the poet's "Lovesong of J. Alfred Prufrock." One of Lewis's poems, published in *Punch* magazine, confessed: "I am so coarse, the things the poets see / Are obstinately invisible to me. / For twenty years I've stared my level best / To see if evening—any evening—would suggest / A patient etherized upon a table; / In vain. I simply wasn't able."[53] Lewis suggested the cardinal problem of Eliot's poetry concerned whether it was "possible to distinguish poetry about squalor and chaos from squalid and chaotic poetry."[54]

Lewis also satirized those who maintained that only poets could validly critique other poets. Such nonsense was comparable to saying only cooks could judge whether a dish was worthy of eating. "For who could endure a doctrine which would allow only dentists to say whether our teeth were aching, only cobblers to say whether our shoes hurt us?"[55]

The consciousness of poets of their elevated status occurred between Chaucer's time and that of Alexander Pope. Since Pope's time, Lewis wrote sarcastically, the arts have become even more self-conscious. "One almost foresees the day when they may be conscious of little else."[56] We have come to the predicament where our "most esteemed poets and critics are read by our most esteemed critics and poets . . . and nobody else takes any notice."[57] Lewis's critical system would banish those literary debunkers and elitist critics for whom all the great names in English literature, except the fashionably chosen few, are "as to many lamp-posts for a dog."[58] One such critic was F. R. Leavis of Cambridge, who approached all literature so seriously. (Back in the early 1980s I stayed in the Kilns (Lewis's home) with caretaker Michael Piret—now Dean of Divinity at Magdelen College, who had picked up an old story from an old neighbor of Lewis, known as Dennis. Dennis remembered Guy Fawkes Day in 1960 when Lewis, his brother, and the boys merrily hung an effigy that looked remarkably like Leavis. Much laughter, it is reported, accompanied the burning.)

Along with modern poetry, Lewis satirized modern political philosophical movements in his early work *The Pilgrim's Regress*. Marx, Kant, Steiner, and Spinoza were all caricatured as frivolous philosophers, playing at life with their empty games of philosophy—a sort of serious leapfrog or running to and fro chasing moths. They try to solicit pilgrim John's attention as they are "wrestling with and tickling one another, giggling and making giggle."[59] But there are two sets of dwarfs, "a black kind with black shirts and a red kind who call themselves Marxomanni," who savagely roar with laughter at the prospect of meeting and fighting worldly, clever men. "When the Cruels meet the Clevers," the Savage laughed, "there will not be even the ghost of a tug of war."[60]

Atheists were another odd and amusing breed for Lewis. He accused them of being "strangely unsuspicious people when it came to the whispers of the universe."[61] Having been one himself, he could see atheists maintaining a deadly earnestness about their predicament. Inviting many to speak at the Socratic debating club, he "discovered there was an undersupply of atheists willing to speak without pay."[62]

Worse than unbelievers, however, were the liberal theologians like Rudolph Bultmann and others seeking the true personality of the Messiah—wanting to know the facts of Jesus's life like "what you'd get in a Dictionary of National Biography article or an obituary or a Victorian Life and Letters of Yeshua Bar-Yoself in three volumes with photographs."[63] Lewis sarcastically commented that "we had to wait nearly 2,000 years to be told by a theologian called Vidler that what the Church has always regarded as a miracle, was, in fact, a parable."[64] In *The Pilgrim's Regress*, the modern theologian, Mr. Broad, aims at making friends with the world; he seeks no truth, only wildflowers.

Religious people without a sense of humor were most dangerous. The stern and dour Pharisees deny the good news by their solemnity. As Conrad Hyers has said, if "laughter without faith leads to cynicism," then "faith without laughter tends to dogmatism and self-righteousness."[65] This attitude is incarnated in the spiritually bankrupt fictional character of the Reverend Straik, who, unlike Lewis himself, never drank nor smoked nor adapted himself to the ribald and realistic tone of his colleagues. He would not "join in the joke" when his colleagues laughed, but would move aside and "utter religious solemnity."[66] Such Manichaean prudes Lewis found more insidious to genuine holiness than happy saints like Chesterton's wise and merry fuddy-duddy Father Brown, a short, almost bubbly Roman Catholic priest with a face as round (and one might almost say as merry) as a Norfolk dumpling. God's true saints do not try to be holier and more solemn than God.

For those who would be mystics and deal in hermetic dreams or visions alone, Lewis leaves another lesson. At the end of *The Great Divorce*, the dreamer Lewis is told to make it plain that this tale of heaven and hell was but a mere dream. The Scot tells him: "Give no poor fool the pretext to think ye are claiming knowledge of what no mortal knows. I'll have no Swedenborgs and no Vale Owens among my children."[67] (Swedenborg had received "new divine revelations" in which he felt free to reject traditional doctrines such as original sin, eternal punishment, or a devil. Ironically, Lewis attacked this man whose 1758 work, *Heaven and Hell*, maintained that these were not places but states of mind, in a fictional heaven that was geographical and actual.)

Apostate bishops and other spuriously devout church leaders also come under attack by Lewis. Those who have left the faith or watered down the doctrine were fair game for satirical unmasking. As such, churchmen and clergy were legitimate objects for satirical barbs and arrows. When one is admonished not to "touch" the Lord's "anointed," it does not mean the anointed is protected from inquiry and, if necessary, satirical admonishment. From Tartuffe to traveling evangelists, hypocrisy and greed can be uncovered. In particular, Lewis sought to sting those modernists who would empty the faith of its substance. They hold a theology, he said, which "after the camel of the Resurrection strains at such gnats as the feeding of the multitudes." Such theologians "claim to see a fern-seed and can't see an elephant ten yards away in broad daylight."[68] Thus, Mr. Broad in *The Pilgrim's Regress* or Reverend Straik at the N.I.C.E. were sketches of liberal, gas-filled, even Unitarian churchmen—much like Lewis's opinions of Rudolph Bultmann or the Bishop of Woolwich, the Rt. Rev. J. A. T. Robinson, who appeared as an expert defense witness in the obscenity trial regarding *Lady Chatterley's Lover* and D. H. Lawrence. Lewis believed that twelve good men in a jury could tell right and wrong better than this professional moral expert. His foremost qualification for the court record was that "he had read ethics." Of the adulterous sex relationship in *Lady Chatterley's Lover*, Robinson said: "I think Lawrence tried to portray this relation as in a real sense something sacred, as in a real sense an act of holy communion."[69] Lewis judged such ethical posturing as folly. Bishop Woolwich, Lawrence, and other moderns succeeded only in making sex a solemn bore. "Poor Aphrodite! They have sandpapered most of the Homeric laughter off her face."[70]

In *The Great Divorce*, a fat apostate bishop wearing gaiters condescendingly addresses a former colleague who "became rather narrow-minded" toward the end of his life, "coming to believe in a literal Heaven and Hell!" He wishes to discuss hell reverently and seriously, though not to believe in it. He feels libeled when the Bright, Solid Person exposes his desire of popularity and fashionable modernity. The apostate bishop prefers his "little Theological Society down there" to the hard, sharp truths of heaven. He suggests that, had Jesus lived to a more mature age, He would have outgrown some of His earlier views. The clerical ghost turns away from paradise, "humming softly to itself 'City of God, how broad and far.'"[71] Lewis combatted such men in direct and indirect ways. The latter tactic he adopted humorously in *The Horse and His Boy*. The horse, Bree, mouths liberal theology as he expounds on Aslan.

> "No doubt," continued Bree, "when they speak of Him as a Lion they only mean he's as strong as a lion or (to our enemies, of course) as fierce as a lion. Or something of that kind. Even a little girl like you, Aravis, must see that it would be quite absurd to suppose he is a real lion. Indeed it would be disrespectful. If he was a lion he'd have to be a Beast just like the rest of us. Why!" (And here Bree began to laugh) "If he was a lion he'd have four paws and a tail, and Whiskers! . . . Aie, ooh, hoo-hoo! Help!" For just as he said the word Whiskers one of Aslan's had actually tickled his ear.[72]

Lewis felt a stronger spiritual kinship with the devout faithful of other denominations than he did with the skeptical fringes of his own Anglican communion. A commitment to Christ, no matter if one were Episcopal, Roman, Greek, or (even) Baptist, was more crucial than a church membership. Screwtape explained to Wormwood what to do if "men become Christians at all. Keep them in the state of mind I call 'Christianity And.' You know—Christianity and the Crisis, Christianity and the New Psychology, Christianity and the New Order, Christianity and Faith healing, Christianity and Psychical Research, Christianity and Vegetarianism, Christianity and Spelling Reform."[73]

Lewis felt the nominal members of Christendom were too smug, familiar, and even cheeky in their theology. The worldly church people are too much at ease in Zion, like Lewis's grandfather who supposedly "looked forward to having some very interesting conversations with St. Paul when he would go to heaven." The image of "two clerical gentlemen talking at ease in a club!" contrasted vividly with Dante's view of the apostles in heaven; they were like "mountains."[74] One suspects part of the inspiration of J. B. Phillips's *Your God Is Too Small* came from Lewis's observation that people wanted, not so much a Father in heaven, as a sweet, generous, senile grandfather in heaven.

Lewis believed that those who were at the heart of their communions were closer to each other than any were to those on the liberal fringe. He joined those who resisted novelty in liturgy as an attempt to become more relevant: "I wish they'd remember that the charge to Peter was Feed my sheep; not Try experiments on my rats, or even, Teach my performing dogs new tricks."[75]

Lewis's satire swayed somewhere between that of the genial Chesterton and the trenchant Swift. His weapon was not the rapier of biting anger and scathing abuse of the latter; neither was it charitable largesse or the feathery, soft blow of the former. Where his works are explicitly satirical, Lewis drew his broadaxe with hurrahs from his side, usually winning the battle. But there are more ways than this of winning a battle—you can win the enemy instead of the fight. Or, as Chesterton was wont to do, you could take a weapon that once belonged chiefly to your opponent. This very useful weapon may have been as small as a slingshot, but it was mighty enough to bring down giants. His simple weapon was laughter.

Biographer Maisie Ward showed how such a weapon used by Voltaire and his followers to mock moral and doctrinal orthodoxy was wrested away and seized by Chesterton. Ward wrote that when "Bishop Barnes of Birmingham said that St. Francis was dirty and probably had fleas many Catholics were furious and spoke in solemn wrath." Chesterton answered with the simple verse ("A Broad-minded Bishop Rebukes the Verminous Saint Francis"): "If Brother Francis pardoned Brother Flea / There still seems need of such strange charity / Seeing he is, for all his gay goodwill / Bitten by funny little creatures still."[76]

Lewis's blunt satires against certain women or literary critics struck but didn't dent well-armored souls. But in those laughing satires against his own heart, he pierced the vulnerable flesh of all men and women. By gleefully battling the dragons of his own heart, as in

The Screwtape Letters, he was able to bleed the rampant monsters of all humanity. When Lewis looked to his own soul, he saw, like Pogo, that "we have met the enemy and he is us." "Some have paid me an undeserved compliment," Lewis wrote, "by supposing that my Letters were the ripe fruit of many years' study in moral and ascetic theology. They forgot that there is an equally reliable, though less creditable, way of learning how temptation works. 'My heart'—I need no other's—'sheweth me the wickedness of the ungodly.'"[77]

Laughter in heaven differs from the noise in hell as delicious, fresh spring waters differ from poisonous gases. The first laughter one hears in *The Great Divorce* is in hell at the bus line where the damned are waiting for the bus to heaven. The competitive desire to be first eventually results in pushing and shoving. (In *Mere Christianity* Lewis viewed such quarrels over seats on a bus or spots in a queue as funny. It was funny in the sense that all the riders were assuming a moral law and standard—that the others should recognize and obey!) The crowd roars with laughter when one woman is bilked of her place in line; it is a mean, malicious, and harsh laughter, directed at the cheated victim. Those dim ghosts from hell are either laughing at others or feeling laughed at.

One hard-bitten, paranoid ghost sees heaven as a cosmic, sadistic joke, where "every raindrop will make a hole in you, like a machine-gun bullet. That's their little joke, you see. First of all tantalize you with ground you can't walk on and water you can't drink and then drill you full of holes. But they won't catch me."[78] For such an unbeliever, the hope of heaven was false, and thus, the cruelest comedy of all.

The ghosts from hell mock and scorn. They perpetually put down and degrade everything, especially their fellow travelers. One respectable, cultured ghost (who was fat and wearing gaiters) took this holiday to avoid unpleasant riffraff. All carried some sense of self-conceit and their own self-importance, or simple pride. The bus passengers' faces were stripped of pretty masks. They told cruel and hollow stories. One would shrink from these "fixed faces, full not of possibilities, but of impossibilities, some gaunt, some bloated, some glaring with idiotic ferocity, some drowned beyond recovery in dreams; but all, in one way or another, distorted and faded." Then, writes the author, catching a look in a mirror on the bus, "I caught sight of my own." The face betrays a state of mind—and, as a guide tells the dreamer, "every state of mind, left to itself, every shutting up of the creature within the dungeon of its own mind—is, in the end, Hell."[79]

George MacDonald (to whom Lewis paid tribute as his imagination's guide, and who was as well an influence on Lewis's conversion, baptizing Lewis's imagination) tells the dreamer that "the damned have holidays—excursions, ye understand." They can haunt old houses, play tricks on daft old women called mediums, or "hang about public libraries to see if anyone's still reading their books."[80]

One big ghost meets a solid spirit who was a bloody murderer, though now a forgiven one. The face of this solid spirit made the dreamer "want to dance, it was so jocund, so established in its youthfulness." The big ghost ironically declares: "Well, I'm damned." He claims he only wants his rights, his just desserts, only what he has earned and deserved. "I'm not asking for anybody's bleeding charity." The grand paradox of the Christian faith is laid out here, as the forgiven spirit responds: "Then do. At once. Ask for the Bleeding Charity. Everything here is for the asking and nothing can be bought." Sadly, however, the big ghost grumbles and refuses to join the bloody clique: "I'd rather be damned than go along with you." His wish is granted. Lewis echoed MacDonald's notion that in the end either we say to God, "Thy will be done"—or God says to us, "Thy will be done."[81]

The practice of humor and reason are almost enough to compel resistant ghosts to laugh at their pride and persuade them into the joy of heaven. Almost, but not enough. A ghost husband, by now a dwarf ghost, has been dominated by his theatrical self-image as a tragedian. (Lewis's view of actors and their puffed-up self-importance was quite low.) The haughty tragedian leads the actual husband ghost around on a chain, like a monkey with its grinder. His saintly wife tries to separate the dwarf husband from his acting role.

"Frank! Frank!" she cried in a voice that made the whole wood ring. "Look at me. *Look* at me. What are you doing with that great, ugly doll? Let go of the chain. Send it away. It is *you* I want. Don't you see what nonsense it's talking?" Merriment danced in her eyes. She was sharing a joke with the Dwarf, right over the head of the Tragedian. Something not at all unlike a smile struggled to appear on the Dwarf's face. For he was looking at her now. Her laughter was past his first defenses.[82]

As the wife tries to help the husband see how absurd and ridiculous his posturing is (for at one time there must have been a gleam of humor in him), he still struggles against the laughter and joy offered him. The tragedian storms against being made to look foolish, even a folly that is embraced in grace and forgiven in mirth. His self is offended, and as his hubris and feigned wounding grows, his real self in the dwarf ghost shrinks to the size of an insect (just as each of us is turning that small seed within our self into something spoiled and weedy).

But the self-willed wretchedness and abuse of the tragedian cannot threaten the joy of heaven. The lady tells him: "Here is joy that cannot be shaken. Our light can swallow up your darkness: but your darkness cannot now infect our light."[83] Love and laughter and joy cannot be held captive by frowns and sighs. Joy of heaven prevails over misery and the cunning tyranny of hell. Self-pity will pass away with self-conceit, and the tears of weeping will be wiped away and disappear. What will be left when the human vapors dissipate will be the solid laughter and gladness of the saints in paradise.

In the heavenly spirits, laughter inhabits their voices as twinkles dance in their eyes. They expect joy in every bit of play and work. The laughter is gigantic and loud. Laughter arrives when one allows oneself to be carried into glory. If one would confess one's pride or wrath or mere meanness (simply one's sin), admitting one was wrong, "and had a good laugh at himself he could have begun all over again like a little child and entered into joy."[84]

When an obsessive, possessive mother ghost (that sort of woman who lives for others) complains that a solid spirit is making her out to be wrong ("Everything I say or do is wrong, according to you"), the bright spirit, "shining with love and mirth so that my eyes dazzled," responds, "But of course! That's what we all find when we reach this country. We've all been wrong! That's the great joke. There's no need to go on pretending one was right! After that we begin living."[85]

Laughter and joy follow repentance as a glorious sunrise follows night. Lewis's splendid depiction of the man haunted by a little red lizard of lust sitting on his shoulder vividly illustrates the transformation from sin and guilt to glory and joy. The burdened ghost gives an angel permission to kill the beast, even though he fears the torturous pain—and even death—that may occur in purging his sin. When the bright and burning angel grips the ugly little reptile, the ghost screams in agony. The angel twists it while it bites and writhes, and then flings it, breaking its back, onto the turf. The ghost man then begins to grow more solid and bright, his face shining with tears, and the lizard is transformed into a great white stallion with a gold mane and tail. Sickly, whimpering lust is converted into healthy, virile sexuality. "In joyous haste the young man leaped up on the horse's back."[86] That which is submitted to death is reborn in the fullness of life.

Of the joy of heaven, an enormous measure can be found in one such humble little lady, "Sarah Smith, who quietly tended any boy or girl, dog and (even cat) that strayed her way." The abundance of life she has in Christ from the Father flows over "into all her beasts and children. . . . But already there is joy enough in the little finger of a great saint such as [this] lady to waken all the dead things of the universe into life."[87]

The proper posture toward evil is to mock it. God scoffs at the wicked. "He who sits in the heavens laughs, The Lord scoffs at them"

(Ps. 2:4). "The LORD laughs at him; for He sees his day is coming" (Ps. 37:13). Lewis garnered support from a Roman Catholic and a Reformer to buttress his use of satire as a weapon against evil. "The devil . . . the prowde spirit . . . cannot endure to be mocked," announced Thomas More, whom Lewis admired in other contexts as well. Luther echoed this sentiment, writing, "The best way to drive out the devil, if he will not yield to texts of Scripture, is to jeer and flout him, for he cannot bear scorn."[88] In *TheScrewtape Letters*, Screwtape becomes the object of such laughter when Wormwood's patient falls in love with a Christian girl. Screwtape detests what he finds.

> I have looked up this girl's dossier and am horrified at what I find. Not only a Christian but such a Christian—a vile, sneaking, simpering, demure, monosyllabic, mouselike, watery, insignificant, virginal bread-and-butter miss! The little brute! She makes me vomit. She stinks and scalds through the very pages of the dossier. It drives me mad, the way the world has worsened. We'd have had her in the arena in the old days. That's what her sort is made for. Not that she'd do much good there, either. A two-faced little cheat (I know the sort) who looks as if she'd faint at the sight of blood, and then dies with a smile. A cheat every way. Looks as if butter wouldn't melt in her mouth, and yet has a satirical wit. The sort of creature who'd find ME funny! Filthy, insipid little prude—and yet ready to fall into this booby's arms like any other breeding animal. Why doesn't the Enemy blast her for it, if He's so moonstruck by virginity—instead of looking on there, grinning.[89]

Lewis punctuated the power of a "satirical wit" against evil by inducing in this devil such an outburst of noise, insanity, horror, and disgust that Screwtape cannot even finish his letter. His mockery of the girl he is vilifying—one of God's simple, little saints—undoes him. In the heat of the preceding composition, Screwtape discovers that he has inadvertently allowed himself to become a large centipede. This apt

Miltonic punishment, meted out by his creator, parallels the judgment in Genesis upon the serpent. Part of the curse upon the serpent was that he would forever grovel in the dust, crawling upon his belly—something like centipedes do. Finding himself in this fix, Screwtape finishes his letter by dictation. (Lewis briefly satirized George Bernard Shaw in this letter, allowing Screwtape to corroborate his interpretation of his serpentine transformation as an outworking or "glorious manifestation of that Life Force" introduced by a "more modern writer—someone with a name like Pshaw.") As More predicted, Lewis's devil cannot stand to be mocked. (Screwtape later mutters, "I wish Slumtrimpet could do something about undermining that young woman's sense of the ridiculous."[90])

In a similar vein, Chesterton was inspired to satirize an occurrence in the garden of Eden when he read somewhere that good salesmanship makes "everything in the garden beautiful." Pointing back to Genesis, he exposed one of its ancient actors who had a real slippery talent for salesmanship.

> He seems to have undertaken to deliver the goods with exactly the right preliminaries of promises and praise. He knew all about advertisement: we may say he knew all about publicity, though not at the moment addressing a very large public. He not only took up the slogan of Eat More Fruit, but he distinctly declared that any customers purchasing his particular brand of fruit would instantly become as gods. And as this is exactly what is promised to the purchasers of every patent medicine, popular tonic, saline draught, or medicinal wine at the present day, there can be no question that he was in advance of his age.[91]

Chesterton thought it extraordinary that the record ends with a remarkable scene where one "pursuing the bright career of Salesmanship is condemned to crawl on his stomach and eat a great deal of dirt."[92] Chesterton aimed one of his satiric arrows at a more vulnerable and amusing modern target: American advertisers.

Only a very soft-headed, sentimental and rather servile generation of men could possibly be affected by advertisements at all. People who are a little more hard-headed, humorous, and intellectually independent, see the rather simple joke; and are not impressed by this or any other form of self-praise. Almost any other man in almost any other age would have seen the joke. If you had said to a man in the Stone Age, "Ugg says Ugg makes the best stone hatchets," he would have perceived a lack of detachment and dis-interestedness about the testimonial. If you had said to a medieval peasant, "Robert the Bowyer proclaims, with three blasts of a horn, that he makes good bows," the peasant would have said, "Well, of course he does," and thought about something more important. It is only among people whose minds have been weakened by a sort of mesmerism that so transparent a trick as that of advertisement could ever have been tried at all.[93]

Lewis's satire radiated with luminous sparks in his gentle friction with the modern world, in part because his satire was grounded in the Light of the world. As he took the doctrines of the church seriously, he could take the doings of culture lightly. All the silly notions, errors, and arrogant attitudes of contemporary thought were like so much hay, wood, and stubble to be burned off, needing only the kindling of incendiary wit to reduce them to ashes.

The laughter of this inflammatory satire incited more than a witty thump on the back or sudden blow in the face, as the old Victorian author George Meredith observed. Its sharp jolt awakened thought and conscience. When the divine comedy does stir the hearts of men and women, it often rouses them with violence. Satire is the electricity of laughter. The satire of the Lord to Pharisees and lawyers was not low voltage, but stunning, provocative, and fierce. Such satire shakes and shocks the very being of us sinners and hypocrites, inflaming and igniting self-righteous rage. It holds us upside down, joshing and jos-tling any loose and excess junk out of the pockets of our souls. God mocks the proud and arrogant, and if we are to be like God, we may find an opportunity and invitation to mock the high and mighty, but only insofar as we are holy and humble like our Lord. Otherwise, as Lewis foresaw, our moral satire would be no more than stinging, poisonous flippancy. Without its moral base, satire would be a grinning tragedy—a mocking of all life with no hope for the curative or restorative role of good satiric laughter.

32

Flippancy

But Thou, O LORD, dost laugh at them;
Thou dost scoff at all the nations.
—PSALM 59:8

I shall take no bull from thy house.
—PSALM 50:9 (AUTHOR'S PARAPHRASE)

In 1811 bachelor English bishop Richard Hurd complained that laughter "obscures truth, hardens the heart, and stupefies the understanding."[1] The complaint and accusations against laughter are legion—and with good cause.

Laughter, like any other good gift bestowed by God, can be corrupted, bent, spoiled, ruined. This happens when it exceeds the pleasant part of life it was meant to be and becomes life itself. When laughter is thus exalted, it strays from being one's servant to being one's master. Having escaped the bounds of good judgment, it sets itself up as judge—particularly as a kangaroo court judge: sentencing the good, the virtuous, and the moral to endless mockery.

"There is but one good," the George MacDonald character in *The Great Divorce* warns a visiting Lewis:

> That is God. Everything else is good when it looks to Him and bad when it turns from Him. And the higher and mightier it is in the natural order, the more demonic it will be if it rebels. It's not out of bad mice or bad fleas you make demons, but out of bad archangels. The false religion of lust is baser than the false religion of mother-love or patriotism or art: but lust is less likely to be made into a religion.[2]

In the same way, the higher the pretensions of laughter, the more defiled and spoiled it becomes when it falls. Such laughter is laced with the poisons of patronizing superiority, cruelty, and cynicism. The wanton cruelty of making a mean joke about another becomes equivalent to weaving a verbal crown of thorns without pricking our own fingers. Cold-blooded hatred masquerading as laughter kills more callously than passionate anger. As Lewis put it: "Lilies that fester smell far worse than weeds."[3] Laughter begins to be a demon the moment it begins to be a god. When the laugh is valued above love for one's neighbors, when it becomes the ego expressing itself in superiority over others, it becomes sin. Even as any human love can be elevated onto an altar or pedestal, so, too, the comic spirit can make claims for itself as a divine spirit.

For Lewis, this demon laughter is known as flippancy. It is the wicked rival to the holy and hearty laughter of joy, fun, and even the joke proper. The flippant person, in Lewis's definition, fits Chesterton's second category in respect to the "two types of men who can laugh when they are alone. He is either confiding the joke to God or confiding it to the Devil."[4] Flippancy belongs to the latter. It is along these lines that the devil, Screwtape, pontificating (if one can use this word in such a context) about the causes of laughter, makes the following declaration at the end of his eleventh epistle:

But flippancy is the best of all. In the first place it is very economical. Only a clever human can make a real Joke about virtue, or indeed about anything else; any of them can be trained to talk as if virtue were funny. Among flippant people the Joke is always assumed to have been made. No one actually makes it; but every serious subject is discussed in such a manner which implies that they have already found a ridiculous side to it. If prolonged, the habit of Flippancy builds up around a man the finest armour plating against the Enemy that I know, and it is quite free from the dangers inherent in the other sources of laughter. It is a thousand miles away from joy; it deadens, instead of sharpening the intellect; and it excites no affection between those who practice it.[5]

The habit of flippancy blinds the eyes to goodness, even as its loud, unhappy laughter deafens the ears to truth. Paradoxically, flippancy dilutes the pleasures of good laughter, gradually becoming, like an addictive drug, the only thing one has an appetite for. Screwtape points this out to Wormwood in his letters. As the habit of flippancy becomes established in the human heart and mind, he says, it "renders the pleasures of vanity and excitement and flippancy at once less pleasant and harder to forgo (for that is what habit unfortunately does to pleasure)."[6] The habit of flippancy deadens the exercise of quick wit, of playful jesting, of delight in people and ideas. It separates laughter from the merry community into an elite individualism. It pops balloons rather than juggling or jostling them. For the flippant there is no more joyful laughter, no more jolly fun, no more leg-slapping jokes; the world is a pale and lifeless place fit only to be chuckled or cackled at, knowingly.

Several of Lewis's evil fictional characters laugh nothing but this kind of twisted laughter. The Prophet of Ecclesiastes' view of laughter as madness—as the noise of hell—is realized in two members of the N.I.C.E. when, with shoulders twitching, Wither and Frost gradually began to laugh, "louder and louder, a crackling noise that seemed in the end rather an animal than a senile parody of laughter."[7] On Perelandra, a demonic Weston eked out a similar "cackling laughter, almost an infantile or senile laughter."[8] Such laughter—artificial, cruel, strained, wicked—is as far from genuine laughter as poison is from a mother's milk.

Lewis excavated what he saw as the theological origins of flippancy. To pluck out the weed of flippancy from our garden of laughter, we must dig out its grubby theological root: pride. Pride sucks all life into itself without producing any fruit itself, and it kills all that is beautiful and good around it. The root of pride strangles the flowers of kindness, joy, goodness. Pride places the self on the throne of the heart's castle, where its favorite hunchback jester is flippancy. The decline of real laughter inherent in flippancy is merely a by-product of what Chesterton saw as the decline and fall of human nature. He "always maintained that men were naturally backsliders; that human virtue tended of its own nature to rust or to rot; I have always said that human beings as such go wrong, especially happy human beings, especially proud and prosperous human beings."[9]

Where human beings go wrong is in this one vice, which everyone loathes and from which no one is exempt. Pride, or self-conceit, is the core vice, the utmost evil in Christian morality. It is the "movement whereby a creature . . . tries to set up on its own, to exist for itself."[10] In *Mere Christianity*, Lewis called it "The Great Sin," of which no man or woman in the world is free. "Unchastity, anger, greed, drunkenness, and all that, are mere flea bites in comparison: it was through Pride that the devil became the devil."[11] The chief cause of misery and pain in this world is this competitive desire to be brighter, richer, or more beautiful than others. "A man who is eating or lying with his wife or preparing to go to sleep in humility, thankfulness, and temperance, is, by Christian standards, in an infinitely higher state than one who is listening to Bach or reading Plato in a state of pride."[12]

The proud person looks down on people and things. He or she takes that superior vantage point to see others as inferior, and thus can take license to treat them as trifles. Pride, standing high and mighty, does not bow nor bend the knee, and so ignores those below itself, or condescends and patronizes. It does not recognize God, who is above it, because it is always looking down, comparing how it is better. Pride is a purely spiritual cancer; it comes, Lewis wrote, "direct from hell." In fact, left to itself, pride becomes hell. It eats up love, humility, and all that is good. "Other vices," wrote Lewis, "may sometimes bring people together: you may find good fellowship and jokes and friendliness among drunken people or unchaste people. But Pride always means enmity—it is enmity. And not only enmity between man and man, but enmity to God."[13] Its effect upon character, Chesterton observed, is that it "dries up laughter" and wonder.[14]

This enmity is a fact of the Fall, even as pride is the cause of the Fall. But what is the Fall? asked Lewis.

The Fall is simply and solely Disobedience—doing what you have been told not to do: And it results from Pride—from being too big for your boots, forgetting your place, thinking that you are God. . . . "The great moral which reigns in Milton," said Addison, "is the most universal and most useful that can be imagined, that Obedience to the will of God makes men happy and Disobedience makes them miserable."[15]

Satan suffered from a "sense of injur'd merit" as we see in "domestic animals, children, film-stars, politicians, or minor poets; and perhaps nearer home." When wounded pride appears "unable to hurt, in a jealous dog or a spoiled child, it is usually laughed at."[16]

All that is said about Milton's "sympathy" with Satan, his expression in Satan of his own pride, malice, folly, misery, and lust, is true in a sense, but not in a sense peculiar to Milton. The Satan in Milton enables him to draw the character well just as the Satan in us enables us to receive it. Not as Milton, but as man. . . . A fallen man is very like a fallen angel. That, indeed, is one of the things which prevents the Satanic predicament from becoming comic. It is too near us.[17]

Comedy stops before ultimate damnation, before the pain of pride is perfected. A wish to be oneself, to live in and for oneself, is a wish God can grant. Yet this wish cannot bring laughter, but, rather, only a hell of infinite boredom where one lives in unending autobiography. The only joke one sees is in the mirror, and, ironically, it is not funny to its audience.

Milton's "Satan wants to go on being Satan. That is the real meaning of his choice. 'Better to reign in Hell than serve in Heav'n.' Some, to the very end, will think this a fine thing to say; others will think that it fails to be roaring farce only because it spells agony."[18] If one could come out of oneself, to be free and self-forgetting in the presence of God, one could find comedy; yet one is locked in the tragedy of the self.

What is one to do about the selfish, exploitative person who laughs at the simplicity of his victims and who oppresses even his own accomplices with jeering and mocking? "Suppose he will not be converted?" asked Lewis. "Can you really desire that such a man, remaining what he is . . . should be confirmed forever in his present happiness—should continue for all eternity, to be perfectly convinced that the laugh is on his side?" For those who will not repent and come out, Lewis wrote, "that door out of Hell is firmly locked, by the devils themselves, on the inside."[19]

Lewis sketched a possible outline for the origins of flippancy in his discussion of the Fall in Milton's *Paradise Lost*.

No man, perhaps, ever at first described to himself the act he was about to do as Murder, or Adultery, or Fraud, or Treachery, or Perversion; and when he hears it so described by other men he is (in a way) sincerely shocked and surprised. Those others "don't understand." If they knew what it had really been like for him, they would not use those crude "stock" names. With a wink or a titter . . . the thing has slipped into his will as something not very extraordinary, something of which, rightly understood and in all his highly peculiar circumstances, he may even feel proud.[20]

Pride can beat down lesser vices; "many a man has overcome cowardice, or lust, or ill-temper by learning to think that they are beneath is dignity—that is, by Pride. The devil laughs."[21]

And, warned Lewis by quoting from eighteenth-century spiritual author William Law's *Serious Call*, "You can have no greater sign of a confirmed pride than when you think you are humble enough." We can hear the false tone of our own heart's confession or excusing. "The very act of confessing—an infinitesimally hypocritical glance—a dash of humor—all this contrives to dissociate the facts from your very self."[22] It is a wide and easy path that leads from flippancy to pride; yet one can refuse to recognize the direction one is headed on the road of laughter. Lewis saw the slippery descent of this folly in a broad spectrum of experiences from the wagging of tongues to the sly wink.

Eve's and Adam's responses to disobedience are different. Eve, who would not bow (it was beneath her dignity) to Adam or to God, "now worships a vegetable." Adam becomes less "primitive" as a "man of the world, a punster, an aspirant to fine raillery. He compliments Eve on her palate and says the real weakness of Paradise is that there were too few forbidden trees." He becomes the father of flippancy, of "all the bright epigrammatic wasters."[23] Even the wit of Oscar Wilde pales in comparison.

The pride over one's sinful life, rather than repentance leads inexorably to hell, away from God. In *The Screwtape Letters*, Lewis invented a modern image of hell in which pride is the overweening concern. Since he liked "bats much better than bureaucrats," he made his symbol for hell "something like the bureaucracy of a police state or the offices of a thoroughly nasty business concern." Rather than paint hell as one of Dickens's sordid "dens of crime," or even a concentration camp, he saw the greatest evil being done in "clean, carpeted, warmed, and well-lighted offices, by quiet men with white collars and cut fingernails and smooth-shaven cheeks who do not need to raise their voice."[24] The operating principle of this superficially suave and sophisticated society is "dog eat dog." This image not only includes the competitive goal of trying to discredit and ruin others, but the drive to devour others, to dominate, to digest, to eat one's fellows. The practical name for this spiritual cannibalism is pride. And flippancy is its small table talk and hungry laughter before the meal.

Flippancy, in fact, produces an atmosphere of conniving. It selects an inner ring that is "in the know," more clever and superior to all the common others. One characteristic of this type of group is its tendency to condone vice, "by our words, looks and laughter, to 'consent.'"[25] Unfortunately, such an attitude is infectious, and mere contact with those "in the know" is problematic. At one time or another, everyone finds himself in the company of such priggish or "smug" people. Lewis pointed out that such situations present an unavoidable difficulty.

> We shall hear vile stories told as funny; not merely licentious stories but (to me far more serious and less noticed) stories which the teller could not be telling unless he was betraying someone's confidence. We shall hear infamous detraction of the absent, often disguised as pity or humor. Things we hold sacred will be mocked. Cruelty will be slyly advocated by the assumption that its only opposite is "sentimentality." The very presuppositions of any possible good life—all disinterested motives, all heroism, all genuine forgiveness—will be, not explicitly denied (for then the matter could be discussed), but assumed to be phantasmal, idiotic, believed in only by children.[26]

Lewis recalled an example of this sort of thing from his own experience. Attending a conference, he found himself in the company of two modern clergymen, "obviously very close friends.

> [They] began talking about "uncreated energies" other than God. I asked how there could be any uncreated things except God if the Creed was right in calling Him the "maker of all things visible and invisible." Their reply was to glance at one another and laugh. I had no objection to their laughter, but I wanted an answer in words as well. It was not at all a sneering or unpleasant laugh. It expressed very much what Americans would express by saying "Isn't he cute?" It was like the laughter of jolly grown-ups when an *enfant terrible* asks the sort of question that is never asked . . . it conveyed the impression that they were fully aware of living habitually on a higher plane than the rest of us, of coming among us as Knights among churls or as grown-ups among children.[27]

Lewis takes a fairly tolerant tone to flippancy here, or seems to, but Chesterton would not have. He points out that the disregard of virtue and truth is wrong whether it is flippant or solemn. Writing of the French author Emile Zola, Chesterton asked:

> Is indecency more indecent if it is grave, or more indecent if it is gay? For my part, I belong to an old school in this matter. When a book or play strikes me as a crime, I am not disarmed by being told that it is a serious crime. If a man has written something vile, I am not comforted by the explanation that he meant to do it. I know all the evils of flippancy; I do not like the man who laughs at the sight of virtue. But I prefer him to the man who weeps at the sight of virtue and complains bitterly of there being any such thing.[28]

Lewis did not like a man who laughed at the sight of virtue, either. He incorporated many examples of this diseased form of wit in his work. In *The Pilgrim's Regress*, John is on his backward pilgrimage when he stumbles upon the Clevers, among whom "every shrewd turn was exalted among men . . . and simple goodness . . . was mocked away."[29] The city of Eschropolis, where the Clevers dwelled, despised normal values and promoted obscenity and satire. Goodness, virtue, and love were all debunked and had vanished from the Clevers' society. The general tone of flippancy about such noble things infected all other relations (as it always will do); slander and gossiping behind other's backs was *sine qua nom* in their conversations.

In *The Silver Chair*, a bewitched prince mocks the people of Narnia in the same Clever-fashion. He is boasting about the upcoming invasion and domination of Narnia when some visiting children object to this on moral grounds. The Prince listens, but not for long. "Fie on gravity," he flippantly exclaims. "Is it not the most comical and ridiculous thing in the world to think of them all going about their business and never dreaming . . . there is a great army ready to break out upon them?"[30] Jill refuses to be a victim of flippancy and retorts that she does not think that defeat or tyranny are funny at all. Rather, when evil or suffering is real, it is the season to cease flippant and silly laughter.

The laughter that lashes out against virtue is also a laughter that hides one from truth. It often tries to cover our own nakedness. Lewis found certain societies where laughter was "nothing but a drinking, guffawing cry of barbarians" who continually cackled at every bawdy reference, even tragic ones. "If one spent much time with these swine one would blaspheme against humor itself as being nothing but a kind of shield with which (the) rabble protect themselves from anything which might disturb the muddy puddle inside them."[31]

What we proud sinners, stubbornly resistant to our own transformation, need most is to have "our noses rubbed," like puppies, in our pride.[32] This may be God's tactic for treating mockers: to mock those who scoff at Him or His children. He does laugh from the heavens easily, quickly, and judiciously at those whose necks are stiff, noses are high, eyes are haughty, and tongues are wagging. It is a laugh to humble, nay, to humiliate our pride. One could almost say that God is the Cosmic Satirist, bringing out and down pride with His laughter in order to bring in life with His Spirit.

But men and women cannot bridle their own tongues, so they defile the body and set the whole world on fire. The tongue is, as the apostle James warns, a restless evil and full of poison. It unleashes a torrent of flippancy. The same tongue that articulates the good laughter is also that organ that clucks and mocks. It pours forth both sweet and bitter waters. This small instrument can be the most violent of weapons, doing more evil than "the knife, the big stick, and the firebrand." Lewis listed an inventory of its cruel and flippant evils, collected from the Psalter, but relevant for any age:

> Their throat is an open sepulcher, they flatter (5:10), under his tongue is ungodliness and vanity, . . . (10:7), deceitful lips (12:3), lying lips (31:20), words full of deceit (36:3), the "whispering" of evil

men (41:7), cruel lies that "cut like a razor" (52:3), talk that sounds "smooth as oil" and will wound like a sword (55:21), pitiless jeering (102:8). . . . One almost hears the incessant whispering, tattling, lying, scolding, flattery, and circulation of rumors. No historical readjustments are here required, we are in the world as we know. We even detect in that muttering and wheedling chorus voices which are familiar. One of them may be too familiar for recognition.[33]

In *That Hideous Strength*, Lewis almost personified flippancy in the silver-tongued character, Lord Feverstone. The novel's hero, Mark Studdock, is a promising young fellow of Bracton College. He is a newcomer, though, an outsider, and is enamored of Feverstone and of the mysterious and elitist inner circle, the "we" of the college's Progressive Element of which Feverstone is the chief. The members of this inner ring laugh in ironical and knowing tones about all outsiders. In their company, Mark begins to pick up their metallic and unreal laughter—laughter polluted with flattery, malice, backbiting, and toadeating. Among the in-crowd, Lord Feverstone is particularly known for his mocking banter, which often cruelly nettles others. He has "an extremely virile and infectious laugh." In exchanges like the following, he baits lesser colleagues—in this case one who hopes to write a book on military history but wants first to attend to college politics. "'I see,' said Feverstone. 'In order to keep the place going as a learned society, all the best brains in it have to give up doing anything about learning.' 'Exactly!' said Curry. 'That's just—' and then stopped, uncertain whether he was being taken quite seriously. Feverstone burst into laughter."[34]

Lord Feverstone had always been impertinent, shallow, and flashy, even before he attained his peerage (at which time he went by the name Devine and so appeared in the first two books of Lewis's space trilogy). He is an infectious model of a fashionable and flippant fellow of infinite jest, viewing what is solid and simple as trifles. Ransom remembers him from school, where Devine "had learned just a half a term earlier than anyone else that kind of humour which consists in a perpetual parody of the sentimental or idealistic clichés of one's elders." From childhood on, Lewis tells us, Devine simply "didn't give a damn" about anything or anyone. He mocks Ransom's fondness for the creatures of Malacandra, the brutes. "When the time comes for cleaning the place up we'll save one or two for you, and you can keep them as pets or vivisect them or sleep with them or all three—whichever way it takes you. . . . Yes, I know. Perfectly loathsome. I was only joking. Good night."[35]

The laughter of Feverstone and his friends entrances Mark, who, since childhood has always wanted to belong to such a group. (Credit must be given to Mark's wife, Jane, for not only intuiting the true nature of this "man with the loud unnatural laugh and mouth like a shark, and no manners," but even more so for finding him repellent.) Now Feverstone seduces Mark into feeling "that he was somehow being included in the fun."[36] Mark falls for the age-old ploy that Screwtape describes when he encourages Wormwood to get his charge to laugh at the sight of virtue. The real business of a demonic tempter is to undermine and subvert faith and "prevent the formation of virtues." Screwtape craftily recommends that the patient be encouraged to mingle with a certain sort of people—"rich, smart, superficially intelligent, and brightly sceptical [sic] about everything in the world."[37] Connive, Screwtape advises, to get him committed to such fashionable people through his "social, sexual, and intellectual vanity," whereby he will be seduced into evil without his realizing. The recipe should be as follows:

> A subtle play of looks and tones and laughs by which a mortal can imply that he is of the same party as those to whom he is speaking. . . . [Let him] be silent when he ought to speak and laugh when he ought to be silent. He will assume, at first only by his manner, but presently by his words, all sorts of cynical and sceptical [sic] attitudes which are not really his. But if you play him well, they may become his.[38]

Smug, self-satisfaction would result from such training, Screwtape advises. Most people, today, are not warned about the world as much as about the flesh and the devil. So Screwtape dictated to his pupil to inculcate in his patient such worldly vanities as becoming urbane and mocking, allowing him to still feel spiritually superior to others who "enjoy the bawdy and blasphemy over the coffee." To those people, he will feel he is doing some "'good' by the mere fact of drinking their cocktails and laughing at their jokes, and that to cease to do so would be 'priggish,' 'intolerant,' and (of course) 'Puritanical.'"[39]

In *That Hideous Strength* Mark follows this tempter's plan perfectly. He passes a moral point-of-no-return when he is told to fabricate a news report. When he asks how he can write about a riot before it happens, "everyone bursts out laughing.

> This was the first thing Mark had been asked to do which he himself before he did it, clearly knew to be criminal. . . . But, for him, it all slipped past in a chatter of laughter, of that intimate laughter between fellow professionals, which of all earthly powers is strongest to make men do very bad things before they are yet, individually, very bad men.[40]

For Lewis, Rudyard Kipling—the literary spokesman of the pleasures of freemasonry and confederacy against the wicked Baboons—was the author of this type of "inner ring." Such an inner ring, with its secret handclasp, esoteric comedies, and highly specialized smiles, opens a private door into the great world of sophistication and cynicism. Kipling's favorite joke was the hoax played upon a confused outsider. Yet an innocent member could be initiated into the corruption of such bad society simply by a quiet, confidential, knowing glance. "'It's always done,' they say, and so, without any 'scenes' . . . with a nod and a wink, over a couple of whiskies and soda, the Rubicon is crossed."[41]

For this reason, Screwtape advised Wormwood to encourage the sweet "idea of belonging to an inner ring, of being in a secret. . . . Play on that nerve. Teach him . . . to adopt an air of amusement at the things the unbelievers say."[42] As Screwtape knew, the flippant disregard of virtue combined with the proud self-delusion of superiority is the one-two punch that will knock the patient to hell. Such flippancy, though seemingly innocuous, is exposed as thoroughly wicked. It demeans others and mocks what is good. As one later discovers, it is laughter shared with the devil.

Although the glance and the laugh did not seem inoffensive or intended to wound or exult, the seeds of a shared superiority were obvious. The flippant flaunts her superiority by not meeting those "below itself" as real people, by excluding others, or, in an image Lewis borrowed, spraying insecticide on those outside the circle.

Scoundrelism and its invitation to flippancy follow quietly. One is drawn in and seduced "over a drink or a cup of coffee, disguised as a triviality and sandwiched between two jokes." And then, "next week it will be something a little further from the rules . . . but in the jolliest, friendliest spirit."[43]

The addictive taste of Turkish Delight and the spurious sweetness of the White Witch draw Edmund into derisive behavior. A spiteful Edmund "sneered and jeered at Lucy and kept on asking her if she'd found any other new countries in other cupboards all over the house." In a sillier and more flippant mood—one immediately following the relief of finding a lion was only a stone statue—he "scribbled a moustache on the lion's upper lip and then a pair of spectacles on its eyes. . . . 'Yah! Silly old Aslan!' . . . but in spite of the scribbles on it the face of the great stone beast still looked so terrible and sad and noble . . . that Edmund didn't really get any fun out of jeering at it."[44]

Lewis recognized the first buds of flippancy sprouting from small, cheeky boys, such that "half an hour in the society of a French thirteen-year-old makes most of us feel that there is something to be said for fagging after all." Otherwise, the system produces the natural extension of this impertinent and snotty child of the public schools—"truculent, skeptical, debunking, and cynical intelligentsia."[45] Nip the little proud sprouts in the bud.

Eustace Clarence Scrubb was a complainer, a sulker, and stinker. He was also an apprentice of flippancy. He was a proud little sprout needing to be nipped in the bud. His name, Lewis noted, was not only apt, but also almost fully deserved. He mocked his Pevensie cousins with a nasty limerick: "Some kids who played games about Narnia / Got gradually balmier and balmier—."[46]

Eustace is a sort of whiny, miniature Tartuffe, the kind of cheeky kid that Lewis believed could be improved with a bit of discipline. His idea of a good joke is being mean. He thinks it would be delightful, for example, to catch hold of Reepicheep's tail, swing the mouse "round by it once or twice upside-down, then run away and laugh." It is to Scrubb's credit, however, that when he is turned into a selfish dragon, he repents of his old ways and wants what is good: friends and the shared laughter and discourse of friends. After Aslan has transformed him back to his human form, "Eustace laughed—a different laugh from any Edmund had heard him give before."[47] Humility and humor enter his life together, hand in hand.

Lewis denounced flippancy so thoroughly because it was so close to home. It was a disease, a thorn, that beset his own heart. In Lewis's inner circle, one of the most familiar voices was his own, usually booming, jovial, and merry, but one also that could jab and cut with a quick parry and thrust. Flippancy was an enemy Lewis knew, and he felt qualified to combat its temptations because he knew them so well. He quoted Samuel Butler on the natural human tendency: "Compound for sins we are inclined to / By damning those we have no mind to."[48]

Lewis believed that one should censure only what one deeply knows and (in some sense) loves. "Just as I, for instance, who have no taste for cards, could not find anything very useful to say by way of warning against deep play. They will be like the frigid preaching chastity, misers warning us against prodigality, cowards denouncing rashness. . . . Who wants to hear a particular claret abused by a fanatical teetotaler, or a particular woman by a confirmed misogynist?"[49]

One should denounce those vices one knows so intimately. Vices do gratify. If you have never enjoyed a thing, you will hardly understand its attraction. Lewis, with his own prohibitions against and tendencies toward flippancy, enjoyed it, especially as a young man. He felt properly suited thus to rail against it. (Dreams provide a sneaky way to enjoy one's vices. The dreaming mind, Lewis confided, is "regrettably immoral." One could be caustic or flippant in dreams where such behavior would be wrong when awake. [This may be why St. Augustine thanked God that he was not responsible for his dreams.] Lewis once dreamed that "he saw a ship of meddling busybodies going plop-plop into the deep blue sea. I could do nothing but laugh. My punishment was that the laughter woke me up."[50])

In Lewis's early personal correspondence, flippancy oozes through various comments, betraying his youthful vanity and pride. He was becoming the kind of person he detested—that sly, furtive, knowing, and self-satisfied sort, with a "tipping-the-wink-ness." The young Lewis did not, in Owen Barfield's phrase, strut "in the puddle of his great naughtiness," but he practiced a smug meanness. In a postscript to one letter, he scribbled: "Haven't heard from my esteemed parent for some time; has he committed suicide yet?"[51]

While Lewis later loathed the flippancy of newspapers during World War II (they were, he felt, sensational and exploitative about life and death issues), he himself could be flippant about his own father. His letters are frequently bruised with punches thrown at his father, whom he nicknames "Excellenz." But his father was not his only victim. Lewis once wounded his dear friend, Arthur, with his flippancy. Writing to Arthur later, Lewis offered an apology not without its own bite: "I should have spared my 'sarcasm' if I had known that it would 'cut you to the heart,' that susceptible and sorely-tried organ of yours should not offer itself so readily to the knife." In later life, when Lewis reread some of his letters, he was struck by their egotism, affectation, and intellectual and social priggery. Such a realization, however, did not mean that he never again made the same mistake. When Sir Herbert Read gave Lewis's *An Experiment in Criticism* a very favorable review, Lewis wrote: "I always thought Herbert R. an ass, so I don't know whether to conclude that my book is bilge or to revise my opinion of H. R." (Perhaps Lewis would adopt Bailey's "amusing" disclaimer when the latter lectured on Lucretius. He would preface his remarks by saying: "I hope none of you gentlemen have got my edition of this book as it was written in my unregenerate days."[52] Lewis might excuse himself on similar grounds.)

In his autobiography, Lewis identified one of the sources of his tendency to posturing: a funny fellow called "Pogo." Pogo was a dressy and witty man about town, a fashionable and flashy version of a Saki or a Wodehouse. "We learned from him all the latest jokes; where we did not understand he was ready to give us help."[53] This faddish and friendly model did not cause Lewis to stumble from virtue; he was not a key influence in drawing the potential rake into the flesh, but he did help make a young and impressionable Lewis into a fop, a cad, and a snob. (Lewis counseled against a harsh judgment of Pogo as he was young and naïve himself.)

Lewis won his battle with flippancy and left behind a guide for those who want to be cured and to help cure others (the former must come before the latter). "The real way of mending a man's taste," Lewis wrote, "is not to denigrate his present favorites but to teach him how to enjoy something better."[54] Flippancy may disguise insecurity or fear, and can be diluted both by showing the patient how to find good laughter and by holding a comic mirror back up to the mocker. Even to urge a flippant person to progress from maligning other people to laughing about institutions or ideas would be a step in the right direction. Peccadilloes are preferred over mortal or venial sins. Actually, nothing evil is desired—but as Screwtape observed: "I have known a human defended from strong temptations to social ambitions by a still stronger taste for tripe and onions."[55] It is best, however, to purge and wash out any stinking scurrility, and to fill the rooms of the soul with fragrant laughter.

When one is tempted by the flippancy of others, Lewis recommended silence as a good response. It keeps us from participating in flippancy's mockery and protects us, at the same time, from being contentious. It protects us also from the temptation to make a priggish comment, showing that, like Queen Victoria, "one is 'not amused.'" Another good response to temptation is the soft, reasonable answer of disagreement, out of which discussion of the real issue may follow. It is a rhetorical trick recommended by Cicero to answer raillery with sobriety (and contrawise, for wiseacres). Silence or a gentle answer, however, does not always work, as Lewis pointed out: "[There] comes of course a degree of evil against which a protest will have to be made, however little chance it has of success. There are cheery agreements in cynicism or brutality which one must contract out of unambiguously. If it can't be done without seeming priggish, then priggish we must seem."[56]

The laughter of flippancy is as old as the scoffers of God, and like the other forms of laughter it is contagious. Therefore, the psalmists advise prudence in avoiding its infection. The good man should eschew "the seat of the scornful" and refuse "to consort with the ungodly lest he should 'eat of' (shall we say, laugh at, admire, approve, justify?) 'such things as please them.'"[57] This kind of laughter is, in one sense, very gratifying. It puts one above others and above morality. It connects one to fascinating contacts and brilliant fashions, "which I so often, at such risk, desire." It allows one to stay detached and safe from the risk of commitment to goodness.

In *The Last Battle*, certain dwarfs refuse to be taken in. "The Dwarfs are for the Dwarfs," they sneer. They refuse to be made fools of joy committing themselves to an idea. They refuse to be made part of a joke, even if the joke is for their benefit. And be assured, Chesterton observed, if a man cannot make a fool of himself, the effort might be quite superfluous.[58] These dwarfs become eternal fools, creatures that look "at one another with grins; sneering grins, not merry ones." Their habit of self-centeredness results in their own self-destruction. They refuse even to be taken into paradise. They will not believe because faith may make them fools, even if holy fools. So they remain secular skeptics, flippant and mocking, and outside the divine comedy of a new Narnia. With glib confidence, they concoct their own country of the blind. Aslan defines their decision, "They will not let us help them. They have chosen cunning instead of belief. Their prison is only in their minds, yet they are in that prison; and so afraid of being taken in that they can not be taken out."[59]

A flippant disregard of virtue combined with the self-delusion of pride ushers the laughter into the dark halls of hell. Each flippant look or each mean joke inches us toward the discourtesy of hell. In *The Lion, the Witch, and the Wardrobe*, the wicked laughter of the leering hags, vultures, ogres, and evil apes is only the prologue to their wicked action of binding, shearing, and sacrificing Aslan. The jeerings of the brutes, "Puss, Puss! Poor Pussy," and, "how many mice have you caught to-day, Cat?" decorate the more despicable deed of the killing of an innocent victim.[60] Flippancy enables one to excuse the evil lurking in the soul and gives it an eerily articulate voice.

Flippancy is the laughter that keeps one out of the kingdom of God. For those who would feast on tainted laughter, and not be satisfied with daily bread, it is the sad, cotton-candy taste of death. Flippancy does not nourish, but devours and even cannibalizes others, and eventually the self. And yet at the table of this earthly life, when one is hungry for a laugh, it appears the tastiest and most tempting dessert, and the easiest to make.

Lewis, who knew the temptation to flippancy so well, gave those of us with the same problem this model prayer to pray:

> *From all my lame defeats and oh! much more*
> *From all the victories that I seem to score;*
> *From cleverness shot forth on Thy behalf*
> *At which, while angels weep, the audience laugh;*

From all my proofs of Thy divinity,
Thou, who wouldst give no sign, deliver me.[61]

The deliverance of laughter from the tormenting demons of flippancy that smirk and scoff could only come through grace. And here
Lewis placed laughter under the liberating discipline of love.

Part 6

Conclusion: The Laughter of Love

A sour religion is the devil's religion.
—John Wesley

For I have found a joy that is full, and more than full. For when heart, and mind, and soul, and all the man, are full of that joy, joy beyond measure still will remain. Therefore, the whole of that joy shall not enter into those who rejoice; rather, they who rejoice shall wholly enter into that joy.
—Anselm of Canterbury

33

A Divine Comedy

He will yet fill your mouth with laughter, and your lips with shouts of joy.
—JOB 8:21 (NRSV)

Laughter by itself is not innately good; it does not necessarily improve us. Human nature, unfortunately, has always had the tendency to drift and go bad in its laughter as well as in other things. As an egg rots or a painted fence chips and buckles, so human nature has a tendency to degenerate and take its laughter with it.

As we have seen, every time we laugh we are not necessarily sharing our joy or our fun or even our jokes with one another. Rather, we may be laughing at each other in the cruelest kind of way. Indeed, laughter can be an expression of evil as well as of good. Each time I laugh, I am either sharing my laughter with God or with the devil. And, Lewis said, as each of us faces life with all its innumerable choices, we are turning either into a creature that is in harmony with God—and with other creatures, and with itself—or else into one that is in a state of war and hatred with God, and with its fellow creatures, and with itself.

To be the one kind of creature is heaven—that is, it is joy and peace and knowledge and delight. To be the other means madness, horror, idiocy, rage, impotence, and eternal loneliness.[1] Laughter alone, therefore, is not enough for life. To laugh only is not to live, but to become a stark-raving lunatic—a human hyena. A life that consists only of laughter may be compared to Chesterton's description of his good but unconverted friend, George Bernard Shaw: "All the virtues he has are heroic virtues. Shaw is like the Venus de Milo; all there is of him is admirable."[2] All there is of laughter, too, is admirable, but more is required. More is needed. Laughter may be one's response to the play, but it must not be the reason for being in the theater; the play's the thing. Our response to the whole play, and to the author behind it, is paramount. A parable by Søren Kierkegaard serves as warning: "It happened that a fire broke out backstage in a theatre. The clown came out to inform the public. They thought it was just a jest and applauded. He repeated his warning; they shouted even louder. So I think the world will come to an end amid general applause from all the wits, who believe that it is a joke."[3]

The general applause and laughter cajole us to forget that such pleasant moments on life's pilgrimage are, after all, only momentary. The end of the road, like the apocalyptic end of life's dramatic variety show, looms before us. Each of us travels this road, trotting toward becoming a heavenly creature or a hellish one. On the right road you see and pay attention to the signposts, reminding you of your destination. Lewis wrote regularly about the roads we all travel: Any path leads both to and away from Jerusalem. It goes in both directions, toward heaven or toward hell, and every step moves us closer toward one place or the other. Lewis warned through Screwtape that it doesn't matter how big our steps are or how fast we travel:

> It does not matter how small the sins are, provided that their cumulative effect is to edge the man away from the Light and out into the Nothing. Murder is no better than cards if cards can do the trick. Indeed, the safest road to Hell is the gradual one—the gentle slope, soft underfoot, without sudden turnings, without milestones, without signposts.[4]

On Perelandra, Ransom sees the difference. We either walk toward some Person, some Face, who will give us our faces or toward some spirit that would erase and devour all that we are:

> As there is one Face above all worlds merely to see which is irrevocable joy, so at the bottom of all worlds that face is waiting whose sight

alone is the misery from which none who beholds it can recover. And though there seemed to be, and indeed were, a thousand roads by which a man could walk through the world, there was not a single one which did not lead sooner or later either to the Beatific or the Miserific Vision.[5]

The warnings are posted along the way. Those who have eyes to see and ears to hear will understand the Preacher in Ecclesiastes when he calls laughter madness: "For as the crackling of thorn bushes under a pot, so is the laughter of the fool; and this too is futility" and "I said of laughter, 'It is madness'" (Eccl. 7:6; 2:2).

We may enjoy laughter on our way, but laughter is not where we are headed; we have seen where laughter alone will lead us. On the other hand if our laughter is submitted to something greater, to a higher end, then it will never be able to lead us astray. As expressed in Gerard Manley Hopkins's poem, "The Leaden Echo and the Golden Echo," the beauty that is offered back to God returns more golden and glorious than that which is kept, hoarded, corroded, corrupted, and killed. Laughter must submit to love.

"Laughter and love are everywhere," wrote Chesterton in *The Napoleon of Notting Hill*. "The cathedrals, built in the ages that loved God, are full of blasphemous grotesques. The mother laughs continually at the child, the lover laughs continually at the lover, the wife at the husband, the friend at the friend."[6] The cathedrals, as monuments of stone grace, reflected the laughter that is natural in the heart of love. Gargoyles grin because they sit on God's house of love.

As in the holy church, love and laughter abide in the holy family, which is the safest and sanest place for laughter. There it is free and fearless. When there are problems, love, like a surgeon, can cleanse and heal and remove suffering; and laughter, in love's hands, can be its scalpel or its healing balm. Laughter in love's hands is never used amiss, never mocks, never hurts. Just as human beings are at their best when they love, so, too, laughter is at its best when it arises out of love.

Love and laughter ripen and bloom together in the Day of the Lord, or on any holy day.

The designated season to laugh with the love of God is, in fact, the holy day, which is also a holiday. The word *holiday* remains as a promise, Chesterton argued, as an answer to "the ignorant slander which asserts that religion was opposed to human cheerfulness; that word will always assert that when a day is holy it should also be happy."[7]

Laughter and love flourish in the shared garden of earthly delights. But Lewis recognized that while a garden is a good and fruitful thing, it needs constant weeding and pruning to keep it from becoming a wilderness. These natural loves, with their attendant laughter, cannot suffice. When William Morris published a poem entitled "Love Is Enough," a reviewer succinctly critiqued it with the words: "It isn't." So for Lewis, all natural loves need to be submitted in obedience to God. In this blessed yoke, they find their true freedom to bring life and laughter. They "are taller when they bow" and find their ripe fruition.[8] When they attempt to satisfy all our deepest longings, however, they fail. They fall short of their own vows. And one discovers that it is not that we love others too much, but that we love God—and even others—too little.

In planting our loves and laughter in the charity of God we find they have "for the first time a firm basis. Emerson has said, 'When half-gods go, the gods arrive.' That is a very doubtful maxim. Better say, 'When God arrives (and only then) the half-gods can remain.' Left to themselves they either vanish or become demons. Only in His name can they with beauty and security 'wield their little tridents.'" In surrendering to the full grace of God, in humbling ourselves and confessing our absolute starvation before Him, we find a living refreshment. Grace brings a "full, childlike, and delighted acceptance of our Need, a joy in total dependence. We become 'jolly beggars.'"[9]

Pride and fear have kept us from the rewards of divine joy, fun, and laughter; they have "kept us from being happy. We have been like bathers who want to keep their feet—or one foot—or one toe—on the bottom, when to lose that foothold would be to surrender themselves to a glorious tumble in the surf."[10]

When perfect love casts out fear, there is room for laughter. The freedom from fear is a freedom to enjoy. Thus, George MacDonald discovered holy laughter is such a freedom: "It is the heart that is not yet sure of its God that is afraid to laugh in His presence."[11] Laughter may even aid in the divine purpose and *telos* of the individual, as Screwtape prophesied about such an end:

> The Enemy wants him, in the end, to be so free from any bias in his own favor that he can rejoice in his own talents as frankly and gratefully as in his neighbor's talent—or in a sunrise, an elephant, or a waterfall. He wants each man, in the long run, to be able to recognize all creatures (even himself) as glorious and excellent things. He wants to kill the animal self-love as soon as possible; but it is His long-term policy, I fear, to restore to them a new kind of self-love— a charity and gratitude for all selves, including their own; when they have really learned to love their neighbors as themselves, they will be allowed to love themselves as their neighbors.[12]

We are created for our neighbors, to be in a loving and joyous community with one another. And here we discover that both good laughter and love have a tendency to be inclusive rather than exclusive. Jokes are shared and passed on. Laughter draws and gathers a sad world to its center. The sounds of laughter heard in another room will jerk the interest and curiosity of the hearer, and may, without any logic, draw the stranger in and elicit a sympathetic smile.

The inclusive nature of comedy unites high and low. All humble creatures are exalted by membership in a glorious community. Aslan honors another ordinary lion by announcing that "us" lions must be at the front. The lion is ecstatic with delight: "Did you hear what he said? *Us lions.* That means him and me. *Us lions.*" But honor involves the responsibility of *noblesse oblige*. So Aslan loads up this newly exalted and excited beast with "three dwarfs, one Dryad, two rabbits, and a hedgehog. That steadied him a bit."[13]

Some humor strives to isolate or drive away a victim just as some "love" seeks to construct a shining barrier that would keep the world from just us two or three. Private jokes exclude, not because they're jokes, but because they're private. The joke has a tendency, like young lovers, to be public even in its secrecy. Laughter cannot be hid under a bushel, a bed, or behind closed doors. Its communal chorus is heard escaping prisons, hospitals, confessional booths, and even university classrooms. It spreads like a good infection, a cheerful contagion. Even Mark Twain acknowledged that "the best way to cheer yourself up is to try to cheer somebody else."[14] Like the widow's jar that Elijah blessed so it would not run dry, so laughter does not run dry when shared with the saints.

Laughter exhibits a goodness that seems divinely planted and grown. Yet it is a goodness that is natural, that does not convey a special redemptive blessing. As Lewis noted, "I enjoyed breakfast this morning, and I think that was a good thing and do not think it was condemned by God. But I do not think myself a good man for enjoying it."[15] (Being good does not always go with having fun, Lewis wrote to an American girl. "A martyr being tortured by Nero [was] being good but not having fun. And even in ordinary life there are things that would be fun to me but I mustn't do them because they would spoil other people's fun. But of course you are quite right if you mean that giving up fun for no reason except that you think it's 'good' to give it up, is all nonsense."[16])

Laughter and enjoyment are good in themselves, but they do not make us good. They do not make us better in the sense of gaining meritorious or moral goodness. Rather, there is a *non*moral goodness to it all. "As a well-grown healthy toad is 'better' or 'more perfect' than a three-legged toad," in this sense, a clever or laughing man is better than a dull or miserable one, "or any man than a chimpanzee."[17]

For this reason we are by no means more acceptable or pleasing to our Maker when we approach Him with a readiness to laugh. If we expect laughter to keep us from getting into a terrible jam on Judgment Day, we have an unpleasant surprise awaiting us. The Proverbs warn against the person who would wiggle out of responsibility or righteousness with a wave of a hand and a jest. Such a wag and knave is aptly described: "Like a madman shooting firebrands or deadly arrows is a man who deceives his neighbor and says, 'I was only joking!'" (Prov. 26:18–19 NIV).

In *The Four Loves*, Lewis illuminated the role of laughter in the various kinds of loving relationships people have. The fundamental ethic of these relations is love, and, therefore, the laughter that rises out of it is the hearty sign of a healthy communion, an echo from the heart of God. The humblest of the four loves is the love of the family—the *storge*, or "affection, especially of parents to offspring." This type of love carries with it a nondiscriminating and easy humor. We laugh at those we love, not because they are funny, necessarily, but because they are ours. There is a warm, happy comfortableness in being together, like the comfort of a pair of old slippers. Lewis pointed out how affection binds people together, even diverse personalities, like the comic literary couples, Don Quixote and Sancho Panza, Pickwick and Sam Weller, and the amazing foursome of Mole, Rat, Badger, and Toad in *The Wind in the Willows*. Each humbly accepts and enjoys the other, no matter what differences exist—even, for example, in the surprising affection between a dog and a cat. Yet as a friend speculated to Lewis: "I bet no dog would confess it to the other dogs."[18]

Like Christianity itself, Lewis wrote, affection can open the public, communal side of our experiences; it can "teach us humility and charity towards simple low-brow people who may be better Christians than ourselves. I naturally *loathe* all hymns; the face and life of the char-woman in the next pew who revels in them, teaches me that good taste in poetry and music are not necessary to salvation."[19]

Affection lives with old jokes by the fireplace. It places before the hearth a number of people whom you would not have invited but who happen to be there for the warmth. The broadening of our sense of humor comes, in part, from encountering a wide cross section of people with whom we are thrown together. Humor and love grow together in our being stuck with a different, broader sort of people in our churches, schools, military service, and in-laws. We receive a more democratic education in being with these others. Lewis wrote that it is affection that creates a truly wide taste in humanity, "teaching us first to notice, then to endure, then to smile at, then to enjoy, and finally to appreciate, the people who 'happen to be there.' Made for us? Thank God, no. They are themselves, odder than you could have believed and worth far more than we guessed."[20]

Lewis presents an amusing example of how this simple, happy love can become obsessive and perverse. He facetiously invented an example of the loving maternal instinct gone berserk in a Mrs. Fidget who recently died. "It is really astonishing how her family have brightened up. The drawn look has gone from her husband's face; he begins to be able to laugh." The two sons and the daughter have turned out to be not sickly, delicate, peevish creatures, but active, productive, healthy humans. "Even the dog who was never allowed out except on a leash is now a well-known member of the Lamp-post Club in their road." Mrs. Fidget was a woman who inexorably "lived for her family," not allowing them to live for themselves. "The Vicar says Mrs. Fidget is now at rest. Let us hope she is. What's quite certain is that her family are."[21] In a similar vein, Lewis wrote a poetic epitaph: "Erected by her sorrowing brothers / In memory of Martha Clay / Here lies one who lived for others / Now she has peace, and so have they."[22]

One wonders if Lewis's own predicament with a nagging, interrupting Mrs. Moore did not provide ample material for such an invention. Screwtape even described this "sort of woman who lives for others—you can always tell the others by their hunted expression."[23] Yet affection even has a way of making suffering sufferable and humorous.

If the laughter of affection is a chuckle, the laughter of friendship is a roar. In friendship, particularly in male friendships, Lewis found some of his happiest moments and his loudest laughter. His brother remembered him as "a man with an outstanding gift for pastime with good company, for laughter and the love of friends—a gift which found full scope in any number of holidays and walking tours. . . . Indeed a remarkable talent for friendship, particularly for a friendship of an uproarious kind."[24] Lewis himself acknowledged: "My happiest hours are spent with three or four old friends in old clothes tramping together and putting up in small pubs—or else sitting up till the small hours in someone's college rooms talking nonsense, poetry, theology, metaphysics over beer, tea and pipes. There's no sound I like better than adult male laughter."[25]

Lewis pointed back to early communities, where men, as hunters and fighters, shared esoteric jokes as well as dangers—"away from the women and children. As some wag has said, Paleolithic man may or may not have had a club on his shoulder but he certainly had a club of the other sort."[26]

Lewis has been accused of being a male chauvinist. His limited experience of women persuaded him not that women were inferior or deficient to men, but mainly *different*. Even a modern woman, by "learning to drink and smoke and perhaps to tell risqué stories . . . has not . . . drawn an inch nearer to the men than her grandmother."[27] For the Oxford don, women using bawdy humor in mixed company was an alien and discomforting idea. Lewis tried to imagine what "any sensible woman would make of such a wooing as Donne's nasty poem, 'The Extasie.'" It is "difficult to imagine," he acknowledged, "or would be difficult if we forgot the amazing protective faculty which each sex possesses of not listening to the other."[28]

As a creature conditioned by and immersed in the dominant culture of a patriarchal university system, Lewis believed it best to let members of each gender find friends among their own gender and find the kind of laughter that is proper to their sex.

Only the riff-raff of each sex . . . wants to be incessantly hanging on the other. Live and let live. They laugh at us a good deal. That is just as it should be. Where the sexes, having no real shared activities, can meet only in Affection and Eros—cannot be Friends—it is healthy that each should have a lively sense of the other's absurdity. Indeed it is always healthy. No one ever really appreciated the other sex—just as no one really appreciates children or animals—without at times feeling them to be funny. For both sexes are. Humanity is tragi-comical; but the division into sexes enables each to see in the other the joke that often escapes it in itself—and the pathos too.[29]

Cockney humorist Charles Lamb expressed a truth about friendship. For three or four friends, he said, losing one member means losing more than that friend's opinion. "In each of my friends there is something that only some other friend can fully bring out. . . . Now that Charles is dead, I shall never again see Ronald's reaction to a specifically Caroline joke."[30] The loss of a friend divides and robs us of delight even as the addition of a friend multiplies our fun. As Dante hears the blessed souls say: "Here comes one who will augment our loves," so we hear laughter explode in a full community of friends.

The more we share laughter, the more we all shall have. Each of us also feels fortunate to be included among our friends. Lewis saw each friend, in his secret heart, "humbled before all the rest. Sometimes he wonders what he is doing there among his betters. He is lucky beyond dessert to be in such company. Especially when the whole group is together, each bringing out all that is best, wisest, or funniest in all the others."[31]

In addition, in friendships between men and women the unexpected may happen. The love and laughter of friendship sometimes turn magically into that of Eros, much as fairytale goose-girl may turn into a princess, a sexy one who leaves her prince breathless. The love between the sexes offers the most hilarious sense of proportion that humor can bestow: For here we see through the eyes of a creature so like but so unlike ourselves, that, if we did not laugh, we must assuredly go crazy. Chesterton exclaimed that the wonder of knowing one real woman—not put on a pedestal but simply and unexpectedly met—and marrying her—was a glorious miracle of mythic dimensions; even "keeping to one woman is a small price for so much as seeing one woman."[32]

In the last decade of his life, Lewis discovered this startlingly joyful reality of love and laughter with a woman. Joy Davidman, a divorced Jewish American who converted to Christianity, interrupted and surprised C. S. Lewis with a carnival of new laughter. Her supple intellectual skills, not to mention her unrivaled rough-and-ready— even coarse—Brooklyn humor, matched Lewis's own quick wit. Her brain tumbled with his in interest, analysis, and "above all in humor and sense of fun. . . . She shared his delight in argument for argument's sake, whether frivolous or serious, always good-humored yet always meeting him trick for trick as he changed ground."[33] Lewis said that on one occasion, he praised Joy "for her 'masculine virtues.' But she soon put a stop to that by asking how I'd like to be praised for my feminine ones. It was a good riposte, dear."[34]

But in the final analysis, family, friends, lovers, all these loves and their accompanying laughter, are emphatically penultimate concerns for Lewis. One Other Treasure is first and foremost. It is God Himself who deserved the fruits of his love, adoration, and laughter. He was Lewis's first love. And, Lewis reminded us, "When first things are put first, second things are not suppressed but increased."[35] Our laughter, therefore, increases when we keep it in its proper place. It is at its greatest when we remember it is on loan from God. We humans, Screwtape noticed, are "always putting up claims to ownership which sound equally funny in Heaven and in Hell." We deceive ourselves with such curious assumptions as "This is my body," or, "These are my boots, my dog, my wife, my country, even, My God." Or "my joke." Rather, the joke is, Screwtape explains, that "the word 'mine' in its fully possessive sense cannot be uttered by a human being about anything."[36] In the long run, everything will be either God's or Satan's—laughter included. Thus, we must give back to God our joy, our play, our humor and wit, for they belong to Him. We are only stewards of such laughter, to use and invest for Him. And as stewards we will be called to task, called to account for every laugh, even whether we multiplied it tenfold or buried it in fear of looking foolish. Inasmuch as we give it to a stranger or widow or orphan or the least of these, we give it unto God. Our laughter then is a cup of water given to sad and thirsty children, who may then drink "sadly" and fully of abundant, laughing waters. In his sermon "The Weight of Glory," Lewis proclaimed: "There are no *ordinary* people."

> You have never talked to a mortal. But it is immortals whom we joke with . . . immortal horrors or everlasting splendors. This does not mean that we are to be perpetually solemn. We must play. But our merriment must be of that kind (and it is, in fact, the merriest kind) which exists between people who have, from the outset, taken each other seriously—no flippancy, no superiority, no presumption. And our charity must be real and costly love, with deep feeling for the sins in spite of which we love the sinner—no mere tolerance or indulgence which parodies love as flippancy parodies merriment.[37]

If this is true, then in heaven there will be great merriment—merriment that rises from the greatest example ever of "real and costly love." And in heaven the great laugh over Satan will be that God truly loves His creatures—loves them personally, individually. Screwtape could never believe it. It appalled him to have to admit that God "really likes the little vermin,

> and sets an absurd value on the distinctness of every one of them. . . . We must never forget what is the most repellent and inexplicable trait in our Enemy; He *really* loves the hairless bipeds He has created. . . . He really *does* want to fill the universe with a lot of loathsome little replicas of Himself—creatures whose life, on its miniature scale, will

be qualitatively like His own, not because He has absorbed them but because their wills freely conform to his. We want cattle who can finally become food; He wants servants who can finally become sons.[38]

In this sense, then, as His sons and daughters, we will one day laugh with God. As part of His family we will someday participate in the laughter we know typifies loving families. After all, if God is love, as the Bible says He is, then laughter in His family must be loving. And if it is loving, then it is good. Having this assurance, Chesterton battled with boisterous cheerfulness to correct the solemn mask given to the Christian faith by dour churchmen and grim Pharisees. Chesterton believed that the Man of Sorrows kept within Himself a colossal secret. Lewis caught a glimpse of that secret while writing of a quality in our Lord's "human character which is, in fact so visible in His irony," "His *argumenta ad homines*, and His use of the *a fortiori*, which I would call the homely, peasant shrewdness. Donne points out that we are never told He laughed; it is difficult to believe in reading the Gospels not to believe, and to tremble in believing, that He smiled."[39]

Chesterton saw even greater joy:

Joy, which was the small publicity of the pagan, is the gigantic secret of the Christian. And as I close this chaotic volume I open again the strange small book from which all Christianity came; and I am again haunted by a kind of confirmation. . . . The Stoics, ancient and modern, were proud of concealing their tears. He never concealed His tears; He showed them plainly on His open face at any daily sight, such as the far sight of His native city. Yet He concealed something. . . . I say it with reverence there was in that shattering personality a thread that must be called shyness. There was something that He hid from all men when He went up a mountain to pray. There was something that He covered constantly by abrupt silence or impetuous isolation. There was some one thing that was

too great for God to show us when He walked upon our earth; and
I have sometimes fancied that it was His mirth.[40]

To know God's mirth, however, one must first know Him and
His love. He then forgives those who come to Him. It is the act of
forgiveness that transforms those who would submit to the comedy of
His grace. Therefore, laughter must be linked to love and forgiveness
if it would last. Its total transformation into a mode of charity will not
be quick or easy, but then neither is forgiveness. Lewis says there is
no use talking as if it were: "We all know the old joke, 'You've [only]
given up smoking once; I've given it up a dozen times.' In the same
way I could say of a certain man, 'Have I forgiven him for what he
did that day? I've forgiven him more times than I can count.' For we
find that the work of forgiveness has to be done over and over again."[41]

The practice of forgiveness must be inexorable and gracious (for
grace is needed most deeply here). Would we not rather, Lewis asks,

> live with those ordinary people who get over their tantrums (and
> ours) unemphatically, letting a meal, a night's sleep, or a joke mend
> all? . . . We have not got far enough if we play a game of cards
> with the children "merely" to amuse them or to show that they are
> forgiven. If this is the best we can do we are right to do it. But it
> would be better if a deeper, less conscious, Charity threw us into a
> frame of mind in which a little fun with the children was the thing
> we should at that moment like best.[42]

Laughter and rejoicing flood scenes where people are forgiven,
restored, rescued. When the spring thaw begins in Narnia, little groups
of talking creatures enjoy gathering together for picnics. Every reunion
is a tiny homecoming. School chums meeting for summer vacations
or a chance bumping into an old friend at a railway station quickens
laughter. When Lucy is reunited with the thawed little faun, they hold
each other by both hands and dance round and round for joy.

Just as angels rejoice when a sinner is saved, so when Eustace is changed from dragon to boy there is great rejoicing around the campfire. After narrowly avoiding the encircling knot of a stupid but hostile Sea Serpent, the crew of the Dawn Treader first start reliving their rescue with talk and then begin to laugh about it. (Then, appropriately, as their laughter accelerates, rum is served, all around, and "they even raised a cheer.") The escape from the terror of the dark island where dreams come true was an experience of moving from fear to joy.

> Just as there are moments when simply to lie in bed and see the daylight pouring through your window and to hear the cheerful voice of an early postman or milkman down below and to realize that *it was only a dream: it wasn't real*, is so heavenly that it was very nearly worth having the nightmare in order to have the joy of waking.[43]

In *Prince Caspian*, the results of the liberation of laughter turn Narnia into a playground. Unnecessary and uncomfortable clothes are shed. "Sad old donkeys who have never known joy grew suddenly young again; chained dogs broke their chains; horses kicked their carts to pieces and came trotting along with them—clip-clop—kicking up the mud and whinnying."[44] A boy being beaten is rescued, and his crying is transformed into laughing. A weary girl teaching arithmetic to little boys who look like pigs hears the music of the revelers and "a stab of joy" goes through her heart, as Aslan frees her enslavement.

In *The Lion, the Witch, and the Wardrobe*, the resurrected strength of Aslan as he leaps over the girls causes Lucy to laugh (though she didn't know why). New life releases ineffable, inexplicable laughter. The joy of resurrection breaks into a wild romp and madcap chase, with Aslan tossing the girls "in the air with his huge and beautifully velveted paws and catching them again, and now stopping unexpectedly so that all three of them rolled over together in a happy laughing heap of fur and arms and legs."[45]

Later when statues in the courtyard come to life, the scene resembles a zoo more than a museum, ringing with the "sound of happy roarings, brayings, yelpings, barkings, squealings, cooings, neighings, stampings, shouts, hurrahs, songs and laughter."[46] After the Calormenes are defeated in another Narnian story, and peace is restored, a great feast is held and the real fun begins: "The wine flowed and tales were told and jokes were cracked."[47]

The liberation of the Earthmen from the enchanted enslavement by the queen of the Underland is cause for riotous celebration and laughter. The gnome Golg explained how glum and gloomy things were under the Witch's reign. "I've nearly forgotten how to make a joke or dance a jig," he says. Once the wicked spell is broken and they are free to return to the deep crack of the earth's core, they ignite all sorts of firecrackers and rockets and stand on their heads for joy. Discovering the good news that the wicked Witch was dead, the whole of Underland took only a few minutes to explode in gladness, "ringing with shouts and cheers, and gnomes by hundreds and thousands, leaping, turning cartwheels, standing on their heads, playing leap-frog, and letting off huge crackers."[48]

The pains of adventures and quests are always worth the cost in Narnia. "Such cheering and shouting, such jumps and reels of joy, such handshakings and kissings and embracings of everybody by everybody else broke out" when Prince Rilian was rescued, that "tears came into Jill's eyes."[49] Rejoicing—usually with squirrels leaping and dancing somewhere nearby—was a sign of *eucatastrophe* and a good ending.

The turn from tears to joy occurs frequently in Narnia. Eustace, Jill, and Aslan weep over dead King Caspian. After Aslan's paw is pierced by a thorn and his blood splashes on the dead body, the dead king is revived; "his sunken cheeks grew round and fresh, and the wrinkles were smoothed, and his eyes opened, and his eyes and lips both laughed, and suddenly he leaped up and stood before them—a very young man, or a boy." When he turns to the children, he gives a "great laugh of astonished joy." When asked if Caspian hadn't died, the great lion speaks in a voice that sounds as if he were laughing: "He has died. Most people have, you know. Even I have. There are very few who haven't."[50] The victory over death invites the laughter of resurrection—a laughter reborn and blessed.

Lewis teaches both the importance and the value of surrendering our laughter to the sovereignty of the God who vanquished death with His resurrection. In light of His death and resurrection, we may think that our laughter is only a trifle, and such a natural one at that. But to Lewis,

> Nothing is either too trivial or too animal to be thus transformed. A game, a joke, a drink together, idle chat, a walk, the act of Venus— all these can be modes in which we forgive or accept forgiveness, in which we console or are reconciled in which we "seek not our own." Thus in our very instincts, appetites, and recreations, Love has prepared for Himself "a body."[51]

To follow Christ and give up our lives for His service is a calling to take up His yoke. But His yoke is light, not grave. His burden is easy, not heavy. As Lewis wrote to his friend Griffiths, "We must, if it so happens, give our own lives for others, but even while we're doing it, I think we're meant to enjoy our Lord, and in him, our friends, our food, our sleep, our jokes, and the birds and the frosty sunrise."[52]

For this reason, just as hell is the only place outside of heaven where we can be safe from the dangers of love, heaven is the only place where we can be endlessly immersed in the laughter of love. The charity of God transforms natural laughter into a "tuned and obedient instrument" of Love Himself. It is a work of marvelous mystery that heavenly laughter is not something beyond us, kept from us, hidden and limited, until Christ returns. It began with the Creation, was lost in the Fall, but was gloriously reclaimed through the Resurrection and dispersed through Pentecost. Its reign began when His did, which means it has already begun, in the already, but not yet; it exists right now in the present, in every humble word and deed that springs from love and yet awaits the Parousia for the consummate and hearty laughter of the cosmos.

Our task is to humbly serve God with our laughter. Does He, in turn, laugh with us? Is there merriment with God? We may not know whether there is—yet. But if we are ever to find out, we must first know Him and know His love. There is a vision of what is to come in a Chesterton poem entitled "The Wise Men": "Hark! Laughter like lion wakes / To roar to the resounding plain / And the whole heaven shouts and shakes / For God Himself is born again, / And we are little children walking / Through the snow and rain."[53]

We may find in our final encounter with Almighty God that every idea of Him and His world we have formed, He, as the Great Iconoclast, must in mercy shatter. He unmakes us with joy. When the gods came to judge Orual in *Till We Have Faces*, she experienced a glorious transformation. "Each breath I drew let into me new terror, joy, overpowering sweetness. I was pierced through and through with the arrows of it. I was being unmade."[54] So, too, in *That Hideous Strength*, Jane Studdock encounters supernatural goodness and joy and finds herself unmade and radically changed. Our meetings with God will unmake and remake us all. Lewis wrote that the most blessed result of meeting Him would be our surprise: "But I never knew before. I never dreamed. . . . I suppose it was at such a moment that Thomas Aquinas said of his own theology: "It reminds me of straw.'"[55] Indeed, the Grand Surprise of God ushers us with inescapable humility into the Grand Comedy of God. And the agape love of God interrupts and surprises us in ways we might never expect.

Most people expect the worst from an encounter with God. Our guilt and shame chase us away from the gladness of His presence. He must then become the Hound of Heaven pursuing us, not simply to chide, rebuke, or punish us, but to embrace us and lick us with love. This sort of misperception Lewis remembered in an incident involving his wife, Joy:

Long ago, before we were married, [Joy] was haunted all one morning as she went about her work with the obscure sense of God (so to speak) "at her elbow," demanding her attention. And of course, not being a perfected saint, she had the feeling that it would be a question, as it usually is, of some unrepented sin or tedious duty. At last she gave in—I know how one puts it off—and faced Him. But the message was, "I want to *give* you something" and instantly she entered into joy.[56]

But those who see laughter as a gift, empty in itself without the Giver, will enjoy it for just what it is—for the quiddity of itself. But there is more. Lewis ended his autobiography, *Surprised by Joy*:

But what, in conclusion, of Joy? For that, after all, is what the story has mainly been about. To tell you the truth, the subject has lost nearly all interest for me since I became a Christian. I cannot, indeed, complain like Wordsworth, that the visionary gleam has passed away. I believe (if the thing were at all worth recording) that the old stab, the old bittersweet, has come to me as often and sharply since my conversion as at any time of my life whatever. But I now know that the experience, considered a state of my own mind, had never had the kind of importance I once gave it. It was valuable only as a pointer to something other and outer. While that other was in doubt, the pointer naturally loomed large in my thoughts. When we are lost in the woods the sight of a signpost is a great matter. He who first sees it cries, "Look!" The whole party gathers round and stares. But when we have found the road and are passing signposts every few miles, we shall not stop and stare. They will encourage us and we shall be grateful to the authority that set them up. But we shall not stop and stare, or not much, not on this road, though their pillars are of silver and their lettering of gold. "We would be at Jerusalem." Not, of course, that I don't often catch myself stopping to stare at roadside objects of even less importance.[57]

The final danger of our treatise occurs on these last pages: the temptation to take the principles of laughter set forth in this book too solemnly. Older authors would introduce a palinode after their writing, a sort of passage of repentance after the book was over, just in case it was needed. "Even Ovid had furnished a model by writing a *Remedium Amoris* to set against *Ars Amatoria*."[58] Thus, a palinode for this work is not out of order, and may yet rescue me, if not this book.

But the rescue from solemnity has its escape hatch in laughter itself. We must make our own pronouncements and insights lightly, very lightly. Lewis proposed an example from the *Paradiso* (XXVIII) that undoes any pretension that may arise. It seems that when poor Pope Gregory was ushered into heaven, he "discovered that his theory of the hierarchies, on which presumably he had taken pains, was quite wrong. We are told how the redeemed soul behaved; '*di sé medesmo rise*.' It was the funniest thing he'd ever heard."[59]

So, too, I conclude, like the redeemed Pope Gregory, I must be ready to humbly and hilariously acknowledge all these discoveries and inventions as askew. My own sense of reason and humor persuade me to regard the frailty and finitude of my own pronouncements. I have simply done a work of exhumation. I am content to submit to a line like that penned by Groucho Marx reviewing an early work by S. J. Perelman: "From the moment I picked up your book until I laid it down, I was convulsed with laughter. Someday I intend reading it." If some friend does read and then proves this comic work wrong (or even, heaven forbid, solemn), I must be free to laugh at all my vain labors. For at the end, the laughter will be all grace and joy.

Notes

Introduction

1. Lewis, *Discarded Image*, viii.
2. Lewis, *On Stories and Other Essays*, 150, 133.
3. Lee, Judith Yaross, *Defining New Yorker Humor* (University Press of Mississippi, 2000).
4. Lewis, *Preface to Paradise Lost*, v.
5. White, *Subtreasury of American Humor*, xvii.

Chapter 1

1. Lewis, *Studies in Words*, 103.
2. Aristotle, *Poetics*, 59.
3. Walsh, *Apostle to the Skeptics*, 241.
4. Lewis, *God in the Dock*, 65–66.
5. Lewis, *Medieval and Renaissance Literature*, 17.
6. Lewis, "Meditation in a Toolshed," *God in the Dock*.
7. Lewis, *Grief Observed*, 38.
8. Shakespeare, *Love's Labour Lost* in *Plays and Sonnets of William Shakespeare*, 5.2.869.
9. Lewis, *Letters of C. S. Lewis*, 132.
10. Ibid., 132–133.
11. Lewis, *God in the Dock*, 102.
12. Lewis, *Letters to Malcolm*, 48.

Chapter 2

1. Lewis, *Selected Literary Essays*, 103.
2. Chesterton, *Everlasting Man*, 46.
3. Lewis, *Experiment in Criticism*, 81.
4. Ibid.
5. Lewis, *Medieval and Renaissance Literature*, 26.
6. Lewis, *They Stand Together*, 445.
7. Lewis, *Essays Presented to Charles Williams*, xii.
8. Ibid., x.
9. Ibid., xiii.
10. Lewis, *Fern-seed and Elephants*, 54.
11. Chesterton, *Everlasting Man*, 59.
12. Lewis, *Fern-seed and Elephants*, 66.
13. Chesterton, *Orthodoxy*, 158.

14. Lewis, *Experiment in Criticism*, 44.
15. Lewis, *Surprised by Joy*, 148–49.
16. Lewis, *God in the Dock*, 208.
17. Ibid., 213.
18. Lewis, *Pilgrim's Regress*, 60–61.
19. Lewis, *Selected Literary Essays*, 293.
20. Ibid., 288.
21. Lewis, *Reflections on the Psalms*, 99–100.
22. Lewis, *God in the Dock*, 204.
23. Ibid., 181.
24. Lewis, *Reflections on the Psalms*, 121.
25. Lewis, *Christian Reflections*, 171.
26. Lewis, *English Literature in the Sixteenth Century*, 222–23.
27. Lewis, *Christian Reflections*, 10.
28. Lewis, *God in the Dock*, 279.
29. Lewis, *Christian Reflections*, 10.
30. Lewis, *Discarded Image*, 33–34.
31. Kierkegaard, *Kierkegaard Anthology*, 7.
32. Lewis, *Preface to Paradise Lost*, 95.
33. Lewis, *That Hideous Strength*, 299, 310.
34. Kierkegaard, *Concluding Unscientific Postscript*, 413.
35. Chesterton, *Everlasting Man*, 104.
36. Ibid., 104–5.
37. Ibid., 106.
38. Lewis, *Miracles*, 100.
39. Chesterton, *Tremendous Trifles*, 215.

Chapter 3

1. Lewis, *God in the Dock*, 285.
2. Lewis, *Surprised by Joy*, 122–23.
3. Ibid., 120.
4. Ibid., 121.
5. Ibid., 38.
6. Lewis, *Silver Chair*, 33–34.
7. Ibid., 47.
8. Lewis, *Surprised by Joy*, 123.
9. Ibid., 122.
10. Chesterton, *Everlasting Man*, 68.
11. Lewis, *Letters of C. S. Lewis*, 126.
12. Lewis, *Surprised by Joy*, 4–5.
13. Lewis, *Letters of C. S. Lewis*, 123.
14. Griffin, *Clive Staples Lewis*, 55.

Chapter 4

1. Lewis, *Discarded Image*, 5.
2. Lewis, *Surprised by Joy*, 191.
3. Lewis, *God in the Dock*, 259.
4. Lewis, *Surprised by Joy*, 190.
5. Ibid., 227.
6. Ibid., 223–24.
7. Chesterton, *All Things Considered*, 12.
8. Ibid., 13.

Chapter 5

1. Ward, *Gilbert Keith Chesterton*, 585.
2. Ibid., 596.
3. Lewis, *Surprised by Joy*, 47.
4. Ibid., 48.
5. Lewis, *Horse and His Boy*, 150.
6. Ibid., 185.
7. Lewis, *Surprised by Joy*, 48.
8. Ibid., 94.
9. Lewis, *Letters to an American Lady*, 79.
10. Ibid., 43.
11. Lewis, *Experiment in Criticism*, 71.
12. Lewis, *Letters to an American Lady*, 15.
13. Ibid., 110.
14. Ibid., 67–68.
15. Lewis, *Letters to Malcolm*, 58.
16. Chesterton, *All Things Considered*, 131.
17. Lewis, *Grief Observed*, 8.
18. Chesterton, *Orthodoxy*, 11–12.
19. Ward, *Gilbert Keith Chesterton*, 567.
20. Lewis, *Lion, the Witch and the Wardrobe*, 148.
21. Ibid., 66.
22. Lewis, *Allegory of Love*, 322.
23. Lewis, *English Literature in the Sixteenth Century*, 185.
24. Lewis, *Selected Literary Essays*, 2.
25. Lewis, *English Literature in the Sixteenth Century*, 79.
26. Ibid., 81.
27. Ibid., 450.
28. Lewis, *Selected Literary Essays*, 137.
29. Lewis, *Christian Reflections*, 39.
30. Lewis, *Medieval and Renaissance Literature*, 126.
31. Lewis, *That Hideous Strength*, 33.
32. Lewis, *Letters of C. S. Lewis*, 98.
33. Gibb, *Light on C. S. Lewis*, 76.
34. Lewis, *Letters of C. S. Lewis*, 90.

35. Como, *At the Breakfast Table*, 93.
36. Ibid., 209.
37. Lewis, *Letters of C. S. Lewis*, 110.
38. Ibid., 55.
39. Ibid., 108.
40. Keefe, *Speaker and Teacher*, 80.
41. Ibid., 83.
42. Green and Hooper, *C. S. Lewis: A Biography*, 139.
43. Ibid., 140.
44. Keefe, *Speaker and Teacher*, 89.
45. Ibid., 98.
46. Ibid., 99.
47. Lewis, *Letters of C. S. Lewis*, 217.
48. Keefe, *Speaker and Teacher*, 100.
49. Lewis, *Fern-seed and Elephants*, 112.
50. Lewis, *Letters of C. S. Lewis*, 174.
51. Ibid., 103.
52. Lewis, *Letters to an American Lady*, 16.
53. Lewis, *That Hideous Strength*, 26.
54. Lewis, *Last Battle*, 170.
55. Lewis, *Christian Reflections*, 152.
56. Lewis, *Selected Literary Essays*, 88.
57. Ford, *Companion to Narnia*, xxii.
58. Lewis, *Letters to Malcolm*, 65.
59. Ibid., 74.
60. Ibid., 68–69.
61. Lewis, *They Stand Together*, 474.
62. Chesterton, *As I Was Saying*, 271.

Part 2 Introduction

1. Buechner, *Wishful Thinking*, 47.
2. Lewis, *Screwtape Letters*, 50.
3. Lewis, *Present Concerns and Other Essays*, 53.
4. Ibid., 52–53.
5. Lewis, *Surprised by Joy*, 169.
6. Ibid., 140.
7. Ibid., 20.
8. Gibb, *Light on C. S. Lewis*, 82.
9. Lewis, *Surprised by Joy*, 61, 20.

Chapter 6

1. Lewis, *They Stand Together*, 311.
2. Ibid., 316, 385.
3. Lewis, *Letters of C. S. Lewis*, 289.
4. Lewis, *Weight of Glory*, 12.
5. Lewis, *Till We Have Faces*, 74–76.
6. Lewis, *Discarded Image*, 84.

7. Lewis, *Present Concerns and Other Essays*, 24–25.
8. Lewis, *Surprised by Joy*, 17.
9. Ibid.
10. Ibid.
11. Lewis, *Weight of Glory*, 4–5.
12. Lewis, *Surprised by Joy*, 21.
13. Ibid., 63, 66.
14. Ibid., 73.
15. Ibid., 75.
16. Ibid., 77.
17. Ibid., 78.
18. Lewis, *Present Concerns and Other Essays*, 54.
19. Lewis, *Surprised by Joy*, 213.
20. Ibid., 223, 228.
21. Ibid., 228.
22. Ibid., 237.
23. Moynihan, *Latin Letters of C. S. Lewis*, 44.
24. Lewis, *Letters of C. S. Lewis*, 166.
25. Lewis, *Poems*, 108.
26. Lewis, *Grief Observed*, 40.
27. Ibid., 22.
28. Ibid., 50.
29. Ibid., 59.
30. Ibid., 46.
31. Ibid., 14.
32. Moynihan, *Latin Letters of C. S. Lewis*, 48.
33. Lewis, *Problem of Pain*, 146–47.
34. Lewis, *Letters to an American Lady*, 119.

Chapter 7
1. Lewis, *They Stand Together*, 435.
2. Lewis, *Problem of Pain*, 96.
3. Ibid., 90.
4. Ibid., 115.
5. Lewis, *God in the Dock*, 58.
6. Ibid.
7. Bonham, *Humor: God's Gift*, 251.
8. Lewis, *God in the Dock*, 252.
9. Lewis, *Problem of Pain*, 93.
10. Lewis, *God in the Dock*, 168.
11. Lewis, *Problem of Pain*, 107.
12. Ibid., 105.
13. Ibid., 44.
14. Lewis, *Mere Christianity*, 169.
15. Lewis, *Letters to Malcolm*, 110.

16. Lewis, *God in the Dock*, 123.
17. Ibid., 153.
18. Ibid., 112.
19. Lewis, *Mere Christianity*, 174.
20. Lewis, *Reflections on the Psalms*, 52.
21. Lewis, *Essays Presented to Charles Williams*, 81.
22. Ibid.
23. Ibid., 84.
24. Lewis, *Letters to an American Lady*, 115, 119.
25. Lewis, *Problem of Pain*, 116.

Chapter 8
1. Lewis, *Letters of C. S. Lewis*, 10.
2. Lewis, *They Stand Together*, 324.
3. Lewis, *Present Concerns and Other Essays*, 71.
4. Lewis, *Out of the Silent Planet*, 73.
5. Lewis, *Prince Caspian*, 23.
6. Ibid.,25.
7. Griffin, *Clive Staples Lewis*, 306.
8. Lewis, *Last Battle*, 138.
9. Ibid., 182.
10. Ibid., 170.
11. Ibid., 183–84.

Chapter 9
1. Chesterton, *All Things Considered*, 132.
2. Lewis, *Letters to Children*, 100.
3. Lewis, *Fern-seed and Elephants*, 35.
4. Lewis, *Problem of Pain*, 153.
5. Lewis, *That Hideous Strength*, 149.
6. Lewis, *Perelandra*, 203.
7. Ibid., 209.
8. Lewis, *Preface to Paradise Lost*, 81.
9. Lewis, *Miracles*, 129.
10. Lewis, *Fern-seed and Elephants*, 211.
11. Lewis, *Preface to Paradise Lost*, 17.
12. Ibid.
13. Ibid., 21.
14. Lewis, *Selected Literary Essays*, 65.
15. Lewis, *Essays Presented to Charles Williams*, x.
16. Lewis, *Preface to Paradise Lost*, 75.
17. Lewis, *Prince Caspian*, 78.
18. Lewis, *Spenser's Images of Life*, 96.
19. Lewis, *Silver Chair*, 193.
20. Ibid., 45.

Chapter 10

1. Lewis, *Letters of C. S. Lewis*, 28.
2. Ibid., 209.
3. Lewis, *They Stand Together*, 434.
4. Lewis, *The Four Loves*, 48.
5. Lewis, *They Stand Together*, 95.
6. Ibid., 112.
7. Ibid., 84.
8. Ibid., 77.
9. Ibid., 152.
10. Lewis, *Preface to Paradise Lost*, 21.
11. Lewis, *Letters of C. S. Lewis*, 205.
12. Lewis, *Screwtape Letters*, 50.
13. Lewis, *They Stand Together*, 475.
14. Lewis, *Experiment in Criticism*, 22.
15. Griffin, *Clive Staples Lewis*, 337.
16. Lewis, *Selected Literary Essays*, 65.
17. Lewis, *Studies in Medieval Literature*, 85.
18. Chesterton, *Tremendous Trifles*, 201.
19. Ibid., 198.
20. Ibid., 200.
21. Ibid., 199, 201.
22. Lewis, *Experiment in Criticism*, 23.
23. Kierkegaard, *Kierkegaard Anthology*, XX.
24. Lewis, *Experiment in Criticism*, 23.
25. Ibid., 24.
26. Ibid., 25.
27. Lewis, *God in the Dock*, 62.
28. Lewis, *Christian Reflections*, 96.
29. Lewis, *God in the Dock*, 62.
30. Lewis, *Silver Chair*, 192.
31. Lewis, *Magician's Nephew*, 101.
32. Ibid., 107.
33. Ibid.
34. Ibid., 113, 114.
35. Lewis, *Letters of C. S. Lewis*, 268.
36. Ibid., 269.
37. Chesterton, *Orthodoxy*, 160.

Chapter 11

1. Chesterton, *All Things Considered*, 27.
2. Lewis, *Prince Caspian*, 104.
3. Lewis, *Reflections on the Psalms*, 44.
4. Ibid., 46, 47.
5. Ibid., 48.
6. Ibid., 51–52. Commas changed to colons in Bible references.
7. Bonham, *Humor: God's Gift*, 128.

8. Lewis, *Reflections on the Psalms*, 90.
9. Ibid., 98.
10. Ibid., 92.
11. Ibid., 92, 94.
12. Ibid.
13. Ibid., 95.
14. Ibid.
15. Lewis, *Letters to an American Lady*, 82.
16. Lewis, *Reflections on the Psalms*, 96.
17. Lewis, *Christian Reflections*, 140.
18. Lewis, *Grief Observed*, 49.
19. Chesterton, *St. Francis of Assisi*, 156.
20. Ibid., 78.
21. Lewis, *Poems*, 35.

Chapter 12

1. Lewis, *Voyage of the Dawn Treader*, 179.
2. Lewis, *Letters of C. S. Lewis*, 262.
3. Lewis, *Letters to Malcolm*, 28.
4. Ibid., 28–29.
5. Ibid., 91.
6. Lewis, *Letters of C. S. Lewis*, 227.
7. Lewis, *Preface to Paradise Lost*, 137.
8. Lewis, *Screwtape Letters*, 59.
9. Lewis, *Medieval and Renaissance Literature*, 85.
10. Lewis, *Mere Christianity*, 120.
11. Lewis, *Problem of Pain*, 61.
12. Lewis, *Mere Christianity*, 121.
13. Davies, *Laughter in a Genevan Gown*, 13.
14. Lewis, *Mere Christianity*, 130.
15. Lewis, *Letters of C. S. Lewis*, 248.
16. Lewis, *Mere Christianity*, 80.
17. Lewis, *Letters to Malcolm*, 94–95.
18. Lewis, *Medieval and Renaissance Literature*, 130.
19. Ibid., 373.
20. Lewis, *Allegory of Love*, 153.
21. Lewis, *Weight of Glory*, 14.
22. Lewis, *Miracles*, 165.
23. Lewis, *Weight of Glory*, 2.
24. Lewis, *Last Battle*, 134.
25. Ibid., 157.
26. Ibid., 179.
27. Lewis, *Surprised by Joy*, 32.
28. Lewis, *Last Battle*, 183.
29. Lewis, *Great Divorce*, 103.
30. Ibid., 49.
31. Lewis, *Letters to Malcolm*, 124.

Part 3: Introduction
1. Lewis, *Screwtape Letters*, 50.
2. Lewis, *Mere Christianity*, 51.
3. Lewis, *Screwtape Letters*, 50.
4. Lewis, *Problem of Pain*, 40.
5. Lewis, *Prince Caspian*, 149.
6. Lewis, *Screwtape Letters*, 41–42.
7. Ibid., 101.
8. See the astute reflections on Lewis and pleasure in Stewart Goetz's *C. S. Lewis on Pleasure and Happiness* and David A. Horner's *C. S. Lewis is a Eudaimonist: Response to Goetz* in *Christian Scholar's Review* XL: 3 (Spring 2011), 283–310.
9. Lewis, *Screwtape Letters*, 60.
10. Ibid., 102.
11. Lewis, *Christian Reflections*, 33.
12. Lewis, *God in the Dock*, 152.
13. Ibid., 154.
14. Ibid.
15. Ibid., 54.
16. Chesterton, *What's Wrong with the World*, 3.
17. Lewis, *Perelandra*, 42, 43.
18. Lewis, *Miracles*, 169.

Chapter 13
1. Lewis, *Surprised by Joy*, 66.
2. Ibid., 199.
3. Ibid.
4. Lewis, *Letters of C. S. Lewis*, 256.
5. Gibb, *Light on C. S. Lewis*, 52.
6. Lewis, *Letters of C. S. Lewis*, 171.
7. Lewis, *Reflections on the Psalms*, 77.
8. Lewis, *Letters of C. S. Lewis*, 150.
9. Lewis, *Grief Observed*, 17.
10. Lewis, *That Hideous Strength*, 113.
11. Barker, *G. K. Chesterton: A Biography*, 102–3.
12. Chesterton, *All Things Considered*, 26.
13. Chesterton, *Orthodoxy*, 10.
14. Chesterton, *Tremendous Trifles*, 267.
15. Eastman, *Enjoyment of Laughter*, 37.
16. Lewis, *On Stories and Other Essays*, 34–35.
17. Ibid., 35.
18. Lewis, *Silver Chair*, 205.
19. Ibid., 71–72.
20. Ibid., 44.

21. "Don v. Devil," *Time Magazine* 50 (September 8, 1947), 65–66, 68.
22. Lewis, *Screwtape Letters*, 116.
23. Chesterton, *Orthodoxy*, 60.
24. Ibid.
25. Lewis, *On Stories and Other Essays*, 120.
26. Chesterton, *All Things Considered*, 26–27.
27. Ibid.
28. Ward, *Gilbert Keith Chesterton*, 643.

Chapter 14
1. Lewis, *Weight of Glory*, 32.
2. Lewis, *Perelandra*, 83.
3. Lewis, *Letters to an American Lady*, 69.
4. Lewis, *Perelandra*, 69.
5. Lewis, *Screwtape Letters*, 41.
6. Chesterton, *Common Man*, 157–58.
7. Chesterton, *Handful of Authors*, 28–29.
8. Chesterton, *Alarms and Discursions*, 201.
9. Lewis, *Medieval and Renaissance Literature*, 6.
10. Lewis, *Studies in Words*, 178.
11. Chesterton, *Heretics* in *Collected Works I*, 129.
12. Lewis, *Letters of C. S. Lewis*, 80.
13. Lewis, *Letters to an American Lady*, 29.
14. Lewis, *Mere Christianity*, 114.
15. Lewis, *Studies in Words*, 178.
16. McDonald, *Poems of Stephen Crane*, 2.
17. Lewis, *Screwtape Letters*, ix.
18. Ibid., 63.
19. Lewis, *Problem of Pain*, 67.
20. Bonham, *Humor: God's Gift*, 246.
21. Lewis, *Reflections on the Psalms*, 121.

Chapter 15
1. Chesterton, *Tremendous Trifles*, 146, 148.
2. Ward, *Gilbert Keith Chesterton*, 497.
3. Chesterton, *All Things Considered*, 7–8.
4. Chesterton, *Heretics*, 159–60.
5. *Webster's Seventh New Collegiate Dictionary*, 338.
6. Lewis, *Studies in Words*, 75.
7. Ibid., 79.
8. Lewis, *On Stories and Other Essays*, 151.
9. Lewis, *They Stand Together*, 372.
10. Lewis, *On Stories and Other Essays*, 152.

11. Lewis, *Studies in Words*, 83.
12. Chesterton, *Orthodoxy*, 121.
13. Lewis, *Screwtape Letters*, ix.
14. Lewis, *Four Loves*, 127.
15. Lewis, *Medieval and Renaissance Literature*, 6.
16. Lewis, *Letters to an American Lady*, 95.
17. Lewis, *Perelandra*, 68.
18. George MacDonald, *Gifts of the Christ Child II*, 13.
19. Chesterton, *Heretics*, 96.

Chapter 16

1. Lewis, *Letters to an American Lady*, 28.
2. Lewis, *God in the Dock*, 216.
3. Lewis, *Letters of C. S. Lewis*, 96.
4. Lewis, *Selected Literary Essays*, 307.
5. Lewis, *They Stand Together*, 490.
6. Lewis, *God in the Dock*, 304.
7. Lewis, *Out of the Silent Planet*, 17.
8. Lewis, *God in the Dock*, 29.
9. Lewis, *Miracles*, 141.
10. Chesterton, *What's Wrong with the World*, 7.
11. Chesterton, *All Things Considered*, 148.
12. Ibid.
13. Lewis, *Letters of C. S. Lewis*, 236.
14. Chesterton, *All Things Considered*, 167.
15. Chesterton, *Heretics*, 103.
16. Ward, *Gilbert Keith Chesterton*, 382.
17. Pascal, *Pensees*, 181.
18. Lewis, *Narrative Poems*, 19.
19. Lewis, *Prince Caspian*, 5.
20. Ibid., 79.
21. Lewis, *Voyage of the Dawn Treader*, 139, 148.
22. Lewis, *Perelandra*, 42.
23. Ibid., 49.
24. Lewis, *That Hideous Strength*, 214.
25. Lewis, *Perelandra*, 49.

Chapter 17

1. Lewis, *Discarded Image*, 185.
2. Lewis, *Allegory of Love*, 300.
3. Ibid., 307.
4. Ibid., 301.
5. Ibid., 302.
6. Ibid., 299, 303.
7. Lewis, *Experiment in Criticism*, 37.

8. Lewis, *Magician's Nephew*, 37–38.
9. Lewis, *Out of the Silent Planet*, 45.
10. Ibid., 93, 99.
11. Ibid., 75.
12. Chesterton, *Orthodoxy*, 11.
13. Chesterton, *All Things Considered*, 190.
14. Chesterton, *Orthodoxy*, 59.
15. Lewis, *Surprised by Joy*, 75, 81.
16. Lewis, *Present Concerns and Other Essays*, 35.
17. Lewis, *Surprised by Joy*, 80.
18. Lewis, *Letters of C. S. Lewis*, 259.
19. Ibid.
20. Chesterton, *Tremendous Trifles*, 18.
21. Ibid.
22. Berger, *Rumor of Angels*, 58.
23. Lewis, *Miracles*, 96.
24. Aquinas, *Ethicorum Aristotelis and Nicomachum*, 16.
25. Lewis, *Surprised by Joy*, 130, 129.
26. Lewis, *Fern-seed and Elephants*, 35, 37.
27. Ibid., 31.
28. Lewis, *They Stand Together*, 292, 319.
29. Chesterton, *All Things Considered*, 64.
30. Ibid., 66.

Chapter 18

1. Lewis, *Miracles*, 66.
2. Ibid., 170.
3. Ibid., 173.
4. Ibid., 68.
5. Moynihan, *Latin Letters of C. S. Lewis*, 24.
6. Howard, *Novels of Charles Williams*, 17.
7. Lewis, *Miracles*, 118–19.
8. Ibid.
9. Ibid., 67.
10. Ibid., 88, 67.
11. Lewis, *Letters of C. S. Lewis*, 242.
12. Ibid., 217.
13. Ibid., 28.
14. Lewis, *Letters to an American Lady*, 97.
15. George MacDonald, *Princess and Curdie*, 72.
16. Lewis, *Poems*, 98.
17. Lewis, *Magician's Nephew*, 131.
18. Ibid., 132.
19. Lewis, *Letters of C. S. Lewis*, 150.
20. Chesterton, *Everlasting Man*, 37.

21. Gibb, *Light on C. S. Lewis*, 61.
22. Aristotle, *Poetics*, 202.
23. Lewis, *Miracles*, 107.
24. Lewis, *Letters to an American Lady*, 112.
25. Ibid., 119.
26. Lewis, *Poems*, 122.
27. Lewis, *Letters to an American Lady*, 115.
28. Lewis, *Letters to Children*, 57, 59.
29. Lewis, *Last Battle*, 174.
30. Lewis, *Prince Caspian*, 196.
31. Lewis, *Surprised by Joy*, 163.
32. Lewis, *They Stand Together*, 24.
33. Lewis, *Letters to an American Lady*, 82, 105, 108.
34. Ibid., 40.
35. Lewis, *Letters to Children*, 21.
36. Ibid., 22.
37. Berger, *Rumor of Angels*, 69.
38. Lewis, *Poems*, 2.
39. Lewis, *Letters of C. S. Lewis*, 174.
40. Lewis, *Letters to Children*, 37.
41. Lewis, *Letters of C. S. Lewis*, 262.
42. Lewis, *Essays Presented to Charles Williams*, xii.
43. Lewis, *Problem of Pain*, 142.
44. Ibid., 143.
45. Lewis, *Poems*, 30–31.
46. Lewis, *Letters to Children*, 75.
47. Lewis, *Letters of C. S. Lewis*, 195.
48. Lewis, *Letters to an American Lady*, 109.
49. Lewis, *Problem of Pain*, 139.

Chapter 19
1. Lewis, *God in the Dock*, 67.
2. Ibid., 264.
3. A key contribution for understanding this kind of Rabelasian laughter comes from Orthodox Christian Mikhail Bahktin, who keenly recognized "carnival laughter," a wonderfully ambiguous, grotesque, and communal celebration that marked the Middle Ages. See *Rabelais and His World*, trans. Helene Iswolsky (MIT Press, 1968).
4. Lewis, *Reflections on the Psalms*, 83, 84.
5. Lewis, *Christian Reflections*, 123.
6. Lewis, *God in the Dock*, 143.
7. Lewis, *Selected Literary Essays*, 10.
8. Lewis, *God in the Dock*, 172.

9. Ibid., 86.
10. See Lewis, *Medieval and Renaissance Literature*, 11; and *English Literature in the Sixteenth Century*, 99.
11. Lewis, *God in the Dock*, 143.
12. Lewis, *Allegory of Love*, 52.
13. Lewis, *Prince Caspian*, 152.
14. Lewis, *Lion, the Witch and the Wardrobe*, 13.
15. Lewis, *Prince Caspian*, 153.
16. Lewis, *Letters of C. S. Lewis*, 78.
17. Lewis, *They Stand Together*, 367.
18. This paragraph became a source for my subsequent book, *The Mother of All Laughter: Sarah and the Genesis of Comedy* (Broadman Press, 2003), admittedly the only book of mine that my family read.
19. Lewis, *Reflections on the Psalms*, 89, 128.
20. Lewis, *English Literature in the Sixteenth Century*, 104.
21. Spenser, *Faerie Queene*, (Book I Canto VI) (Encyclopedia Britannica, 1952), 13.
22. Lewis, *Spenser's Images of Life*, 84.
23. Ibid., 89.
24. Ibid., 91.
25. Ibid., 93.
26. Lewis, *Christian Reflections*, 33.
27. Lewis, *Prince Caspian*, 152.
28. Ibid., 154.
29. Lewis, *Spenser's Images of Life*, 140.
30. This stands in stark contrast to Romantic poet/engraver William Blake, whose proverbs of hell exalt the energy of Satan and find the established church a bit too anemic. But then, he may have been right about the latter state of nineteenth-century Christendom.
31. Lewis, *Spenser's Images of Life*, 94.
32. Lewis, *Allegory of Love*, 174.
33. Melville, *Moby Dick*, XX.
34. Lewis, *Surprised by Joy*, 7.
35. Lewis, *Preface to Paradise Lost*, 48–50.
36. Lewis, *Letters of C. S. Lewis*, 137.
37. Lewis, *Allegory of Love*, 331.
38. Ibid., 331.
39. Lewis, *Spenser's Images of Life*, 95.

40. Lewis, *Allegory of Love*, 126.
41. Lewis, *Spenser's Images of Life*, 77.
42. Ibid., 77–78.

Chapter 20

1. Lewis, *On Stories and Other Essays*, ix.
2. Lewis, *They Stand Together*, 91, 93, 123, 474.
3. Ibid., 439.
4. Lewis, *On Stories and Other Essays*, 16.
5. Lewis, *Experiment in Criticism*, 133.
6. Ibid., 138, 140.
7. Ibid., 12.
8. Lewis, *Christian Reflections*, 33.
9. Lewis, *On Stories and Other Essays*, 63.
10. Lewis, *Experiment in Criticism*, 11.
11. Lewis, *On Stories and Other Essays*, 139.
12. Lewis, *Letters of C. S. Lewis*, 201.
13. Lewis, *On Stories and Other Essays*, 14.
14. Ibid., 38.
15. Ibid., 90.
16. Lewis, *Preface to Paradise Lost*, 61.
17. Ibid., 64.
18. Ibid., 64, 65.
19. Lewis, *Experiment in Criticism*, 2.
20. Ward, *Gilbert Keith Chesterton*, 618.
21. Chaucer, *Canterbury Tales*, 212.
22. Lewis, *Selected Literary Essays*, 40.
23. Lewis, *Allegory of Love*, 176.
24. Ibid.,164.
25. Lewis, *Selected Literary Essays*, 35; *Allegory of Love*, 320.
26. Lewis, *Allegory of Love*, 192.
27. Ibid., 171, 193.
28. Ibid., 176; *Selected Literary Essays*, 34.
29. Ibid., 35.
30. Lewis, *Experiment in Criticism*, 63, 66.
31. Rabelais, *Gargantua and Pantegruel*, 1.
32. Lewis, *Letters of C. S. Lewis*, 135.
33. Rabelais, *Gargantua and Pantegruel*, 69.
34. Lewis, *English Literature in the Sixteenth Century*, 417.
35. Lewis, *Letters of C. S. Lewis*, 304.
36. Rabelais, *Gargantua and Pantegruel*, 127.
37. Lewis, *Pilgrim's Regress*, 88.
38. Rabelais, *Gargantua and Pantegruel*, 126.
39. Sterne, *Tristram Shandy*, 189.

40. Lewis, *Studies in Words*, 53, 76, 329.
41. Sterne, *Tristram Shandy*, 294.
42. Ibid., 193.
43. Lewis, *Weight of Glory*, 55–56.
44. Lewis, *They Stand Together*, 142.
45. Ibid., 329.
46. Ibid., 405.
47. Sterne, *Tristram Shandy*, 277.
48. Lewis, *Selected Literary Essays*, 205.
49. Griffin, *Clive Staples Lewis*, 412.
50. Lewis, *Selected Literary Essays*, 154.
51. Ibid., 154, 159.
52. Ibid., 154.
53. Chesterton, *Father Brown Omnibus*, 216.
54. Lewis, *Selected Literary Essays*, 155.
55. Ibid., 167.
56. Ibid., 168.
57. Ibid., 234.
58. Lewis, *Surprised by Joy*, 14.
59. Lewis, *Letters to Children*, 37; *Letters of C. S. Lewis*, 143.
60. Lewis, *Letters of C. S. Lewis*, 114.
61. Lewis, *They Stand Together*, 250.
62. Lewis, *Selected Literary Essays*, 215.
63. Lewis, *They Stand Together*, 446.
64. Lewis, *English Literature in the Sixteenth Century*, 214.
65. Lewis, *They Stand Together*, 410.
66. Lewis, *Studies in Words*, 329.
67. Lewis, *Selected Literary Essays*, 186, 178.
68. Ibid., 185.
69. Lewis, *They Stand Together*, 229.
70. Lewis, *Letters of C. S. Lewis*, 160.
71. Meredith, "An Essay on Comedy" in *Comedy*, 3.
72. Lewis, *They Stand Together*, 410, 239.
73. Lewis, *Letters of C. S. Lewis*, 55–56.
74. Ibid., 255.
75. Ibid., 242, 203, 222.
76. Lewis, *Studies in Words*, 142.
77. Chesterton, "Humour" in *Encyclopedia Britannica*, 883.
78. Hazlitt, *Collected Works VIII*, 11.
79. Lewis, *Discarded Image*, 171.
80. Lewis, *Allegory of Love*, 190.
81. Chaucer, *Canterbury Tales*, 43.
82. Lewis, *That Hideous Strength*, 321.

83. Ibid., 324–27.
84. Lewis, *Discarded Image*, 117, 106. On the role of planets in Lewis' thought, see Michael Ward's illuminating *Planet Narnia: The Seven Heavens in the Imagination of C. S. Lewis* (Oxford University Press, 2010).
85. Lewis, *Poems*, 23.
86. Ibid., 23–24.
87. Ibid., 14.
88. Lewis, *Perelandra*, 37.
89. Green and Hooper, *C. S. Lewis: A Biography*, 140.
90. Lewis, *Studies in Words*, 142.
91. Ibid., 55.
92. Lewis, *English Literature in the Sixteenth Century*, 123.
93. Lewis, *Fern-seed and Elephants*, 10.
94. Lewis, *Surprised by Joy*, 132.
95. Lewis, *Letters to an American Lady*, 83.
96. Lewis, *Christian Reflections*, 106, 156.
97. Lewis, *God in the Dock*, 279.
98. Lewis, *Studies in Words*, 112, 117.
99. Lewis, *Discarded Image*, 122.
100. Lewis, *Present Concerns and Other Essays*, 96.
101. Lewis, *Letters of C. S. Lewis*, 60.
102. Lewis, *Out of the Silent Planet*, 7, 17.
103. Lewis, *On Stories and Other Essays*, 36.
104. Ibid., 13
105. Lewis, *Fern-seed and Elephants*, 16.
106. Lewis, *Letters of C. S. Lewis*, 182.
107. Lewis, *Christian Reflections*, 21.

Chapter 21
1. Lewis, *Letters to Children*, 94.
2. Ibid., 99.
3. Lewis, *They Stand Together*, 64, 104, 110.
4. Lewis, *Letters of C. S. Lewis*, 28.
5. Lewis, *They Stand Together*, 445.
6. Lewis, *On Stories and Other Essays*, 42.
7. Lewis, *Experiment in Criticism*, 93.
8. Lewis, *God in the Dock*, 258.
9. Ibid., 263.
10. Lewis, *On Stories and Other Essays*, 135.
11. Lewis, *English Literature in the Sixteenth Century*, 363; *Selected Literary Essays*, 103.
12. Lewis, *Essays Presented to Charles Williams*, 2–3.
13. Lewis, *On Stories and Other Essays*, 48, 34, 82.
14. Lewis, *Experiment in Criticism*, 37.
15. Lewis, *Out of the Silent Planet*, 128.
16. Ibid., 127–28.
17. Lewis, *Horse and His Boy*, 186, 208, 210.
18. Lewis, *Reflections on the Psalms*, 9.
19. Lewis, *Horse and His Boy*, 211, 213.
20. Lewis, *Magician's Nephew*, 11.
21. Ibid., 124, 126.
22. Ibid., 168, 170, 76.
23. Ibid., 17, 62.
24. Ibid., 57.
25. Lewis, *Horse and His Boy*, 20.
26. Ibid., 94, 95.
27. Ibid., 99.
28. Lewis, *Voyage of the Dawn Treader*, 124.
29. Ibid., 142.
30. Lewis, *Silver Chair*, 70.
31. Lewis, *They Stand Together*, 125.
32. Lewis, *Letters of C. S. Lewis*, 117.
33. Lewis, *English Literature in the Sixteenth Century*, 143, 256, 304.
34. Lewis, *Voyage of the Dawn Treader*, 1. One could easily replace the opening with "There was a boy named Clive Staples Lewis, and he almost deserved it."
35. Ibid., 1–2.
36. Lewis, *English Literature in the Sixteenth Century*, 256.
37. Lewis, *They Stand Together*, 244, 321.
38. Hooper, *Past Watchful Dragons*, 81.
39. Ibid.
40. Lewis, *Essays Presented to Charles Williams*, xii.
41. Lewis, *On Stories and Other Essays*, 27.
42. Lewis, *Silver Chair*, 90.
43. Ibid., 55, 56.
44. Ibid., 64–65.
45. Ibid., 106.
46. Ibid., 123, 139.
47. Lewis, *God in the Dock*, 259.
48. Ibid.
49. Lewis, *Reflections on the Psalms*, 112–13.

Part 4: Introduction

1. Rapp, *Wit and Humor*, 21.
2. Chesterton, *Everlasting Man*, 34.
3. Lewis, *Miracles*, 132.
4. Lewis, *Grief Observed*, 57.
5. Chesterton, *Orthodoxy*, 80.
6. Lewis, *Miracles*, 133.
7. Lewis, *Perelandra*, 40.
8. Ibid., 143.
9. Lewis, *Dark Tower*, 143.
10. Shaftesbury, "Freedom of Wit and Humour," 71.
11. Lewis, *Last Battle*, 166.
12. Plato, *Republic*, III. 326, 338.
13. Ibid., V. 452; and *Philebus*, 48–50.
14. Plato, *Symposium*, 173.
15. Griffin, *Clive Staples Lewis*, 277.
16. Aristotle, *Poetics*, 52, 59.
17. Lewis, *Dark Tower*, 117.
18. Griffin, *Clive Staples Lewis*, 367.
19. Lewis, *Four Loves*, 46.
20. Lewis, *That Hideous Strength*, 59.
21. Lewis, *Letters of C. S. Lewis*, 134.
22. Witty, "The Laugh Makers," 22.
23. Hobbes, *Leviathan IV*, 3: 2.
24. Ibid., 1: 4, 6.
25. Lewis, *English Literature in the Sixteenth Century*, 82.
26. Lewis, *Experiment in Criticism*, 54.
27. Lewis, *Letters of C. S. Lewis*, 96.
28. Lewis, *Till We Have Faces*, 218.
29. Henri Bergson, "La Rire" in Sypher's *Comedy*, 61.
30. Lewis, *Surprised by Joy*, 198.
31. Ibid.
32. Lewis, *They Stand Together*, 281.
33. Lewis, *Studies in Words*, 300; *Selected Literary Essays*, 86; Lewis even remembered Yeats speaking of Henri Bergson, saying, "Ah yes, Bergson. It was his sister who taught me magic." *Letters of C. S. Lewis*, 57.
34. Lewis, *God in the Dock*, 86.
35. Lewis, *Discarded Image*, 17–18.
36. Lewis, *Studies in Words*, 300.
37. Lewis, *God in the Dock*, 86, 251.
38. Lewis, *Present Concerns and Other Essays*, 74.
39. Lewis, *Mere Christianity*, 35.
40. Lewis, *Four Loves*, 152.
41. Ward, *Gilbert Keith Chesterton*, 590.
42. Bergson, "La Rire," 84, 123.
43. Lewis, *Surprised by Joy*, 64.
44. Lewis, *Grief Observed*, 17.
45. Ibid., 26.
46. Chesterton, "Humour," 884.
47. Beattie, *Essays*, 310.
48. Chesterton, *All Things Considered*, 14.
49. Lewis, *Letters of C. S. Lewis*, 115–16.
50. Pascal, *Provincial Letters*, xi.
51. Pascal, *Pensees*, 133.
52. Schopenhauer, *World as Will and Idea*, 76.
53. Hazlitt, *Hazlitt Sampler*, 33.
54. Hazlitt, *Collected Works*, 8.5.
55. Ibid., 1.10; 1.12.
56. Lewis, *Screwtape Letters*, ix.
57. Lewis, *Miracles*, 133.
58. Ibid., 113.
59. Chesterton, *All Things Considered*, 14.
60. Lewis, *Screwtape Letters*, 50.
61. Lewis, *Out of the Silent Planet*, 117.

Chapter 22

1. Lewis, *Studies in Words*, 86.
2. Ibid., 86.
3. Ibid., 147, 88.
4. Ibid., 90, 91.
5. Chesterton, *Orthodoxy*, 18.
6. Boileau, *L'Art Poetique*, 1.36.
7. Lewis, *Studies in Words*, 95.
8. Ibid., 100, 101.
9. Ibid., 101, 102.
10. Ibid., 106.
11. Ibid., 13, 97.
12. Shakespeare, *Much Ado About Nothing*, 1.1 57.
13. Shakespeare, *Henry IV*, II, 1.2.8.
14. Lewis, *Studies in Words*, 98.
15. Ibid., 62, 110.

Chapter 23

1. Lewis, *Magician's Nephew*, 118.
2. Ibid., 119.
3. Lewis, *They Stand Together*, 132.
4. Lewis, *Perelandra*, 60.
5. Lewis, *Of Other Worlds*, 96.
6. Lewis, *Studies in Words*, 20.

7. Ibid., 74.
8. Griffin, *Clive Staples Lewis*, 438.
9. Moynihan, *Latin Letters of C. S. Lewis*, 28.
10. Ward, *Gilbert Keith Chesterton*, 62.
11. Lewis, *Studies in Words*, 134.
12. Ibid., 11–12.
13. Lewis, *They Stand Together*, 368.
14. Lewis, *Studies in Words*, 139.
15. Ibid., 164.
16. Lewis, *Discarded Image*, 69.
17. Lewis, *Letters of C. S. Lewis*, 282.
18. Lewis, *Perelandra*, 47.
19. Lewis, *Studies in Words*, 11.
20. Lewis, *Miracles*, 74.
21. Lewis, *Weight of Glory*, 28.
22. Lewis, *Letters to Children*, 47.
23. Lewis, *Last Battle*, 87.
24. Lewis, *Studies in Words*, 257, 261, 123.
25. Chesterton, *All Things Considered*, 28.
26. Lewis, *Reflections in the Psalms*, 31.
27. Lewis, *Studies in Words*, 321–22.

Chapter 24
1. Lewis, *Prince Caspian*, 75, 174.
2. Lewis, *Till We Have Faces*, 11.
3. Lewis, *Silver Chair*, 12.
4. Lewis, *On Stories and Other Essays*, 42.
5. Lewis, *Horse and His Boy*, 75.
6. Lewis, *Silver Chair*, 173–74.
7. Lewis, *Prince Caspian*, 41.
8. Lewis, *Silver Chair*, 28.
9. Lewis, *Horse and His Boy*, 148.
10. Lewis, *Out of the Silent Planet*, 64.
11. Lewis, *Pilgrim's Regress*, 21.
12. Lewis, *Letters to an American Lady*, 94.
13. Lewis, *Magician's Nephew*, 130–31.
14. Lewis, *Horse and His Boy*, 74.
15. Lewis, *Silver Chair*, 35.
16. Lewis, *Magician's Nephew*, 119–20.
17. Griffin, *Clive Staples Lewis*, 313.
18. Lewis, *Letters to an American Lady*, 45.
19. Lewis, *Selected Literary Essays*, 127.
20. Lewis, *Horse and His Boy*, 63, 107.
21. Lewis, *Till We Have Faces*, 60.
22. Lewis, *Selected Literary Essays*, 86.
23. Lewis, *Letters to Malcolm*, 42.
24. Lewis, *Miracles*, 104.
25. Lewis, *Selected Literary Essays*, 87.

26. Ibid.
27. Lewis, *Silver Chair*, 128.
28. Lewis, *Prince Caspian*, 194.
29. Lewis, *Studies in Words*, 3; *Selected Literary Essays*, 1.
30. Lewis, *Allegory of Love*, 240.
31. Lewis, *English Literature in the Sixteenth Century*, 328.
32. Lewis, *Perelandra*, 75.
33. Lewis, *Prince Caspian*, 66.
34. Lewis, *Pilgrim's Regress*, 72.
35. Lewis, *Horse and His Boy*, 208.
36. Ibid., 216.
37. Lewis, *Prince Caspian*, 105.
38. Ibid., 114–15.
39. Lewis, *Silver Chair*, 139.
40. Lewis, *Voyage of the Dawn Treader*, 174.
41. Lewis, *Lion, Witch, and the Wardrobe*, 101.
42. Lewis, *Prince Caspian*, 42.
43. Lewis, *Lion, Witch, and the Wardrobe*, 11.
44. Ibid., 74.
45. Lewis, *Letters to Children*, 86.
46. Lewis, *English Literature in the Sixteenth Century*, 365; *Medieval and Renaissance Literature*, 132.
47. Lewis, *Surprised by Joy*, 126.
48. Lewis, *English Literature in the Sixteenth Century*, 303.
49. Lewis, *Silver Chair*, 62.
50. Lewis, *Screwtape Letters*, 100–101.
51. Ibid., xii.
52. Lewis, *They Stand Together*, 335.
53. Ibid.
54. Ibid., 336.
55. Lewis, *English Literature in the Sixteenth Century*, 462.
56. Ibid., 437.
57. Griffin, *Clive Staples Lewis*, 93.
58. Lewis, *Selected Literary Essays*, 146.
59. Lewis, Unpublished Papers, September 20, 1985.
60. Ibid.
61. Griffin, *Clive Staples Lewis*, 103.
62. Lewis, *Selected Literary Essays*, 119.
63. Lewis, *English Literature in the Sixteenth Century*, 70.
64. Ibid., 71.

65, Ibid., 70.
66. Lewis, *Mere Christianity*, 55.
67. Lewis, *Surprised by Joy*, 197.
68. Lewis, *Horse and His Boy*, 197.
69. Lewis, *Surprised by Joy*, 194.
70. Lewis, *Mere Christianity*, 36.
71. Lewis, *Miracles*, 142.
72. Lewis, *That Hideous Strength*, 372.
73. Lewis, *Mere Christianity*, 51.
74. Lewis, *Screwtape Letters*, 51–52.
75. Chesterton, *All Things Considered*, 98–99.
76. Ibid., 99.
77. Lewis, *Mere Christianity*, 76.

Chapter 25

1. Berger, *Rumor of Angels*, 70.
2. Lewis, *Selected Literary Essays*, 98.
3. Como, *At the Breakfast Table*, 212.
4. Lewis, *Perelandra*, 151.
5. Ibid., 166.
6. Lewis, *God in the Dock*, 266.
7. Ibid., 312.
8. Lewis, *Preface to Paradise Lost*, 56.
9. Lewis, *Letters of C. S. Lewis*, 140.
10. Lewis, *English Literature in the Sixteenth Century*, 95, 149.
11. Ibid., 94–95.
12. Lewis, *They Stand Together*, 332.
13. Lewis, *English Literature in the Sixteenth Century*, 439.
14. Lewis, *Poems*, 134.
15. Lewis, *Grief Observed*, 10.
16. Ibid., 16, 26.
17. Lewis, *Magician's Nephew*, 21.
18. Lewis, *Grief Observed*, 27.
19. Ibid., 33.
20. Lewis, *Mere Christianity*, 107.
21. Chesterton, *All Things Considered*, 155.

Chapter 26

1. Lewis, *Surprised by Joy*, 5.
2. Lewis, *God in the Dock*, 183.
3. Chesterton, *Heretics*, 89.
4. Chesterton, *Tremendous Trifles*, 20, 202.
5. Ibid., 202–3.
6. Lewis, *Letters of C. S. Lewis*, 272.
7. Lewis, *They Stand Together*, 497.
8. Lewis, *Christian Reflections*, 155.
9. Lewis, *Letters of C. S. Lewis*, 272.
10. Lewis, *Miracles*, 158.
11. Lewis, *Letters of C. S. Lewis*, 286.
12. Lewis, *They Stand Together*, 70–71.
13. Ibid., 73.
14. Lewis, *Miracles*, 75.
15. Lewis, *God in the Dock*, 71.
16. Lewis, *Miracles*, 75.
17. Lewis, *Mere Christianity*, 155.
18. Ibid., 65.
19. Ibid., 63.
20. Lewis, *Screwtape Letters*, 101–102.
21. Chesterton, *Tremendous Trifles*, 203–4.
22. Lewis, *Letters to Children*, 48.
23. Chesterton, *All Things Considered*, 15.
24. Lewis, *Studies in Words*, 16.
25. Lewis, *Reflections in the Psalms*, 79.
26. Chesterton, *All Things Considered*, 14.
27. Lewis, *English Literature in the Sixteenth Century*, 194.
28. Lewis, *God in the Dock*, 259.
29. Lewis, *Miracles*, 133.
30. Lewis, *English Literature in the Sixteenth Century*, 99.
31. Lewis, *They Stand Together*, 312.
32. Lewis, *Christian Reflections*, 78.
33. Chesterton, *Illustrated London News* (August 13, 1932), 224.
34. Cited in *Saturday Review* (March 27, 1987), XX.

Chapter 27

1. Lewis, *Four Loves*, 143.
2. Lewis, *Present Concerns and Other Essays*, 90–91.
3. Lewis, *Selected Literary Essays*, 272.
4. Lewis, *English Literature in the Sixteenth Century*, 466.
5. Lewis, *Selected Literary Essays*, 111.
6. Lewis, *Four Loves*, 143.
7. Lewis, *Perelandra*, 55.
8. Ibid., 59, 79.
9. Lewis, *Four Loves*, 29.
10. Lewis, *Screwtape Letters*, 50.
11. Kierkegaard, *XXXXX*, 69.
12. Lewis, *Present Concerns and Other Essays*, 89.
13. Lewis, *Selected Literary Essays*, 169–70.
14. Ibid., 173, 174.

15. Ibid., 171.
16. Lewis, *Horse and His Boy*, 106.
17. Lewis, *Voyage of the Dawn Treader*, 82.
18. Lewis, *Letters of C. S. Lewis*, 18; Lewis mentions Bannatyne CLXVII and CCI.
19. Lewis, *English Literature in the Sixteenth Century*, 74.
20. Lewis, *Discarded Image*, 205.
21. Lewis, *God in the Dock*, 98.
22. Lewis, *Letters of C. S. Lewis*, 146–47.
23. Ibid.
24. Lewis, *Allegory of Love*, 148.
25. Ibid., 149.
26. Ibid.
27. Lewis, *Christian Reflections*, 30, 31.
28. Lewis, *Studies in Words*, 324.
29. Lewis, *Allegory of Love*, 172.
30. Ibid.
31. Ibid., 172–73.
32. Lewis, *English Literature in the Sixteenth Century*, 317.
33. Lewis, *Selected Literary Essays*, 189–90.
34. Ibid., 192, 193.
35. Ibid.
36. Lewis, *English Literature in the Sixteenth Century*, 540.
37. Como, *At the Breakfast Table*, 47.
38. Lewis, *Selected Literary Essays*, 275.
39. Lewis, *English Literature in the Sixteenth Century*, 105, 138.
40. Ibid., 412.
41. Lewis, *Selected Literary Essays*, 214.
42. Lewis, *Medieval and Renaissance Literature*, 111.
43. Lewis, *Selected Literary Essays*, 273.
44. Ibid., 270.
45. Lewis, *English Literature in the Sixteenth Century*, 149.
46. Lewis, *Selected Literary Essays*, 117.
47. Muggeridge, *Third Testament*, 37.
48. Lewis, *God in the Dock*, 320.
49. Lewis, *Selected Literary Essays*, 169.
50. Lewis, *God in the Dock*, 265.
51. Lewis, *Experiment in Criticism*, 61.
52. Lewis, *Studies in Words*, 287–88.
53. Ibid., 299.
54. Chesterton, *Everlasting Man*, 31.
55. Lewis, *God in the Dock*, 253.
56. Lewis, *Mere Christianity*, 89.
57. Ibid., 89, 91–92.
58. Lewis, *World's Last Night*, 37.
59. Lewis, *God in the Dock*, 31, 26.
60. Lewis, *Screwtape Letters*, 50–51.
61. Lewis, *English Literature in the Sixteenth Century*, 488.
62. Lewis, *Screwtape Letters*, 51.
63. Lewis, *Letters of C. S. Lewis*, 18.
64. Como, *At the Breakfast Table*, 212.
65. Ibid., 212.
66. Lewis, *Letters of C. S. Lewis*, 146.
67. Como, *At the Breakfast Table*, 212.

Chapter 28

1. Chesterton, *All Things Considered*, 15.
2. Griffin, *Clive Staples Lewis*, 430, 201.
3. Lewis, *That Hideous Strength*, 168.
4. Lewis, *Allegory of Love*, 144.
5. Ibid., 158.
6. Chaucer, *Canterbury Tales*, 277.
7. Lewis, *Allegory of Love*, 145–46, 18–20.
8. Ibid., 212.
9. Lewis, *Selected Literary Essays*, 60.
10. Lewis, *Medieval and Renaissance Literature*, 498.
11. Lewis, *Selected Literary Essays*, 62.
12. Lewis, *Mere Christianity*, 102.
13. Lewis, *Letters to an American Lady*, 107.
14. Chesterton, *All Things Considered*, 15–16.
15. Chesterton, *Tremendous Trifles*, 104.
16. Chesterton, *All Things Considered*, 17, 18.
17. Lewis, *Studies in Words*, 4.
18. Ibid., 57.
19. Lewis, *Surprised by Joy*, 8–9.
20. Lewis, *Medieval and Renaissance Literature*, 34.
21. Lewis, *Discarded Image*, 52.
22. Lewis, *Spenser's Images of Life*, 105.
23. Ibid., 106.
24. Ibid.
25. Lewis, *Medieval and Renaissance Literature*, 101.
26. Ibid., 93, 106.
27. Lewis, *Allegory of Love*, 145.

Chapter 29

1. Chesterton, *What's Wrong with the World*, 37.

2. Lewis, *Spenser's Images of Life*, 38.
3. Lewis, *Selected Literary Essays*, 118.
4. Lewis, *Perelandra*, 62–63.
5. Lewis, *Letters of C. S. Lewis*, 141.
6. Lewis, *Out of the Silent Planet*, 116.
7. Lewis, *Preface to Paradise Lost*, 84.
8. Lewis, *Mere Christianity*, 99.
9. Lewis, *Four Loves*, 142.
10. Lewis, *English Literature in the Sixteenth Century*, 305.
11. Lewis, *Letters to an American Lady*, 74.
12. Lewis, *That Hideous Strength*, 13.
13. Ibid., 76.
14. Ibid., 199, 200.
15. Ibid., 380–81.
16. Ibid., 382.
17. Lewis, *Four Loves*, 138.
18. Ibid., 127.
19. Ibid., 139.
20. Lewis, *Allegory of Love*, 6.
21. Lewis, *Surprised by Joy*, 65.
22. Lewis, *Allegory of Love*, 6–7.
23. Lewis, *Four Loves*, 141.
24. Ibid., 144.
25. Lewis, *That Hideous Strength*, 301.
26. Lewis, *Allegory of Love*, 193–194.
27. Lewis, *Four Loves*, 151.
28. Ibid.
29. Lewis, *Till We Have Faces*, 21.
30. Lewis, *Four Loves*, 140–41.
31. Lewis, *God in the Dock*, 320.
32. Lewis, *Allegory of Love*, 8.
33. Lewis, *Letters of C. S. Lewis*, 203.
34. Lewis, *That Hideous Strength*, 376.
35. Ibid., 378.
36. Lewis, *Allegory of Love*, 237.
37. Lewis, *That Hideous Strength*, 379.

Part 5: Introduction
1. Chesterton, *Illustrated London News*, 224.
2. Lewis, *Mere Christianity*, 17.
3. Chesterton, *Tremendous Trifles*, 98–99.
4. Lewis, *Christian Reflections*, 65, 43.
5. Ibid., 61.
6. Lewis, *Miracles*, 23.
7. Lewis, *Abolition of Man*, 60.
8. Chesterton, *Orthodoxy*, 18.
9. Lewis, *God in the Dock*, 234

10. Lewis, *Abolition of Man*, 34.
11. Ibid., 35.
12. Lewis, *Miracles*, 38.
13. Lewis, *Christian Reflections*, 56, 47.
14. Lewis, *Mere Christianity*, 21.
15. Lewis, *God in the Dock*, 182.
16. Chesterton, "Humour," 883.
17. Lewis, *Selected Literary Essays*, 185.
18. Lewis, *Studies in Words*, 199.
19. Lewis, *Fern-seed and Elephants*, 99.
20. Lewis, *Screwtape Letters*, 141, 149.
21. Lewis, *Silver Chair*, 76, 114.
22. Lewis, *Last Battle*, 83.
23. Lewis, *Poems*, 135.
24. Lewis, *Till We have Faces*, 249.
25. Lewis, *Christian Reflections*, 47.
26. Lewis, *God in the Dock*, 264.
27. Lewis, *Allegory of Love*, 267.
28. Ibid., 267, 270, 100.
29. Lewis, *God in the Dock*, 50.
30. Ibid., 156.
31. Ibid., 158.
32. Ibid., 101, 158; See also *Mere Christianity*, 56; and for the original source in Chesterton, see *Tremendous Trifles*, 98.
33. Griffin, *Clive Staples Lewis*, 297.

Chapter 30
1. Lewis, *English Literature in the Sixteenth Century*, 167.
2. Ibid., 167, 168.
3. Ibid., 161.
4. Ibid., 173.
5. Ibid., 175.
6. Ward, *Gilbert Keith Chesterton*, 579.
7. Lewis, *English Literature in the Sixteenth Century*, 175–76.
8. Ibid., 180.
9. Ibid., 181.
10. Ibid., 191, 185.
11. Ibid., 192.
12. Ibid., 210.
13. Lewis, *God in the Dock*, 53.
14. Lewis, *English Literature in the Sixteenth Century*, 37.
15. Ibid., 33–34, 35. Hilaritas was one of the original eight blessed virtures, with its vice as sadness.

16. Lewis, *Selected Literary Essays*, 116–17.
17. Ibid.
18. Ibid., 18, 24.
19. Ibid., 117.
20. Bonham, *Humor: God's Gift*, 245.
21. Lewis, *Studies on Words*, 305.
22. Ibid.
23. Lewis, *English Literature in the Sixteenth Century*, 405.
24. Ibid.
25. Ibid., 404.
26. Ibid., 110.
27. Ibid., 93.
28. Ibid., 93, 97.
29. Ibid., 98, 94.
30. Ibid., 413.
31. Ibid., 415, 416.
32. Ibid., 416.
33. Ibid., 415.
34. Ibid., 416.
35. Ibid., 413.
36. Ibid.
37. Ibid., 354.
38. Ibid., 449.
39. Lewis, *Christian Reflections*, 119.
40. Ibid., 127–28.
41. Lewis, *Studies on Words*, 323, 324.
42. Lewis, *English Literature in the Sixteenth Century*, 477.
43. Ibid., 469, 470.
44. Ibid., 473, 472.
45. Ibid., 472.
46. Ibid., 476.
47. Ibid.
48. Lewis, *Selected Literary Essays*, 154.
49. Lewis, *Christian Reflections*, 17.
50. Lewis, *Letters of C. S. Lewis*, 135.
51. Lewis, *On Stories and Other Essays*, 103.
52. Lewis, *Medieval and Renaissance Literature*, 95.
53. Chesterton, *Heretics*, 170.
54. Ibid., 171.
55. Kiley and Shuttleworth, *Satire*, 28. More recently, Ruben Quintero edited a most impressive *A Companion to Satire, Ancient and Modern* (Blackwell, 2007).
56. Wells, *An Outline of Humor*, 111.
57. Lewis, *Medieval and Renaissance Literature*, 95.
58. Ibid.

Chapter 31

1. Lewis, *English Literature in the Sixteenth Century*, 415.
2. Lewis, *God in the Dock*, 301–2.
3. Ibid., 303.
4. Lewis, *Present Concerns and Other Essays*, 96.
5. Lewis, *English Literature in the Sixteenth Century*, 14.
6. Lewis, *Experiment in Criticism*, 109.
7. Lewis, *Of Other Worlds*, 76–77.
8. Lewis, *Out of the Silent Planet*, 123.
9. Lewis, *Of Other Worlds*, 77.
10. Lewis, *Perelandra*, 95.
11. Lewis, *Of Other Worlds*, 77.
12. Ibid., 78.
13. Lewis, *On Stories and Other Essays*, 152.
14. Lewis, *Of Other Worlds*, 81.
15. Ibid., 81, 82.
16. Ibid., 79, 82.
17. Lewis, *Of Other Worlds*, 80.
18. Lewis, *Letters to Children*, 64.
19. Ward, *Gilbert Keith Chesterton*, 566.
20. Lewis, *On Stories and Other Essays*, 110–12.
21. Lewis, *That Hideous Strength*, 346.
22. Ibid., 351.
23. Chesterton, *Tremendous Trifles*, 62.
24. Green and Hooper, *C. S. Lewis: A Biography*, 206.
25. Lewis, *That Hideous Strength*, 100, 135.
26. Lewis, *Present Concerns and Other Essays*, 57.
27. Lewis, *Experiment in Criticism*, 28.
28. Lewis, *Letters to an American Lady*, 62.
29. Moynihan, *Latin Letters of C. S. Lewis*, 64.
30. Lewis, *Poems*, 59.
31. Ibid.
32. Lewis, *World's Last Night*, 42.
33. Lewis, *Voyage of the Dawn Treader*, 1, 47–48.
34. Lewis, *Silver Chair*, 1, 8.
35. Ibid., 216.
36. Lewis, *Letters to Children*, 88.
37. Lewis, *Narrative Poems*, 8.
38. Ibid., 9.

39. Ibid., 10.
40. Lewis, *Last Battle*, 6, 29.
41. Ibid., 30.
42. Lewis, *English Literature in the Sixteenth Century*, 366.
43. Lewis, *Poems*, 55.
44. Lewis, *Letters of C. S. Lewis*, 179
45. Lewis, *Fern-seed and Elephants*, 124.
46. Lewis, *Pilgrim's Regress*, 54, 5, 10.
47. Lewis, *Poems*, 134.
48. Lewis, *World's Last Night*, 62.
49. Lewis, *Dark Tower*, 111.
50. Griffin, *Clive Staples Lewis*, 397.
51. Lewis, *Great Divorce*, 5.
52. Lewis, *Selected Literary Essays*, 227.
53. Lewis, *Poems*, 1.
54. Lewis, *Selected Literary Essays*, 199.
55. Lewis, *Preface to Paradise Lost*, 11.
56. Lewis, *Discarded Image*, 214.
57. Lewis, *God in the Dock*, 251.
58. Lewis, *Experiment in Criticism*, 112.
59. Lewis, *Pilgrim's Regress*, 131–32.
60. Ibid., 108.
61. Griffin, *Clive Staples Lewis*, 242.
62. Ibid., 285.
63. Lewis, *Christian Reflections*, 157.
64. Lewis, *Fern-seed and Elephants*, 104.
65. Hyers, *Holy Laughter*, 24
66. Lewis, *That Hideous Strength*, 127–28.
67. Lewis, *Great Divorce*, 127.
68. Lewis, *Christian Reflections*, 153, 157.
69. Lewis, *Present Concerns and Other Essays*, 108.
70. Lewis, *Letters of C. S. Lewis*, 16.
71. Lewis, *Great Divorce*, 46.
72. Lewis, *Horse and His Boy*, 192.
73. Lewis, *Screwtape Letters*, 115.
74. Lewis, *Letters of C. S. Lewis*, 15.
75. Lewis, *Letters to Malcolm*, 6.
76. Ward, *Gilbert Keith Chesterton*, 612.
77. Lewis, *Screwtape Letters*, xii.
78. Lewis, *Great Divorce*, 57.
79. Ibid., 25, 69.
80. Ibid., 66.
81. Ibid., 72.
82. Ibid., 114.
83. Ibid., 118.
84. Ibid., 71.
85. Ibid., 95.

86. Ibid., 103.
87. Ibid., 108–9.
88. Lewis, *Screwtape Letters*, 5.
89. Ibid., 101.
90. Ibid., 124.
91. Ward, *Gilbert Keith Chesterton*, 506.
92. Ibid.
93. Chesterton, *As I Was Saying*, 35–36.

Chapter 32

1. Hurd, *Works of Richard Hurd*, 6.362.
2. Lewis, *Great Divorce*, 98.
3. Lewis, *World's Last Night*, 48.
4. Chesterton, *Father Brown Omnibus*, 758.
5. Lewis, *Screwtape Letters*, 52.
6. Ibid., 55.
7. Lewis, *That Hideous Strength*, 243.
8. Lewis, *Perelandra*, 94.
9. Chesterton, *Orthodoxy*, 116.
10. Lewis, *Problem of Pain*, 75.
11. Lewis, *Mere Christianity*, 109.
12. Lewis, *Letters of C. S. Lewis*, 183.
13. Lewis, *Mere Christianity*, 111.
14. Chesterton, *Heretics*, 107.
15. Lewis, *Preface to Paradise Lost*, 70–71.
16. Ibid., 96.
17. Ibid., 101.
18. Ibid., 103.
19. Ibid., 121, 105.
20. Ibid., 126.
21. Lewis, *Mere Christianity*, 112.
22. Lewis, *Problem of Pain*, 55, 59.
23. Lewis, *Preface to Paradise Lost*, 127–28.
24. Lewis, *Screwtape Letters*, x.
25. Lewis, *Reflections in the Psalms*, 71.
26. Ibid., 72.
27. Lewis, *Four Loves*, 119.
28. Chesterton, *All Things Considered*, 59.
29. Lewis, *Pilgrim's Regress*, 49.
30. Lewis, *Silver Chair*, 138.
31. Lewis, *Letters of C. S. Lewis*, 112.
32. Lewis, *Christian Reflections*, 119.
33. Ibid., 75. Commas changed to colons in Scripture references.
34. Lewis, *That Hideous Strength*, 36.
35. Lewis, *Out of the Silent Planet*, 15, 34.
36. Lewis, *That Hideous Strength*, 48, 35.
37. Lewis, *Screwtape Letters*, 25, 45.

38. Ibid., 46.
39. Ibid., 48.
40. Lewis, *That Hideous Strength*, 130.
41. Lewis, *Selected Literary Essays*, 248.
42. Lewis, *Screwtape Letters*, 113.
43. Lewis, *Weight of Glory*, 63.
44. Lewis, *Lion, Witch, and the Wardrobe*, 23, 92.
45. Lewis, *Surprised by Joy*, 106.
46. Lewis, *Voyage of the Dawn Treader*, 5.
47. Ibid., 26, 87.
48. Lewis, *They Stand Together*, 405.
49. Lewis, *On Stories and Other Essays*, 56, 57.
50. Lewis, *Present Concerns and Other Essays*, 40.
51. Lewis, *They Stand Together*, 411, 254.
52. Ibid., 439, 262, 561, 242.
53. Lewis, *Surprised by Joy*, 68.
54. Lewis, *Experiment in Criticism*, 112.
55. Lewis, *Screwtape Letters*, 60.
56. Lewis, *Reflections in the Psalms*, 73.
57. Ibid., 74.
58. Chesterton, *As I Was Saying*, 266.
59. Lewis, *Last Battle*, 71, 148.
60. Lewis, *Lion, Witch, and the Wardrobe*, 150.
61. Lewis, *Poems*, 129.

Chapter 33

1. Lewis, *Mere Christianity*, 86.
2. Chesterton, *As I Was Saying*, 284–85.
3. Kierkegaard, *Either/Or*, 30.
4. Lewis, *Screwtape Letters*, 56.
5. Lewis, *Perelandra*, 111.
6. Chesterton, *What's Wrong with the World*, 62.
7. Chesterton, *All Things Considered*, 141–42.
8. Lewis, *Four Loves*, 166.
9. Ibid., 166, 180.
10. Ibid., 181.
11. Lewis, *George MacDonald: An Anthology*, 132.
12. Lewis, *Screwtape Letters*, 64–65.
13. Lewis, *Lion, Witch, and the Wardrobe*, 172.
14. Bonham, *Humor: God's Gift*, 247.
15. Lewis, *Christian Reflections*, 36.
16. Lewis, *Letters to Children*, 72.
17. Lewis, *Christian Reflections*, 19.
18. Lewis, *Four Loves*, 56.
19. Lewis, *Letters of C. S. Lewis*, 224.
20. Lewis, *Four Loves*, 60.
21. Ibid., 73–74, 76.
22. Lewis, *Poems*, 134.
23. Lewis, *Screwtape Letters*, 123.
24. Lewis, *Letters of C. S. Lewis*, 13.
25. Lewis, *Perelandra*, book dust jacket.
26. Lewis, *Four Loves*, 95.
27. Ibid., 108.
28. Lewis, *Selected Literary Essays*, 118.
29. Lewis, *Four Loves*, 110–11.
30. Ibid., 92. (Cf. Charles as Charles Williams and Ronald as J. R. R. Tolkien)
31. Ibid., 105.
32. Chesterton, *Orthodoxy*, 57.
33. Lewis, *Letters of C. S. Lewis*, 23.
34. Lewis, *Grief Observed*, 39.
35. Lewis, *Letters of C. S. Lewis*, 248.
36. Lewis, *Screwtape Letters*, 97, 98.
37. Lewis, *Weight of Glory*, 15.
38. Lewis, *Screwtape Letters*, 59, 65, 38.
39. Lewis, *Christian Reflections*, 4.
40. Chesterton, *Orthodoxy*, 160.
41. Lewis, *Reflections on the Psalms*, 24–25.
42. Lewis, *Four Loves*, 185.
43. Lewis, *Voyage of the Dawn Treader*, 160.
44. Lewis, *Prince Caspian*, 195.
45. Lewis, *Lion, Witch, and the Wardrobe*, 160.
46. Ibid., 16.
47. Lewis, *Horse and His Boy*, 213.
48. Lewis, *Silver Chair*, 177, 179–80.
49. Ibid., 199.
50. Lewis, *Silver Chair*, 212, 213.
51. Lewis, *Four Loves*, 184.
52. Griffin, *Clive Staples Lewis*, 266.
53. Chesterton, *What's Wrong with the World*, 6.
54. Lewis, *Till We Have Faces*, 307.
55. Lewis, *Letters to Malcolm*, 84.
56. Lewis, *Grief Observed*, 38.
57. Lewis, *Surprised by Joy*, 238.
58. Lewis, *Allegory of Love*, 43.
59. Lewis, *Christian Reflections*, 11.

Bibliography

Aquinas, Thomas. *In decem libros Ethicorum Aristotelis ad Nicomachum expositio.* Chicago: Encyclopedia Britannica, 1952.

Aristotle. *Poetics.* Translated by S. H. Butcher. New York: Hill and Wang, 1961.

Bakhtin, Mikhail. *Rabelais and His World.* Translated by Helene Iswolsky. Cambridge, MA: MIT Press, 1968.

Barker, Dudley. *G. K. Chesterton: Biography.* New York: Stein and Day, 1973.

Beattie, James. "An Essay on Laughter and Ludicrous Composition." *Essays.* London, 1779.

Berger, Peter L. *A Rumor of Angels.* New York: Anchor, 1970.

Bettelheim, Bruno. *The Uses of Enchantment: The Meaning and Importance of Fairy Tales.* New York: Vintage, 1977.

Boileau, Nicolas. *L'Art Poetique.* French Pbns, 1965, 1.36.

Bonham, Tal D. *Humor: God's Gift.* Nashville: Broadman Press, 1988.

Bretall, Robert, ed. *A Kierkegaard Anthology.* New York: The Modern Library, 1946.

Buechner, Frederick. *Telling the Truth: The Gospel As Tragedy, Comedy, and Fairy Tale.* New York: Harper and Row, 1977.

———. *Wishful Thinking.* New York: Harper & Row, 1973.

Caputi, Anthony. *Buffo: The Genius of Vulgar Comedy.* Detroit: Wayne State University Press, 1978.

Carnell, Corbin Scott. *Bright Shadow of Reality*: C. S. Lewis and the Feeling Intellect. Grand Rapids, MI: Eerdmans, 1974.

Carroll, Lewis. *Alice's Adventures in Wonderland.* New York: New American Library, 1960.

Chaucer, Geoffrey. *The Canterbury Tales.* Chicago: Encyclopedia Britannica, 1952.

Chesterton, G. K. *Alarms and Discursions.* London: Library Press, n.d.

———. *All Things Considered.* Philadelphia: Dufour, 1969.

———. *As I Was Saying: A Chesterton Reader.* Edited by Robert Knille. Grand Rapids, MI: Eerdmans, 1985.

———. *The Ball and the Cross.* New York: Trow Press, 1909.

———. *Charles Dickens.* London: Methuen, 1907.

———. *The Club of Queer Trades.* London and New York: Penguin, 1984.

———. *Collected Words Vols. I-XXVII.* San Francisco: Ignatius Press, 1987.

———. *The Common Man.* London: Sheed and Ward, 1950.

———. *The Everlasting Man.* Garden City, NY: Doubleday, 1955.

———. *The Father Brown Omnibus.* New York:Dodd, Mead, 1982.

———. *A Handful of Authors: Essays on Books and Writers.* New York: Sheed and Ward, 1953.

———. *Heretics.*In *Collected Words I.* San Francisco: Ignatius Press, 1986.

———. "Humour." *Encyclopedia Britannica.*14th ed. Vol. 2. New York (1929): 883–885.

———. *Illustrated London News,* Aug. 13, 1932, 224.

———. *A Miscellaney of Men.* Philadelphia: Dufours, 1959.

———. *Orthodoxy.* Garden City, NY: Doubleday, 1956.

———. *St. Francis of Assisi.* Garden City, NY: Doubleday, 1956.

———. *St. Thomas Aquinas: "The Dumb Ox."* Garden City, NY: Doubleday, 1956.

———. *Tremendous Trifles.* London: Methuen, 1927.

———. *What's Wrong with the World.*In *Collected Works IV.* San Francisco: Ignatius Press, 1987.

———. *Wit and Wisdom of G. K. Chesterton.* New York: Dodd, Mead, 1911.

Cicero. *De Oratore II*. Translated by E. W. Sutton and H. Rackman. Cambridge, MA: Harvard University Press, 1942.

Como, James T., ed. *At the Breakfast Tale and Other Reminiscences*. New York: Macmillan, 1979.

Conington, John. *Satires, Epistles, and Art of Poetry of Horace*. London: George Bell and Sons, 1892.

Corrigan, Robert W., ed. *Comedy: Meaning and Form*. San Francisco: Chandler, 1965.

Cote, Richard G. *Holy Mirth: A Theology of Laughter*. Whitinsville, MA: Affirmation Books, 1986.

Cousins, Norman. *Anatomy of an Illness*. New York: Norton, 1979.

Dale, Alzina Stone. *The Outline of Sanity: A Life of G. K. Chesterton*. Grand Rapids, MI: Eerdmans, 1982.

Davies, Marie-Helene. *Laughter in a Genevan Clown: Works of Frederick Buechner, 1970–1980*. Grand Rapids, MI: Eerdmans, 1983.

Eastman, Max. *The Enjoyment of Laughter*. New York: Simon and Schuster, 1936.

Eco, Umberto. *The Name of the Rose*. New York: Warner, 1980.

Ford, Paul F. *Companion to Narnia*. San Francisco: Harper and Row, 1980.

Frazer, Sir James George. *The Golden Bough*. New York: Macmillan, 1963.

Freud, Sigmund. *Jokes and Their Relation to the Unconscious*. Translated and edited by James Strachey. New York: Norton, 1963.

Gibb, Jocelyn, ed. *Light on C. S. Lewis*. New York: Harcourt, Brace and World, 1965.

Grahame, Kenneth. *The Wind in the Willows*. New York: Dell, 1969.

Green, Roger Lancelyn and Walter Hooper. *C. S. Lewis: A Biography*. New York: Harcourt Brace Jovanovich, 1974.

Griffin, William. *Clive Staples Lewis: A Dramatic Life*. San Francisco: Harper and Row, 1986.

Hazlitt, William. *Collected Works VIII*. Edited by A. R. Walter and Arnold Glover. London: J. M. Dent, 1902.

———. *The Hazlitt Sampler*. Edited by Herschel M. Sikes. New York: Fawcett, 1961.

———. *Lectures on English Comic Writers III*. London: George Bell, 1885.

Hobbes, Thomas. *The English Works of Thomas Hobbes*. London: Bohn, 1839.

Hooper, Walter. *Past Watchful Dragons*. London: Macmillan, 1971.

Howard, Thomas. *The Achievement of C. S. Lewis*. Wheaton, IL: Shaw, 1980.

———. *The Novels of Charles Williams*. New York: Oxford University Press, 1983.

Huizinga, Johan. *Homo Ludens: A Study of the Play-Element in Human Culture*. London: Routledge and Kegan Paul, 1949.

Hurd, Richard. *The Works of Richard Hurd*. London: T. Cadell and W. Davies, 1811.

Hyers, Conrad. *The Comic Vision and the Christian Faith*. New York: Pilgrim Press, 1981.

———, ed. *Holy Laughter: Essays on Religion in the Comic Perspective*. New York: Seabury, 1969.

Johnston, Robert K. *The Christian at Play*. Grand Rapids, MI: Eerdmans, 1983.

Keefe, Carolyn, ed. *C. S. Lewis: Speaker and Teacher*. Grand Rapids, MI: Zondervan, 1971.

Kierkegaard, Søren. *The Concept of Irony*. New York: Harper and Row, 1966.

———. *Concluding Unscientific Postscript*. Translated by David F. Swenson. Princeton, Princeton University Press, 1941.

———. *Either/Or*. Translated by David F. Swenson and Lillian Marvin Swenson. Princeton, Princeton University Press, 1971.

Kilby, Clyde S., and Marjorie Lamp Mead, eds. *Brothers and Friends: The Diaries of Major Warren Hamilton Lewis*. San Francisco: Harper and Row, 1982.

Kiley, Frederick, and J. M. Shuttleworth, eds. *Satire*. New York: Bobbs-Merrill, 1971.

Lee, Judith Yaross. *Defining New Yorker Humor.* Jackosn, MS: University Press of
  Mississippi, 2000.
Lewis, C. S. *The Abolition of Man.* New York: Macmillan, 1965.
———. *A Grief Observed.* New York: Seabury, 1961.
———. *The Allegory of Love.* New York: Oxford University Press, 1958.
———. *Christian Reflections.* Edited by Walter Hooper. Grand Rapids, MI: Eerdmans, 1967.
———. *The Dark Tower and Other Stories.* Edited by Walter Hooper. New York: Harcourt
  Brace Jovanovich, 1977.
———. *The Discarded Image.* Cambridge: Cambridge University Press, 1964.
———. *English Literature in the Sixteenth Century, Excluding Drama.* London: Oxford
  University Press, 1973.
———. *Essays Presented to Charles Williams.* London: Oxford University Press, 1947.
———. *Experiment in Criticism.* Cambridge: Cambridge University Press, 1961.
———. *Fern-seed and Elephants.* Edited by Walter Hooper. London: Fontana Books, 1975.
———. *The Four Loves.* New York: Harcourt Brace Jovanovich, 1960.
———. *George MacDonald: An Anthology.* New York: Geoffrey Bles, 1946.
———. *God in the Dock: Essays on Theology and Ethics.* Grand Rapids, MI: Eerdmans, 1970.
———. *The Great Divorce.* New York: Macmillan, 1946.
———. *The Horse and His Boy.* New York: MacMillan, 1954.
———. *The Last Battle.* New York: Macmillan, 1956.
———. *Letters of C. S. Lewis.* Edited by W. H. Lewis. New York: Harcourt, Brace and
  World, 1966.
———. *Letters to an American Lady.* Grand Rapids, MI: Eerdmans, 1975.
———. *Letters to Children.* Edited by Lyle W. Dorsett and Marjorie Lamp Mead. New
  York: Macmillan, 1985.
———. *Letters to Malcolm: Chiefly on Prayer.* London: Fontana Books, 1966.
———. *The Lion, the Witch, and the Wardrobe.* New York: Macmillan, 1950.
———. *The Magician's Nephew.* New York: Macmillan, 1955.
———. *Mere Christianity.* New York: Macmillan, 1952.
———. *Miracles: A Preliminary Study.* New York: Macmillan, 1947.
———. *Narrative Poems.* New York: Harcourt Brace Jovanovich, 1969.
———. *Of Other Worlds: Essays and Stories.* Edited by Walter Hooper. New York: Harcourt,
  Brace and World, 1967.
———. *On Stories and Other Essays.* Edited by Walter Hooper. New York: Harcourt Brace
  Jovanovich, 1982.
———. *Out of the Silent Planet.* New York: Macmillan, 1965.
———. *Perelandra.* New York: Macmillan, 1965.
———. *The Pilgrim's Regress: An Allegorical Apology for Christianity, Reason and
  Romanticism.* Grand Rapids, MI: Eerdmans, 1958.
———. *Poems.* Edited by Walter Hooper. New York: Harcourt Brace Jovanovich, 1964.
———. *Preface to Paradise Lost.* New York: Oxford University Press, 1961.
———. *Present Concerns and Other Essays.* Edited by Walter Hooper. New York: Harcourt
  Brace Jovanovich, 1986.
———. *Prince Caspian.* New York: Macmillan, 1951.
———. *The Problem of Pain.* New York: Macmillan, 1962.
———. *Reflections on the Psalms.* New York: Harcourt Brace Jovanovich, 1958.
———. *The Screwtape Letters.* New York: Macmillan, 1968.
———. *Selected Literary Essays.* Edited by Walter Hooper. London: Cambridge University
  Press, 1969.

————. *The Silver Chair*. New York: Macmillan, 1953.

————. *Spenser's Images of Life*. Cambridge: Cambridge University Press, 1967.

————. *Studies in Medieval and Renaissance Literature*. New York: Cambridge University Press, 1979.

————. *Studies in Words*. Cambridge: Cambridge University Press, 1967.

————. *Surprised by Joy: The Shape of My Early Life*. New York: Harcourt Brace Jovanovich, 1955.

————. *That Hideous Strength: A Modern Fairy Tale for Grown-ups*. New York: Macmillan, 1946.

————. *They Asked for a Paper: Papers and Addresses*. London: Geoffrey Bles, 1962.

————. *They Stand Together: The Letters of C. S. Lewis to Arthur Greeves*. Edited by Walter Hooper. New York: Macmillan, 1979.

————. *Till We Have Faces*. Grand Rapids, MI: Eerdmans, 1956.

————. *Transposition and Other Addresses*. New York: Macmillan, 1949.

————. Unpublished Papers. Bodleian Library, Oxford.

————. *The Voyage of the Dawn Treader*. New York: Macmillan, 1952.

————. *The Weight of Glory*. Grand Rapids, MI: Eerdmans, 1949.

————. *The World's Last Night and Other Essays*. New York: Harcourt Brace Jovanovich, 1959.

Lindvall, Terry. *The Mother of All Laughter: Sarah and the Genesis of Comedy*. Nashville: Broadman and Holman, 2003.

Lynch, William F. *Christ and Apollo: Dimensions of the Literary Imagination*. New York: Sheed and Ward, 1969.

MacDonald, George. "The Light Princess." *Gifts of the Christ Child II*. Edited by Glenn Edward Sadler. Grand Rapids, MI: Eerdmans, 1973.

————. *The Princess and Curdie*. New York: Penguin, 1969.

Macdonald, Michael H., and Andrew A. Tadie, eds. *The Riddle of Joy: G. K. Chesterton and C. S. Lewis*. Grand Rapids, MI: Eerdmans, 1989.

McDonald, Gerald D., ed. *Poems of Stephen Crane*. New York: Thomas Crowell, 1964.

Meilaender, Gilbert. *The Taste for the Other: The Social and Ethical Thought of C. S. Lewis*. Grand Rapids, MI: Eerdmans, 1978.

Melville, Herman. *Moby Dick or, The Whale*. New York: Modern Library, 1950.

Meredith, George. "An Essay on Comedy." In *Comedy*. Edited by Wylie Sypher. New York: Doubleday, 1956.

Morreall, John, ed. *The Philosophy of Laughter and Humor*. Albany, NY: SUNY Press, 1987.

————. *Taking Laughter Seriously*. Albany, NY:SUNY Press, 1983.

Moynihan, Martin. *The Latin Letters of C. S. Lewis*. Wheaton, IL: Crossway Books, 1987.

Muggeridge, Malcolm. *The End of Christendom*. Grand Rapids, MI: Eerdmans, 1980.

————. *A Third Testament*. Boston: Little, Brown and Company, 1976.

Nesbit, E. *Five Children and It*. London: Octopus Books, 1979.

Pascal, Blaise. *Pensées*. Translated by W. F. Trotter. Chicago: Encyclopaedia Britannica, 1952.

————. *Provincial Letters*. Translated by Thomas M'Crie. Chicago: Encyclopaedia Britannica, 1952.

Pearson, Hesketh. *Lives of the Wits*. London: Heinemann, 1962.

Percy, Walker *Lost in the Cosmos: The Last Self-Help Book*. New York: Washington Square Books, 1983.

Plato. *Philebus*. In *The Dialogues of Plato*. Translated by Benjamin Jowett. Chicago: Encyclopaedia Britannica, 1952.

————. *Republic*. In *The Dialogues of Plato*. Translated by Benjamin Jowett. Chicago: Encyclopaedia Britannica, 1952.

————. *Symposium*. In *The Dialogues of Plato*. Translated by Benjamin Jowett. Chicago: Encyclopedia Britannica, 1952.

Polhemus, Robert M. *Comic Faith: The Great Tradition from Austen to Joyce*. Chicago: University of Chicago Press, 1980.

Rabelais, Francois. *Gargantua and Pantagruel*. Chicago: Encyclopaedia Britannica, 1952.

Rapp, Albert. *The Origins of Wit and Humor*. New York: Dutton, 1951.

Samra, Cal. *The Joyful Christ: The Healing Power of Humor*. San Francisco: Harper and Row, 1986.

Schakel, Peter J. *Reading with the Heart: The Way into Narnia*. Grand Rapids, MI: Eerdmans, 1979.

Schopenhauer, Arthur. *The World as Will and Idea*. Translated by E. F. J. Payne. New York: Dover, 1969.

Shaftesbury, Lord Anthony. "An Essay on the Freedom of Wit and Humour." In *Characteristicks of Men, Manners, Opinions, Times*, 4th ed. London: John Darby, 1727.

Shakespeare, William. *Love's Labour Lost*. In *The Plays and Sonnets of William Shakespeare*. Chicago: Encyclopaedia Britannica, 1952.

————. *Much Ado About Nothing*. In *The Plays and Sonnets of William Shakespeare*. Chicago: Encyclopaedia Britannica, 1952.

Siedman, Steve. *Comedian Comedy*. Ann Arbor, MI: University of Michigan Research Press, 1981.

Spenser, Edmund. *Selections from the Poetical Works of Edmund Spenser*. Boston: Houghton Mifflin, 1970.

Spenser, Edmund. *The Faerie Queene*. Book I. Canto VI. Chicago: Encyclopaedia Britannica, 1952.

Sterne, Laurence. *Tristram Shandy*. Chicago: Encyclopaedia Britannica, 1952.

Sypher, Wylie, ed. *Comedy*. New York: Doubleday, 1956.

Thigpen, Thomas Paul. *A Reason for Joy*. Colorado Springs, CO: NavPress, 1988.

Tolkien, J. R. R. *The Hobbit*. Boston: Houghton Mifflin, 1966.

Trueblood, Elton. *The Humor of Christ*. New York: Harper and Row, 1964.

Vanauken, Sheldon. *A Severe Mercy*. San Francisco: Harper and Row, 1977.

Walsh, Chad. *C. S. Lewis: Apostle to the Skeptics*. New York: Macmillan, 1949.

Ward, Maisie. *Gilbert Keith Chesterton*. New York: Sheed and Ward, 1943.

Webster's Seventh New Collegiate Dictionary. Springfield, IL: G. & C. Merriam Co., 1967.

Wells, Carolyn. *An Outline of Humor*. New York: G. P. Putnam's Sons, 1932.

White, E. B., and K. S. White. *A Subtreasury of American Humor*. New York: The Modern Library, 1941.

Willis, John Randolph. *Pleasures Forevermore*. Chicago: Loyola University Press, 1983.

Williams, Margery. *The Velveteen Rabbit*. Garden City, NY: Doubleday, 1970.

Wilson, A. N. *C. S. Lewis: A Biography*. New York: Norton, 1990.

Whitty, Susan. "The Laugh Makers." *Psychology Today*, August 1983, 22–29.

About the Author

Terry Lindvall (PhD University of Southern California) occupies the C. S. Lewis Chair of Communication and Christian Thought at Virginia Wesleyan College. He is the author of six books, including *Celluloid Sermons* (NYU Press, 2011), *Sanctuary Cinema* (NYU Press, 2007), and *The Mother of All Laughter: Sarah and the Genesis of Comedy* (Broadman/Holman, 2003). An ordained Congregational minister, Lindvall has taught at Duke University School of Divinity, College of William and Mary, Fuller Seminary, and other universities. He is currently writing *In the Seat of Scoffers: A History of Religion and Satire from the Hebrew Prophets to Steven Colbert*. He lives in Virginia Beach, Virginia, with his wife Karen, with son Christopher at the University of Virginia and daughter Caroline finishing her senior year at First Colonial High School.

Index